Critical Library Instruction

Critical Library Instruction

Theories and Methods

Edited by

Maria T. Accardi, Emily Drabinski, and Alana Kumbier

Library Juice Press
Duluth, Minnesota

Editorial contributions copyright Maria T. Accardi, Emily Drabinski, and Alana Kumbier, 2009

Articles copyright their respective authors, 2009

Published by Library Juice Press, 2010
PO Box 3320
Duluth, MN 55803
http://litwinbooks.com/

Printed on acid-free paper that meets present ANSI standards for archival preservation.

Cover designed by Alana Kumbier

Library of Congress Cataloging-in-Publication Data

Critical library instruction : theories and methods / edited by Maria T. Accardi, Emily Drabinski, and Alana Kumbier.
    p. cm.
 Includes bibliographical references and index.
 Summary: "A collection of articles about various ways of applying critical pedagogy and related educational theories to library instruction"--Provided by publisher.
 ISBN 978-1-936117-01-7 (acid-free paper)
1. Library orientation for college students. 2. Information literacy--Study and teaching (Higher) 3. Research--Methodology--Study and teaching (Higher) 4. Academic libraries--Relations with faculty and curriculum. 5. Critical pedagogy.
 I. Accardi, Maria T. II. Drabinski, Emily. III. Kumbier, Alana.
 Z711.25.C65C75 2010
 025.5'677--dc22
                                        2009039408

Table of Contents

Introduction

Critical Library Instruction began as good things often do—casually, and largely by accident. Alana mentioned to Emily in between sessions at the 2008 GLBT Archives, Libraries, and Museums conference that she was thinking about putting together a collection about critical approaches to library instruction. Emily, a recent addition to the board of *Radical Teacher*, a journal of socialist, feminist, and anti-racist teaching, found Alana's timing and topic uncanny—as the first teaching librarian on the editorial board, these questions had immediate resonance. Emily mentioned her former colleague Maria, a librarian in Indiana with an extraordinary commitment to student learning, to Alana as a possible addition to the editing team. When Emily and Maria talked, the idea clicked. Alana and Emily met the following weekend at the Thinking Critically conference hosted by the Center for Information Policy Research at the University of Wisconsin, Milwaukee, where they presented together on a wholly unrelated topic. Rory Litwin was there too, so Alana and Emily talked the idea out with him over a conference buffet lunch of meat salads. And now, nearly two years later, we're holding this volume in our hands.

The three of us are practicing instruction librarians working in a variety of higher education settings: a branch campus of a large Midwestern university; a mid-sized private university in urban Brooklyn, New York, and a small liberal arts women's college in the northeast. We all see ourselves as working librarians: we staff service desks and serve on committees; we teach 50 minute one-shot sessions for faculty who just don't get it and multi-session courses for faculty who do; some of us are seeking tenure and others year to year contracts; and we all think about retirement plans and healthcare packages and domestic partnership benefits and the other nuts and bolts of contemporary late-capitalist working life. But we also all read, think, and write. Our work influences our thinking which influences our work; all three of us strive for praxis.

And praxis is what this book seeks as well. Ours is a profession that often splits working and thinking in two—theorizing goes on in LIS doctoral programs while front-line librarians concern themselves with "best practices" at the service desk. When we submitted a proposal to present some of the ideas in this book at the 2009 ACRL conference in Seattle, we struggled to imagine where we might fit in a program that demanded instrumentalist learning outcomes keyed to themes like *Cast a Net!* and *Feel the Buzz!* We wanted to get a group of librarians together to talk about the ideas that background critical practice in the classroom—from Freire's models of liberatory teaching to Kapitzke's criticisms of standards models to Elmborg's blending of literacy theory and library practice. Would ideas that didn't always lead directly to outcomes find a home in our profession?

We think they can, and must. We think there is a difference between teaching the catalog to "remedial" students and an information literacy that respects what each student brings to the classroom. Library faculty in both cases might use problem-based learning (as discussed in these pages by Elizabeth Peterson and Kim Olson-Kopp and Bryan Kopp), but the classroom approach and outcome will, we suspect, be different when a commitment to social justice is present at the front—or at the sides, or in the circle—of the room. In fact, we think of instruction work—especially when it is reflective, as Caroline Sinkinson and Mary Lingold model in these pages—as a kind of thinking-in-action.

The praxis approach modeled in these pages extends that of librarians who adapt approaches from other fields, disciplines, and communities of practice, and make these approaches clearly relevant and useful to library instruction. This volume joins library, information studies, and other scholars whose critiques of epistemological and classificatory practices inspire our conviction that such critiques are necessary and possible. Like them, we build on feminist (Haraway, hooks, Olson), postcolonial (Olson, Said, Stoler), queer (Adler, Anzaldúa, Butler, Drabinski, Roberto, Terry), disability studies (Davis, McCruer), and anti-racist/race-critical (Anzaldúa, Hammonds, hooks, Bowker and Star) frameworks to begin new ways of thinking and teaching in the library context.

Where these theoretical approaches frame out our big picture, the work of librarian-practitioners forms another point of entry for this volume. Elmborg & Hook's *Centers for Learning: Writing Centers and Libraries in Collaboration* (2005) is an important predecessor to this collection, as its contributors describe productive collaborations with writing centers while also enacting a reflexive critical analysis of these relationships, and bringing scholarship in composition and rhetoric into conversation with information literacy and library instruction praxes. As they engage scholarship in composition and rhetoric, librarian-scholars have introduced their colleagues to genre theory (Simmons, 2005), the concept of the ethnographic contact zone (Elmborg, 2006), and theorizations of learning through dialogue and discourse (Elmborg, 2005; 2006), all of which have the power to transform our practice both in the classroom and at the reference desk. For example, we may help students learn about the discursive conventions (e.g., standards for establishing authority; citational practice) of a particular discipline or field by presenting scholars as members of a discursive community whose practices students can study, adopt, analyze, or, vitally, critique or resist.

Our collection is also informed by librarians and scholars who are developing a critical information literacy praxis. This move is itself informed by scholarship in critical literacy studies, which argues that we should understand literacy as more than a set of competencies; more than simply the ability to read and write. Instead of conceptualizing literacy as a "neutral, discrete, context-free skill" (Norgaard, 2003), something that can be measured by a universally-applicable set of standards, critical literacy scholars recognize literacy as a culturally-situated phenomenon, embedded within specific social, political, and economic systems, subject to (and potentially constitutive of) the power relations and ideologies that define particular moments in history (Luke & Kapitzke, 1999; Norgaard, 2003). They argue that our understanding of literacy needs to expand to encompass the multiple literacies students develop in response to new technologies and new media, including "visual literacy, electronic literacy, digital literacy, internet literacy, media literacy, technological literacy and multiliteracies" (Luke & Kapitzke, 1999, p. 2).

They also suggest we attend to the larger contexts in which these technologies and media emerge, including global capitalism (more specifically, the shift to service- and information-based economies) and transnational cultural exchange (Luke & Kapitzke, 1999). Instruction librarians have found this framework useful for a number of purposes: teaching students not only how to find information, but also how to evaluate and contextualize it; helping students conduct research that matters to their personal experience and to the communities to which they belong; dealing with the changing nature of authorship, authority, and publication of content online; negotiating the gap between standards (e.g., the ACRL Information Literacy Competency Standards for Higher Education) and classroom practice; and making sense of (and in some cases, resisting) the privatization of information through subscription- and fee-based licensing and access.

Finally, we are indebted to the work of librarians and scholars who have established the relevance of critical pedagogy to library instruction. We are not the first to imagine ways in which the critical-pedagogical interventions by Paulo Freire, Henry Giroux, bell hooks, Peter McLaren, and Ira Shor can contribute to a library instruction praxis that promotes critical engagement with information sources, considers students collaborators in knowledge production practices (and creators in their own right), recognizes the affective dimensions of research, and (in some cases) has liberatory aims.

We enter into these conversations as both scholars and workers. This volume, then, seeks to disrupt the boundary between theory and practice that we name in order to limn, and invites thinkers to talk about what they do, do-ers to talk about what they think, and all of us to continue to develop a critical praxis of critical library instruction. We've divided the book into five sections that resist this artificial separation, inviting readers to read across and against differing approaches. In section one, we offer a conceptual toolkit for critical library instructors. Bringing together voices that emphasize theoretical orientations, we think these chapters will jumpstart the librarian seeking new ways to conceptualize library instruction. Section two functions as a classroom toolkit, gathering together chapters that blend theoretical approaches with concrete lesson plans and classroom strategies. This section is aimed at the teacher who has a class later this morning. In section three, authors discuss approaches to critical library instruction in specific institutional settings, including service learning programs, community colleges, and in partnership with high schools. Focusing on what's possible in particular environments reminds us that our instruction is always grounded in context. Section four offers strategies for teaching from a range of alternative media, rather than relying on the library catalog and scholarly databases as texts for rote, instrumentalist lessons about authority. By switching up our sources, we can encourage critical engagement with all kinds of materials, including the web resources we traditionally decry and the scholarly sources that too often get an easy pass. Finally, section five aims to directly critique problems of institutional power that necessarily limit what it is possible for librarians—even critical ones—to accomplish, recognizing our precarious and contested position within broader distributions of power, resources, and control.

We end deliberately with a contribution from Cathy Eisenhower and Dolsy Smith. Challenging the idea that a critical approach to library instruction is possible or even desirable, we think they point to the next realm of inquiry. Given the commercialization and privatization of higher education and the elision of public and private lives, work and leisure time, what hope is there for liberatory library instruction? Or is the obsolescence we so often institutionally feel somehow our most valuable asset? Theirs is a provocative piece that challenges us to rethink the purpose of this entire volume, precisely the kind of instability we think lies just underneath what might at first appear to be stable formations of knowledge, theory, and

practice. Like most of our contributors, we think learning happens in
dialogue rather than once and for all, and we hope this collection of
provocative challenges to contemporary practice begins more of that.

August 2009
Maria T. Accardi, Louisville, Kentucky
Emily Drabinski, Brooklyn, New York
Alana Kumbier, Somerville, Massachusetts

References

Adler, M. (2008). The Asian-American bisexual ghetto of LCSH: A
    Cultural history of representation. In E. Buchanan & C. Hansen
    (Eds.), *Thinking critically: Alternative perspectives and methods in information
    studies, 2008 conference proceedings* (pp. 1-12). Milwaukee, WI: University
    of Wisconsin-Milwaukee.
Anzaldúa, G. (1987). *Borderlands: The new mestiza = La frontera* (1st ed.). San
    Francisco: Spinsters/Aunt Lute.
Bowker, G. C., & Star, S. L. (1999). *Sorting things out: Classification and its
    consequences.* Cambridge, MA: The MIT Press.
Butler, J. (1990). *Gender trouble: Feminism and the subversion of identity.* New York:
    Routledge.
Davis, L. (2002). *Bending over backwards: Disability, dismodernism, and other difficult
    positions.* New York: NYU Press.
Drabinski, E. (2008). Queering library space: Notes towards a new
    geography of the library. In E. Buchanan & C. Hansen (Eds.),
    *Thinking critically: Alternative perspectives and methods in information studies,
    2008 conference proceedings* (pp. 30-37). Milwaukee, WI: University of
    Wisconsin-Milwaukee.
Elmborg, J. (2006). Critical information literacy: Implications for
    institutional practice. *Journal of Academic Librarianship, 32*(2), 192-199.
Elmborg, J. (2006). Libraries in the contact zone: On the creation of
    educational space. *Reference & User Services Quarterly, 46*(1), 56-64.
Elmborg, J. K., & Hook, S. (Eds.). (2005). *Centers for learning: Writing centers
    and libraries in collaboration.* Chicago: Association of College and
    Research Libraries.

Elmborg, J., & Pawley, C. (2003). Historical research as critical practice and relationship: The Carnegie Libraries in Iowa Project. *Journal of Education for Library and Information Science, 44*(3-4), 235-245.

Freire, P. (1993). *Pedagogy of the oppressed* (New rev. 20th-Anniversary ed.). New York: Continuum.

Hammonds, E. (1997). New technologies of race. In J. Terry & M. Calvert (Eds.), *Processed lives: Gender and technology in everyday life* (pp. 74-86). New York: Routledge.

Haraway, D. (1997). M*odest_Witness@Second_Millenium.FemaleMan©_Meets_Oncomouse™.* New York: Routledge.

Harris, B. (2008). Communities as Necessity in Information Literacy Development: Challenging the Standards. *Journal of Academic Librarianship, 34*(3), 248-255.

hooks, b. (1994). *Teaching to transgress: education as the practice of freedom.* New York: Routledge.

Luke, A., & Kapitzke, C. (1999). Literacies and libraries—Archives and cybraries. *Pedagogy, Culture & Society, 7*(3), 467-491.

McRuer, Robert. (2006). *Crip theory: Cultural signs of queerness and disability.* New York: NYU Press.

Norgaard, R. (2003). Writing information literacy: Contributions to a concept. *Reference & User Services Quarterly, 43*(2), 124-130.

Norgaard, R. (2004). Writing information literacy in the classroom: Pedagogical enactments and implications. *Reference & User Services Quarterly, 43*(3), 220-226.

Olson, H. (2002). *The Power to name: Locating the limits of subject representation in libraries.* Boston: Kluwer Academic Publishers.

Roberto, K. R. (Ed.). (2008). *Radical cataloging: Essays at the front.* Jefferson, NC: McFarland.

Said, E. W. (1979). *Orientalism* (1st Vintage Books ed.). New York: VintageBooks.

Shapiro, J., & Hughes, S. (1996). Information literacy as a liberal art. *Educom Review, 31*(2).

Simmons, M. H. (2005). Librarians as disciplinary discourse mediators. *portal: Libraries and the Academy, 5*(3), 297-311.

Stoler, A. L. (1995). *Race and the education of desire: Foucault's History of sexuality and the colonial order of things.* Durham, NC: Duke University Press.

Terry, J., & Urla, J. (Eds.) (1995). *Deviant bodies: Critical perspectives on difference in science and popular culture.* Bloomington, IN: Indiana University Press.

Acknowledgements

It is a cliché because it is true that it takes a village to make a book, and ours is no exception. First, we must say hats off to our contributors. Not only did they amaze us with their adherence to deadlines—all editors should be so lucky!—they consistently challenged our own ideas of the boundaries of this book and the questions that can be asked of ourselves and our work. We look forward to what all of us have to say next. This idea would have remained merely an idea without Rory Litwin and his Library Juice Press, like an open door to our fledgling ideas. Rory struck with us the balance so difficult to find in any relationship between freedom and support. We doubt this book would exist in any form without his commitment.

Maria would like to thank her colleagues at the Indiana University Southeast Library for their support, encouragement, and advice. I'd also like to acknowledge the generous collaborative spirit of Dr. Angela M. Salas, the director of the IU Southeast Honors Program, who is always helpful and receptive when I want to try something new with her H103 and H104 students. My 2008-09 students also merit recognition, because it was their astute insights that opened my eyes to the possibilities of critical library instruction. Good friends also offered moral support, especially Erin Kate Ryan and Tony Mick, and my family also deserves thanks for their encouragement and forbearance. Finally, Constance Merritt deserves special acknowledgment for banishing me from the apartment when I needed to get work done, for making life ineffably sweet and blissful when I returned, and for being the one where it rests.

Emily recognizes my fellow teachers and colleagues both at Sarah Lawrence College, where this project began, and at Long Island University, Brooklyn, where it took its final shape, as well as far-flung collaborators who have asked good questions and listened to me talk, particularly Melissa Adler, Lia Friedman, K.R. Roberto, and Laura Wynholds. Thanks also to my family, chosen and given, for cooking me dinner and asking after the project and gossiping when I needed a break, especially Shana Agid, John Drabinski, Kate Drabinski, Abby Lester, Deb Schwartz, Carol Wald, and Liz Wells. I'd choose each of you again and again.

Alana thanks my colleagues in Information Services at Wellesley College—especially members of the Research and Instruction Group—for their warm collegiality, their mentoring, and their investment in developing a reflexive approach to teaching and learning. I thank collaborators and friends who have shared their thoughts about critical instructional praxis with me, especially participants in the 2009 Radical Reference Preconference Unconference in Seattle, students and faculty in Comparative Studies at The Ohio State University, K.R. Roberto, and Cristina Hernandez Trotter. I also thank my former teachers, particularly Mark Corliss, Jane Zanger, Brenda Brueggemann, Timothy K. Choy, and most of all, Maurice Stevens. Their critical pedagogical praxes inspire my own. I come from a family of teachers, and am grateful for their example, as well as for the love and enthusiasm they share with me. Erin Aults, Ariel Berman, Kate Bronstad, Thomas Dodson, Ruby Linhan, Milo Miller, Erica and Ella Tawes, and April West make my life delightful on a daily basis. I wouldn't ask for a better life than the one I'm creating with all of you.

Finally, we would not do the work we do were it not for our students, whose curiosity and commitment never fails to astound us. We're so glad to be in this with you, together.

Section One

Conceptual Toolkit

"There's Nothing on my Topic!" Using the Theories of Oscar Wilde and Henry Giroux to Develop Critical Pedagogy for Library Instruction.

Elisabeth Pankl and Jason Coleman

The Archetypal Scene

It's 9 PM on a Thursday evening early in fall semester. The campus library has yet to hum with the activity of the twenty thousand students at a rural, land grant university. A fresh-faced female undergraduate, in a tight t-shirt emblazoned with her beloved school's name, approaches the Help Desk.

"There's nothing on my topic!" she states with a defeated yet defensive air of entitlement. The reference librarian, who had been checking her Facebook, looks up wearily.

"What's your topic?" she asks for perhaps the thousandth time since she graduated two years ago from library school.

"The impact of single motherhood on kids," the girl mumbles.

"Where have you looked?"

"The library person who talked to our class told us to type our topic into the library site and I can't find anything! My paper is due tomorrow and I need three resources" she chokes.

The undergraduate is nearly on the verge of tears, and the librarian wonders why library instruction isn't more effective.

Positivism and Knowledge

This vignette illustrates typical encounters in academic libraries across the country. The fundamental problem in such scenarios is that the student has failed to properly conceptualize the research process and lacks the cognitive sophistication to articulate and imagine her topic in a manner that is meaningful and dialectical. The hypothetical student truly believes that academic research is merely a process of punching some random terms into an electronic apparatus and then receiving, perhaps by the will of God, a magical and sizable list of sources that are all perfectly relevant to what she is writing about (and, ideally, these sources all have titles that closely match her *own* title). Such situations are attributable to education that is bound and constrained by positivism. Positivism is the belief and practice that valid knowledge is objective, empirical, and static. Unfortunately positivism is the dominant paradigm for most educational efforts in the U.S. and has been since the Enlightenment. Educational systems within the U.S. are committed to marketing knowledge as something outside of the individual, and treat the individual's fundamental character as instrumental rather than imaginative and creative. Such an educational ideology produces agents that are incapable and, for the most part, unwilling to construct their own knowledge—knowledge that might in turn liberate them from the tyranny of facts.

Critical pedagogy attempts to combat the positivistic stranglehold on the educational system. Its fundamental project is to emancipate all people from overt and hidden forms of oppression by denaturalizing dominant ideologies and systems as historically produced human constructs that are far reaching in their impacts and, perhaps more importantly, subject to change. One of the primary targets of critical pedagogy is the over-simplified construction of rationality within the educational framework and its cultural/social context. Rationality is often presented as a mere technical ability used to solve discreet problems as efficiently as possible. In contrast, the critical pedagogy articulated and advanced within this analysis seeks to place ethics and aesthetics at the forefront of the educational enterprise. Thus, it, in many ways, is a reinvention and expansion of Arnoldian humanism—an educational philosophy that locates the development of the whole individual in the exposure to "the best which has been thought and said in the world" (Arnold, 1865/1994, p.5). Although Arnold is often reviled for his absolute insistence on the centrality of the canon, his assertion that the individual is developed ethically via aesthetic encounters persists in current educational theory. For example, Abowitz (2007) contends that "[m]oral perception and imagination can be developed through experiences that center on an aesthetic experience" (p. 290). In the educational pursuit, she advocates, like Arnold, exposure to the aesthetic realm and postulates that moral and ethical development grow naturally from that exposure.

This chapter explores the necessity of critical pedagogy in library instruction. The ideology behind the type of critical pedagogy espoused in this chapter is grounded in the principles of aesthetics and ethics. The argument is developed by first introducing two theorists, Oscar Wilde and Henry Giroux, who each advocate substantive revision of educational practice and policy to liberate human minds from the calcified structures of learning. Their relevance to librarianship is highlighted by juxtaposing their ideals against the ACRL *Information Literacy Competency Standards for Higher Education.* Finally, the chapter provides concrete suggestions for incorporating critical pedagogy in library instruction.

Wilde and Giroux

Two theorists whose ideas and writings address the fallacy of positivism are Oscar Wilde and Henry Giroux. Although Wilde and Giroux are divided by time and space, they are united by a passionate commitment to the individual and his/her active role within the learning process. Wilde, although widely regarded as merely an aesthete and writer of comedies of manners, continues to be an influential theorist of the modern dilemma. Wilde is considered one of the more influential fin de siècle writers in British literature. Education, in particular, was extremely important to Wilde and he looked with dismay upon what he termed the "rubbish and facts" (as cited in Wright, 2008, p. 98) that dominated the English educational system. His education, first at Trinity College Dublin and then at Magdalene College Oxford, shaped Wilde profoundly. For instance, Wilde was a great fan of Cardinal Newman whose text *The Idea of the University* (Newman, 1888) critiqued the insidious and pervasive role of testable knowledge. Giroux is a contemporary educational philosopher who has written numerous essays and books critiquing the United States' educational system. He has been a staunch proponent of politicizing pedagogy and developing an ideology of education that promotes democracy and opposes oppression (Aronowitz & Giroux, 1991, 1993; Giroux, 1997, 2001, 2005, 2007). A central hallmark of his thinking is its unyielding idealism and unabashed promotion of utopian goals. Fundamentally, Wilde and Giroux share a vocal distaste for any educational agenda that is primarily rooted in positivism.

Positivism works against the ideal that each theorist holds dear— aesthetic beauty for Wilde and radical political and social liberty for Giroux. Wilde's aestheticism recognizes the growth of the individual as the greatest good whereas positivism, in the form of a radical utilitarianism, pursues, almost relentlessly, predetermined, measurable outcomes. The products of an educational philosophy grounded in a utilitarian framework are individuals who cannot imagine nor experience an existence outside of their own immediate physicality. Individuals produced in such a utilitarian context remain in an imaginative desert and are frozen by passivity; thus they are fundamentally hindered by a lack of orientation toward growth. In his dialogic essay "The Critic As Artist," Wilde celebrates the ideal of self-consciousness and likens it to both the imaginative and critical faculties.

Gilbert, the dominant voice of the essay, asserts, "The longer one studies life and literature, the more strongly one feels that behind everything that is wonderful stands the individual, and that it is not the moment that makes the man, but the man who creates the age" (Wilde, 1923, p. 137). The worship of individuality is paramount in Wilde's thinking and the development of the individual is, in his opinion, the highest educational pursuit. Individuality is achieved, according to Wilde, via intense and continual participation in the dialogic process. The teacher's role is to both model and participate in this process of creation.

Giroux, on the other hand, focuses less on the opposition between positivism and individuality as he does on positivism's insidious role in impeding the development of critical reasoning. In his book *Pedagogy and the Politics of Hope: Theory, Culture, and Schooling*, Giroux (1997) argues that positivism's privileging of technocratic rationality reduces questions of ethics and morality to a trivial status. As a consequence, in curricula informed by positivism, students are not taught that knowledge can be self-constructed. Giroux is unequivocal on this point. He contends, "Adulating 'facts' and empirically based discourse, positivist rationality provides no basis for acknowledging its own historically contingent character. As such, it represents not only an assault on critical thinking, it also grounds itself in the politics of 'what is'" (Giroux, 1997, p. 20). As an alternative to positivism, Giroux proposes that teachers assume the role of "transformative intellectuals" who engage students in dialogue to help them understand how power operates in society and to reveal "concrete possibilities for empowering people" (Giroux, 2005, p. 103). In his view, teachers should base class content on the experiences and problems students bring with them to the classroom and help students learn to interrogate the bases of their perceptions so they understand how to construct social structures conducive to democracy (Giroux, 2005). Although Wilde and Giroux each have unique perspectives and emphases, both champion the absolute necessity of active participation in the creation of new knowledge. For each, experience is the essence of learning.

Library Conference Vignette

It is 7 PM on the second day of a typical, large library conference in a bustling, overpriced city. Several instruction librarians from various institutions are milling around aimlessly at one of the many happy hours, suffering from acute 'conference nausea'.

Librarian 1: "I hate to say this, but I don't feel like I've learned anything new so far," he admits sheepishly. "This is a rehash of last year's conference—just leftovers and chop suey!"

Librarian 2: "I know!" she exclaims. "I wish someone would have a session about what it really takes to teach and connect with students. I just can't seem to get through to them. I know that library instruction can be engaging."

Librarian 1: "Right! We are more than animated database tutorials and encyclopedias of truncation symbols. For goodness sake, most of us are members of the faculty at our institutions."

Librarian 2: "And there's no reason we shouldn't act like it! When I get back I'm going to start searching for some way to make information literacy meaningful and alive."

Librarian 1: "Yes, there has to be a means to encourage students to think imaginatively about the research process. What we really need to do is figure out how the ACRL Standards can serve our pedagogy rather than limit it."

Librarian 2: "Definitely email me about where you're going with this once you get back. Now, enough talking about work, let's get out of here."

Although many instruction librarians attend conferences and other development opportunities faithfully, these "opportunities" seldom transform the static nature of library instruction. While conference conversations allow librarians to articulate this problem, they often do not provide means for transforming instructional practice. This lack of transformative material is attributable to both the conference format itself, which features one-way communication and offers few opportunities to produce knowledge and develop instructional praxis, and to instruction librarians' over-reliance on a formulaic approach to addressing information literacy standards. Whether intentionally or not, IL standards are often presented as an ends rather than a means. They are constructed as an objective path rather than a fluid inspiration. Thus, IL instructors struggle to make these standards come alive for students.

ACRL Standards and Critical Library Instruction

The recent proliferation of information literacy standards and guidelines is principally motivated by librarians' recognition of the need to expand library instruction from a strict focus on retrieval tools and techniques to critical analysis of the match between information documents and the searchers' proximal goals. While this constitutes movement away from an over-simplified pedagogy that characterizes the universe of knowledge as a static body of objective facts for harvesting—and does little more than equip students to achieve externally-supplied goals—the new terrain of instruction is still far from utopian. For instance, the Association of College and Research Libraries' (2000) *Information Literacy Competency Standards for Higher Education* largely ignore elements of dialogue, discovery, and mutability of purposes. For information seeking to assist in the process of knowledge creation, dialogue is absolutely necessary. Essentially, all information seeking behavior should be located in a rhetorical context (Andersen, 2006). A rhetorical context is established when students are required to produce and articulate their research within a dialogic community. Means by which this context is established include requiring discussion, presentation, and other forms of language-driven interaction with the researchers' peers.

As well, information seekers must continually be engaged in the act of discovery during research. 'Static' information seeking only leads to flat and perfunctory research and contributes very little to the growth of the researcher's intellectual identity. Thus, the mutability of purpose is perhaps the most significant concern within the context of IL; without it, dialogue and discovery are unlikely to occur. Unfortunately, the Performance Indicators listed under each ACRL Standard do not fully address the individuality and creative functionality of the researcher—they, in effect, bypass the agency of the researcher. Fundamentally these standards favor an instrumental approach. They are predicated upon the idea of using information to achieve purposes, rather than highlighting the purposiveness of the researcher. Thus, they construct research as an accretion of knowledge that can be added to a pre-existing 'knowledge base' that is divorced from any new knowledge creation. Consequently, by promoting (to the letter) the ACRL Standards, the IL instructor is hindering the transformation of her students and inhibiting their impact on the world. Yet, library instruction is not doomed to always be limited in these ways. The passivity of the ACRL Standards (as they are written) is contrary to the ideals promoted by Wilde and Giroux, for each theorist continually constructs the cruciality of the engaged rhetorical subject in the educational endeavor.

Both Wilde and Giroux promote dialogue as the central vehicle for self-discovery and transformation. Giroux (1997) sees self-expression, connections with peers, and active exploration of reasons for action as vital pre-requisites for engaged learning. He presents dialogue that is founded on students' concerns and stories as the center-piece of classroom activity because dialogue engages the classroom community, ensures that the content of classroom discourse has relevance to daily lives, and invites the teacher and the students' peers to interrogate language choice and contradictions. As well, not only did Wilde write plays composed almost entirely of conversation, he also employed the format of dialogue for his essays—most notably "The Critic As Artist" and "The Decay of Lying". Wilde's intellectual upbringing in the salons of his mother, Francesca, endeared him to the instructional and entertaining value of dialogue.

The most imperative paradigm shift for library instructors involves placing the individual, the researcher, at the center of the research process rather than demanding that the researcher bend to a static and arbitrary outcome. To accomplish this radical, conceptual shift, the IL instructor must make her classroom activities malleable to the passions of each student. There are clear steps that she can take to create such a classroom environment. The first step is to establish an environment that encourages sharing and dialogue among the students. For instance, rather than have each student hide behind his or her computer monitor, the instructor can create a space where the students must face each other. As well, to further foster dialogue, the instructor can promote research that is relevant to the students' personal and academic lives. Too often there is a disconnect between the students' conception of leisure and education. By demonstrating the interconnectedness of the intimate and the academic, IL instructors can engender an intellectual curiosity within their students. Before any lessons about skills or objective facts about the information universe are imparted, students' curiosity must be whetted and they must realize that the act of researching is authentic and representative of their own selves.

English 101

The despondent students file into the library's cramped technology classroom. Their instructor, a graduate student, slumps behind them in a similarly dejected manner.

IL Instructor: "Before you get comfortable, let's move to the adjacent classroom."

The students, along with their instructor, silently moan and wonder how they'll accomplish anything without computers at hand.

IL Instructor: "Now, let's discuss some of the topics you developed for your research papers."

In the example above, the IL instructor disrupts the normative hierarchy of tools over humanistic individuality by severing the student from the security of simply carrying out an instrumental task. Often students enter the library classroom with the assumption that the subsequent experience will be entirely oriented toward accessing information; and understand research as a practice that is independent from creating knowledge. Such an attitude creates barriers for the IL instructor and contributes to the most common frustrations voiced by student researchers. By forcing a pedagogical change, the IL instructor subverts the place of positivism within the realm of research.

Praxis and the Art of Library Research

One of the most common student complaints librarians hear is that there is "nothing" on a particular topic. This complaint is rooted in the positivistic world view that meaning is external to perception and is to be inductively assembled from facts encountered in the outside world. However, when students are taught they are, in fact, knowledge creators, they begin to understand that they are responsible for producing the "evidence" that will support their assertions. Thus, students will learn that their ideas and their opinions stand not in the shadow of others. Instead, students will act as agents of change and discovery. This relationship between researcher and research is similar to Wilde's summation of the relationship between critic and work of art. In "The Critic As Artist" Gilbert contends, "The critic occupies the same relation to the work of art that he criticizes as the artist does to the visible world of form and colour, or the unseen world of passion and of thought" (Wilde, 1923, p. 152). Here, Wilde elevates the critic's engagement with the artwork to the level of the artist's act of creation. Likewise, students need to re-conceptualize the relationship between themselves and their research to one that is fundamentally creative and experiential. Giroux, like Wilde, seeks to overturn the traditional hierarchy. Giroux (2005) urges teachers to "work with the knowledges that students actually have" (p. 197) and root viable instruction in their problems and needs, rather than the teacher's ideas of what their problems and needs should be. By emphasizing students' individuality, creativity, and agency, teachers can then help students interact with external knowledge in a way that presents it not as superseding their understandings, but as intersecting and enriching them.

There are many ways that a library instruction session might incorporate these ideals of individuality, creativity, and liberty. Perhaps the most important step is the construction of the classroom space as a dialogic space. To create space as dialogic the IL instructor must emphasize the rhetorical nature of research. That is, students must realize that their personal and academic language activities (speaking, reading, writing) are inseparable from their information seeking behaviors. To facilitate this realization, the IL instructor must demonstrate that research is not a process of answering questions, but rather a process of formulating questions, ideas, and narratives. In order to conceptualize research in this way, IL instructors must demand that students spend some time really working with their topics in a rhetorical context.

An IL instructor will know that she is being effective when students start taking responsibility for, demonstrating interest in, and projecting ideas about their research. The students will stop "cherry picking" quotes from random research articles and will instead learn to view others' ideas as springboards for their own creativity. They will understand thoroughly that their task is not to answer a question, but instead to pose questions to the academic community to which they belong. In essence, they will be more likely to experience themselves as active produces of knowledge rather than passive consumers/observers. Once IL instructors understand the importance of transforming their students' views of the nature of research, they will recognize that the key to critical pedagogy is placing students at the center of the educational process as opposed to foregrounding the conventional desiderata of search techniques and database idiosyncrasies. Thus, the stronger mentoring relationship between the teacher and the students will inspire the students to create an authentic relationship with their own research. Then the instrumental techniques required for research will become part of the larger narrative of the classroom rather than a presentation of disembodied skill sets.

References

Abowitz, K. K. (2007). Moral perception through aesthetics: Engaging imaginations in educational ethics. *Journal of Teacher Education, 58*(4), 287-298.

Andersen, J. (2006). The public sphere and discursive activities: Information literacy as sociopolitical skills. *Journal of Documentation, 62*(2), 213-228.

Association of College and Research Libraries. (2000). *Information literacy competency standards for higher education.* Chicago: American Library Association.

Arnold, M. (1994). *Culture and anarchy* (Samuel Lipman, Ed.). New Haven, CT: Yale UP. (Original work published 1865).

Aronowitz, S., & Giroux, H. (1991). *Postmodern education: Politics, culture, and social criticism.* Minneapolis: University of Minnesota.

Aronowitz, S., & Giroux, H. (1993). *Education still under siege.* Westport, CT : Bergin &   Garvey.

Giroux, H. (1997). Pedagogy and the politics of hope: Theory, culture, and schooling. Boulder, CO: Westview Publishing.

Giroux, H. (2001). Theory and resistance in education: towards a pedagogy for the opposition. Westport, CT : Bergin & Garvey.

Giroux, H. (2005). Schooling and the struggle for public life: Democracy's promise and education's challenge. Boulder, CO: Paradigm Publishers.

Giroux, H. (2007). The university in chains: Confronting the military-academic-industrial complex. Boulder, CO: Paradigm Publishers.

Newman, J. (1888). *The idea of the university* (8th ed.). London: Longmans, Green, and Co.

Wilde, O. (1923). The Critic As Artist. In *The complete works of Oscar Wilde* (Vol. 5, pp. 107-237). Garden City, NY: Doubleday, Page, and Co.

Wright, T. (2008). *Oscar's books.* London: Chatto & Windus.

Information Literacy and Social Power

Jonathan Cope

A cursory glance at much of the Library and Information Science (LIS) literature written about Information Literacy (IL) reveals its importance to LIS as a discipline. It also illuminates the role that IL plays in creating citizens who are capable of applying learned information skills in their day-to-day lives and in developing an informed, reasoning public capable of participation in a democratic society. However, the acquisition of knowledge is often presented as a linear process in which new knowledge is obtained—or deposited—and tied to a specific task (Elmborg, 2006). LIS commentators tend to shy away from more complicated discussions of social and political power: how it is wielded, maintained, and replicated, and how this affects social actors' search for knowledge. The twentieth century produced many social theorists for whom the issue of social power is central. The work of these thinkers has irrevocably altered the social sciences and the humanities. This has prompted Wayne Wiegand (1999) to suggest that LIS researchers undertake the challenge of integrating the work of these theorists into LIS.

A central tenet of critical pedagogy is the concept that extant social power relationships act to construct social reality in particular ways that limit the parameters of debate and prevent certain questions from being raised. A critical theory of IL—informed by the insights of critical pedagogy—maintains that the development of students' capacity to pose thoughtful questions (as opposed to clear answers) is as important as their ability to locate, access, organize, evaluate, and apply information in the research process. As IL programs become increasingly entrenched in a wide variety of academic institutions, it becomes vital to examine the discursive assumptions of the LIS discourse that has arisen around IL. The development of a theory of critical IL requires that LIS practitioners grapple with the questions raised by theorists of social power. Not only can the work of these thinkers reveal a great deal about how the LIS discipline has approached IL in the past, their work also provides the discipline with a critical lens through which to examine the IL discourse as it develops. Therefore, if LIS is to formulate a coherent critical theory of IL it must ask the following question: How has the LIS literature of IL viewed social power? What do we find when we examine this literature against the concepts and categories established by key theorists of social power?

This work examines a sample of key writings on IL through the lens of social power research as articulated by John Scott (2001) and his differentiation between "mainstream" and "second stream" social power research. Critical pedagogy arose out of and has been heavily informed by some of the key thinkers of the second stream tradition of social power research (Fischman & McLaren, 2005). The presence of second-stream concepts would suggest that information literacy theorists have considered the questions that this tradition poses and are developing a robust and critical theory of IL. Selected LIS literature on IL will be analyzed and placed into one of these categories using the method of discourse analysis.

If, as Buschman (2003) contends, librarianship has been propelled into a "crisis culture" by such disparate phenomena as the decline of the social welfare state and the devaluation of publicly funded institutions in favor of private, market-driven ones—what he describes as a "new public philosophy—these abstract discussions may seem to many LIS practitioners like pointless intellectual exercises ungrounded in the day-to-day realities of library work. However, the prevalence of new technologies and public philosophies, along with the increasing centrality of information literacy in many libraries' missions, elevates the importance discussions about how LIS views IL. If libraries and educational institutions are to be places of critical questioning and intellectual exploration a critical theory of IL must be a part of this conversation.

Historically, much LIS research has utilized the narrowly defined empirical methods of positivist social science (Wiegand 1999). While these methods can be of great use when exploring particular topics and questions, they are less useful in posing larger social questions and analysis. Instrumentalist logic—an interest in the strictly practical and measurable as opposed to the "true" or "universal," or, as Max Horkheimer puts it in *Eclipse of Reason* (1985), a reduction of reason to that which is strictly useful—has tended to dominate LIS research since its inception as an academic discipline (Wiegand). In trying to comprehend the place of the profession in society, this narrow focus on the strictly useful in specific cases diminishes the ability of the LIS practitioner to construct a broad theoretical and intellectual framework in which to situate their labor. The plying of one's intellectual and pedagogical craft requires an intellectual engagement in the social world—and the various theories of what constitutes that world—beyond one's own narrow and specific experience. The craftsperson who builds a chair must have an idea of the whole chair in relation to its constituent parts (e.g., the arm, the legs, etc.). Similarly, the critical information literacy pedagogue must have a broader understanding of the whole social environment in which they teach the particulars of IL. The wrenching forces that continue to transform the ways in which social subjects consume, produce, and analyze information necessitates forms of critique that allow LIS practitioners to pose large and sometimes difficult questions which often lack positivist, empirical answers. In order to do so, the LIS discipline must take a more expansive view of social power and its role in IL if it is to develop a critical theory of its practice. Theory and practice are both vital parts of a critical whole.

Social Power

Scott defines social power as being the relation between two agents. One of these agents can be described as the "principal" and the other as the "subaltern." The principal is the agent that wields power and the subaltern is the agent that is affected by this power. Power is also understood as the capacity to influence; a principal may not have to act in order to get a subaltern to behave in a particular manner. Consider the example of the librarian who is trying to decide whether or not to add to the collection a book that is critical of a large donor to their library. The donor may not actually withdraw their funding, and the librarian may still decide to add that book to the collection regardless of the risk, but the donor constrains the actions of the subaltern agent (in this case the librarian) because of the principal's *perceived* power. According to Scott, "acts of power occur when principals are able to restrict the choices that subalterns are able to make" (p. 3).

Focusing on power relationships between social actors represents a fundamental shift in thinking about IL. Most discussions of IL stress the development of applied skills that assume a rational, unconstrained information-seeking agent operating in an environment free of social hierarchies. A critical IL will see information-seeking as situated within particular contexts (relationships to power determined by social characteristics such as class, ethnicity, gender, etc.) and in particular societies with their attendant constraints, pressures, and structures. Commentators such as Pawley (1998) and Harris (1986) have observed that pluralism—the strain of social power research that Scott labels "mainstream"— influences many of the assumptions in LIS research and commentary.

The Mainstream Tradition

The mainstream—or pluralist—strain of social power research arose in the early part of the twentieth century. In this view, social institutions in Western liberal democracies are neutral terrain in which different groups, interests, and blocs vie for power through conflict and dialogue. This view sees "the sovereign power of the state as its exemplar" (Scott, p. 6) and social actors as rational subjects that are able to choose between various courses of action (Lukes, 1974). In pluralist thought, individual subjects align themselves with particular groups. Power is exercised by group pressure, although the state may play an important role in a particular conflict. Pluralists see the state as an actor with capacities similar to those of other groups that exercise power in political systems (Bailey & Braybrooke, 2003). Social subjects choose between competing groups and coalesce to exert pressure in order to achieve particular outcomes. For pluralists, constant interplay of groups and alliances is the essence of democratic decision making. What makes a society democratic as opposed to totalitarian is that it allows for this process of negotiation. In this theory, liberal democracies are governed by the action of dispersed blocs that compete and form temporary alliances to influence political outcomes. For this system to operate effectively, the various blocs must see the institutions and frameworks in which they operate as legitimate and the "rules of the game" as fair and transparent. Postwar American pluralist thinkers celebrated the United States' liberal and moderate character when compared to the totalitarianism of the right (e.g., Nazism) and left (e.g., Stalinism).

A theory of IL that focuses on the application of acquired skills reflects a mainstream/pluralist conception of social power. If pluralism sees social institutions in liberal democracies as being a neutral, open space in which all social actors may freely participate in debate, then it follows that those structures will not be as closely scrutinized in conceptions of IL informed by the tradition of pluralistic inquiry. Students are asked by educators to use "authoritative" sources without critically examining the systems in which that "authority" is established and articulated. In order for the pluralist/mainstream view of power to be practiced effectively, citizens must view social institutions as neutral. Large, abstract social questions are addressed as dichotomous choices (e.g., should one vote for a Republican or a Democrat?), because the heart of democratic expression is found in alliances that coalesce within a framework everyone agrees upon. To question the nature of such a framework would threaten the stability of such a social system and view of social power.

Additionally, such a world view—like much IL literature—stresses the acquisition of specific workplace skills, especially for non-elites. The development of such skills is one of the key functions of pluralist educational systems. As information technology continues to transform the ways in which workers labor, IL has often taken on this vocational, applied character. Pawley finds that the "Simple possession of computer skills still confers status. Just as mid-nineteenth-century clerks obtained better paying jobs because of their clear handwriting skills, so late twentieth-century clerks still enjoy a slight premium by virtue of their facility with word-processing, database, and spreadsheet manipulation" (p. 137). Teaching these kinds of skills is the focus of most of IL literature and practice.

Pawley finds that an LIS curriculum that centers on the acquisition of vocational IL skills—and does not question the world views from which they are born—will not enhance the lot of the historically subaltern. This approach to IL fails to create avenues that allow students to explore questions that address the causes of subalternity. This conception of IL acts as a hegemonic force in that it subtly reinforces a framework that primarily serves the interests of the middle class and wealthy by presenting extant social institutions as being neutral. Pawley argues that LIS has shied away from utilizing a class analysis and has continually used mainstream/pluralist perspectives as a way to understand its historical role. Pawley identifies LIS's links with the corporate world, its interest in professionalization, and its aspiration to a scientific status as the key components of a perspective that fits well within the mainstream/pluralist tradition of social power research. Using E. P. Thompson's concept of social class as "defined in terms of how people actively make sense of their experiences, values, and traditions and how groups of people act to create and maintain a sense of identity" (p. 126), Pawley finds that a class analysis would lead to a critical IL that encourages students to explore broad social issues such as the lack of good paying, fulfilling jobs instead of simply developing vocational skills for the few jobs that do exist. If the mainstream tradition of social power research offers a problematic framework for those who wish to develop a critical theory of IL what does the second-stream tradition offer?

The Second Stream

It is impossible to speak of the second-stream of social power research without discussing the work of two key figures: Antonio Gramsci and Michel Foucault. Gramsci's "Hegemony" and Foucault's "Governmentality" can be viewed as the two key divergent paths that second-stream power research has taken. Although there have been many other articulations of social power that would fit within the category of the second-stream tradition of research, these two concepts have been hugely influential. Therefore, if we are to observe the presence of the second-stream of power research in the IL literature, the appearance—or absence—of these concepts should serve as a benchmark by which to determine if such considerations exist.

The writing of Antonio Gramsci has cast a long shadow over the work of subsequent social theorists working within the second-stream of power research. As mentioned earlier, the second stream of power research is primarily concerned with the capacity of principals to influence and constrain the choices of the subaltern. In his *Prison Notebooks* (1971), Gramsci argues against the traditional Marxian tendency to reduce class power to solely economic factors. When the "inevitable" socialist revolution predicted by orthodox Marxism failed to materialize in the early twentieth century in Western Europe, Gramsci examined the role that culture played in securing the power of the ruling class. He argued that principals monopolize the field of options that subalterns have to choose from. He saw that the dominant ideas of a society are not only embedded in its political institutions, but also in its social institutions, or "civil society"—institutions such as the church, school, factory, trade union, or library. Through the consistent reiteration of dominant concepts and narratives, the principals naturalize certain concepts and ideas. Subalterns then assume that the options presented to them are the only options possible. It is through this iterative process that principals— in Gramsci's argument the ruling class—secure the consent of subalterns— in this case the working class. For Gramsci, the interests of the subaltern lie in organizing collectively in opposition to the power of capital. However, hegemony restricts individuals from the working class to a set of paths (or perceived paths) that better their individual lot only within the framework of the capitalist order. For Gramsci, the "organic intellectual," the social actor that is able to consider its own situation and act autonomously, is the key vehicle for disrupting this hegemonic framework. For Gramsci, the mass political party and the organic intellectual can create an alternative—or counter-hegemony—through collective mobilization (Day, 2005).

Gramsci's concept of hegemony contributed heavily to the development of Lukes's (1974) "three-dimensions of power." Lukes developed these concepts as a way to critique the shortcomings that he found in the mainstream of power research. These dimensions may be categorized thusly:

The First Dimension: The principal exerts power over the subaltern through the use of superior resources in a terrain of open conflict over articulated issues.

The Second Dimension: Principals act to exclude certain actors and issues and they act to confine the terms of debate.

The Third Dimension: The power of the principal is exercised over the subaltern through the creation of myths and beliefs that serve the interests of the principals resulting in the "internalization of the values, beliefs, or rules of the game of the powerful as a further adaptive response" (Gaventa, 1980, p. 17) on the part of the subalterns.

Although Lukes borrows from Gramsci, this multidimensional approach to the study of power was a major development in the discourse surrounding social power and created the context for a great deal of subsequent research.

If the domination of one group is secured through the production of ideology in the civil society of liberal democracy, it presents LIS and information literacy practitioners with many issues to consider. Raber (2003) posits that, by using Gramscian methods of analysis, librarians may be seen as organic intellectuals and participants in what Gramsci called a war of position. For Raber, libraries and librarians have the ability to act in counter-hegemonic ways. Gramsci's "work suggests that librarians might manifest a contradictory theoretical consciousness. On one hand, their activity implies a progressive transformation of the world. On the other hand, they uncritically absorb a theoretical consciousness from the past" (p. 50). Raber notes that "Even within a single library it is likely that one will discover some professional practices that represent capitalist hegemony at work and others that challenge that hegemony" (p. 49). A critical IL informed by Gramscian concepts will seek to develop students' capacity for social questioning and act to denaturalize the social structures and world views that they inhabit. In this context, strict "neutrality" is an illusory position for an educator to take, because to be neutral within the context of a specific hegemonic historic bloc is to lend support to that structure. A failure to foster students'capacity to question the dominant values and beliefs of a given society is akin to an endorsement of those concepts.

Unquestionably, the other key figure in second-stream power research is Michel Foucault (Scott, 2001). For Foucault, power is a pervasive, yet amorphous, fundamental aspect of the human condition. It exists everywhere, and yet it is difficult to isolate with any precision. Foucault conceives of power as something that exists beyond the formal structures of the state, economy, and civil society. Foucault's response to an interviewer's question about the use of the metaphor of war to explain power in society is revealing of his general view of power:

> Isn't power simply a form of warlike domination? Shouldn't one therefore conceive all problems of power in terms of relations of war? Isn't power a sort of generalized war which assumes at particular moments the forms of peace and the state? (1984, p. 65)

However, for Foucault, power relationships are in a constant state of flux. When power relations are altered they are transformed as individuals become social subjects through discourse. To use Foucault's metaphor of battle, discourse is one of power's key weapons. Individuals become discursively incorporated into power relationships as hierarchies based on expertise and discipline are continually created, contested, and then reinforced. This is fundamentally different from the Gramscian notion of hegemony—Foucault does not view this action through the lens of Marxian class struggle. Gramsci sought to establish a new hegemony, or historic bloc, in which socialism would serve as the hegemonic formation. Foucault's examinations of psychiatry, sexuality, and discipline took place in very a different paradigm. According to Foucault, "the eighteenth century [The Enlightenment] invented, so to speak, a synaptic regime of power, a regime of its exercise *within* the social body, rather than *from above* it" (1972, p. 39). He saw all discourse as being thoroughly entwined with the exercise of, and the resistance to, power.

Assessments of Foucault's work have been as numerous as they have been contentious. Many have seen Foucault, and the postmodern and post-structuralist thinkers with whom he is associated (Jacques Derrida, among others), as advocates of a nihilistic form of politics that sees every action as the product of an internalized power relationship. One of the most notable debates has been between Foucault and Jurgen Habermas about the notion of public participation and the possibilities of a public sphere (Buschman, 2003; Day, 2005). In his review of Foucaultian ideas in LIS, John Buschman (2007) finds that the application of Foucaultian theory to LIS theory has led to a kind of stasis. Foucault's work is a "conceptual import with its own discursive agenda that rules out all or most of the end purposes of such a critique" (p. 40). In other words, Foucault's form of analysis only leads to more analysis. The instrumentalist focus of most LIS scholarship resists such a divergence from practice.

If discourse frames the ways in which social actors conceptualize relationships within society, then it might be fruitful for IL pedagogues to ask themselves how they participate in particular discourses. If a critical theory of IL is interested in developing within students an ability to question common sense notions of society, then a Foucaultian unpacking of a particular discourse can help analyze the ways in which society examines a certain topic or question. By seeking to understand how social subjects have been prevented from asking particular kinds of questions in certain discourses, critical IL can generate new types of social analysis that serve to situate its practice within a broader social context. Using some of Foucault's critical techniques in the particular contexts where they might be useful does not necessitate a wholesale adoption of his methodology or thinking. Surely, the use of some of his concepts does not require librarians to abandon the rational classification and organization of information in order to make it publicly accessible. As with any thinker, Foucault's methods and ideas can be used as a conceptual toolkit to address specific issues and questions in specific contexts. There are occasions when critical IL calls more for the asking of new questions than it does for the provision of clear, instrumental answers.

As this brief discussion of thinkers from the second-stream tradition of social power research indicates, this tradition provides LIS with concepts that can facilitate the development of a critical theory of IL. This is because critical IL—and critical pedagogy—sees the instructor as a part of the social and cultural context in which they practice. The second stream of social power research problematizes social subjects' relationships to social and educational institutions; the mainstream tradition does not. The mainstream/pluralist tradition places a greater emphasis on the importance of consensus building and the importance of subjects choosing from available options. The second stream is interested in opening new avenues for critique and analysis. Examining some of the major LIS writings about IL against the divergent traditions of social power research unpacks some of the ideological underpinnings of IL research and helps LIS determine how it views social power.

The Study

As of 2002, more than 5,000 articles related to IL had been published in scholarly LIS journals. More than 300 publications about IL were printed in both 2001 and 2002 (Rader, 2002). Due to the sheer volume of IL publications, I selected the ten most cited LIS articles in the *ISI Social Science*

Citation Index that contained the term "information literacy" in their title or abstract. Results from journals that did not conform to this author's understanding of what constitutes an LIS journal (e.g., *The Journal of the Medical Informatics Association*) were excluded. These ten articles cannot serve as a representative sample; the purpose of this inquiry is simply to examine how a small selection of the most discussed IL-related LIS articles approach theoretical frameworks of social power. The method employed is that of discourse analysis. In this case, the discourse analysis examines how the LIS literature discusses social power. This examination does not suggest that every LIS or IL research inquiry necessarily need engage questions posed by theorists of social power in order to be methodologically sound or informative. The purpose of this inquiry is simply to see if the second-stream concepts that have stirred so much debate in other disciplines appear in the IL literature. By scrutinizing the most cited articles, a general understanding of how information literacy researchers approach social power emerges.

The literature examined displayed several general tendencies. First, several of the works struggled with the issue of simply defining the term IL (Bawden, 2001; Behrens, 1994; Grafstein, 2002; Marcum, 2002; Webber & Johnston, 2000). Although the term was first used in the 1970s, it did not gain widespread currency until the early 1990s (Rader). Several of the works examined offered a thorough historical analysis of the term (Bawden; Behrens; Webber & Johnston) and sought to clarify its precise meaning. This suggests that the term is highly contested and still subject to redefinition. Bawden—noting the large amount of ink spilled over defining terms such as "information" and "computer literacy"—advocates a "Popperian position of explaining, rather than defining, terms" (p. 251) as a parse of the often-conflicting underlying meanings attached to these labels. The sample examined reflects this tendency in that five of the ten articles spent a considerable amount of energy reviewing the various definitions of IL and their various histories. Although official library organizations have adopted IL as a central professional goal in need of promotion (e.g., the Association of College and Research Libraries's IL standards), the contentious definitional debate in the literature suggests that LIS has yet to develop a rigorous and multifaceted understanding of the concept. It should be noted that the increase in LIS literature on IL is concomitant with the development and widespread adoption of the Internet (Rader, 2002). This suggests that efforts to codify and define IL are reactions to the external forces of a changing information environment.

Second, any discussion of social power played an incredibly small role in the literature. A great deal of the literature reflected an instrumentalist approach to the acquisition of knowledge. Although several of the examined writings discuss the importance of life-long learning, much of the discussion focuses on the development of specific skills and is tied to specific tasks for application in specific contexts. For example, Webber and Johnston (2000) described literature that discussed how the perspectives of students and teachers differ when it comes to the importance of IL. Additionally, in Dunn's (2002) report on California State University's assessment program, a component of the institutional information competency aimed to develop within students "the ethical, legal and sociopolitical issues surrounding information" (p. 27). However, none of these writers engage in social power as something that would play a role in the construction of students' world view. With a few notable exceptions, there was practically no mention of social structure. These articles reflect a conception of social power that consistently fails to address the questions posed by both the mainstream and second stream of power research.

Several exceptions in this sample approach social power in a slightly more multifaceted manner and suggest a small measure of engagement in issues raised by the second stream of power research. Of the ten articles examined, only two explicitly explored questions of social power. Fisher, Durrance & Hinton's (2004) work on needs-based services for subaltern immigrants in Queens, New York, presents the development of IL in these library users based on a building-block and personal gains model. The building-block outcomes approach is a linear model that begins with the discovery of the library and ends with trust in the library's staff. Fisher, Durrance & Hinton define an immigrant's success primarily in terms of "personal gains outcomes" as opposed to more collective or social gains. The authors claim that because "outcomes accrue to and belong to individuals, as such, their fairest articulation comes from the users themselves" (p. 758). One of the outcomes described by the authors is "immigrants prepare to become citizens," a section that included an anecdote about the immigrant's participation in a lobbying trip to the state capital in support of library services. Yet, there is no mention of the immigrants lobbying on behalf of immigrants as a social group. The authors explicitly describe how library services better prepare immigrants for employment, provide immigrants with technological skills, and build self-confidence, among other things. While allowing the subjects to speak for themselves is sound methodology, the authors' reluctance to examine the subaltern political role of immigrants suggests a lack of engagement in the issues raised by the second-stream tradition. While the article soundly evaluates particular important services offered by a particular library to particular immigrants, it lacks an interest in developing programs and services that the subaltern immigrants could use to examine and question their social position.

Grafstein's (2002) call to situate IL within the other academic disciplines is the second work in the sample that addresses questions of social power. Grafstein discusses the role of "unacknowledged bias" (p. 201) in the development of generic critical thinking skills. The concept of unacknowledged bias suggests some engagement in second-stream issues. Grafstein suggests that "prejudices or bigotry" (p. 201) can be presented as fact and that there are occasions when research that is presented as unbiased and neutral can be influenced by the "financial, career, or personal interests" (p. 201) of the author. This suggests that social institutions play a role in how information and knowledge are socially constructed, reflecting the concerns raised by the second stream of social power research. However, without a more thorough explanation of what is meant by unacknowledged bias it is difficult to classify this work in the mainstream/second-stream schema.

Discussion

It is important to note that in recent years a small body of literature has emerged that seeks to develop a critical theory of information literacy. Writers such as Elmborg (2006) and Simmons (2005) have addressed questions of social power and discourse as they relate to information literacy. Elmborg specifically proposes a critical IL based on the insights of theorists such as Paulo Freire, Peter McLaren, and Henry Giroux, whereas Simmons suggests that librarians can act as mediators between different communities of discourse. However, these writings remain on the margins of LIS's IL discourse. This examination of ten of the most cited LIS articles on IL revealed practically no engagement in the debates from the second stream of social power research. Nine of the ten articles reviewed in this inquiry did not address conceptions of social power developed in Scott's second stream, and one held an ambiguous perspective.

One of the key insights of critical pedagogy is that there is no such a thing as an "apolitical" educational exchange. The decision of an educator to present "neutral" content as facts to be deposited into the heads of students is a political decision. A critical theory of IL does not seek to indoctrinate students with an educator's particular viewpoints. Instead, it entails a deep and fundamental embrace of the centrality of questioning in any educative process. To confine one's perspective to that which is strictly measurable diminishes the ability to conceptualize the social whole and the role of specific IL practices within it. A critical theory of IL seeks to engage students as active social subjects charged with interrogating the social world and developing their own capacity for informed questioning. In the classroom, a critical IL would entail a move away from the demonstration of technical search processes and simplistic claims that certain sources are "authoritative" because authorities have decided that they are. It would embrace a collective questioning of how information is constructed, disseminated, and understood. It would view the library instructor more as a facilitator of collectively generated insight and knowledge than as a sagacious depositor of facts and inherited wisdom. As more institutions embrace IL as a part of their institutional mission, it is vital that IL practitioners advocate for an IL that values the role of this questioning as much as it values a set of fixed IL competencies.

References

Bailey, M. & Braybrooke, D. (2003). Robert A. Dahl's philosophy of democracy,   exhibited in his essays. *Annual Review of Political Science, 6*, 99-118.

Buschman, J. (2003). *Dismantling the public sphere: Situating and sustaining librarianship in the age of the new public philosophy.* Westport, CT: Libraries Unlimited.

Buschman, J. (2007). "Transgression or Stasis? Challenging Foucault in LIS Theory." *Library Quarterly 77*(1), 21-44.

Dahl, R. (1961). *Who governs? Democracy and power in an American city.* New Haven: Yale University Press.

Day, R. J. F. (2005). *Gramsci is dead: Anarchist currents in the newest social movements.* London: Pluto Press.

Elmborg, J. K. (2006). "Critical information literacy: Implications for instructional   practice." *Journal of Academic Librarianship, 32*(2), 192-199.

Fishman, G. & McLaren, P. (2005). Rethinking critical pedagogy and the Gramscian and Freirean legacies: From organic to committed intellectuals or critical pedagogy, commitment, and praxis. *Cultural Studies - Critical Methodologies, 5*(4), 425-447.

Foucault, M. (1977). *Discipline & punish: The birth of the prison.* New York: Random House.

Foucault, M., & Gordon, C. (1980). *Power/knowledge: Selected interviews and other writings, 1972-1977.* New York: Pantheon Books.

Foucault, M., & Rabinow, P. (1984). *The Foucault reader*. New York: Pantheon Books.

Gaventa, J. (1980). *Power and Powerlessness: Quiescence and rebellion in an Appalachian valley*. Urbana, IL: University of Illinois Press.

Gramsci, A. (1971). *Selections from the prison notebooks of Antonio Gramsci*. New York: International Publishers.

Harris, M. (1986). State, class and cultural reproduction: Toward a theory of library service in the United States. *Advances in Librarianship, 14,* 211-252.

Horkheimer, M. (1985). *Eclipse of reason*. New York: Continuum.

Lukes, S. (1974). *Power*. London: Macmillan Press Ltd.

Pawley, C. (1998). Hegemony's handmaid? The library and information studies curriculum from a class perspective. *Library Quarterly, 68*(2), 123-144.

Rader, H. B. (2002). Information literacy 1973-2002: A selected literature review. *Library Trends, 51*(2), 242-259.

Raber, D. (2003). Librarians as organic intellectuals: A Gramscian approach to blind spots and tunnel vision. *Library Quarterly, 73*(1), 33-53.

Scott, J. (2001). *Power*. Cambridge, UK: Polity Press.

Simmons, M. H. (2005). Librarians as disciplinary discourse mediators: Using genre theory to move toward critical information literacy. *Portal: Libraries and the Academy, 5*(3), 297-311.

Wiegand, W. (1999). Tunnel vision and blind spots: What the past tells us about the present; reflection on the twentieth-century history of American librarianship. *Library Quarterly, 69*(1), 1-32.

Articles examined in discourse analysis.

Bawden, D. (2001). Information and digital literacies: A review of concepts. *The Journal of Documentation, 57*(2), 218-259.

Behrens, S. J. (1994). A conceptual analysis and historical overview of information literacy. *College and Research Libraries. 55*(4), 309-322.

Dunn, K. (2002). Assessing information literacy skills in the California State University: A progress report. *The Journal of Academic Librarianship. 28*(1) 26-35.

Edmunds, A. & Morris, A. (2000). The problem of information overload in business organisations: A review of the literature. *International Journal of Information Management, 20,* 17-28.

Fisher, K. E., Durrance, J. C., & Hinton, M. B. (2004). Information grounds and the use of need-based services by immigrants in Queens,

New York: A context-based, outcome evaluation approach. *Journal of the American Society for Information Science and Technology, 55*(8), 754-766.

Foster, A. (2003). A nonlinear model of information-seeking behavior. *Journal of the American Society for Information and Technology. 55*(3) 228-237.

Grafstein, A. (2002). A discipline-based approach to information literacy. *The Journal of Academic Librarianship, 28*(4), 197-204.

Hirsh, S. (1999).Children's relevance criteria and information seeking on electronic resources. *Journal of the American Society for Information Science, 50*(14), 1265-1283.

Marcum, J. W. (2002). Rethinking information literacy. Library Quarterly, 72(1), 1-26

Webber, S. & Johnston, B. (2000). Conceptions of information literacy: New perspectives and implications. *Journal of Information Science, 26*(6). 381-39

Breaking the Ontological Mold: Bringing Postmodernism and Critical Pedagogy into Archival Educational Programming

Lisa Hooper

> The archive was part of the apparatus of social rule and regulation, it facilitated the governance of the territory and population through accumulated information... the construction of archives can be seen as furthering governmentality and the regulation of internal and colonial populations. (Featherstone, 2006, p. 591)

> Systems of classification which reproduce, in their own specific logic, the objective classes, i.e., the divisions by sex, age, or position in the relations of production, make their specific contribution to the reproduction of the power relations of which they are the product, by securing the misrecognition, and hence the recognition, of the arbitrariness on which they are based: in the extreme case, that is to say, when there is a quasi-perfect correspondence between the objective order and the subjective principles of organization (as in ancient societies) the natural and social world appears as self-evident. This experience we shall call *doxa*. (Bourdieu, 1994, p. 159-160)

Tracing the beginnings of Paulo Freire's critical pedagogy to the Frankfurt School, Henry Giroux wrote that the Frankfurt School focused on "the issues of how subjectivity was constituted and how the spheres of culture and everyday life represented a new terrain of domination" (2003, p. 30). While the Frankfurt School blossomed from the late writings of Walter Benjamin, coming to fruition during the 1950s and 1960s, similar concepts of subjectivity, culture, and domination did not enter the archival literature until the mid-1990's with Jacques Derrida's seminal conference presentation, "Archive Fever, a Freudian Impression." Derrida's book version of this presentation, published in 1996, became the touchstone of contemporary archival theory. The disciplines of archival theory and critical pedagogy have shared strikingly similar understandings of symbolic capital, knowledge, cultural memory, and the role of institutions such as archives and education in supporting hegemonic structures. Despite these similarities, the paths of archival theory and critical pedagogy largely have yet to cross. Indeed, the postmodern identity of archives lags in the theory and practice of educational programming, which unquestioningly continues in its capitalistically-rooted, positivist modernist paradigm. Archival educational programming can, however, accommodate the profession's capitalistic survivalism as well as its postmodernist identity through the incorporation of elements from critical pedagogy.

Proponents of critical pedagogy view educational institutions as places of indoctrination, of orthodoxy with the goal of rendering hegemonic relationships doxic. Barry Kanpol views this in terms of market value, writing "Schools, it has been argued, in direct relationship with social efficiency ideology, prepare students for the market economy" (1994, p. 25). Henry Giroux broadened the influence of education within the positivist modernist paradigm to include social consciousness:

> Instrumental rationality extended its influence from the domination of nature to the domination of human beings. As such, mass-cultural institutions such as schools took on a new role in the first half of the twentieth century as 'both a determinant and fundamental component of social consciousness (Aronowitz, 1976)'... This meant that the cultural realm now constitutes a central place in the production and transformation of historical experience. (2003, p. 40)

Education serves as the linchpin of any given community of practice, indoctrinating youth with moderated knowledge as well as defining social interactions through the constructs of race, religion, class, sexuality and geographic boundaries. As Ronald E. Day observed, "the uniqueness of human individuals, however, is not due to any a priori qualities in themselves or in their humanness, but like all other animals and all other living beings in general, is due to their social, cultural, and historical specificity of development" (2007, p. 333); individual identity is moderated by communities of practice (Wenger, 2000, p. 207). An educational focus on the hard sciences, rote memorization of proscribed histories, and literary inclusions and exclusions all contribute to a hegemonic, socio-politically structured cognitive model which students are expected not only to navigate but to also read as a social map defining societal roles.

Archives are equally complicit in this production of cultural and historical experience. At once a representative and receptacle of power, archives have a dual identity: they are an institutional place, a building designed by those in power (archons) to house and protect evidences confirming archontic authority; archives are also the documents to which historical and evidential value have been assigned.

As architectural structures, archives function as physical symbols of archontic power and authority. Filling an orthodoxic role within a hegemonic doxic system,[1] archives became extensions of court, which "could serve as a propaganda machine, advertising national glory and demonstrating the prince's command of his leading subjects" (Dewald, 1996, p. 122). These symbolic archival buildings are accordingly built with fortress-like grandeur and impenetrability. Built and stocked by the archon, the place of archives becomes, in Derrida's words, a place of domiciliation, where paper documents become factual representatives of truth and bestow interpretive authority on the archon as well as on the archives itself.[2] Warfare exposes the institutionalizing role of archives; from the rubble of the French Revolution, the new government quickly rebuilt archives and began stocking them with new documents in order "to assist historical understanding, to redefine the notion of posterity, and to glorify the new Republic" (Cox and O'Toole, 2006, p. 50). The archives and its role in nation-building following the French Revolution became the model for national archives in democratic countries, particularly in North America.[3]

Archives are more than symbolic structures, archives are also documents, or memory artifacts. Within the archival community, the primary characteristics of a document remain essentially unchanged since Theodor R. Schellenberg redefined archival principles in the mid-1900s. Accordingly, archives are "those records of any public or private institution which are adjudged worthy of permanent preservation for reference and research purposes and which have been deposited or have been selected for deposit in an archival institution" (Schellenberg, 1956, p. 16). This seemingly straight-forward definition obscures a three-fold process of value

---

[1] This binary relationship referenced here refers to Pierre Bourdieu, who wrote "Orthodoxy, straight, or rather *straightened*, opinion, which aims, without ever entirely succeeding, at restoring the primal state of innocence of doxa..." (Bourdieu, 1994, p. 165).

[2] Archons are "those who commanded. The citizens who thus held and signified political power were considered to possess the right to make or represent the law... The archons are first of all the documents' guardians. They do not only ensure the physical security of what is deposited and of the substrate. They are also accorded the hermeneutic right and competence. They have the power to interpret the archives" (Derrida, 1996, p. 2).

[3] A contemporary example of the nation-building power of archives is found in Iraq and the struggles and personal tragedies Iraqi archivists have experienced trying to maintain the safety of their building and the integrity of their collections in face of Western occupying forces and political agendas.

assignation: the creator assigns value to information through inclusions and exclusions in the original document; the archivist through surface-level interpretation during selection and arrangement; the researcher through deep-level interpretation during history writing. The final historical record derived from these selective processes completes the orthodoxic function of the archive as place. Derrida refers tangentially to this process as the power of consignation, which "aims to coordinate a single corpus, in a system or a synchrony in which all the elements articulate the unity of an ideal configuration" (1996, p. 3).

In this authoritative and authorial position of archives, documents become the centerpiece of an historical consciousness which is "rooted in the identification of the past with external, material symbolic storage and with 'artificial' mnemonic systems, that is, with temporally marked written documentation" (Brothman, 2001, p. 59). The archivist's intention of neutrality through passive interaction with creators and records feeds into the positivist modernist theorem of accepting history without critique,[4] enforcing the paradigmatic pattern of collecting and classifying facts (Giroux, 2003, p. 33-34). Archivists ascribing to these tacit relationships (un)consciously participate in strengthening existing hegemonic structures, allowing the symbolic memory objects of the dominant culture to become sole proprietor of historical cultural memory.

The introduction of post-modernism to the archival profession led to a dramatic paradigm shift. Mark Greene's statement that "our work is about providing the building blocks and tools for assembling and interpreting the past—history and/or memory" (2003-2004) fairly expresses this shift. Derrida cut to the heart of archivists' struggle to reconcile the positivist-modernist archival legacy with their new post-modernist values:

> In their epistemology, in their historiography, in their operations as well as in their object, what should the classical archivists or historians make of this distinction between 'repression' and 'répression,' between Verdrängung and Unterdrücken, between repression and suppression? If this distinction has any relevance, it will be enough to disrupt the tranquil landscape of all historical knowledge, of all historiography, and even of all self-consistent 'scholarship'. (1996, p. 28).

---

[4] "The social function of the ideology of positivism was to deny the critical faculty of reason by allowing it only the ground of utter facticity to operate upon. By so doing, they denied reason a critical Moment." (Giroux, 2003, p. 32).

From this disrupted archival landscape, Terry Cook prodded archivists to "understand better our own politics of memory, the very ideas and assumptions that have shaped us, if we want our 'memory houses' to reflect more accurately all components of the complex societies they allegedly serve" (1997, p. 19). Archivists began recognizing archives as reflections of "the characteristics of their time and place" (Cook, 2001, p. 19), or, as Francis X. Blouin phrased it, "history is in some ways an official expression derived from institutions (archives) that have official responsibilities. Social memory, this new mode of looking at the past, goes beyond the archives to a validation of situational perspectives on the past" (1999, p. 109). These realizations have given rise to a generation of self-named 'activist archivists' such as Verne Harris, Carol Bernstein, Diane Britton, Barbara Floyd, Patricia Murphy, and Sue McKemmish among many others.[5] These activist archivists have blazed a path allowing archivists to engage the silenced, repressed, oppressed, and underrepresented in gathering and preserving their documental heritage.

The archival post-modernist movement is in its infancy compared to many other academic disciplines. Archivists are just now resolving the identity crisis brought on by post-modernism and are actively seeking to rectify the absence of the Other[6] from the physical archives. Despite these efforts, archival outreach and educational programming remain rooted in a lingering modernist educational praxis. At the heart of many conversations on archival educational programming is a fear of becoming irrelevant in an increasingly commercialized information industry. Speaking at the 1983 annual meeting of the Society of American Archivists, David B. Gracy II voiced this fear: "The threat to our programs and our profession resulting from our unsatisfactory image is real, and it is here now" (1984, pp. 8-9). This foreboding of professional death found its rejuvenating draught in the repurposing of educational programming to promote increased patronage and, consequently, public financial support:

> The principle [of use] remains today: To the extent that the public understand that archives exist to be used for reasons that affect their lives, property, civic well-being, and political influence, the public will be disposed to support and encourage archives. (Finch, 1994, p. 1)

[5] See Harris, V. (2004a; 2004b); Bernstein, C. L. (2007); Britton, D. F., Floyd, B. & Murphy P. A. (2006); McKemmish, S. (1996).
[6] The term Other denotes any socio-cultural group existing external to the dominant power; these groups, including subalterns, are often repressed and excluded from the dominant narrative.

This basic principle, observed in 1994 by Elsie Freeman Finch, noticeably begins with an altruistic call to archivists' democratic duty. Terry Eastwood later crystallized this mantra of democratic obligation to inform citizens of "how they have ruled themselves, and to allow them to build understanding of their place in the communities to which they consider themselves to belong, including of course the national community" (2002, p. 66). Reminiscent of Rousseau's *Les Droits de l'homme*, Ian Wilson offered "to venture the opinion that in a democratic, information-based society, there exists a basic social right to equitable and free access to archival services" (1990-91, p. 92). In 1990, Wilson saw this as the fundamental goal of the sea-change in archival outreach Gracy set off less than a decade earlier. Ironically, these calls to democratic equity represented by Finch, Gracy, and Wilson, invariably conclude with observations of the fiscal stability and social viability that public outreach generates.

Many of the educational programs growing out of these capitalistic calls for archival education remain mired in positivistic pedagogic formulae. Given the traditional identity of archives as places of research, programs often have as their primary objective "the instruction of actual and prospective users in research strategies and techniques" (Blais and Enns, 1990-91, p. 107). A secondary and more profound branch of archival education, however, creates an integral role for positivist archives within the educational enterprise:

> But the primary value of archives is their role as part of the cultural heritage, the contribution they make to a better understanding of the past, of the historical roots of human environment, of national identities and of international interdependencies. With this in mind it must be in the best interests of archivists to intervene at the moment when human ideas and convictions are formed, which means at the stage of primary or secondary education. (Franz, 1986, p. 9)

Within this dual paradigm of teaching youth the value of archives while presenting society's 'historical roots' with all their ontological power structures, archivists have developed three primary types of educational programming: presentation of selected documentation, exhibition, and digital archives. These typologies have the potential to be as much a source of hegemonic stabilization as they do to become intellectual spaces for contestation and critical self-discovery.

According to the 1986 *Archives and Education RAMP* study, the archivist must select documents for educational purposes that are "understandable in themselves and representative of a certain problem or historical phenomenon" (Franz, 1986, p. 13). Marcus Robyns similarly believes that the "guided use of primary resources in education can have an empowering effect on students," made more effective by the archivist's role of "guiding students through the process of critical thinking" (2001, p. 264-265).[7] This apparently simple process of document selection, however, is entwined with layers of social marking and bias, the same interpretive constructs Terry Cook identified in the process of archival appraisal: the "theories of value of societal significance an archivist brings to the records" (1992, p. 41). Imbedded within the archivist's culturally defined mental state,[8] these selections authenticate specific "historical phenomenon" which often represent the events, conventions, and social contexts of the dominant power and remain inaccessible within the socio-cultural frame of the Other. As Juan Flores phrased it, "without authentic dialogue [between all social groups], knowledge must be imparted through the monocultural, that is, highly suspect soliloquy of one voice" (2000, p. 193).

A critical selection of documents, however, can transform the classroom into a space of contestation and identity exploration through the multi-cultural voices of the Other. Margaret LeCompte's warnings for the researcher apply equally well to the archivist:

> To go beyond conscious-raising requires a greater commitment. If researchers truly wish to empower those whom they study, they must redefine informants to be those with whom they study, and redefine their own activities far beyond the production of a document describing events experienced, recorded and analyzed. (1993, p. 14)

As archivists become activists, they are confronted with the same dangers facing cultural anthropologists: falsely naming a cultural group;

---

[7] Robyns adopts Richard Paul's definition of critical thinking: "the intellectual disciplined process of actively and skillfully conceptualizing, applying, analyzing, synthesizing, and/or evaluating information gathered from, or generated by, observation, experience, reflection, reasoning, or communication, as guided to belief and action." (2005, p. 365).

[8] This use of mental states is drawn from Ronald Day (2007), who writes: "persons develop various types of personal potentials for using cultural tools, and that these potentials, when performed in either relatively solitary or social situations, then are traditionally seen as reflecting various types of mental 'states' ('knowledge,' 'feelings,' 'beliefs,' etc.) and their contents." He continues with the observation: "the psychological study of different cognitive 'states' is... a study of cultural grammars and groupings of what are considered to be mental events (i.e., materials and actions understood as 'beliefs,' 'knowledge,' 'reason,' imagination,' etc.).

unconsciously imposing a proscribed world view on a group; of 'liberating' a subaltern or Other that does not perceive a need for 'being saved.' With these cautions in mind, how might an archivist go beyond the representation of dominant society in their educational programming?

Recognizing a need for (de)selection in order to accommodate the limitations of students' knowledge base and curricular needs, there must nonetheless be a fundamental shift in the approach to document selection and in the conceptualization of the educational goals of archival outreach. In the classroom setting particularly, the need to advance beyond simply showing commemorative documents of an unchallenged history is of great presence. Rather than presenting a class with documents from which a unified, uncontested story may be derived, the archivist should consciously work to provide documents from a broad spectrum of perspectives that not only challenge their own authoritative legitimacy, but that also provide insight into events from the perspective of the subaltern and Other in addition to that of the dominant force. By remaining cognizant of students' mental models, presenting such a varied group of documents and engaging in critical discussion, students are challenged to "perceive and challenge dominant ideology, unmask power, contest hegemony, overcome alienation, pursue liberation, reclaim reason, and practice democracy" (Brookfield, 2005, p. 2). Similarly, archivists can follow the model of Juan Flores, replacing standard literature or historical frames with substitutions of corresponding meaning yet created within the contexts and mental states familiar to the class. A third option for the activist archival educator is to embrace the participatory nature of critical pedagogy and invite students to create their own documents. Classroom discussion of these documents can demonstrate what makes them archives and exploration of how they might be organized and accessed fits into the goal of critical awareness through the discursive self-awareness paradigm of critical pedagogy.

Exhibitions within archives have, generally speaking, been adopted from museums. While archival exhibitions were encouraged as a means of making the archives a destination point,[9] they are primarily conceived of as educational tools. Within the RAMP study, discussion of exhibitions took on a decidedly hegemonic, commemorative tone: "A well-conceived 'museum' exhibition will combine the illustration of various periods, aspects, and major events of national, regional or municipal history" (Franz, 1986, p. 17). Literature from the 1990s follows suit, with Susan Saidenberg identifying

---

[9] See Blais, G. & Enns, D (1990-1991); Wilson, I. E. (1990-1991); Gracy, D. B. (1984); Finch E. F. (1994); Saidenberg, S. F. (1991).

nine exhibition categories, including: institutional treasures, "historical themes, often in conjunction with anniversaries of major events," enduring ideas and issues, and community interest and leisure activities (1991, p. 129). Saidenberg's discussion hardly raises the questions of whose stories are selected and through what narrativistic lens they are told. Instead, positivistic exhibitions of unchallenged, authoritative documents are presented as facts doxically framed by the dominant historical narrative.

Exhibitions can, however, become highly effective modes of contestation and self-validation for under-represented populations. One approach is to create exhibitions focusing on controversial issues through the cognitive frame and documentary voice of the Other. Gwendolyn Reece describes such an exhibition featuring the Palestinian point of view on the Palestinian/Israeli conflict. This exhibition was created with the understanding that "representations are always created for library exhibits and they can therefore be sites in which the 'voice' of the subaltern is constructed by others" (Reece, 2005, p. 370). Reflecting the crisis of authority such exhibitions may invoke, the exhibition drew a certain amount of criticism from those who felt the library was legitimizing the Palestinian argument.[10] As Reece noted in retrospect, "many of the viewers brought the preferred meaning [i.e. pro-Israeli], often because the viewers brought their privileged epistemology to their viewing experience and read the exhibit through that lens" (2005, p. 370). The presentation of a minority voice challenged viewers to question the authority of their own mental models and, in some cases, revealed the orthodoxic undercurrents in dominant culture media and education. Simply challenging viewers' preferred epistemology promotes a certain level of critical self-awareness. In this case, the emotionally charged display encouraged viewers to review their presumed subject knowledge which led either to confirmation or continued questioning of the status quo. The point is not necessarily to change a viewer's mind, but to make the observer question him or herself.

In tandem with socially aware collection development, the activist archivist can similarly utilize exhibitions to bring representations of the Other to wider audiences, pushing both participants and observers to question their mental models and the doxic structures they navigate. The Centennial History Project in Chicago accomplished something quite similar to this goal. Sponsored by the East Chicago Public Library, the

---

[10] As Reece observed from the comment book, "the implication is that, because of its display in an official university setting, the exhibit would therefore 'carry the weight and implicit authority' of the whole American University"(2005, p. 368).

project had a notable undercurrent of regional commemoration, approaching the topic not from a dominant textbook perspective, but rather from that of a broad spectrum of minority groups, or Others, residing in Chicago. As with public archeology, the goal was "the creation of a sense of community and social identity" (Baumann, Hurley, and Allen, 2008, p. 70) through the active engagement of unrepresented community groups in collecting their memory artifacts and "information that cannot be found elsewhere about their social, economic, and political history" (Rodriguez, 1991, p. 1026) and allowing them to narrate their story in the form of self-created exhibitions. Once the project librarian-archivists established lines of communication with underrepresented groups, community members voluntarily came forward with their memory artifacts. This approach allowed the librarian/archivist to avoid naming, instead permitting these groups to name themselves through their own mental models. This practice of naming the Other is an intrinsic element of documenting a community, as LeCompte noted, "naming something may make it real; that reality becomes more apparent when the naming is done by those for whom it has become salient" (1993, p. 11). Though not consciously pursued, the conceptualization and manifestation of the History Project approaches Freire's ideal of teaching literacy through the symbols and knowledge structures of culturally unique groups. While self-education was not the primary concern in this case, groups organized their cultural symbols to construct historical representations accessible within their own mental state rather than filtered through the hegemonic framing of the dominant power.

Closely related to exhibitions are digital archives. While the online forum solves some problems of equitable access,[11] the issue of selection in which the archivist determines, typically within his/her own mental state or cognitive frame, what is included and excluded from these digital learning environments persists. From these databases of images linked to description, web-display developers seek to create "generative, problem-based, creative play and expository methodologies that help learners to build on their own knowledge structures (schema) to construct new knowledge and understanding" (Sumption, 2001). In such cases, "the material is reduced to emblematic functions" (Dalbello, 2004, p. 274) which hardly have the opportunity to break from the symbolic capital of the dominant hegemonic force, as both the digital space and the intellectual cognitive frame with which students are expected to view digital archives are created within a

---

[11] The archival world has largely yet to address the issue of the digital divide and its implications for representation, silencing, contestation, cultural ownership, etc.

doxic understanding of historical and educational purposes. At issue is whether these online displays are spaces of contestation or extensions of the symbolic capital of archives.

Principles of critical pedagogy brought to exhibitions can be incorporated into the online knowledge-space of digital archives. Rather than selecting documents to represent an uncontested dominant history, the activist archivist can use Freirian pedagogy to provide a forum in which the Other may bring their contested history to the surface of society via the most widely accessible media available. Darcy Alexandra of the Dublin Institute of Technology provides an excellent model of a critical digital archive through which she gives presence to the stories of undocumented immigrants living in Dublin, Ireland. The project promotes participant "storytelling that engages processes of remembering, meaning making and the re-constituting of lived experiences through the creation of a digital story" (2008, p. 103). To accomplish this, Alexandra created workshops that engaged participants in dialog through speech, still image, moving image, and other forms of artistic self-expression. These workshops resulted in several online displays. The participants, as well, concluded the workshop series with a rejuvenated sense of identity and a more critical understanding of the socio-political structures they navigate.

These suggestions for pedagogically critical archival education programming offer only a glimpse into what can be done. If the archival profession is to fully shed the mantle of positivism, activist archivists must also accept their role as educators and seek to bring the profession's post-modern values into archival educational programming. The parallel philosophical convictions grounding critical pedagogy provide a facile paradigmatic transition for the activist archivist and an entry into critical archival education. While such endeavors undoubtedly consume already scarce time and resources, the efforts to provide a forum for the disenfranchised, to render previously doxic ideals and convictions heterodoxic, and to inspire the intellectual tools necessary for individuals to critically navigate their socio-political environment have far-reaching consequences already embraced by the post-modernist archival profession.

References

Alexandra, D. (2008). Digital storytelling as transformative practice: Critical analysis and creative expression in the representation of migration in Ireland. *Journal of Media Practice 9*(2), 101-112.

Baumann, T., Hurley, A. & Allen, L. (2008). Economic stability and social identity: Historic preservation in Old North St. Louis. *Historical Archeology* 421, 70-87.

Bernstein, C.L. (2007). Beyond the archive: Cultural memory in dance and theater. *Journal of Research Practice* 3(2), 1-14.

Blais, G. & Enns, D. (1990-1991) From paper archives to people archives: Public programming in the management of archives. *Archivaria* 31.

Blouin, F. X. (1999). Archivists, mediation, and constructs of social memory. *Archival Issues* 24(2), 101-112.

Bourdieu, P. (1994). Structures, habitus, power: Basis for a theory of symbolic power. In N. Dirks et al, (Eds.), *Culture/Power/History, a Reader in Contemporary Social Theory* (pp. 155-199). Princeton, NJ: Princeton University Press.

Britton, D. F., Floyd, B. & Murphy, P. A. (2006). Overcoming another obstacle: Archiving a community's disabled history." *Radical History Review* 97, 213-227.

Brookfield, S. D. (2005). *The Power of critical theory: Liberating adult learning and teaching.* San Francisco: John Wiley and Son.

Brothman, B. (2001). The Past that archives keep: Memory, history, and the preservation of archival records." *Archivaria* 51, 48-80.

Cook, T. (1992). Mind over matter: Towards a new theory of archival appraisal. In B. Craig (Ed.). *The Archival imagination: Essays in honour of Hugh A. Taylor.* Ottawa: Association of Canadian Archivists.

Cook, T. (1997). What is past is prologue: A History of archival ideas since 1898, and the future paradigm shift." *Archivaria* 43, 17-63.

Cook, T. (2001) Fashionable nonsense or professional rebirth: Postmodernism and the practice of archives. *Archiviaria* 51, 14-36.

Cox, R. & O'Toole, J. (2006). *Understanding archives and manuscripts.* Chicago: Society of American Archivists.

Dalbello, M. (2004). Institutional shaping of cultural memory: Digital library as environment for textual transmission. *Library Quarterly* 74(3), 265-298.

Day, R. E. (2007). Knowing and indexical psychology. In McInerney, C. R. & Day, R. E. (Eds.), *Rethinking knowledge management: From knowledge artifacts to knowledge processes* (pp. 331-347). Berlin: Springer

Derrida, J. (1996) *Archive fever: A Freudian impression.* Chicago: University of Chicago Press.

Dewald, J. (1996). *The European nobility, 1400-1800.* Cambridge: Cambridge University Press.

Eastwood, T. (2002) Reflections on the goal of archival appraisal in democratic societies." *Archivaria* 54, 59-71.

Featherstone, M. *Theory, Culture, and Society 23*(2-3), 591-596.

Finch, E. F. (1994) *Advocating archives: An introduction to public relations for archivists*. Metuchen, NJ: Society of American Archivists and Scarecrow Press.

Flores, J. (2000). Authentic multiculturalism and nontraditional students: Voices from the 'contact zone'. In Steiner, F., Krank. H. M., McLaren, P. & Bahruth, R. E. (Eds.), *Freirian Pedagogy, Praxis and Possibilities: Projects of the New Millennium* (pp. 193-202). New York: Falmer Press.

Franz, E. G. (1986) *Archives and education: A RAMP study with guidelines*. Paris: General Information Programme and UNISIST, United Nations Educational, Scientific and Cultural Organization.

Giroux, H. (2003). Critical theory and educational practice. In Darder, A., Baltodino, M. & Torres, R. D. (Eds.), *The Cultural Pedagogy Reader* (pp. 27-56). New York: Routledge.

Gracy, D. B. II. (1984). Archives and society: The First archival revolution." *American Archivist 47*(1), 7-10.

Greene, M. A. (2003/2004). The Messy business of remembering: History, memory, and archives. *Archival Issues 28*(2), 95-103.

Harris, V. (2004a). Concerned with the writings of others: Archival canons, discourses, and voices. *Journal of the Society of Archivists 25*(2), 211-220.

Harris, V. (2004b). History after apartheid: Visual culture and public memory in a democratic South Africa/Apartheid's festival: Contesting South Africa's national past. *Public Historian 26*(4), 115-118.

Heaney, T. (2000). Politics of explanation: Ethical questions in the production of knowledge." In Steiner, F., Krank. H. M., McLaren, P. & Bahruth, R. E. (Eds.), *Freirian Pedagogy, Praxis and Possibilities: Projects of the New Millennium* (pp. 101-118). New York: Falmer Press.

Kanpol, B. (1994). *Critical pedagogy, An introduction*. Westport, CT: Bergin and Garvey.

LeCompte, M. (1993). A Framework for hearing silence: What does telling stories mean when we are supposed to be doing science? In McLaughlin, D. & Tierney, W. G. (Eds.), *Naming Silenced Lives: Personal Narratives and Processes of Educational Change* (pp. 9-27). New York: Routledge.

McKemmish, S. (1996). Reflections of me. *Australian Library Journal 45*(3), 174-187.

Reece, G. J. (2005). Multiculturalism and library exhibits: Sites of contested representation. *Journal of Academic Librarianship 31*(4), 366-372.

Robyns, M. C. (2005). Archivist as educator: Integrating critical thinking skills into historical research methods instruction. *The American Archivist* 64, 366-372.

Rodriguez, G. (1991). Forging civic pride in the Rust Belt: East Chicago's History Project. *American Libraries*, 1026-1029.

Saidenberg, S. F. (1991). Displaying our wealth: Exhibitions make an auspicious comeback. *American Libraries*, 128-132.

Schellenberg, T. R. (1956). *Modern archives: Principles and techniques*. Chicago: University if Chicago Press.

Sumption, K. (2001). Beyond museum walls—A Critical analysis of emerging approaches to museum web-based education. *Papers: Museum and the web 2001.* Retrieved December 31, 2008, from http://www.archimuse.com/mw2001/papers/sumption.html

Wenger, E. (2000). Communities of practice: The Structure of knowledge stewarding. In Despres, C. & Chauvel, D. (Eds.), *Knowledge horizons: The Present and the promise of knowledge management* (pp. 205-223). Boston: Butter-Worth Heinemann.

Wilson, I. E. (1990-1991). Towards a vision of archival services. *Archivaria* 31, 91-100.

Grand Narratives and the Information Cycle in the Library Instruction Classroom

Sara Franks

Grand Narratives and Higher Education

In the early 1980's, historian and philosopher Jean Francois Lyotard wrote *The Postmodern Condition: A Report on Knowledge*, a text that has since become quintessential in defining and investigating the postmodern across disciplines and discourses. Within this work, he announced that the modernist days of "grand narratives" were soon to be over. These narratives, centered on scientific development as the primary propeller for the advancement of humanity, attempted, within educational as well as other cultural institutions, to link all of the narratives of human progression back to several large threads of historical development. (These could be religious narratives of progression, such as Christianity, social narratives of progression, such that Marx lays out, or the epic story of scientific inquiry and development that, we are sometimes told, drives us forward.) In modern classrooms, critical pedagogists have called into question the legitimacy of these grand narratives as representative of all human experience, and have come to critique the educational structures that uphold the retellings of these narratives as silencing and shutting out the voices of the repressed and oppressed: a narrative centered around biblical constructions of history and progress, for instance, ignores other religions and ethnicities; a telling of advancement through scientific inquiry might glorify technological and industrial progress at the expense of discussing the concurrent history of labor and environmental exploitation that this type of progress has caused; examining events or concepts solely through a Marxist lens, even though many would consider this an emancipatory framework, might bypass important discussions about the constructions of gender and race that complicate the class system. Instructors who wish to reframe education around individual and more fragmented histories argue that teaching these grand narratives distorts students' understanding of reality and presents historical veins of progress as natural, the only truth worth telling; they ignore the very real need to recognize the diverse and dissenting voices that come from outside the borders of these narratives (Lankshear, C., Peters, M., & Knobel, M., 1996; McLaren, P., & Farahmandpur, R., 2005).

Within the postmodern era, though, and with the rise of alternative outlets for historical documentation, Lyotard projects, these Western-centric and limiting grand narratives would fray, breaking apart and giving way to other, smaller and more fragmented veins of historical knowledge; this condition would ultimately create a plethora of vastly different ways of seeing and thinking about historical and scientific progress. He suggests that this breakdown of the grand narrative will be driven forward by information technology, as the construction of what knowledge is and, therefore, how we teach it, changes with new channels of access. Within this new postmodern era, Lyotard suggests that the system of memorizing content in educational institutions would be replaced by learning about the process of finding information- in fact, the very skills library professionals and information literacy specialists seek to impart to students (Elmborg, 2005; Lyotard 1982).

Many "canonical" resources in the humanities and social sciences, sources that have long defined intellectual subjects and constituted foundational reading for students in a given discipline, might be considered relics of the past in a Lyotardian framework of scholarship, as they, in some ways, represent an age when students were asked to build a knowledge of these grand narratives to which Lyotard refers. And, as some critical pedagogy theorists would agree, researchers and educators who follow a Lyotardian framework will be stepping into a new era of liberationist, postmodern pedagogy, in which disciplines and instructors must undergo a thorough questioning of the way curriculums and knowledges are constructed (Peters & Lankshear, 1996; Luke & Kapitzke, 1999), in which they must unpack the grand narratives and see them not as the ultimate truth of progression but as one of many truths that should be properly situated alongside oppressed voices that have often been silenced within the traditional classroom. Colin Lankshear, Michael Peters, and Michele Knobel (1996), within an insightful discussion of the critical pedagogical possibilities of cyberspace, in fact, criticize the texts of the traditional classroom as "'sub-institutions' of...modernist spaces of enclosure," suggesting that by separating literacy from the context of the real world, educational institutions have long taught isolated, decontextualized, and linear histories that often leave students disengaged and alienated (p. 165).

It is very evident that grand narratives are still ingrained in the academic disciplines that make up higher education, particularly in the construction of specific disciplines. Many professors, in fact, work to preserve and uphold not only disciplinary boundaries and practices, but also the traditional curricular framework of the past (Klein, 1999). Yet, as college and university communities evolve, we should also be aware of how the grand narratives are being challenged. It is undeniable that higher education in the U.S. continues to become more experimental. Faculty are encouraged and rewarded to specialize deeper and more narrowly than ever before, resulting in, as James Davis (1995) terms, an "isolation" within the disciplines; at the same time, though it seems rather paradoxical, this isolation sometimes increases the need for true interdisciplinarity, rooted in collaboration and communication (p. 35), as researchers find their base of knowledge lacking for truly large-scale projects. Interdisciplinary departments have sprouted up in response, partly, to the breakdown of the more rigid grand narratives of the disciplines: women's and gender studies departments, for instance, as well as American and African-American studies departments, usually depend on the expertise of a wide range of scholars, from sociologists to fine arts specialists. This is due, in large part, to recognition by scholars of the insufficient job traditional departments within academia have done in examining the issues surrounding these subjects (Klein, 2005). Davis reminds us, as well, that scholars' pedagogical choices reflect and follow their collaborative pursuits, suggesting that scholars learn to value teaching in these types of programs because, within interdisciplinary courses: "...the focus is on developing critical thinking skills, employing multiple perspectives, and relating information to some larger conceptual framework than the concerns of a specific discipline" (p. 38). In this spirit, standard survey courses and hierarchical curriculums are being replaced with classes like freshmen first-year experience courses that combine and link disciplines, and problem-based, team-taught courses, representing a major migration within higher education towards interdisciplinarity (Klein, 1999). This is a sure indication that the academy is gradually growing tired, itself, of at least some of the grand narratives to which it used to ascribe, pulling away into specialized paths of knowledge that often do not feed students the same Western arc of "truth" from which colleges and universities used to insist their students began.

Grand Narratives and Information Literacy

Regardless of whether or not grand narratives are still pedagogically embedded within higher education curriculums, our focus as information literacy specialists needs to be not only on imparting how to find resources, as Lyotard insists, but also on teaching how to think critically about the resources that are found. Within an age where information channels are changing so rapidly, this would have two purposes: because students are often surrounded by cultural and educational material (including material collected through their libraries) that *do* still perpetuate grand narratives, they need to learn to think critically about whose voices are not represented within a text that they find; because, on the other end of the spectrum, they are also often confronted with texts that *challenge* traditional grand narratives, they need to learn to question the ability of any given work to capture a concept completely, to be skeptical of any telling that claims to be representative of others. This would, ultimately, show them how they themselves can participate fully in the breakdown of grand narratives while also preventing new ones from solidifying.

In order to tackle these issues effectively, we need to translate the theoretical base that Lyotard gives us into practical applications that we can adopt when working with students. We as information literacy professionals need to reflect upon our own behavior within the classroom, as well as individually with students, as we either encounter them at the reference desk or through research consultations. How do we either perpetuate or try to break free of the "grand narratives" that might prevent students from taking a truly critical perspective towards their culture? This reflexive approach needs, in my opinion, to include: a discussion of the types of sources we are suggesting to students and how they may reinforce or release themselves from disciplinary constraints and problems, an investigation of the way we frame our discussions of information flows and exchanges, and a look into how we ourselves suggest critical analysis of the processes of searching for and evaluating information. Students need to know that the production of any text is a highly political act, with choices along the way that will affect how information users, just like them, will reflect on the topic addressed. Ultimately, we need to challenge students to ask themselves: as information is situated through the publication hierarchy, discussed initially, perhaps, on the web, placed within academic journals and, then, introductory works like encyclopedias, how are decisions made about what should be represented, and, as information is carefully filtered out for the more selective publications, and sliced up for recombination and redefinition, what is deemed important enough to include and why? Who is supported by such decisions in terms of both disciplinary boundaries and the larger hierarchy of social power?

In the following sections, I will discuss how we can translate a critical stance of grand narrative structures into good pedagogical applications. I will begin with what is termed by many information literacy specialists as "the information cycle" and its assumptions about information flows. I will then move on to three popular publication types often discussed within the information cycle and explored by librarians in the classroom, and will present some of the complications, while suggesting some good practices, of introducing such sources in a postmodern and critical framework that questions the grand narratives that still linger in our educational practices.

The Information Cycle

The information cycle is often used within library instruction to challenge students to think of how information flows from initial events, ideas, experiments, or studies, into the popular press (newspapers, news magazines), into scholarly articles, books, and finally reference sources like encyclopedias, readers and handbooks.[1] Of course, different disciplines would represent the information cycle in different ways, but the very typical example often used in introductory library sessions consists of showing how an event unfolds from its initial occurrence, how it is reported on by the popular press (the open web, followed by newspapers, then news magazines), then "flows" into discussions within scholarly articles, followed by academic books and, after several years, if it were of enough significance, how it would then begin to appear in reference works. Within our discussion of such a "cycle," we often *describe* the publishing mediums without probing the assumptions about information flows that we make along the way: the very term "information cycle," in fact, suggests to the researcher or student that it is a passive, natural process, like the "water cycle" or the "cycle of seasons." In the same vein, we discuss "information flows" and frame the process of gradually revisiting the same event or concept within each stage of the cycle as information "trickling" through the cycle. Our initial terminology, and certainly the way we describe the steps of creation and publication of texts, reflects our own preconceptions of the process as something so established and so ingrained in the way we talk about information that it takes on an apolitical, manifest and predetermined quality, much like the grand narratives of Lyotard's discussion, rather than the value–ridden and strategic acts that the processes actually represent as information is carefully situated at each level of this so-called cycle. Students must come to question how the natural presentation of "realities" within

---

[1] Popular instructional tutorials online on the information cycle include one from Pennsylvania State University Libraries: http://www.libraries.psu.edu/instruction/infocycle/infocycle.html, and one from Northwest Missouri State University: http://www.nwmissouri.edu/library/courses/research/timeline.htm

such texts is actually contingent on a myriad of dimensions: historical, social, hegemonic, and even material (as, for instance, within the print genre, by virtue of its materiality, fewer voices could be represented) (Andersen, 2006; McLaren & Hammer, 1996). If we were to reframe our discussion of such processes of publication with vocabulary of action and agency, we could begin to place students in the position of considering the choices that are made along the way in such processes: the event happens, people of all kinds report on it, newspapers and magazines comb through these initial occurrences and commentaries and slice up the information to make a story, academics carefully review the events for research questions from which they could construct a discussion, centered around their particular disciplines and interests. Lastly, encyclopedia editors and writers think carefully about what to include in a short entry on the subject, and most likely edit such an entry substantially, years later. By changing our vocabulary, we can begin to instigate among our students an important realization that information is not a prepackaged thing that naturally reappears in various sources over years. It is actively constructed, according to interests intellectual, commercial, and hegemonic, and it is reformed because of these interests continually (Sholle & Denski, 1995; Hammer, 1995).

The Open Web

By beginning with the open web, students should be challenged to think of both the complications and the potential of a boundariless and instantly updatable forum of communication. Asking questions about whose voices are represented, and particularly how those voices are found in the "infoglut" of the web, can be a powerful point of discussion (Luke & Kapitzke, 1999, p. 477). Students should learn to question the structure of search results and the commercialization of the web, and to investigate questions of sponsorship and corporate connections, not only by criticizing pages with advertisements and questioning their content, but by investigating even how commercialization might play a role in what is situated at the top of search results pages (Buschman & Brosio, 2006). Certainly, as many theorists have argued, while we should aim to gradually break down the grand narratives that made up educational practice for many years, we also don't want to create a new grand narrative that naturalizes capitalism and commercialization—students need to always be probing and questioning the way they themselves participate in a new but rapidly expanding market of information that often asserts itself, both overtly and covertly, on the web (McLaren & Farahmandpur, 2005, p. 169).

Certainly, the possibilities of the web in breaking down grand narratives should also be discussed as well: opinions and assertions of the everyday citizen, including sources like blogs, wikis, and discussion lists, might be considered tools for empowering and strengthening dissenting voices. A searcher's navigation around, between, and through such communication on the web can be fodder for getting an overall sense of how the public is engaging a particular subject. This exploration could yield differing opinions on the topics at hand, help searchers imagine how the subject might have been exploited by corporations or even non-profit organizations, or illustrate to searchers how different audiences are framing and discussing the subject (e.g.—by examining how amateur web pages might show it's a subject schools have taught, or in which a particular population has shown interest).

Scholarly Books and Academic Journal Articles

Often, information literacy librarians insist on jumping in to a discussion of popular versus scholarly resources as an initial introduction into the academic world of information. There are several reasons for doing so, including our desire to introduce students to the most reputable information to which they have access, and our plans to orient them within the realm of their new disciplinary community and the channels of communication that flow therein. Librarians and professors often suggest that the struggle with complex and specialized language that students face resulting from such disciplinary materials is not only healthy, but is needed in order for students to fully be inducted into the discipline that they study (Elmborg, 2006; Simmons, 2005).

It is important, though, to also be frank with students about the possibilities and limitations of such texts. When we introduce scholarly materials such as academic journals and books, we should make students aware that the publication of scholarly articles, while offering quality information, is often, in fact, influenced by the trends and styles of disciplines and subjects as much as popular publications (Simmons, 2005). (How might grant funding influence a study? How might a scholar be influenced by the institution in which they are researching or the tools to which they have access? How might the fact that a particular subject is broached mostly by male authors influence one's perception of the work?). In our initial differentiation for students between popular and scholarly material, we need to make sure we don't, as Troy Swanson (2004) puts it, "candy-coat" the distinction for them, indisputably equating popular with "bad" and scholarly with "good," a distinction that perpetuates a naturalized image of scholarly material as infallible (p. 267). Rather, we need to place these different types of materials on a sliding-scale without avoiding discussions of how scholarly materials sometimes do face the same questions of bias or falsely-constructed information as their popular counterparts.

College-level instructors, including information literacy librarians, must also acknowledge that the general movement towards more interdisciplinary and problem-based classes often means students approach subjects of which they have very little background knowledge. Most scholarly publications, for all their benefits, do a poor job of providing such introductory material. As stated above, a sweeping trend in academia encourages and rewards extremely deep and narrow specialization, making scholars in any given discipline and with any given specialization more "isolated" and versed with a particular vocabulary that becomes increasingly difficult to impart to new community members, whether they be upcoming scholars, scholars trying to venture into new intellectual territory, or students (Davis, 1995, p. 36). In fact, the trend for the past several decades has been to publish journals on more narrowly-defined topics and for smaller audiences within the academic community, making them often more laced with jargon and even less suited for preliminary reading than in the past (Peek & Newby, 1996). Presenting students with introductory materials such as reference works can certainly alleviate the problem, but promoting the use of these reference sources—without also suggesting that we should unequivocally accept their "truths" (thereby reinstating the paradigm of grand narratives)—then becomes a challenge.

Reference Sources

The instinct, mentioned at the top of the last section, to jump into an introduction to resources by pushing students towards academic material might also reflect (for some of us) our own reluctance to rely on introductory sources like encyclopedias, handbooks and readers. Such materials might mark, to the critical information literacy librarian, the remains of an age that clung to grand narratives, that reduced all stories to a single, overarching voice, and that asserted authority in a supposedly neutral tone. Luke and Kapitzke (1999) suggest further that encyclopedias "privileged and reinforced disciplinary boundaries," declaring that "[t]he very historical structure and organization of the library thus expresses a will towards permanence and canonicity" (p. 472). As Christine Pawley points out, also:

> Many encyclopedia articles appear without accompanying justification in the form of references or citations. The information encapsulated in an article stands alone, authoritative by virtue only of its presence in the volume. Legitimacy is conferred by its place on the library shelf… (2003, p. 435)

As more and more reference sources are made available digitally, these books are deemed legitimate now because of their place on the *digital* library shelf: in our collection of databases and on our subject pages. The move towards digital collections is often discussed within the framework of the democratization of information: as digital collections grow, so remote access to valuable information is possible for anyone with access to a computer, and so dynamic and evolving uses of information are possible.[2] Yet, we also must acknowledge that the filters we provide through the library, even digitally, dictate to a large degree what resources our students end up using. And here is where a large dilemma of our profession lies: by pointing students to encyclopedias and handbooks, we risk imposing on them the idea that "authoritative" knowledge of introductory sources is to be trusted as laying out the "general truth" of ideas and concepts, events and histories, and yet we are also aware of their need for such resources.

We might, then, reframe our discussion of these resources around how these texts are culturally constructed. The question of what gets *left out* of such work becomes an important point of discussion, in order to search for unanswered questions, for minor players that might not be fully represented, and for how an entry might be aligning itself with a particular discipline, group, or interest. (How, for instance, might dimensions of gender or race be left unexamined within an encyclopedia entry? How might such an entry assume a cultural knowledge of a largely accepted "truth" or grand narrative?) These resources should also be probed for what they do not include at all. Students should be encouraged to view the *absence* of a topic from these resources not as a sign that they should change their topic, but largely as an opportunity to criticize the work in front of them, and to probe their own research question further with other sources—how might they be able to create a new vein, a new, localized and situated description of what they are searching that *isn't* represented in such works?

---

[2] For an early discussion of the pedagogic and democratic potential of the information revolution, particularly in the humanities, see Lanham, 1993.

In discussing introductory resources, we now also have the luxury of seeking out online resources as opposed to their print counterparts. There are several justifications for doing so. Most significantly for this discussion is the obvious benefit of searching across numerous sources in one gesture— allowing students, often, to probe how numerous *disciplines* define a particular topic. Seeing the definition for *postmodernism* in a literature encyclopedia, an architecture handbook and a history of science reader may, at least, initiate a reflection on how rigid academic disciplines might become permeable and interact, encouraging students to step outside their own disciplinary comfort zone to probe areas and connections they wouldn't have even considered. At least, then, if students aren't treading new ground in creating true interdisciplinarity, they will be considering their topics from a *cross*-disciplinary perspective.[3]

Conclusion

By initially taking a critical stance in the classroom about the information cycle, librarians can impart to students the importance of critically probing new pathways for those veins of knowledge that have already been reconstructed in a postmodern (and post-grand narrative) context, while also unraveling and questioning the grand narratives that still exist within our educational structures. Ultimately, if we arm them with these critical skills, they will be much more fully prepared to participate in their own educational experience, and to participate fully in the world of knowledge they have entered.

Within this chapter, I have put forward interdisciplinarity as one framework for encouraging students to think critically about concepts because an interdisciplinary perspective is vital in probing an issue or concept from all angles and investigating all voices that examine, experience, or write about a particular topic. Further investigation of how information literacy professionals might incorporate interdisciplinarity into their lessons, and a special focus on encouraging professors to see the value in allowing their students the freedom to explore texts outside of their discipline, have not been explored within the literature on information

---

[3] In *Interdisciplinarity: History, Theory and Practice,* Julie Thompson Klein argues that a *cross-disciplinary perspective* includes complicating one's view of an idea, issue, or concept by looking at it through the lens of another discipline, as opposed to true *interdisciplinarity*, which requires communication and true collaboration among researchers of different fields.

ANKS

literacy, and would benefit our reflection on the disciplines themselves, and our work within the classroom.

References

Andersen, J. (2006). The public sphere and discursive activities: Information literacy as sociopolitical skills. *Journal of Documentation, 62*(2), 213-288.

Bichel, R., & Cheney, D. (2001). *The information cycle.* Pennsylvania State University Libraries. Retrieved January 3, 2009, from http://www.libraries.psu.edu/ instruction/infocycle/infocycle.html

Buschman, J., & Brosio, R. A. (2006). A critical primer on postmodernism: Lessons from educational scholarship for librarianship. *Journal of Academic Librarianship, 32*(4), 408-418.

Davis, J. R. (1995). *Interdisciplinary courses and team teaching: New arrangements for learning.* Phoenix, AZ: American Council on Education and the Oryx Press.

Elmborg, J. (2005). Libraries and writing centers in collaboration: A basis in theory. In J. Elmborg, & S. Hook (Eds.), *Centers for learning: Writing centers and libraries in collaboration* (pp. 1-20). Chicago: Association of College and Research Libraries.

Elmborg, J. (2006). Critical information literacy: Implications for instructional practice. *Journal of Academic Librarianship, 32*(2), 192-199.

Elmborg, J. (2006). Libraries in the contact zone. *Reference & User Services Quarterly, 46*(1), 56-64.

Fister, B. (1993). Teaching the rhetorical dimensions of research. *Research Strategies, 11*(4), 211-219.

Giroux, H. A. (1996). *Counternarratives : Cultural studies and critical pedagogies in postmodern spaces.* New York: Routledge.

Hammer, R. (1995). Rethinking the dialectic: A critical semiotic meta-theoretical approach for the pedagogy of media literacy. In P. McLaren, R. Hammer, D. Sholle & S. Smith Reilly (Eds.), *Rethinking media literacy: A critical pedagogy of representation* (pp. 33-85). New York: Peter Lang.

Ishii, A. (2002). *Information cycle timeline.* Northwest Missouri State University, Owens Library. Retrieved January 3, 2009, from http://www.nwmissouri.edu/library/courses/research/timeline.htm

Klein, J. T. (2005). Humanities, culture and interdisciplinarity: The changing American academy. Albany, NY: State University of New York Press.

Klein, J. T. (1990). *Interdisciplinarity: History, theory, and practice*. Detroit: Wayne State University Press.

Klein, J. T. (1999). *Mapping interdisciplinary studies: The academy in transition*. Washington, DC: Association of American Colleges and Universities.

Lanham, R. (1993). *The electronic word: Democracy, technology, and the arts*. Chicago: University of Chicago Press.

Lankshear, C., Peters, M., & Knobel, M. (1996). Critical pedagogy in cyberspace. *Counternarratives: Cultural studies and critical pedagogies in postmodern spaces* (pp. 149-188). New York; London: Routledge.

Luke, A., & Kapitzke, C. (1999). Literacies and libraries: Archives and cybraries. *Curriculum Studies, 7*(3), 467-491.

Lyotard, J. F. (1984). *The postmodern condition : A report on knowledge*. Minneapolis,MN: University of Minnesota Press.

McLaren, P., & Farahmandpur, R. (2005). *Teaching against global capitalism and the new imperialism: A critical pedagogy*. Lanham; Boulder; New York; Toronto; Oxford: Rowman & Littlefield Publishers, Inc.

McLaren, P., & Hammer, R. (1996). Media knowledges, warrior citizenry, and postmodern literacies. In H. A. Giroux, C. Lankshear, P. McLaren & M. Peters (Eds.), *Counternarratives: Cultural studies and critical pedagogies in postmodern spaces* (pp. 81-116). New York; London: Routledge.

Pawley, C. (2003). Information literacy: A contradictory coupling. *Library Quarterly, 73*(4), 422-452.

Peek, R. P., & Newby, G. B. (Eds.). (1996). *Scholarly publishing: The electronic frontier*. Cambridge, MA: MIT Press.

Peters, M., & Lankshear, C. (1996). Postmodern counternarratives. In H. A. Giroux, C. Lankshear, P. McLaren & M. Peters (Eds.), *Counternarratives: Cultural studies and critical pedagogies in postmodern spaces* (pp. 1-39). New York; London: Routledge.

Sholle, D., & Denski, S. (1995). Critical media literacy: Reading, remapping, rewriting. *Rethinking media literacy: Critical pedagogy of representation* (pp. 7-31). New York: Peter Lang.

Simmons, M. H. (2005). Librarians as disciplinary discourse mediators: Using genre theory to move toward critical information literacy. *Portal: Libraries and the Academy, 5*(3), 297-311.

Swanson, T. A. (2004). A radical step: Implementing a critical information literacy model. *Portal: Libraries and the Academy, 4*(2), 259-273.

Depositories of Knowledge: Library Instruction and the Development of Critical Consciousness

Bryan M. Kopp and Kim Olson-Kopp

While classrooms may be found anywhere at a college or university, students and teachers wandering from one to the next, libraries are few, often centrally located. While librarians (people who live in The Library) may be dispatched to classrooms on and off campus, ultimately they return to the hive. Their bee-like behavior is what students sometimes emulate. When they need a peer-reviewed source on the effects of cardiovascular disease in aging diabetics or the effects of music on learning in elementary education, they wisely visit the depository of accumulated learning, online or in person.

Although librarians may satisfy the immediate needs of these information users, they may find themselves, despite their good intentions, working within the logic of an underlying educational structure—namely, the banking concept, in which knowledge is treated as a thing to be received, filed, and stored rather than as an ongoing process of transformation. Paulo Freire (1993) argued, "The more students work at storing the deposits entrusted to them, the less they develop the critical consciousness which would result from their intervention in the world as transformers of that world" (p. 54). Elmborg (2006) asked, "Is the library a passive information bank where students and faculty make knowledge deposits and withdrawals, or is it a place where students actively engage existing knowledge and shape it to their own current and future uses?" (p. 193). To what extent may classroom and reference-based library instruction resist banking education, facilitate student engagement, and foster the development of critical consciousness?

From Barriers to Opportunities: The Limit-Situations of Library Instruction

Library educators interested in the development of critical consciousness, or the transformation of an individual's awareness of, and action toward, real problems in the world, must acknowledge numerous barriers, some of which are external to the practice of library instruction itself. Freire (1993; 1998) referred to these barriers or obstacles as "limit-situations," which are the boundaries of what we can imagine as possible or feasible. If people are aware of their limit-situations, they may respond to them in various ways ranging from denial and despair to hope and commitment. Jacobs (2008) stated that "if we are going to address the issues of librarians' roles within educational endeavors systemically, we, as a discipline, need to foster reflective, critical habits of mind regarding pedagogical praxis within ourselves, our libraries, and our campuses" (p. 256). Below we problematize habitual ways of thinking about the work of libraries so that critical librarians may challenge and move beyond them in their instructional practices.

In broad terms, library instruction functions within the banking concept of education to the extent it can be described merely as *a transfer of objects that fosters the development of skills in the service of others*. This description stands in dialectical opposition to an alternative, problem-posing orientation, which defines library instruction as a dialogic process, a collaborative praxis in the face of authentic problems.

Transfer of Objects

To the undiscerning eye, the interior of a library resembles the warehouse of a large book dealer. Lines of shelves contain boxes and books, each stamped with numbers to facilitate sorting and retrieval. The total number of items, whether circulated or sold, is used as a brute indicator of quality and success. Both librarians and booksellers keep things, so to speak, albeit for different purposes. What sorts of things do librarians keep? These objects, whether called information, knowledge or simply research, may be purchased and cataloged, circulated and mailed, shelved and lost, borrowed and returned—in short, they may be treated as any material object. What do people do with these things? Teachers tell students they need them and students, sometimes unaware of the fact, proceed to gather them in much the way consumers take items off shelves and put them into their shopping carts. If we call these objects "contents" and the shopping carts "minds," then we have realized the banking concept of education perfectly.

If we look closely at either these objects or at the people who use them, however, the object-container metaphor fails to describe anything but the physical structure of libraries. After all, the words of a peer-reviewed article are what researchers find most interesting, and even if we are not language theorists, we can see that these words have a referential dimension, having implications for how we see and act in the world, and a social function, having a bearing on how we identify ourselves and relate to other people. The development of critical consciousness in a library setting depends first and foremost on *humanizing*, or putting a face on, research, and grounding it in the realities which shape it.

Inasmuch as research involves the exchange of words by people in particular situations, it is a form of dialogue. Students may be unaware of the dialogic quality of the sources they use, but the researchers, theorists, and practitioners who produce them generally are not. A student may view a source as an absolute authority to which they must passively defer, as in the banking model of education, or they may view it as an embodied voice in a conversation, one that occupies a position in space and time and thus a political perspective in relation to real problems in the world. Librarians are not in a position to notice the difference between banking and problem-posing kinds of research if they see themselves merely providing materials to students, delivering items from point A to point B.

Critical educators strive toward praxis, which Freire (1993) defined as "word-work" or reflection-action-reflection, but in the research process, as in life in general, sometimes reflection is practiced at the expense of action and vice versa. Indeed students are often overwhelmed to the point of alienation when they first confront the sheer quantity of words on a given topic. Such verbosity can have silencing effect, making dialogue impossible, a situation worsened when the words are strings of unfamiliar terms and disciplinary jargon. "To exist, humanly, is to *name* the world, to change it. Once named, the world in its turn reappears to the namers as a problem and requires of them a new *naming.*" (Freire, 1993, p. 69) This transformative, wor(l)d-changing potential cannot be realized when research is detached from dialogic processes, when students are reduced to passive roles.

Development of Skills

Although people across campus may view libraries as places where information is stored and librarians as people who keep and transfer information, library instructors usually define their work differently, focusing instead on the development of student abilities and lifelong learning skills. Librarians generally pursue broader goals such as "information literacy," defined as a set of abilities requiring students to "recognize when information is needed and have the ability to locate, evaluate, and use effectively the needed information" (American Library Association, 1989).

This is not the place to critique the notion of information literacy in its entirety but rather to question how the conventional goals of library instruction relate to the development of critical consciousness. In a document entitled, "Information Literacy Competency Standards for Higher Education" (2000), specific aspects of information literacy are articulated as standards, with performance indicators and respective outcomes. An "information literate individual" can, for example, "access the needed information effectively and efficiently" (p. 2). At first glance, this standard seems to focus on the transfer of information-objects, but the lists below it suggest the development of discrete skills is the ultimate goal. Consider, for example, outcomes such as the following: "Constructs a search strategy using appropriate commands for the information retrieval system selected (e.g., Boolean operators, truncation, and proximity for search engines; internal organizers such as indexes for books)" (p. 10). It is at the level of such outcomes that much library instruction takes place and by which its successes or failures are gauged.

The value of constructing search strategies with Boolean operators, and the higher-order thinking skills upon which such construction depends, should not be questioned. However, when learning outcomes are couched primarily in mechanistic and behavioral terms, we should not be surprised if students remain uncritical. Although students may play a visibly active role when they complete a hands-on task such as using truncation in a search, they are for the most part developing technical expertise—learning how to operate machines, as it were, without considering their purposes, functions, or effects on others. Technical skills, when they are taught in the absence of the particular human contexts which give them significance, may seem hollow or pointless. Ettinger (2008) underscored one consequence of the emphasis on skills development:

> Some students simply do not take kindly to library instruction. They are reluctant participants, coming to our sessions begrudgingly, under duress, and expecting soporific canned expressions of boring library skills. On more occasions than we probably care to admit, we don't fail to disappoint them. (p. 60)

If students are not engaged, they can scarcely develop critical consciousness, but there are many different types of engagement. An analogy may help illustrate the importance of these differences. A student athlete may work, under a coach's direction, to improve her strength by lifting weights or her aerobic capacity by jogging. Working on these isolated skills may or may not help improve her game play because actual performance involves the coordination of multiple skill sets, adopted spontaneously during a game. If we listed these different skill sets, including abilities to work as a team player, to perceive the relative strengths and weakness of other players, etc., we would have a list as impressive as ALA's standards and outcomes for information literacy. No matter how thoroughly discrete skills are itemized, targeted, and checked off by the coach, the student athlete's success depends largely on her abilities to combine her skills as holistic responses to complicated situations; that she may lift weights is perhaps less important than how she acts *in* the game, when actions lead to consequences, and *after* the game, when she may reflect on those actions with others.

What is most interesting about this analogy, though, is how it may be contrasted with another kind of engagement, a kind that may accompany the development of critical consciousness. Neither student athlete nor coach needs to ask fundamental questions about the significance, relevance, or implications of playing sports in various social and historical contexts. Why, for example, is winning so important? Why must losers accept responsibility for their defeat? How do competitive sports reproduce ideologies such as free market capitalism? Awareness of and reflection on "bigger pictures" and how we reproduce, negotiate, or resist them seems to be an important aspect of critical consciousness, yet standards and outcomes rarely place them at the center of instruction, perhaps because they are inherently complex and difficult to measure.

Many library educators, of course, pursue complex goals even though they are hard to assess, but is "critical consciousness" asking a bit much of us and our students? The answer is clearly "yes" if we have before us information literacy standards and outcomes. "There is too much to cover in too little time, with no guarantee that what is presented will benefit the student" (Ettinger, 2008, p. 60). Jacobs (2008) cautioned:

> For librarians working directly with information literacy programs, it is particularly easy in the midst of a busy teaching load to lose sight of the fact that what we are doing goes far beyond Boolean searching and Library of Congress Subject Headings. The work we do is part of a broader educative project that works to empower individuals both locally and globally. (p. 261)

What is this broader educative project? What does local and global empowerment look like in a library instruction setting? These questions serve as problem spaces that must be investigated anew in each situation. If library instruction is too structured around learning standards, performance indicators, and outcomes, there may not be room for such questions in the first place. Critical consciousness develops when real problems are posed in a dialogic atmosphere, with all their ethical, moral, and human dimensions. Goals such as information literacy, if they are to be progressive and empowering, must be situated likewise to help students "become dynamic learners and thinkers who are creative, analytical and efficient, instead of mere regurgitators of facts" (Mokhtar & Majid, 2006, p. 32) or, we might add, "mere developers of skills."

Offering of Services

Circulation clerks may find themselves, as they scan barcodes on books, performing tasks quite similar to those performed by sales associates in any retail business. Although library and information science has attained disciplinary status equivalent to other academic and professional fields, a service orientation frequently defines library positions, including those in reference and library instruction. An attitude of service informs many instructional practices, and even though library staff may not wear uniforms with "How may I help you?" printed on the back, in both a library or a commercial environment, the customer, as they say, is always right; determining what students and teachers want or need is thus a perennial concern.

We might notice an important difference between the critical educators who work in libraries and those who work in academic departments: the latter seldom think of themselves as "offering services" even when they are teaching what are sometimes disparagingly called "service courses." Higher education has become more consumerist in recent times, to be sure, but relations among teachers, and between teachers and students, are not so narrowly defined. Although teachers across the disciplines may encourage students to play an active role in their education, they do not make customer satisfaction a sole indicator of success, nor do they relinquish the ability to judge or determine what is desirable or necessary in a given situation. Through assignments, syllabi, and the curriculum in general, teachers continue to have a leading voice in the educational process. Numerous reform efforts have worked to include student voices in the conversation, but what about the librarians? Whether teacher-centered or student-centered, curriculum has a tendency to leave librarians in supporting roles in the educational process.

A service orientation itself is not a barrier; the problem is when good service is equated with the delivery of objects or the development of skills and nothing else. To question such assumptions is to challenge the at times bureaucratic institutions within which we dwell, which define our roles through a distribution of power and responsibilities and status distinctions. Freire (1993) argued for breaking down the walls that traditionally separate students and teachers, leaving in their places teacher-students and student-teachers. Where do librarians fit into this scheme? Freire (1993) described how "the problem-posing educator constantly re-forms his reflections in the reflection of the students. The students—no longer docile listeners—are now critical co-investigators in dialogue with the teacher" (p. 62). When librarians are also in dialogue with students and teachers, they, too, become critical co-investigators.

We must acknowledge, however, the distance between this collaborative ideal and the realities many library instructors face. They, after all, rarely determine the curriculum or make assignments; like students in the banking model of education, they defer to the authority of teachers. Whether in a classroom or during a reference interview, librarians must negotiate the needs of students within a small window of time. During this brief period, which frequently contains interruptions, librarians must not only point students to resources, but also provide necessary technical instruction (e.g. "click this box" or "select this database"). In addition, they must combat unrealistic expectations and misconceptions about the library (e.g. that it is like a department store). Given all the limit-situations described above, how much can a librarian feasibly contribute to the challenges of empowering students to understand and transform their worlds?

The Untested Feasibilities of Transformative Library Instruction

Ana Maria Araujo Freire, in her notes to *Pedagogy of Hope*, wrote the "untested feasible" is "something the utopian dreamer knows exists, but knows it will be attained only through a practice of liberation—which can be implemented by way of Freire's theory of dialogical action" (1998, p. 206). Dialogic action may take many forms in and out of the classroom, ranging from Freire's "culture circles" to other cooperative methods of learning. In the remainder of this article, we will discuss two such models that have been used in library settings: problem-based learning and lesson study.

According to Barbara Ferrer Kenney (2008), problem-based learning helps students think and retain library instruction lessons. Problem-based learning (PBL) encourages the librarian to shift from instructor to guide, allowing students to discover resources with encouragement, not outright instruction, from the librarian. "Perhaps the most challenging aspect of incorporating PBL into one's teaching repertoire is taking on the role of guide, facilitator, or tutor. As the learning activity becomes user-centered, the librarian must step aside to allow the students to take responsibility for their own learning" (Kenney, 2008, Challenges section ¶ 6).

When Reeves (2008) and her colleagues embraced PBL, the goal was to create a structured session in which small groups teach each other. Like Kenney, these librarians had to step aside to allow students to become teachers (p. 78). In this case, the goal of the session was to encourage students to learn and use research methods that would be utilized outside the classroom. Starting with a broad research question and a five-minute introduction to the library's online resources, the class divided into small groups, each with a resource to explore. After a set amount of time, groups presented findings to the class, allowing enough time for individual research and exploration on the initial question (p. 82). According to Reeves:

> Students enjoy the lesson because it involves an interesting, real-world topic, and because they are actively engaged and working together collaboratively. Students tend to pay more attention to a fellow student explaining how to use a resource than they would to a librarian. Knowing that they will have an individual exercise at the end of the class also keeps students attentive. (p. 82-83)

Such attentiveness depends upon the meaningfulness of the question posed at the beginning of the session. Spence (2004) stated, "students would not take library research assignments seriously unless they were part of the intellectual architecture of courses and curricula" (p. 491-492). Everyone involved in library instruction sessions (librarians, teachers, and students) needs to go through a learning process:

> Instructors and librarians need to demonstrate the process they so much want their students to learn. Instructors who can demonstrate to their students the thinking and questioning process they themselves go through as they seek and read information are providing the best examples of how to use and locate information. (Cheney, 2004, p. 506)

Many challenges, including the time required to develop and revise the lesson, face library instructors who implement PBL. Snavely (2006) stated that "developing information literacy problems appropriate to the content of a class requires significantly more course instructor and librarian consultation and development time than is normally devoted to these activities. However, this is time well spent." (p. 526).

PBL provides an excellent example of how librarians have already overcome some of the limit-situations described above. Students are encouraged to play active roles and to enter into dialogue with their peers during their research process rather than simply retrieve objects or gather sources. Although the focus is largely on skills development, not unlike those listed as standards and outcomes for information literacy, there is an increased emphasis on the contexts in which skills are used, the purposes they fulfill, and the authenticity of problems. Librarians no longer merely serve the external needs of students and teachers. Although library instructors play a more central role in the educational process, they may or may not collaborate with teachers in both preparation and implementation of the session.

These are real gains, but is PBL equivalent to problem-posing education? Is PBL sufficient to develop critical consciousness among critical co-investigators? Jacobs (2008) described a core challenge faced by critical educators in the library and elsewhere:

> The dialogues we have surrounding information literacy instruction strive to find a balance in the daily and the visionary, the local and the global, the practices and the theories, the ideal and the possible…. This means thinking about pedagogy and talking about how we might work toward making the global local, the visionary concrete, the theoretical practicable, and, perhaps, the ideal possible. (p. 258)

A central goal of Freirean critical pedagogy is indeed to make the visionary concrete and the ideal possible. To be aware of limit-situations and countless constraints but nonetheless seek, through dialogue with others, to transform local and global realities though the practice of liberation is an ambitious project, to say the least. PBL as well as other pedagogical techniques may be important tools for the critical educators but they do not in and of themselves substitute for this broader emancipatory project. In PBL, students face problems, but the problems may be contrived by teachers and librarians in advance simply as tricks to get students to develop skills and thus achieve learning outcomes. Critical pedagogy in Freire's terms:

> Requires that the investigators and the people (who would normally be considered objects of that investigation) should act as *co-investigators*. The more active an attitude men and women take in regard to the exploration of their thematics, the more they deepen their critical awareness of reality and, in spelling out those thematics, take possession of that reality. (1993, p. 87)

For such awareness to be developed, problems must be authentic, grounded in the existential realities of human beings through what Freire (1993) called "meaningful thematics" or "generative themes." Although there is not space to explore these strategies in depth, we might highlight a couple characteristics: they focus on human issues, are grounded in a total (not partial) view of reality, and involve a process of becoming among all participants, not just students. Problem-posing education, when it shares these qualities, can be quite different from PBL.

What might these differences look like for library educators in the space of, for example, a one-hour classroom session? One answer may be found in combining PBL with a collaborative teaching and learning process known as lesson study. Built on collaboration and dialogue among teachers and students, lesson study focuses on the development of brief instructional sessions, such as those common in library instruction. In the context of American higher education, lesson study (Cerbin & Kopp, 2006) involves a team of instructors designing, teaching, and refining a single class lesson, a process which includes articulating learning goals, planning instructional activities, observing teaching and learning interactions, and reflecting on them on an ongoing basis. For librarians, lesson study is an ideal way to bridge the gap between teacher and librarian goals for an instruction session (Desai et al, 2007, p. 292). The process of creating the lesson, enacting it in front of peers, and revising it "fostered increased collaboration" (p. 293) and allowed building a better understanding of library instruction (p. 293).

What is intriguing about the lesson study cycle from the standpoint of critical pedagogy is how it models praxis as a process of reflection-action-reflection, asking how the visionary may be made concrete, the theoretical practical, and the ideal possible. Reflecting on our goals as educators in the library and in the disciplines is valuable in itself, but perhaps of more consequence is how we can "bring the goals to life" (Lewis, 2000) in an actual instruction session. Such sessions may be highly constrained, as discussed above, but real problems may nonetheless be posed and meaningful dialogue can take place. Below is a brief outline of how lesson study might be fused with critical pedagogy in library instruction sessions. This sketch leaves out many important details because 1) they are still being explored, and 2) they ideally emerge from the local conditions of the participants involved in the instructional sessions.

A team of co-investigators, which may include teachers, librarians, and even students, might begin the lesson study process by reflecting on the overarching goals of critical pedagogy. Developing a shared understanding of key terms such as "critical consciousness" seems to be an important entry point into the conversation. What does "critical consciousness" look like? How do we know it when we see it—or feel it—in ourselves or others? This question defies easy answers, which is perhaps why it can motivate an inquiry process. Such discussions invite participants to reflect not only on their professional and personal identities but also their hopes and fears and, in the process, their underlying commitments. We are presented with an opportunity to articulate and develop our philosophies of education, but our work does not end in diffuse conversations about consciousness.

We must, after all, bring our answers down to earth—what might critical consciousness look like before, during, or after an instruction session? To answer this question, we need to turn to the substance of sessions themselves, examining not only whether they provide occasions for dialogue among participants, but also the extent to which such dialogue seems to facilitate the development of critical consciousness. Rather than artificially constructing problems, library educators and teachers would look to the existential experiences of students (and themselves) to develop instructional activities. What makes one problem "real" and another contrived? One indication is the degree to which it connects to the concrete realities of human beings in particular situations. In a few meetings, critical lesson study practitioners could generate a number of problems and approaches to teaching the session, but they would need to choose and implement only one at time, given the limitations of time for librarians, teachers, and students alike. Whichever problem is chosen, it may become the focus of the instruction session and then posed in a manner that invites sustained inquiry with others.

When the session actually takes place, other members of the lesson study group actively listen, observe, and reflect on what happens (e.g. how students interact with one another, the kinds of dialogue that take place) and how it fosters critical consciousness. A session developed with a lesson study approach may not be perfect or predictable, but it could be improved over time, making it more probable that transformative educational experiences will occur.

Whether confronting limit-situations or exploring untested feasibilities, librarians may play a key role in the development of critical consciousness. The questions we have posed in this essay may seem daunting, but they can help focus future conversations about critical pedagogy in a library setting. In any case, the greatest challenge facing librarians is perhaps not so much imagining the transformative potential of library instruction as much as it is finding the opportunities to exercise our imaginations in the first place.

References

American Library Association. Presidential committee on information literacy. Final report. (Chicago: American Library Association, 1989.) http://www.ala.org/ala/acrl/acrlpubs/whitepapers/presidential.htm

Cerbin, W., & Kopp, B. (2006). Lesson study as a model for building pedagogical knowledge and improving teaching. *International Journal of Teaching and Learning in Higher Education, 18*(3). p. 250-157.

Cheney, D. (2004, October). Problem-based learning: Librarians as collaborators and consultants. portal: *Libraries & the Academy, 4*(4), 495-508. Retrieved April 1, 2009, from Project Muse database.

Desai, S., Freeland, M., & Frierson, E. (2007, May). Lesson study in libraries. *College & Research Libraries News, 68*(5), 290-293. Retrieved April 1, 2009, from Wilson Select Plus database.

Elmborg, J. (2006, March). Critical information literacy: implications for instructional practice. *Journal of Academic Librarianship, 32*(2), 192-199.

Ettinger, D. (April 1, 2008). The librarian as bibliotherapist. (BACKTALK). *Library Journal, 133*(6), 60. Retrieved December 18, 2008, from Academic OneFile via Gale.

Freire, P. (1998). Pedagogy of Hope. New York: Continuum.

Freire, P. (1993). Pedagogy of the Oppressed. New York: Continuum.

Information literacy competency standards for higher education. (2000). [Brochure]. Chicago: Association of College & Research Libraries.

Jacobs, H. (2008, May). Information literacy and reflective pedagogical praxis. *The Journal of Academic Librarianship, 34*(3), 256-262. Retrieved Jan 10, 2009, from ScienceDirect database.

Kenney, B.F. (2008). Revitalizing the one-shot instruction session using problem-based learning. *Reference & User Services Quarterly, 47*(4), 386-391. Retrieved Feb 22, 2009, from Academic Search Premier database.

Lewis, C. (2000, April). Lesson study: The core of Japanese professional development. Paper presented at the American Educational Research Association Meeting, New Orleans.

Mokhtar, I., & Majid, S. (2006, March). Teaching information literacy for in-depth knowledge and sustained learning. *Education for Information, 24*(1), 31-49. Retrieved Feb 22, 2009, from Academic Search Premier database.

Reeves, L., McMillan, J., & Gibson, R. (2008). Keep them engaged: Cooperative learning with the jigsaw method. In Cook, D., & Sittler, R. (Eds.), *Practical pedagogy for library instructors: 17 innovative strategies to improve student learning* (pp. 77-86). Chicago: Association of College & Research Libraries.

Snavely, L. (2004, October). Making problem-based learning work: Institutional challenges. *portal: Libraries & the Academy*, *4*(4), 521-531. Retrieved April 1, 2009, from Project Muse database.

Spence, L. (2004, October). The usual doesn't work: We need problem-based learning. *portal: Libraries & the Academy*, *4*(4), 485-493. Retrieved April 1, 2009, from Project Muse database.

Section Two

Classroom Toolkit

Problem-based learning as teaching strategy

Elizabeth Peterson

"I'd like my students to know about all the resources available to them in the library, both print and online, and microfilm and special collections too, and to be comfortable using all the search tools. We just have time for one session, though. The class meets for 50 minutes. Will that work?"

Ah, the typical library instruction request. For the librarian who wants to be an effective teacher—that is, for her students to actually learn about research—while also incorporating the principles of critical pedagogy into library instruction, this is a daunting prospect. I receive this email several times each term, and each time I try to meet these expectations despite all of the inherent problems. There is not enough time. There are too many resources. The systems are too complex. How can I expect students to interrogate the systems when they don't even understand them? How can I both cover relevant material *and* engage in activities that encourage students to question the underlying political hegemony of the classroom/library/university/society—in 50 minutes?

In the past I have spent many of these sessions telling students about ten different things and asking them to follow along as we rush from catalog to database. The instructor may be satisfied because the students "as least heard about ten things," but I feel very unsatisfied as a teacher. And I know I shortchange students with this approach, behaving as if I just keep talking and pointing and clicking in *some new special way* the students will stay engaged and leave the classroom competent and comfortable with the library. And the whole hegemony thing? Forget about it.

The other side effect of this lecture-demonstration, cram-it-all-in approach is distance. When I teach this way, I don't have to engage with the students beyond a superficial level. It's all show and tell on my part with no discussion or active reflection with the group. I am the expert at the podium in the front of the classroom and the students are the passive receptacles. For introverted librarians who prefer predictable structure in a teaching situation, this format probably feels fine, especially since they never have to see the students again or run the risk of being accountable to them.

None of this works for a librarian who wants to incorporate critical pedagogy into library instruction. Critical pedagogy demands that teachers loosen their control in the classroom and get out from behind the podium, literally and figuratively. Critical pedagogy reminds us that students come to us with a host of previously learned knowledge and experiences. An effective critical classroom has a climate of trust developed over time through discussion and reflection. Students in a critical classroom engage in activities that encourage challenging and disruptive questions about the nature of privilege, inequality, access, and exclusion. Critical pedagogy reveals libraries to be cultural institutions that are shaped by, and reflect the prejudices of, the society as a whole: "they embody representations and practices that construct as well as block the possibilities for human agency among students" (Giroux, 1988, p. 98-99). Like school itself, the library "is far from being neutral" and is a "particular representation of a dominant culture" (Giroux, 1988, p. xxx).

Faced with the competing constraints of the one-shot instruction session on the one hand, and the deeper demands of critical pedagogy on the other, what's a well-intentioned librarian to do?

First, some assumptions. While library instruction takes many forms—at the reference desk, in one-on-one consultations, in credit courses, and in online tutorials—the majority of instruction occurs as single sessions in a library classroom as an add-on to a credit course. Thus, this paper will focus on that format. Most librarians agree that this approach is "broken" and that meaningful research instruction is embedded throughout course material. However, instructors continue to request this approach, so it seems appropriate to use it to frame this discussion.

Also, as already suggested, true critical pedagogy requires more time than a single 50-minute session allows, particularly when there is other content to cover. One can incorporate some elements of this approach, as I will demonstrate, but real transformation and student empowerment of the kind described by Paulo Freire and other theorists are beyond the limitations of such a brief meeting.

All of that said, as a methodology for critical pedagogy in library instruction, Problem-Based Learning (PBL) is a natural fit. PBL breaks down the traditional hierarchy of the classroom and shifts the focus from lecture to active learning. It uses open-ended questions to encourage exploration and independent conclusions. PBL assumes that students come to the library classroom with previous experiences and builds on them to develop new skills and knowledge. It is also a tidy way to incorporate multiple skills and sources into the typical one-shot session.

PBL got its start at McMaster University's medical school. Rather than learn material according to the traditional approach of memorizing vast quantities of information, students were placed in small teams and presented with cases—or problems—to solve. Students broke the problems into its various issues, assessed what they already knew about the issues, made lists of areas needing further investigation, and went about seeking information to fill in the gaps in their knowledge. "The emphasis is not on memorization, rather it is on asking the necessary questions and knowing how to find appropriate answers" (Tooey, 1993, p. 86). PBL has since spread to all areas of education, from K-12 to graduate schools. The library literature is rife with examples of its effectiveness as an approach for teaching information literacy skills to students, whether as an integrated part of course instruction (Baker, 1999; Carder, Willingham, and Bibb, 2001; Cheney, 2004; Macklin Smith, 2001; Pelikan, 2004) or in one-shot sessions (Ferrer Kenny, 2008; Munro, 2006; Snavely, 2004). Noticeably absent from the PBL literature, however, is any explicit mention of the political implications of this teaching strategy.

This is an intriguing omission, particularly given how well it aligns with the goals of critical pedagogy, such as teachers ceding control as the sole experts in the classroom. As Macklin Smith (2001) writes, "In PBL there is no teacher, *per se*. An expert facilitator replaces the traditional role of lecturer as primary instructor. This person is responsible for helping the learners discover what they already know and guiding them to new knowledge through problem-solving. The learning process is really about thoughtful trial and error" (p. 309). This echoes the goals of critical pedagogy, which aim to have students themselves take an active part in their own learning process in the classroom, not just to receive knowledge, but also to create new information (Giroux, 2007; Huerta-Charles, 2007).

In both PBL and critical pedagogy, giving students an active role in the classroom also encourages them to call upon previous knowledge and apply it to new situations (Ferrer Kenney, 2008; McLaren, 1988). Constructivist learning theory affirms that students come to us with a variety of experiences related to research; they are not starting from scratch. In other words, they are not empty vessels waiting to be filled with our expert knowledge. Incorporating the students' own experience into lesson plans has a twofold benefit. When students can find themselves and their own interests in the material and concepts, the instruction is more likely to be relevant and engaging to them. Also, it brings the student and instructor onto a more equal footing. It says to the student: what you know and what you have experienced is relevant and important. It says: I know something, you know something, so let's work together to learn more. Acknowledging this prior experience is a profound act of respect in the classroom, and it is a small step toward equipping students with the power to further transform their own educational experience, "to intervene in their own self-formation" (McLaren, 1988, p. xi).

As with any lesson plan, one designs a **PBL** lesson by constructing learning outcomes: what will students know and be able to do as a result of this lesson? How will those skills help the students accomplish the research objectives of the course? In a traditional 50-minute library instruction session, **PBL** or not, one cannot be overly ambitious, despite the often high expectations of instructors. For the librarian attempting to incorporate critical pedagogy and **PBL** into her teaching, an important first step is letting go of the temptation to cover as much material in a single session as we know students need. But take heart: a **PBL** approach may not cover as much material, but students will likely understand and retain more of the skills and information once they leave the classroom (Carder, et al., 2001, p. 188).

As with learning outcomes, **PBL** questions should relate to the course content. If the course is interdisciplinary, current events or controversial topics also work well. Good **PBL** questions are open-ended enough for students to arrive at different conclusions based on their research. This is in keeping with Hinchey's (2004) description of a critical classroom as a place where research is "not something done by distant authorities...but by students themselves" (p. 15), and where students are not just "passive recipients of familiar knowledge," but rather those who "critically engage diverse ideas [and] transform and act on them" (Giroux, 2007, p. 3). Carder, et al. (2001) suggest some guidelines for forming **PBL** questions: "(1) The problem should relate to the real world and be complex enough to require the students to cooperate with one another in order to complete the exercise; (2) The problem should be interesting or controversial enough to draw students' interest; (3) Learning objectives should be incorporated into the problem and should include concepts that have been covered in previous classes so students can apply what they have learned to a real-life situation" (p. 188).

A well-designed **PBL** lesson has enough structure for students to stay focused and meet their learning objectives but is still open-ended enough for students to come to independent conclusions. Likewise, based on the learning outcomes, students should have an annotated list of the sources the librarian wants them to know and use for the assignment. This is especially important for first-year or inexperienced students who would otherwise fall back on the tools they know best, i.e., broad searches in Google, which don't help them learn how to find scholarly journal articles in a particular discipline or when to use subject-specific encyclopedias. "Students who are not given any support or structure to begin the research process only use what they already know (the Internet), because the unknown is too unknown or too invisible to their untrained eye" (Cheney, 2004, p. 497).

For example, rather than letting students pick any topic, one should provide a short list to choose from based on the course content. Without this structure, students may spend an inordinate amount of time waffling about a topic, rather than focusing on searching for information and evaluating its usefulness. This is especially important with a 50-minute session. I learned this lesson well after an experiment with a class of first-year students in a film studies class. Their scenario/problem was as follows: *You are part of a production team that is looking for a new film to do. This is your chance to make a splash with the studio heads and wow them with your insight and creativity. You decide to do a remake of an iconic film. In your pitch to the studio heads, describe who will play the main roles, how you will update the story, setting, costumes, and themes. Use relevant research to support your choices.*

The students spent a full 25 minutes in their groups simply debating which films to remake and only stopped when I told them they'd have to "make their pitch" to the rest of the class, since we were quickly running out of time. The discussions were lively and entertaining, but the students never progressed into the rest of the assignment. The results were shallow, focusing on superficial elements rather than more substantial conclusions based on research (example: "Anne Hathaway as Dorothy in *The Wizard of Oz*! Of course because she is so cute and hot!").

The next time I tried this assignment I gave the students a list of three films from which to choose, and the results were much more successful. This strategy also adapts well to other subject areas (see Appendix A and B).

Students can work individually or in groups in PBL, but I prefer the latter. The efficiency of group work is well suited to the time constraints of the one-shot session, but more importantly, groups allow students to share the work amongst several people. A team-based approach encourages students to rely on and learn from each other as they work through the assignment and to capitalize on "individual strengths by allowing the whole group to tackle problems that would normally be too difficult for any student alone" (Hmelo-Silver, 2003, p. 1174). From a critical pedagogy standpoint, small, collaborative groups shift the locus of control in the classroom from the teacher to the students. The librarian can roam and offer help and clarification as needed, but ultimately students discover for themselves how best to solve the problem in the assignment.

With group work, individuals are held accountable to their team members. I like to add an additional layer of accountability by requiring each group to report their findings to the rest of the class. According to Snavely (2004), "Team reporting allows students to compare their results with those of others, to understand how differing strategies produce various results," and to learn how different search tools function (p. 522). The librarian acts as a facilitator here, as well, emphasizing key points and strategies, making connections between the groups, asking questions, and providing clarification. It is important to remember that there are no right or wrong answers in PBL. As Weiner (2004) states, "The critical pedagogue might sometimes have to sacrifice what s/he thinks or knows to be right in an effort to create the conditions for students to investigate the conditions, relations, and contradictions that make things appear right or wrong" (p. 67). Whatever their conclusions, each group should be able to support its claims with appropriate information gleaned from their research.

The group reports also serve as a time for reflection on the entire process, which allows the students to synthesize the skills and new information sources they have learned and how "they might be applied in new situations" (Hmelo-Silver, 2003, p. 1174). This can take the form of a brief discussion in which the librarian asks the students what they learned, what obstacles they encountered, and what questions still remain. I like to write students' responses on the board as a way to validate their perceptions and to reinforce what they learned. Another alternative if there is time, is to pass out 3x5 cards and have students write one thing they learned in the session that they will use next time they need to do research.

Problem-Based Learning is not a cure-all for the woes of library instruction, such as unreasonably high expectations from instructors, time constraints, poor integration with course content, and the complexity of library systems and proprietary databases. Nor is it the best or only way to integrate critical pedagogy into library instruction. Imagine a scenario in which students critique and deconstruct the same library systems and proprietary databases that we spend so much time trying to teach them. Or interrogate the academic library itself as a system of cultural biases that maintain exclusionary policies of intellectual and physical access. Or a cadre of empowered students working alongside librarians to free library resources from the crippling economic structure of commercial publishing. Or an instruction scenario in which students themselves determine which skills, concepts, and resources are most important, and they design their own library instruction.

These scenarios are not beyond the range of possibility, particularly using PBL as a teaching strategy, but they would require more than 50 minutes in a single session with inexperienced library users. But PBL is a move in the right direction. It begins to break down the traditional hierarchy of the classroom, shifting the focus from the librarian and the mechanics of search to a more meaningful engagement with information itself. PBL is learner-centered; students are empowered to "come to terms with their own power as critical agents" (Giroux, 2007, p. 1) as they explore a variety of information sources to help them understand and analyze questions relevant to their own lives. Are students fully competent and efficient researchers after a one-shot PBL library instruction session? No. Does PBL fulfill all the expectations of a critical pedagogical classroom? No. Research remains a complex set of skills and knowledge that requires much practice over time, and the elements of a good critical classroom—a deep engagement with real-world issues through questioning, inclusion, and respect for cultural diversity—are also developed over time. But it is a good start, particularly for a brief library instruction session. As Ferrer Kenney (2008), argues, "The ultimate goal for a one-shot PBL session is to have students actively engage with the librarians and library resources to provide a glimpse into the many ways the library supports student learning" (p. 387).

References

Baker, L. M. (1999). Use of Problem-Based Learning in a basic reference course. *Journal of Education for Library and Information Science, 40*(1), 66-69.

Carder, L., Willingham, P., & Bibb, D. (2001). Case-based, Problem-Based Learning: Information literacy for the real world. *Research Strategies 18*(3), 181-190.

Cheney, D. (2004). Problem-Based Learning: Librarians as collaborators and consultants. *portal: Libraries and the Academy 4*(4), 495-508.

Ferrer Kenney, B. (2008). Revitalizing the one-shot instruction session using Problem-Based Learning. *Reference & User Services Quarterly 47*(4), 386-391.

Giroux, H. A. (1988). *Teachers as intellectuals: Toward a critical pedagogy of learning.* Granby, MA: Bergin & Garvey Publishers.

Giroux, H. A. (2007). Democracy, education, and the politics of critical pedagogy. In. P. McLaren & J.L. Kincheloe (Eds.), *Critical pedagogy: Where are we now?* (pp. 1-5). New York: Peter Lang.

Hinchey, P. H. (2004). *Becoming a critical educator: Defining a classroom identity, designing a critical pedagogy.* New York: Peter Lang.

Hmelo-Silver, C. E. (2003). Problem-Based Learning. In J.W. Guthrie (Ed.), *Encyclopedia of education* (2nd ed., Vol. 4, pp. 1172-1175). New York: Thomson-Gale.

Huerta-Charles, L. (2007). Pedagogy of testimony: Reflections on the pedagogy of critical pedagogy. In. P. McLaren & J.L. Kincheloe (Eds.), *Critical pedagogy: Where are we now?* (pp. 249-261). New York: Peter Lang.

Macklin Smith, A. (2001). Integrating information literacy using Problem-Based Learning. *Reference Services Review 29*(4), 306-313.

McLaren, P. (1988). Foreword: Critical theory and the meaning of hope. In H.A. Giroux, *Teachers as intellectuals: Toward a critical pedagogy of hope* (pp. ix-xxi). Granby, MA: Bergin & Garvey Publishers.

Munro, K. (2006). Modified problem-based library instruction: A simple, reusable instruction design. *College & Undergraduate Libraries 13*(3), 53-61.

Pelikan, M. (2004). Problem-Based Learning in the library: Evolving a realistic approach. *portal: Libraries and the Academy 4*(4), 509-520.

Snavely, L. (2004). Making Problem-Based Learning work: institutional challenges. *portal: Libraries and the Academy 4*(4), 521-531.

Tooey, M.J. (1993). Problem-Based Learning: Getting started-part one. *Medical Reference Services Quarterly 12*, 86.

Weiner, E. J. Critical pedagogy and the crisis of imagination. In. P. McLaren & J.L. Kincheloe (Eds.), *Critical pedagogy: Where are we now?* (pp. 57-77). New York: Peter Lang.

Appendix A

Sample Problem-Based Learning Plan

Course: Freshman Seminar, "The Dark Self: Psychology and Literature"

Learning Outcomes: At the end of the session students will:

1. Be able to find scholarly articles in a periodical database.
2. Use reference tools to find relevant background information on a topic.
3. Use the Library Catalog to find relevant books on a topic.

Problem/Scenario:

A well-known writer of creative fiction has just learned that she has a neurological disorder that is severe enough to affect her daily life. She could take medication to regulate the disease but she is afraid it will affect her creativity. What would you recommend? Use the sources below to find information to support your recommendations.

Neurological disorders (choose one): epilepsy, schizophrenia, bipolar disorder

Recommended Sources:

- *Encyclopedia of Mental Health, Encyclopedia of Psychology, Encyclopedia of* ***Psychiatry, Psychology, and Psychoanalysis***
- *Encyclopedia of Creativity*
- PsycINFO
- MLA International Bibliography
- Library Catalog

Group report requirements:

In presenting your recommendations, be prepared to answer the following questions:

- What is the nature of the disorder or disease you selected, including its causes, symptoms, and treatment?
- What kind of medication is used to treat this disease? What are its possible side effects, especially long-term?
- Which other writers or artists have had this disorder? How did it affect their lives, particularly their ability to do their creative work?
- What research has been done into the relationship between mental illness and creativity?
- Can you find any personal narratives or biographies of artists with mental illness who faced this issue?

Appendix B

Sample Problem-Based Learning Plans

Course: Freshman Seminar, "Shakespeare from Page to Stage"
Learning Outcomes: At the end of the session students will:
   1. Be able to find scholarly articles in a periodical database.
   2. Use reference tools to find relevant background information on a topic.
   3. Use the Library Catalog to find relevant books on a topic.
Problem/Scenario: You are an actor in a new production of "A Midsummer Night's Dream." The director wants to set the play sometime in the 20th century, but is still undecided about which period would be most appropriate to highlight the themes in the play, and how that period would shape the production. She has asked for your advice. What would you recommend? Use the sources below to find information to support your recommendations.
Recommended Sources:
   • *American Popular Culture Through History* series
   • Oxford Companion to Shakespeare (online)
   • MLA International Bibliography
   • Academic Search Premier
   • Library Catalog
Group report requirements:
In presenting your recommendations, be prepared to answer the following questions:
   • What decade did you choose and why?
   • What was going on culturally and politically during this period that makes it especially relevant for "A Midsummer Night's Dream"?
   • What other alternative approaches to this play (or other Shakespeare plays) have been produced? How might those productions influence your own approach? (Hint: try to find reviews or criticism of Shakespeare productions.)
   • What would the production look like as a result of your choice? Describe costumes, sets, lighting, etc.
   • Which of the play's themes would be emphasized as a result of your choice?

Re-visioning the library seminar through a lens of critical pedagogy

Caroline Sinkinson & Mary Caton Lingold

The University of Colorado at Boulder Libraries promotes information literacy through a long-standing collaborative relationship with the Program for Writing and Rhetoric (PWR). All PWR first-year writing classes attend a library seminar for one class period each semester. While the content of writing classes varies, most faculty anticipate that the library seminar will equip students with skills necessary to complete a research paper, including book and article retrieval, source evaluation, and citation. In planning for these classes, we struggled to design a seminar that would fulfill faculty and student expectations while also instilling information literacy's liberating potential. Due to our awareness of first-year students' lack of familiarity with the complex nature of library information systems, we were overwhelmed by the amount of content we wanted to cover. Our goals were to introduce the research process, provide specific strategies, and encourage information literacy, but we were uncertain how to meet these objectives in a 50-90 minute class period. Ultimately, we drew from the *Association of College and Research Libraries' Information Literacy Standards* (2000) to structure the seminar. The standards sequenced information seeking and identified outcomes that we could readily apply to our lesson planning. The compartmentalized framework allowed for a linear demonstration of keyword development, choosing a search system, executing a search, identifying a source as peer-reviewed, and retrieving materials. Despite the clarity that the ACRL standards provided, we were not completely at ease with the seminar structure. We continued to leave our classrooms feeling deflated because we habitually ran out of time and were exhausted by our inability to engage learners. This chapter narrates our process of pedagogical inquiry through an examination and critique of this former seminar model and its ultimate revision. We focus on the ways in which critical pedagogy informed this process and led to meaningful insights into the struggle to align critical pedagogy, critical information literacy, and practiced library instruction.

In the former seminar model, we *explained* library resources and *demonstrated* how to navigate them as students followed along at their own computers. We superficially modeled the research process by moving through sample searches that we knew would produce excellent results while highlighting searching strategies and database features. The clarity of this approach was initially attractive, but we came to recognize that, as Heidi Jacobs put it, "using the ACRL standards to quantify or map information literacy skills or curricula are fraught projects that need to be carefully considered" (p. 258). Troy Swanson (2004) argues that "searching for information is not the simple rules driven process that many of us would like," pointing out one of the essential flaws of our seminar model (p. 260). We knew research to be a messy and iterative process that is often frustrating and surprising, but instead of accurately representing this complexity, we sought to "fix what is fluid" (Jacobs, 2008, p. 258). We compartmentalized information seeking by isolating specific mechanical strategies rather than nurturing a conceptual understanding of information systems.

Our teaching practice undermined the ACRL's (2000) proclamation that information literacy enables learners to "extend their investigations, become more self-directed, and assume greater control of their own learning" (p. 2). Because our classes were teacher-centered and demonstration-based, we were in no manner fostering self-direction for the students. We imposed a research formula on the students that inhibited their active engagement with the seminar content. The ineffectiveness of our teaching practice was compounded by the fact that first-year students are typically not familiar enough with academic research to anticipate the usefulness of the strategies we emphasized in the seminar. Also, while most students lacked academic research experience, they had a great deal of familiarity with popular search engines such as Google, but we did not invite them to reflect upon these past experiences in such a way as to make it transferable to the academic setting. By discouraging this connection, we denied an opportunity to validate student knowledge and to encourage meaningful participation, mimicking what Paulo Freire (2006) called the "banking concept of education," which treats learners as ignorant and positions the teacher as the sole narrator of knowledge (p. 72). Rather than allowing students to explore library resources for themselves, we sought to fill them with what they did not know through demonstration. Discouraged by our struggle to balance traditional expectations and a more progressive set of intentions in our classroom design, we recognized a need to investigate our teaching practice so as to more carefully align it with our pedagogical beliefs.

We view information literacy to be more far-reaching than the academic setting in which we work. Information literacy is not merely necessary for an assignment or the completion of an academic degree. It is a potential source of change and empowerment in today's digital world. We believe, as Heidi Jacobs put it, "information literacy not only incorporates recurrent concepts of identifying, locating, evaluating, and using information ... [it] also encompasses engendering lifelong learning, empowering people, promoting social inclusion, redressing disadvantage, and advancing well-being of all in a global context" (p. 257). Students' information choices will influence their ability to act as information creators, self-directed learners, and indeed as citizens. We sought to develop teaching practices that would empower self-directed learners who actively and critically examine information systems and accepted codes of legitimacy. We worked to revise our classroom structure in order to reflect these beliefs in our teaching practices.

Our commitment to the belief that active student participation is essential to stimulating learning and discovery in the classroom is central to our revised classroom structure. Student participation depends strongly on the teacher's ability to establish a bridge between classroom content and student knowledge and experience. Our seminars lacked active participation and a sense of significance to learners. Furthermore, we did not provide an opportunity for students to think critically about what we were demonstrating or the information we retrieved. As a result, the evaluative and critical stance we wanted students to adopt in their information seeking was contradicted by our own teaching practices. Because students were not authentically experiencing information seeking or investigating their own information use, we were unable to give them a broad perspective of information systems that would allow for critical analysis. Our seminars isolated searching to fulfill assignment demands from the larger information environment and students own information habits; in doing so, we separated these tasks from "the totality that engendered them and could give them significance" (Freire, 2006, p. 71). Becoming increasingly uneasy about the gap between our pedagogical beliefs and our classroom practice, we began to envision a more ideal seminar structure that would incorporate the empowering potential of information literacy. In the process of revision, we were aided by theorists of critical pedagogy such as Paulo Freire, Peter McLaren, and Henry Giroux who promote classrooms in which students are not passive but active "critical co-investigators with the teacher," and where students are "posed with problems relating to themselves in the world and with the world" (Freire, 2006, p. 81). Reinforced by these theories, we sought to adopt problem-posing, dialogic, and reflective teaching strategies in order to empower students through a conceptual understanding of information systems and through the modeling of critical reflective information literacy.

Our revised seminar centers on a student-driven group activity and a class discussion that fosters reflection on information seeking experiences. Students divide into groups of three in which each member has a clearly defined role: the "driver" navigates the computer, the "recorder" documents group answers on a handout, and the "reporter" is responsible for sharing the group's results with the class. We find that specific roles and simple instructions make the activity run smoothly, providing ample time for post-activity dialogue. We introduce the activity by discussing a sample research assignment and topic, urging students to think about the topic as if it were their own. After the brief discussion, each group performs the same keyword search, but in one of three different retrieval systems: Google, the library catalog or an interdisciplinary database. During the activity, the teacher-librarian is available for questions, but we make it a point not to hover. We have found that maintaining a physical distance encourages student leadership. It is important for students to be responsible for their own searches, even if they encounter roadblocks. By approaching challenges without the aid of a librarian, students problem-solve, teach one another, and become aware of the complexity of research and information systems. This results in a more authentic learning experience. The activity is guided by a series of questions that encourage students to draw conclusions based on their findings. Some of the questions students respond to are:

How many results did your search generate?

What kinds of sources (magazines, newspapers, scholarly journals, blogs, etc.)?

Choose the result that looks the most useful and relevant.

- Why did you choose this result?

- What kind of material is your choice (book, website, article)?

- What is the name of the publication?

- What is the publication date?

- Who is the author? Can you find any information about her/him?

•Can you read or access the text? How?

Imagine you are going to revise this search. What might you do differently?

The activity is designed to draw out the students' experience, knowledge, and reflection in order to bring a sense of relevance and meaning, which we believe to be imperative to student engagement. By using Google as a core component of the activity, we are able to bridge known and foreign information systems, legitimating and exercising background student experience. We find that students are able to conceptualize information systems more effectively through an analysis of a familiar interface such as Google, and that by validating the importance of the popular search engine, the classroom content becomes more applicable for students. The activity readies students to offer sophisticated reflection on the research process from a position of authority and expertise while providing a shared context for class discussion.

The class discussion is motivated by a comparison of the results of the groups' searches. Dialogue, not narration, is the communication tool, and the students guide the conversation through an analysis of *their own* findings, thus dismantling the teacher-student hierarchy. By sharing and comparing results, the disparities between the content of sources available in the library catalog, academic databases, and Google become clear. We no longer have to *explain* our teaching-points because the students demonstrate them themselves. Our role is simply to ask students to draw conclusions based on the differences between the resource types by posing questions like, "Why did you get fewer results in the library catalog than the other group got in the database?" Although students are exposed to only one research interface during the group activity, their peers act as mini-experts on each of the research interfaces, pointing out which aspects of search and retrieval among the three databases are unique, and which are transferable.

In the new model, students are no longer banks into which the teacher deposits knowledge, as they were in the previous seminar model (Freire, 2006, p. 72). Instead, they become teacher-learners, finding and evaluating information and thereby creating their own meaning. The teacher uses probing questions to encourage critical analysis, but the classroom is driven by student discoveries and observations of information systems. Each session is then necessarily distinct based on the unique experiences of the individual students. This places the teacher in a position of discovery as well: "The teacher is no longer merely the one-who-teaches, but one who is himself taught in dialogue with the students" (Freire, 2006, p. 80).

Despite our confidence in the theories behind student-centered pedagogy, we struggled to release ourselves from traditional assumptions about what constitutes 'good' teaching. To strengthen our commitment to unconventional teaching practices, we team-taught the first series of seminars. Through co-observation and post-class discussions, we were able to identify moments in the seminar when we reverted to a teacher-centered approach. We became particularly conscious of our desire to expedite student discovery by asserting authority and making directive comments. We listened for teacher-talk that shut-down student participation and developed alternate language that encourages dialogue. We challenge students with questions like, "Why do you think that?" or, "Tell us a little bit more about that." Through this method, even seemingly naïve student comments open into interesting, sophisticated perspectives on information systems. Fighting our urge to deposit knowledge, we are astounded by the quality of student-generated ideas when we allow them to expand in an open-ended, non-judgmental discussion. We no longer follow a strict agenda, but rather rely on the unified content of our activity to evaluate the research process as a group. Some classes delve into a discussion of Wikipedia and its benefits and drawbacks. Others debate standards of academic authority or discuss the process of peer-review. Occasionally our classes are not jaw-dropping, but we remain convinced that a student-centered classroom experience, while unpredictable, is superior to a teacher-centered approach that is comprehensive but depository.

We want students to be aware of their information agency and to understand the impact of source selections, but we avoid making value judgments about the sources students select in the activity. Issues of academic authority are often brought up in discussion, and while we encourage these topics, we try to remain neutral. We do not advocate a blind preference for peer-reviewed publications, nor do we dismiss the value of popular sources. We want students to become critically sensitive to issues of legitimacy and power within information systems and environments. Imposing traditional evaluation criteria or norms of authority would contradict our intention to advance students' critical examination of information. Instead, the activity and dialogue ask students to carefully analyze their own methods of evaluation. We draw this approach from Peter McLaren's (1998) vision of a critical pedagogy "in which students are continually asked to examine various codes—that is, the beliefs, the values, and the assumptions—that they use to make sense out of their world" (p. 226). Through comparison and analysis, students begin to recognize the significance of choosing one system over another and the implications those choices have on potential results, voices represented, audiences addressed, and relevance to specific information needs. We want students to question their own methods of evaluation and to "encourage [them] to be self-reflexive about these questions" (McLaren, 1998, p. 192). Through dialogue, students rehearse thoughtful reflection on their own information seeking habits, the information systems they use, and their own measures of evaluation. This is the kind of critical, reflective information literacy we hope students will develop over time.

Prior to implementing the activity in our new seminar model, we were uncertain that students could draw meaningful conclusions from an analysis of their own searches. We doubted that we could engage in sophisticated, conceptual topics during a brief class period, and most of all, we worried that we would do our students a disservice by not demonstrating the nuts and bolts of library resources. Our new seminar model is more intent on a comparative analysis of information systems than it is on the mechanics of searching because we believe that empowerment through information literacy demands critical evaluation of information tools, sources, and one's own information use. We do not deny that there is an appropriate time and place for teaching specific skill-based strategies where students may gain tremendously from exposure to more sophisticated search manipulation. However, we believe that without a broader conceptual understanding of information systems, mechanical skills do little to empower students. Fortunately, in addition to attending a seminar, our first-year students complete an online tutorial, which introduces many research mechanics. Despite our initial skepticism, after taking a leap of faith and testing out the student-led activity, we were thrilled to observe students transforming into eager mini-experts who have a great deal to say about searching with variant tools, investigating an author or source, limiting searches, and developing new keywords. Indeed, the students began to build methods of critical evaluation, arriving at precisely the conclusions we previously had attempted to drive home through our woefully inauthentic methods.

Realizing that students' information literacy will profoundly impact their lives within the academy and beyond, our allegiance to information literacy education is unwavering. Students' information needs will change and the information environments they use will evolve, but the empowering potential of information literacy will remain. We view information literacy to be a cumulative, developmental process in an individual's life rather than a set of skills to be attained. Incorporating this viewpoint in our revised seminars, we model a critically reflective approach to information that we hope students will continue to practice in future information experiences.

Critical pedagogy has been crucial to our design of teaching strategies that center on student experience, employ problem-posing activities, and foster a dynamic in which students and teachers are co-investigators. We have not exhausted the manner in which critical pedagogy may enlighten us as teachers, feeling that we are only beginning "to find a balance in the daily and the visionary, the local and the global, the practices and the theories, the ideal and the possible" in our work as information literacy educators (Jacobs, 2008, p. 258).

References

Association of College and Research Libraries (2000). *Information literacy competency standards for higher education*. Retrieved 1/1/09, from http://www.ala.org/ala/mgrps/divs/acrl/standards/standards.pdf.

Freire, P. (2006). *Pedagogy of the oppressed* [Pedagogía del oprimido English] (30th anniversary ed.). New York: Continuum.

Giroux, H. (1988). Literacy and the pedagogy of voice and political empowerment. *Educational Theory, 38*(1), 61-75.

Jacobs, H. L. M. (2008). Information literacy and reflective pedagogical praxis. *The Journal of Academic Librarianship, 34*(3), 256-262.

McLaren, P. (1998). *Life in school: An introduction to critical pedagogy in the foundations of education* (3rd ed.). New York: Longman.

Swanson, T. A. (2004). A radical step: Implementing A critical information literacy model. *Portal : Libraries and the Academy, 4*(2), 259.

Negotiating Virtual Contact Zones: Revolutions in the Role of the Research Workshop

Margaret Rose Torrell

The easy accessibility of information through Internet, database, and other electronic searches makes performing research the equivalent of entering into a virtual contact zone. Students are confronted by a multiplicity of often-contradictory opinions, attitudes, and data that reflects social inequalities and frictions between various agendas. As they perform research for their papers, students often enter this conflicted, agenda-inflected zone unaware and with an automatic respect for the published word. Thus, what seems like a quick and easy way to gather information from presumed experts can actually position student researchers as undiscerning consumers of information which can uphold unequal power relationships and advance the status quo. The library workshop that is guided by a critical pedagogy philosophy can be a foundational line of defense against such an uncritical approach to research.

My goal in this chapter is to explore how instructors and librarians, often working together, can use contact zone theory to adjust our pedagogical approach so that we can better prepare our students for critical navigation of the virtual contact zone. I begin with a narrative that highlights the problems of not teaching the research process from such a perspective. In the remainder of the paper, I sketch out the benefits of applying a contact zone approach to the research process, first in theory and second in practice. I end with a sample overview of a research unit I have developed for my English Composition class that can also be adapted for use as a two-part library workshop.

(Not) Teaching the Research Process: A Narrative

In my English Composition classroom in Long Island, New York, it is a few weeks past midterms. I've been teaching from a critical pedagogy perspective all semester, encouraging students to identify and respond critically to agendas embedded in our readings, and my students, second-semester freshmen, seem tuned in to reading and responding to the class-assigned texts in a critical, analytical way. Now, the research paper crunch is on. The library workshop has been scheduled and the bulk of classroom instructional time shifts to the technical aspects of research writing, such as the particulars of Modern Language Association documentation format: documentation because of the crack-down on plagiarism in our college; MLA format because this is an English class. Curiously, very little of my teaching draws on the critical reading and responding skills I've been fostering all semester. I become aware of this change, but can do little about it as I rush to cover the technical aspects of the research paper before the assignment due date.

On the day of our library workshop, class starts a few minutes late as we settle in from our hurried trek across campus to the library. The librarian has little over an hour to get acquainted with the students; teach them the newest methods in finding print articles and books, electronic books, database articles, and the best databases to use; and demonstrate the difference between general internet searching and database searching. The librarian has very skillfully jam-packed the workshop with all of these essentials and has even included a visit to an official-looking white supremacist website on Martin Luther King, Jr.

The students are highly goal-oriented during the one-hour workshop. It is the only time they will perform research in a class setting. They will need to do additional research for their papers, but they will perform this work on their own time and most likely alone. Students want to learn the quickest way to locate a cache of acceptable research materials that can be inserted into the research paper, meeting or exceeding the exact number of sources and source types, the exact number of in-text citations, and the exact number of pages required by the syllabus. This focus on getting and skimming as opposed to seeking and evaluating is a departure from what we've been doing all semester. In my classroom the students mostly form a community of scholars who are ready to be critical readers of everything I assign. Now, however, faced with task of reading the published word by themselves and writing a formal paper that incorporates it, the students morph into survival mode and are ready to accept almost unquestioningly everything they read. Even with the five-minute demonstration of the racist King website, they are not so impressed with the difference between web and database searching, not so excited about attending to the nuanced differences in source agendas. The multidimensional experience of research has collapsed into a shallow, mind-numbing chore. The librarian and I are both aware of this, but we can do little about it in the rush to cover the essential techniques of research.

For my part, I will be just as goal-oriented as my students once I get their papers. I've collected so many in a single day I have to wheel them off campus to get them home to grade. I average twenty-five minutes per paper on a good day, and I'll want to mark them in a two-week period so that students can have them back on the day of the final exam. I evaluate the papers holistically with a focus on source use. The students have submitted photocopies of sources so I can evaluate their integration of research. I look for their ability to enter into critical conversations with the sources—or at least not to lose their voice among the published authors—but not with the same attention to detail I have used on their earlier papers on class-assigned readings. The students may have missed opportunities to identify agendas that conflict with their own beliefs—they may even be reflecting such conflicting opinions as they quote and paraphrase fragments of sources— but I also miss opportunities to find out and let them know.

Even in the rush to get the papers back to the students, this bothers me a lot. I link it to the other missed opportunities—in the classroom and in the library workshop—to make the research paper what it is supposed to be: the culmination of the students' learning where they independently apply the critical reading and responding skills honed in my classroom to their own research projects. Meeting this goal necessitates teaching the research process from a critical pedagogy perspective, but curiously, the research unit is one curricular moment in which my focus on my students' critical reading and responding skills fades into the background.

Getting in the Zone: Understanding the Problem and Proposing a Solution

Theoretically, the problem with the research process described in my narrative can be summed up by Maxine Green's argument in *The Dialectic of Freedom* (1988): "If situations cannot be created that enable the young to deal with feelings of being manipulated by outside forces, there will be far too little sense of agency among them. Without a sense of agency, young people are unlikely to pose significant questions, the existentially rooted questions in which learning begins" (p. 3). In the classroom community, as we discuss the readings as a group, my students may have the sense of agency Green describes. However, because the research paper experience does not create situations that alert students to "being manipulated by outside forces," the research process becomes an exercise in mere reflection of research without evaluation. It is an activity that mutes student voices and shuts down avenues through which they can exercise agency.

Furthermore, as a critical pedagogist, one of my goals is to teach consciously, avoiding the type of education that "sustain[s] asymmetrical relations of power under the guise of neutral and apolitical views of education—views that are intimately linked to ideologies shaped by power, politics, history, culture, and economics" as Antonia Darder, Marta Baltodano, and Rodolfo D. Torres describe it in "Critical Pedagogy: An Introduction" (2003, p. 11). Attending mostly to technique as opposed to substance as I switch gears to teach the research paper, I have risked supporting such status-quo thinking.

As a result of my taking a pedagogical approach that is benignly mind-numbing at best, the papers I get represent very little in educational value. They remind me of one sort of writing that comes out of a contact zone: "Miscomprehension, incomprehension, dead letters, unread masterpieces," writes Mary Louise Pratt, "these are some of the perils of writing in the contact zone" (p. 37). These are also the perils, I find, of not teaching the research process from a critical pedagogy perspective. The solution is to revise my approach to the research process so that students are made sufficiently aware of the virtual information environment as a contact zone.

Theorizing the Zone: The Virtual Research Environment as a Contact Zone

Contact zone pedagogy is a way of teaching the conflicts and connections that arise when cultures meet and grapple for power. These conflicts and connections are captured in many types of writing—some formal and public, some informal and personal; some created by those in dominant social positions, others by members of marginalized cultures. These texts and their diverse agendas form a study in how groups present themselves in the pressured context of unequal power relationships and conflicted social agendas. The concept of the contact zone was first introduced by Pratt in her landmark essay, "Arts of the Contact Zone" (1991), in which she defines contact zones as "social spaces where cultures meet, clash, and grapple with each other, often in contexts of highly asymmetrical relations of power, such as colonialism, slavery, or their aftermaths as they are lived out in many parts of the world today" (p. 34). To illustrate her notion of a contact zone, Pratt uses an example with distinct cultural and historical boundaries: Peru in the sixteenth and seventeenth centuries. However, Pratt's theory more generally applied has been instrumental in advancing the use of critical pedagogy in the college English classroom, where students are trained to discern agendas and assumptions about cultural identities that are often missed because they are hidden within language and metaphor. In subsequent scholarship, in fact, the borders and sizes of contact zones are actually quite varied. A contact zone could be English Studies or the United States (Bizzell, 1994, p. 166), a given school (consider the grappling between administration and instructors, for example), or any classroom (where students represent various cultures and the zone is defined by the boundaries of the course).[1]

The virtual research environment is another type of contact zone. Conceptually, it might function in a way that is similar to Patricia Bizzell's explanation of the United States as a contact zone: "I submit that the United States is another such contact zone, or more precisely, a congeries of overlapping contact zones" (p. 166). Likewise, I consider the Internet to be an umbrella contact zone in which exist smaller, overlapping contact zones that, for example, might cover information on a historical period, culture, piece of literature, etc.

As a macro-level contact zone, the virtual information environment is a repository of cultural conflict and connection captured in word, sound, and image. Pieced together from many unfiltered sources throughout the world, the Internet reflects the same conglomeration of opinions as well as the same social inequalities and struggles to overturn them that exist in society in general. Competing to be heard among them is the same privileged few with the same financial and educational advantages to ensure that their opinions are the most widely broadcast and absorbed. More people can post their opinions, but reader preference is given to sites that are created with enough educational and financial resources to look official, be written in a reader-friendly way, and turn up first in an internet search. For students, electronic research parameters are limited by their pre-college computer knowledge, the quantity and quality of databases to which their college and local libraries can afford subscriptions, and the time they have to perform and evaluate research (the latter is especially a concern for many of my students who work and/or have significant family responsibilities). Thus, as long as social inequality exists, it will be reflected in visible and invisible ways on the Internet, first because the web captures the prejudices and debates of the cultures that produce it, and second because financial resources are a determining factor of information accessibility.

---

[1] See, for example, Patricia Bizzell (1994) on English Studies as a contact zone; Richard E. Miller (1994) on how power hierarchies in the classroom create a contact zone; and Phyllis van Slyck (1997) on how various cultures in the classroom form a contact zone.

Especially in the rush to perform research for major class assignments, students rarely recognize the power hierarchies governing the cultural production of virtual information. This danger is intensified by students' willing acceptance of the authority of the written word, which I interpret as a kind of "narration sickness." The concept of "narration sickness" is developed by Paulo Freire in *Pedagogy of the Oppressed* (1970) to critique the educational model that seated the teacher as the superior holder of knowledge and student as the inferior recipient. The instructor "deposits" knowledge into students who are "passive vaults" for the material (pp. 71-77). Another type of narration sickness is at work when students unskeptically approach the written word without considering its source and agenda. They—and their papers—become passive receptacles of written information, reflections of the dominant agendas most readily accessed on the web.

From an educational standpoint, it is actually a good thing that the Internet is a contact zone. Using the Internet in a classroom environment gives students hands-on, guided experience in intellectually negotiating such a conflicted space. In that way, instructors and librarians don't just "teach the conflicts." Instead, the students themselves gain entrance to a contact zone in which they must critically sift through a range of agendas and opinions with instructors and librarians as ready resources. Such an active experience of a contact zone may even engender the type of agency in students that Green believes is necessary for significant learning to occur. Philip J. Burns in "Supporting Deliberative Democracy: Pedagogical Arts of the Contact Zone of the Electronic Public Sphere" has also argued that the Internet functions as "a contact zone whose power asymmetries reflect the political inequalities of the larger society" (1999, p. 134) and has developed an approach to maximize his students' ability to navigate the information available in such a zone. He creates an electronic contact zone comprised exclusively of students in the class. This, he argues, equips students to become agents of the electronic contact zone at large because it helps students to "enact and develop rhetorical strategies (or 'literate arts') that enhance democratic deliberation among themselves or others as individuals" (p. 130). In what follows, I offer another way of encouraging careful reading and critical responding by engaging students more directly with the literature of the virtual information environment.

The new contact zone-based research process I propose assigns a central role to research performed in a workshop setting and brings a critical pedagogy approach to the entire research unit. Consider that the research paper process described in my narrative places the stress on a "top down" teaching of technique in both the classroom and workshop; it limits the research workshop to a rushed, single hour of class; it does not include opportunities for the students to receive guided instruction throughout the research process; it isolates students as opposed to encouraging peer interaction; it evaluates the students' multi-dimensional process of research writing using a single, formal paper that determines a large part of the course grade; it does little to give students the agency to be active researchers, readers, and responders to sources.

Adapting contact zone pedagogy to the research process offsets many of these downfalls. Whenever possible, the instructional setting is organized so that students discover research principles of the contact zone through a dialog with librarians, instructors, and their peers. The techniques of searching and of formatting will have to be taught, but this can be done in a workshop setting which gives students maximum hands-on experience and allows the librarian or instructor time to work individually with smaller groups of students. Students gather in focus groups as opposed to working alone in order to replicate, on a smaller scale, the community environment of the classroom. Students get multiple exposures to the research process and to strategies for discerning the agendas of research sources. At each step of the process, students write reflective narratives so that they can concretize the intellectual work of the research process in a mode that is conducive to independent thought. Applying contact zone theory to the research process requires a greater commitment of instructional time on both the parts of the classroom instructor and the librarian, but the payoff—greater student agency that allows for learning—is highly desirable.

Teaching in the Zone: A Sample Research Unit

I illustrate how these modifications can take shape by providing an overview of a sample instructional unit in which librarian and classroom instructor work in tandem to guide students in researching the 16th Street Baptist Church bombing of Birmingham, Alabama and the Civil Rights activities surrounding it. The varied perspectives on this historical event demonstrate the necessity of being conscious and careful researchers and give students training in evaluating and voicing responses to such material. I discuss the unit here as part of my English Composition II course to contextualize the interactive role of the library workshop in classroom activities. The unit can be adapted to a two-session research workshop that librarians might develop for other purposes, such as a campus-wide program on critical research abilities.

The 1963 church bombing and the Birmingham, Alabama, civil rights struggles of the early 1960s function as a contact zone and generate cultural documents diverse in genre and agenda. The church bombing is a topic for poetry, other types of literature, music, and art. It is the subject of many newspaper articles, journal articles, and books, and received recent attention in 2002 when the last known bomber was put on trial and found guilty.

I begin the unit with the analysis of Dudley Randall's poem, "The Ballad of Birmingham" (1966).[2] The poem is an excellent starting point for the research experience. It details the imagined reaction of one of the mothers who lost a daughter in the bombing. With heavy emotional impact, the poem vividly depicts the fallout from unequal social relationships and thereby engages students viscerally in questions about social justice. It further sparks student curiosity about the tragedy and the larger circumstances of the Birmingham, Alabama, Civil Rights activities involving Martin Luther King, Jr. Student interest forms the basis for a multi-tiered research experience that fosters student agency, careful reading, and critical response.

The poem opens with the dialogue between a mother and her daughter. The daughter wants to participate in the freedom march downtown instead of going out to play. She asks her mother if she can join other children to "march the streets of Birmingham / To make our country free" (lines 11-12). The mother won't permit her to go to the march because it presents many dangers: "the dogs are fierce and wild, / And clubs and hoses, guns and jails / Aren't good for a little child" (lines 6-8), but offers her the safer option of attending church and singing in the children's choir. The poem's speaker steps in to describe the daughter's meticulous dressing for church and the mother's relief at knowing that her daughter is in "a sacred place" where she would be safe. The speaker remains focused on the mother and her horrified reaction as she hears the explosion and rushes to the church to find her daughter. "She clawed through bits of glass and brick, / Then lifted out a shoe. / 'O, here's the shoe my baby wore, / But, baby, where are you?'" (lines 29-32) are the last pain-filled lines of the poem.

Students come in to class having read the poem and written an informal response on what each student found to be the most powerful lines or moments in it. We discuss the poem and make a list of questions we have

---

[2] I would like to thank Francisco Calo, a peer mentor in my spring 2006 English Composition course, for suggesting that I add "The Ballad of Birmingham" to my syllabus and for his input on research materials for the poem.

about its historical context that we can research. For example, students are curious about the actual dangers associated with participation in the freedom march, why children would be permitted to join the march, why the church was targeted, and what impact the bombing had on Birmingham civil rights activities.

Our next class is held in the library. The librarian runs a workshop on searching for sources, and the focus is on locating a variety of information resources on the church bombing and associated civil rights activities. The librarian takes approximately thirty minutes to demonstrate searching the open web, the book catalog, and journal databases (especially databases which offer decades worth of newspaper articles). The second half of the workshop has the students form focus groups of three to four. The groups complete Research Activity 1 (Appendix A) which has two goals: to locate two websites dedicated to Martin Luther King, Jr., and to locate a *New York Times* article about the parents' reaction to the bombing. Students are asked to read these sources and write a response to them that evaluates their validity. We meet in the classroom the next day to discuss the sources.

The website portion of the assignment has been rigged so that the students locate www.martinlutherking.org, a site sponsored by Stormfront, a white supremacist organization, and www.thekingcenter.org, a site sponsored by King's family and associates. Of the two, the Stormfront site appears to be of most use to researchers. It is entitled "Martin Luther King—A True Historical Examination" and seems to be loaded with information about King. Links point to historical information and writings as well as contemporary raps and an offer to "Bring the dream to life in your town." When clicked on, however, each linked page presents information on King from a white supremacist viewpoint. Student reaction to this site is an excellent gauge of their awareness as researchers. Even if they miss the overt racist agenda of the site on their own, class discussion about the resource underscores the importance of being careful readers.

The lesson about being careful readers is then applied to the newspaper portion of the assignment. Students have located a *New York Times* article by John Herbers entitled "Parents Are Sad but not Bitter" (1963, p. 24) which covers short statements from the parents of the four girls who were killed in the church bombing, and includes a paragraph about "Toots," the cocker spaniel who won't eat because it misses one of the girls. The parents assure Herbers that they aren't bitter about the bombing and express faith that the investigators are working tirelessly to bring the bombers to justice. Students are less likely to be critical of the article since it appeared in the *New York Times* and they have faith that newspapers deal in "the facts." Upon further reflection, however, the parents' subdued reactions and some of the more trivial details in the report seem very strange considering the magnitude of the church bombing. These disconnects generate curiosity about the approach Herbers took when he wrote the article. Frequent questions include: What is Herbers's cultural background and journalistic experience? Who were his readers? How reliable were police investigations of the bombing? What accounts for the parents' guarded reactions: Are they reflecting civil disobedience philosophy? Were their responses skewed by the writer? Can we find other depictions of the parents to compare to Herbers's account of it? We also spend some time talking about emotional versus factual veracity as we compare and contrast Herbers's article and Randall's poem. Students are asked to reflect in informal narratives on their experiences with Research Activity 1 and to develop strategies to be responsible researchers.

We meet again in the library for Research Activity 2. After a refresher in how to locate sources, students work in groups to locate five other newspaper articles on the bombing or on civil rights activities in Birmingham. At least two articles should be from the 1960s and at least two should be written in the last fifteen years. Students read them, group them according to implied agenda, and report on them at the end of the workshop or in the next class. For homework, students are required to write a brief summary of each article and a justification of why they grouped the articles the way they did. This assignment begins the transition toward independent research while continuing to give students guided practice in discerning resource agendas.

We gather in the library for a third research workshop during which students complete Research Activity 3. The students select a research focus from the list of questions generated from reading Randall's poem and Herbers's article and perform research. Their goal is to locate at least four additional sources beyond newspaper coverage of the event. Students read the sources and rate them according to agenda and perceived usefulness for completing the research writing assignment. Students can work in groups or independently at this point. For the next class, students write a personal reflection about the research process and what they learned about being careful researchers. Students are invited to share their thoughts during discussion.

Over the following weeks, students write a documented essay that covers Randall's poem and five of the sources they located during the workshops. During this time, class discussions and workshops address such topics as how to accommodate and respond to opposing viewpoints in a research paper, how to handle competing agendas in a paper, and the more technical aspects of paper presentation, such as proper documentation. Students tend to be invested in the project because they have been shown instances in which readers are "manipulated by outside forces" (Green, 1988, p. 3) and have developed the agency to discover and respond to them. They produce varied types of writing throughout the stages of the research process, including informal reflective narratives and documented essays, and their voices have become stronger and opinions more individualized. Because I receive writing from them almost every class, I can guide them through the critical responding process. I still teach the technical aspects of research writing, but start earlier. I find that when students have a stake in the content, they are also more receptive to applying the format standards of the scholarly field. I still have to wheel the papers off campus to mark them, but it is with a renewed purpose. The assignment matters to the students and has functioned as a research paper should: as the culmination of the learning experience for the class.

The research unit I propose presupposes an interdependence and a shared dedication to critical pedagogy between classroom instructor and librarian. It also assumes that the college library has adequate librarian staff and computerized workshop rooms to cover three library visits per course, something that budget constraints may make challenging at many colleges. If this is the case, the librarian may be able to run Workshop 1 and then dedicate some time to the class during Workshops 2 and 3.

The unit would adapt well to a two-session library workshop run exclusively by library staff. The two sessions might be held on the same day, with a lunch break in between, in order to replicate the type of intensity of coverage that occurs in a classroom setting due to the regularity of class meetings. Session 1 begins with the reading and analysis of the Dudley Randall poem and the generation of questions to research about it (forty minutes). The librarian conducts a class session on locating sources and asks students to work in groups to complete Research Assignment 1 (Appendix A; sixty minutes). Workshop attendees write an informal narrative about their research experiences (in groups or individually) and discuss their findings with the workshop attendees as a whole (approximately sixty minutes). Session 2 begins with a refresher about locating sources and a review of the reasons why it is important to be a careful researcher (thirty minutes). The remainder of Session 2 is dedicated to Research Activity 2, including attendee reports to the entire group (sixty minutes), and Research Activity 3, also with attendee-led reports (sixty minutes). The workshop ends with a summary of the essential points attendees have learned from their research experiences throughout the day (thirty minutes).

For the two-part library workshop, I want to stress the importance of contact zone pedagogy techniques. These techniques require honoring diverse forms of cultural expression in research (such as the Randall poem) and student assignments (such as the personal narratives), and creating learning environments that maximize student agency and engagement. This includes modifying the research instruction components so that students discover for themselves how an uncritical approach to research can lead to "being manipulated by outside forces," and so that open dialogue and hands-on learning are chosen over lecture and instructor-led demonstration.

Such shifts in pedagogical focus can have very promising results. According to Pratt, "Miscomprehension, incomprehension, dead letters, unread masterpieces" and other "perils" represent only one type of writing that comes out of contact zones. Contact zones can also foster the production of more desirable "literate arts" such as "autoethnography, transculturation, critique, collaboration, mediation... denunciation, [and] vernacular expression" (p. 37). Such emancipatory modes of expression are possible from our students. By drawing from contact zone pedagogy in our approaches to teaching the research process, we will provide our students with greater opportunities to become aware researchers, active evaluators, and invested respondents.

Appendix A

Research Activity 1:

1.   Use Google to look up "Martin Luther King, Jr." In the first six
      hits, locate the two sites that are dedicated to him and fill out the
      form, below.

	Web Address of Site 1:	Web Address of Site 2:
Click on the link to get to the webpage. How much useful information does the site seem to provide? What are your first impressions of the webpage?		
Click on some of the webpage's links. From what point of view is the information about Dr. King presented?		

2.   Locate the article entitled "Parents Are Sad, but not Bitter,"
        published in the *New York Times* September 17, 1963.

        A. What are the parents' reactions to the bombing?

        B. Compare and contrast the reaction of the mother in the poem to
           the reaction of the parents in the article. What accounts for
           the difference?

References

Bizzell, P. (1994). Contact zones and English studies. *College English* 56: 163-169. Retrieved October 12, 2008, from JSTOR database.

Burns, P. J. (1999). Supporting deliberative democracy: Pedagogical arts of the contact zone of the electronic public sphere. *Rhetoric Review 18* (1): 128-146. Retrieved October 12, 2008, from JSTOR database.

Darder, A., Baltodano, M., and Torres, R. D. (2003). Critical pedagogy: An introduction. In Darder, A. Baltodano, M. and.Torres, R. D. (Eds.), *The critical pedagogy reader.* (pp. 1-23). New York: Routledge Falmer.

Freire, P. 2000. *Pedagogy of the oppressed.* (M. B. Ramos, Trans.). New York: Continuum. (Original work published 1970)

Freire, P. and Macedo, D. (1987). Rethinking literacy: A dialogue. In Darder, A. Baltodano, M. and.Torres, R. D. (Eds.), *The critical pedagogy reader* (pp. 354-364). New York: Routledge Falmer.

Green, M. (1988). *Dialectic of freedom.* New York: Teachers College Press.

Herbers, J. (1963, September 17). Parents are sad but not bitter, p. 24. Retrieved January 7, 2006, from Proquest Historical Newspapers database.

The King center (n.d.). Retrieved January 18, 2009 from http://www.thekingcenter.org.

Stormfront. (n.d.). Martin Luther King, Jr.—A true historical examination. Retrieved January 18, 2009, from http://www.martinluther.org.

Miller, R. E. (1994). Fault lines in the contact zone. *College English 56*: 389-408.

Pratt, M. L. (1991). Arts of the contact zone. *Profession 91*: 33-40.

Randall, D. (1966). The ballad of Birmingham. *Cities Burning*. Detroit: Broadside Press.

van Slyck, P. (1997). Repositioning ourselves in the contact zone. *College English 59*: 149-70.

Paradigm Shift: Utilizing Critical Feminist Pedagogy in Library Instruction

Sharon Ladenson

What are the critical tenets of feminist pedagogy? What impact can the feminist classroom have on library instruction and the research process? Some traditional bibliographic instruction methods emphasize a patriarchal paradigm, which involves the librarian dominating the classroom by lecturing to students about a plethora of information sources and search strategies. This chapter explores the principles of feminist pedagogy, an educational philosophy that offers a fresh and stimulating approach for motivating students and encouraging them to actively engage in the research process. The chapter also explores how the gender studies librarian at Michigan State University has effectively utilized feminist pedagogical techniques to help students develop and reinforce their information literacy skills.

Feminist Pedagogy: Key Principles

As practitioners of critical pedagogy, feminists resist educational practices that promote and foster passive behavior. Freire (2000/1970) describes the inherently oppressive nature of the "banking concept of education," in which "action allowed to the students extends only as far as receiving, filing, and storing deposits" (p. 72). The banking concept exemplifies a patriarchal paradigm, as the teacher dominates the educational environment, while students behave submissively. Feminist pedagogy resists the banking concept by fostering active learning, and by empowering students to think critically. As Parry (1996) notes:

> Feminist pedagogy promotes the awareness that knowledge is not a discrete body of "truths" that the instructor knows and imparts to students. It reframes the relationship between students and course material by suggesting that students themselves are capable of active learning and that this, rather than passive receiving, is what works best. Feminist teaching encourages classroom interactions that emphasize students' ability to question and explore issues deeply, and nurtures the

development of motivation and skills that allow students to investigate ideas and evidence and arrive at meaning. (p. 45)

Various scholars and practitioners of critical feminist pedagogy further emphasize the fundamental importance of active learning and critical thinking. Chow, Fleck, Fan, Joseph, and Lyter (2003) note that a goal of the feminist approach is "to create an environment where students actively participate in the production of knowledge. This approach challenges the traditional hierarchy of teacher-student relationships and a teacher-centered source of knowledge" (p. 266). Bell, Morrow and Tastsoglou (1999) assert that the critical thinking process causes students to "shift from being passive receivers of knowledge to becoming engaged in a dynamic process of learning" (p. 23).

Feminist teachers seek to actively engage students in learning, and, consequently, they value and encourage sharing diverse personal experiences as part of the educational process. As a practitioner of feminist pedagogy, Fisher (2001) notes that she fosters "a collective, collaborative and ongoing (learning) process that pays special attention to women's experiences, feelings, ideas and actions" (p. 44). Feminist writer bell hooks (1994) recalls that as a student, she learned that women's studies classes "were the one space where teachers were willing to acknowledge a connection between ideas learned in university settings and those learned in life practices" (p. 15). Feminist classrooms and curricula emphasize and value diverse experiences, as Parry (1996) notes: "Feminist pedagogy also makes explicit that how we experience and understand things is rooted in our social position, based on a variety of factors, including gender, race, ethnicity, class and sexual preference" (p. 46). Weiler (1995) also notes that "feminist theorists have increasingly emphasized the importance of difference as a central category of feminist pedagogy" (p. 31).

Instructors who utilize feminist pedagogy seek to foster open discussion and critical inquiry. Consequently, their classrooms are highly participatory and engaging environments where students are encouraged to learn actively and work cooperatively. Shrewsbury (1993) describes the democratic and collaborative nature of the feminist classroom, which becomes "a model of ways for people to work together and accomplish mutual or shared goals, and to help each other reach individual goals" (p. 9). Villaverde (2008) notes that "feminist pedagogy insists on the conditions of a democratic education, such as learning must involve freedom, social justice, participation and community" (p. 127). Parry (1996) also describes the egalitarian and "cooperative and collective" emphasis of feminist pedagogy: "as we become more skilled in devising effective structures for group work and collaborative exercises, the classroom becomes far less competitive and individualistic" (p. 46). Furthermore, Webb, Allen and Walker (2002) identify "building community and cooperation within the classroom" as a core principle of feminist pedagogy (p. 69). The communal and cooperative emphasis subverts traditional classroom dynamics, sometimes shifting the power and sharing of knowledge from the instructor to the students: "students assume more responsibility for teaching and teachers for learning" (Webb et al., 2002, p. 68).

Related Educational Methodologies and Techniques

Practitioners of feminist pedagogy can utilize a variety of educational techniques and methodologies designed to enhance the communal environment, and to foster active engagement and critical thinking. Such techniques may include cooperative and collaborative learning, and inquiry-based and inquiry-guided learning. According to Stanger (1987), collaborative learning does not simply refer to group work: "students in a group are only engaged in collaborative learning if the goal of the task is the learning of high-level critical thinking skills...[and] when the task asks questions that have more than one answer" (p. 37). Although cooperative and collaborative learning methodologies share some common characteristics, they are not synonymous, as the collaborative model supports the feminist pedagogical practice of reforming the traditional relationship between the students and the instructor:

> The collaborative model builds on Cooperative Learning strategies, but extends beyond having the students work together to complete a predetermined task. In collaborative learning, professors and students actively and mutually engage in the learning process. Together they define and create a body of knowledge that informs transforms our world. (Ventimiglia, 1995, p. 21)

Inquiry-*based* teaching and learning also changes the traditional relationship between the instructor and students, as teachers who use this methodology have a preference "for asking instead of answering questions and an eagerness to move away from center stage" (Audet, 2005, p. 14). Inquiry-*guided* learning seeks to stimulate intellectual curiosity, and, consequently, practitioners of this methodology encourage students to actively develop questions (Lee, Greene, Odom, Schechter & Slatta, 2004, p. 5). Four key components of inquiry-guided learning include "critical thinking, independent inquiry, responsibility for one's own learning, and intellectual growth and maturity" (Lee et al., 2004, p. 6).

Feminist Pedagogy and Library Instruction at Michigan State University

Librarians can develop a student's information seeking and evaluation skills effectively by utilizing feminist pedagogy (and related active and cooperative learning methodologies) rather than relying exclusively on a lecture format to teach about information sources and Boolean logic. Fostering an educational environment that promotes critical thinking and independent inquiry is crucial for helping students to hone their information literacy skills. Successful researchers not only know how to effectively locate, evaluate, analyze and utilize information, but also learn to "make relationships between ideas...(transfer) ideas to other contexts...(integrate) what is known with personal experiences...(and think) open-mindedly when considering issues or solving a problem" (Gavin, 2008, p. 2).

Librarians at Michigan State University actively seek opportunities to work with students in order to develop and reinforce their information literacy skills. The library emphasizes the importance of information literacy at all levels of undergraduate and graduate study. Working with first-year students is especially critical, as such students need to develop their skills early in order to have success during their college years and beyond.

Michigan State University has a writing course requirement (involving the development of research skills) for first-year students. The first-year composition courses, offered through the Department of Writing, Rhetoric and American Cultures (WRA), have tracks that focus on various interdisciplinary areas of inquiry, including (among others) "American Radical Thought," "Science and Technology," and "Women in America." The gender studies librarian at Michigan State University works with faculty and students in the "Women in America" track (WRA 140) to foment information literacy at the early stage of the undergraduate course of study.

While the course content varies among the numerous sections of WRA 140, several instructors require students to research and analyze the significant contributions and experiences of a specific woman. Finding and evaluating biographical information on women can present significant challenges. Gross (1994) notes that as recently as the late twentieth century, information on women in specific creative and professional fields (such as theater) was relatively scant and unreliable. She asserts that researchers need to evaluate female autobiographical sources critically, as a woman may place little emphasis on her professional accomplishments in order to please her publisher and/or her audience. Gross recommends that students utilize more recent feminist biographical sources, as well as unpublished diaries and letters which may include more candid descriptions of women's lives and accomplishments.

Given the complexities of locating and assessing biographical information on women, the gender studies librarian works with the faculty who teach WRA 140 classes to ensure that they develop assignments that require students not only to locate a variety of information resources, but also to critically evaluate and analyze them. Some faculty members require their students to research and write a critical analysis of a specific woman's contributions in social and historical context, while other instructors ask students to locate and critically compare numerous primary and secondary sources for the purposes of developing an annotated bibliography. The WRA 140 faculty members regularly bring their students to the library for instruction and guidance on locating and evaluating sources.

As a practitioner of feminist pedagogy, the gender studies librarian appreciates the diversity of women's experiences and contributions. In order to help students acquire books more efficiently, the librarian develops a reserve collection of titles specific to the lives and accomplishments of a diverse group of women, such as (among many others) Mary McLeod Bethune, Bella Abzug, Condoleezza Rice, Gloria Anzaldúa, Wilma Mankiller, and Elizabeth Blackwell. When conducting instruction for WRA 140 classes, the librarian also uses examples of women of color (such as Angela Davis) as possible research subjects.

The gender studies librarian cultivates a feminist classroom environment by utilizing active learning techniques designed to stimulate critical inquiry. At the beginning of each instruction session, the librarian shows students colorful pictures of a prominent woman in popular culture and/or public life (such as Oprah Winfrey). She also shows students pictures of another politically, socially and/or historically significant woman who is less ubiquitous in contemporary culture (such as Angela Davis). After briefly identifying each woman and naming some of her significant accomplishments, the librarian asks students to write down at least one question they would like to ask about each woman, and list at least one information source in which they would expect to find the answer. After generating their ideas, the students share their questions and information sources with the class. Next, the librarian lists the information sources on the board, and engages students in further discussion by asking them to identify which ones are primary, and which ones are secondary. The exercises facilitate the active process of learning how to develop thoughtful research questions, and how to distinguish the differences between various sources of information.

The gender studies librarian also stimulates the process of critical inquiry by implementing cooperative learning techniques in library instruction sessions. Prior to conducting instruction sessions, the librarian compiles numerous primary, secondary, popular and scholarly sources on specific women to distribute to students in class. During the sessions, she asks students to work in small groups in order to compare and contrast the information presented in the various information sources. After discussing and evaluating the sources in small groups, students share their thoughts with the class. The students also discuss the ways in which the various sources could be potentially useful for research. The exercise facilitates the process of learning how to critically evaluate information resources.

Rather than lecturing to the students about how to use the online catalog and other library resources, the gender studies librarian asks students to conduct searches independently during class in order to locate information on specific women. She facilitates this process by developing and directing students to an online research guide that lists tools for finding primary and secondary sources on women. After the students conduct their searches, the librarian encourages them to use the instructor's computer in order to show the rest of the class the tools and techniques they used for finding sources. This effective feminist pedagogical technique subverts traditional classroom dynamics, and engages students by encouraging them to collectively share their ideas for searching. The librarian shares her expertise during this process as well, offering additional strategies for locating information efficiently.

Benefits of Feminist Pedagogy at Michigan State University and Beyond

The feminist pedagogical environment stimulates and engages WRA 140 students during library instruction sessions. As active participants, the students learn about research more effectively by shaping the process themselves. Generating research questions independently, collaboratively evaluating sources, and collectively sharing ideas for various search strategies helps the students develop and reinforce critical information literacy skills. The students also acquire valuable knowledge about the vast diversity of women's experiences and accomplishments.

Utilizing feminist pedagogical techniques can improve library instruction by making the process more stimulating for the students. Rather than responding lethargically and passively with eyes glazed over, the students become actively involved in the research process. The shift from traditional lecture format to a highly active and participatory learning environment can certainly facilitate the development of information literacy skills. Using alternative feminist and active learning techniques not only makes the classroom more engaging for the students, but also for the instructor. Librarians should consider using such techniques in order to make the classroom more dynamic for everyone, to hone the development of information literacy skills effectively, and to encourage students to take ownership of the research process.

References

Audet, R. H. (2005). Inquiry: A continuum of ideas, issues and practices. In R.H. Audet & L.K. Jordon (Eds.), *Integrating inquiry across the curriculum* (pp. 5-15). Thousand Oaks, CA: Sage.

Bell, S., Morrow, M. & Tastsoglou, E. (1999). Teaching in environments of resistance: Toward a critical, feminist and antiracist pedagogy. In M. Mayberry & E.C. Rose (Eds.), *Meeting the challenge: Innovative feminist pedagogies in action* (pp. 23-46). York: Routledge.

Chow, E. N. L., Fleck, C., Fan, G. H., Joseph, J., Lyter, D.M. (2003). Exploring critical feminist pedagogy: Infusing dialogue, participation and experience in teaching and learning. *Teaching Sociology 31* (3), 259-275.

Fisher, B.M. (2001). *No angel in the classroom: Teaching through feminist discourse.* Lanham, MD: Rowman & Littlefield.

Freire, P. (2000). *Pedagogy of the oppressed* (30th anniversary ed.). (M.B. Ramos, Trans.). New York: Continuum. (Original work published in 1970).

Gavin, C. (2008). *Teaching information literacy: A conceptual approach.* Lanham, MD: Rowman & Littlefield.

Gross, B. (1994). Old maids and helpful husbands: Alerting students to gender bias in biography, criticism and autobiography. In S.M. Deats & L.T. Lenker (Eds.), *Gender and academe* (pp. 33-43). Lanham, MD: Rowman & Littlefield.

hooks, b. (1994). *Teaching to transgress: Education as the practice of freedom.* New York: Routledge.

Lee, V.S., Greene, D.B., Odom, J., Schecter, E., & Slatta, R.W. (2004). What is inquiry-guided learning? In V.S. Lee (Ed.), *Teaching and learning through inquiry: A guidebook for institutions and instructors* (pp. 3-16). Sterling, VA: Stylus.

Parry, S. C. (1996). Feminist pedagogy and techniques for the changing classroom. *Women's Studies Quarterly 24* (3&4), 45-54.

Shrewsbury, C.M. (1993). What is feminist pedagogy? *Women's Studies Quarterly 21* (3 &4), 8-15.

Stanger, C. (1987). The sexual politics of the one-to-one tutorial approach and collaborative learning. In C.L.Caywood & G.R. Overing (Eds.), *Teaching writing: Pedagogy, gender and equity* (pp. 31-44). Albany: State University of New York.

Ventimiglia, L.M. (1995). Cooperative learning at the college level. In H.C. Foyle (Ed.), *Interactive learning in the higher education classroom* (pp. 19-40). Washington, D.C.: National Education Association.

Villaverde, L.E. (2008). *Feminist theories and education: Primer.* New York: Peter Lang.

Webb, L.M, Allen, M.W. & Walker K.L. (2002). Feminist pedagogy: Identifying basic principles. *Academic Exchange Quarterly, 6* (1), 67-72.

Weiler, K. (1995). Freire and a feminist pedagogy of difference. In J. Holland, M. Blair & S. Sheldon (Eds.). *Debates and issues in feminist research and pedagogy* (pp. 23-44). Philadelphia: Multilingual Matters.

Section Three

Teaching in Context

Preparing Critically Conscious, Information Literate Special Educators for Alaska's Schools

Thomas Scott Duke, Jennifer Diane Ward and Jill Burkert

Teacher Education as Consciousness Raising

Critical consciousness is characterized by the ability to recognize and take action against the multiple forms of privilege and oppression that contribute to social, political, and economic injustice. *False consciousness* is characterized by the failure to recognize one's own oppression and/or the oppression of others (Freire, 1970). When the awareness of oppression (i.e., critical consciousness) begins, so, too, begins the struggle for liberation (Trask, 1999). In recent years, critical theorists from the disciplines of teacher education, special education, and library and information science have argued that universities, schools, and libraries can (and should) become public institutions where knowledge forms and values are taught for the purpose of empowering individuals to make the journey from false consciousness to critical consciousness (Ah Nee Benham & Heck, 1998; Cannella, 1997; Delpit, 2006; Doherty & Ketchner, 2005; Elmborg, 2006; hooks, 2003; Kapitzke, 2003a, 2003b; Kincheloe, 2003; Lather, 1986; Skrtic, 1995, 2005).

The Brazilian theorist, activist, and educator Paulo Freire (1974) referred to educational processes that empower individuals to recognize and take action against social injustice as *conscientization* (or "consciousness raising"). This essay was written by two teacher educators and an academic librarian who are committed to raising the consciousness of public school teachers who live and work in Alaska's remote, rural, and Alaska Native communities; that is to say, the authors of this essay hope to educate teachers to recognize and take action against social injustice in rural Alaska contexts.

Our Program's Mission

All three authors are faculty members at the University of Alaska Southeast (UAS), where we teach distance-delivered courses to public school teachers enrolled in graduate programs through our university's School of

Education. Jennifer is an academic librarian who supports distance-delivered education and teaches graduate courses in educational research. Thomas coordinates the graduate program in special education and teaches graduate courses in special education and educational research. Jill teaches graduate courses in special education and supervises special education teacher candidates in their school-based clinical practicum settings.

We (Jennifer, Thomas, and Jill) recently collaborated to develop and implement a distance-delivered Master's of Education (M.Ed.) in Special Education degree program that emphasizes critical theory, the disability rights movement, Alaska Native studies, information literacy, and critical approaches to qualitative inquiry. We want to empower our students (the public school teachers) to become strong and effective advocates for their (K-12) students. We believe that knowledge is power. We, therefore, teach our teachers the information literacy skills they need to locate knowledge forms that will empower their (K-12) students and themselves. We teach our teachers the research skills they need to generate such knowledge forms. And we introduce our teachers to theoretical frameworks that empower them to construct knowledge and interpret phenomena from a variety of social justice perspectives.

The mission of the M.Ed. in Special Education program at UAS is to prepare teachers who live and work in Alaska's remote, rural, and Alaska Native communities to provide culturally responsive instructional services to students with disabilities. Social justice for individuals with disabilities, Alaska Natives, and other historically oppressed peoples is central to our program's mission, and our primary goal is to educate critically conscious, information literate special educators for Alaska's schools. All of the courses in our special education teacher preparation program are delivered via audio-conference and augmented with online resources. Jennifer (the librarian) has an important role as a co-instructor and collaborative partner in our program. Information literacy instruction and inquiry-based approaches to teaching and learning are embedded throughout the program, and three research courses are co-taught by Jennifer and Thomas (the program coordinator). Jennifer also serves with Thomas and Jill (the practicum supervisor) on each of our graduate student's Master's Thesis Committee. So, every candidate receives guidance and feedback from the academic librarian *and* the two special education faculty as they engage in the research process.

Our Students—And Their Students

In the summer semester of 2007, the M.Ed. in Special Education program at UAS admitted our first cohort of 30 special education teacher candidates. Some of these candidates live and work in Alaska's urban communities (e.g., Anchorage, Fairbanks, or Juneau); most, however, teach in one of the more than 200 geographically isolated, sparsely populated, and predominately Alaska Native communities that are scattered across Alaska's vast terrain.

The Alaska Native Heritage Center (2009) describes Alaska as a land of diverse Native peoples, including:

> the Athabascan of interior and southcentral Alaska, the Yup'ik Eskimo of southwest Alaska, the Inupiaq and St. Lawrence Island Yupik of northwest to northern Alaska, the Aleut and Alutiiq from Prince William Sound to the end of the Aleutian Island chain, and the Eyak, Tlingit, Haida, and Tsimshian of southeast Alaska. (Retrieved January 6, 2009, from http://www.alaskanative.net/en/main_nav/education/culture_alaska//).

The diverse indigenous peoples of contemporary Alaska represent many languages, creeds, and philosophies, but share common goals and values predicated on a belief in "the interconnectedness of the human, natural and spiritual worlds as reflected in Alaska Native societies" (Assembly of Alaska Native Educators, 1999, p. 4). Alaska's indigenous peoples have inhabited Alaska for approximately 10,000 years, and many Alaska Natives have maintained their customs, languages, and hunting and fishing practices since "the creation times" (Alaska Native Heritage Center, 2009).

Alaska Natives are a historically oppressed cultural group. U.S. and Russian conquests have resulted in the loss of land, language, and spiritual and cultural identity, and contributed to the high rates of poverty, substance abuse, domestic violence, incarceration, suicide, and school failure that continue to plague Alaska Native students and their families (Dauenhauer, 1997; Hope & Thornton, 2000; John, 1996; Kawagley, 1995; Napoleon, 1991). According to the First Alaskans Institute Native Policy Center (2006), 24.3 % of the students enrolled in Alaska public schools are Alaska Native; 26 % of Alaska's Native children live in poverty; and 17.5 % of Alaska Native learners receive special education services (as opposed to 12.4 % of non-Native learners). Alaska Native students score significantly lower on standardized tests in reading, writing, and mathematics than do their non-Native peers; and students of Alaska Native ancestry experience significantly higher dropout rates and lower graduation rates than other ethnic or linguistic groups in Alaska. Alaska's Native youth experience alarmingly high rates of suicide (as do indigenous youth in the continental U.S., Canada, Australia, New Zealand, and in other nations where European and European-American colonizers have marginalized and dominated Native peoples). According to the U.S. Surgeon General, American Indian and Alaska Native youth between the ages of 15 and 24 commit suicide at a rate more than three times the national average (Nieves, 2007).

Special educators who live and work in rural Alaska encounter unique—and often daunting—challenges as they attempt to provide safe, effective, and culturally responsive instructional services to students with disabilities. Our graduate students are often the only special educators in their respective villages, and many of our candidates provide instructional services to students with a wide range of exceptional learning needs and developmental levels. One of our candidates—Judy (not her real name)—teaches in a geographically isolated Yup'ik Eskimo community of approximately 300 people. There are no roads leading into or out of her village. For most of the year, the only way to reach Judy's village is by chartered plane; in the winter months, when the river system is frozen solid, the village is also accessible by snow machine. Judy, who is one of only four certified teachers in this village—and the *only* special educator—provides instructional services to 11 students, including: a pre-school child with developmental delays; a second grader with a hearing impairment and language delays; a medically fragile fourth grader who uses a wheelchair; a fifth grader with a reading disability; another fifth grader with attention deficit hyperactivity disorder (ADHD); three middle school students with specific learning disabilities; an eighth grader with fetal alcohol spectrum disorder (FASD) and severe behavior problems; a sophomore with autism; a nineteen year old with Down syndrome; and a twenty year old with traumatic brain injury. Judy's situation is not unique—many of the teachers in our program are confronted with equally challenging caseloads.

No single special educator can be expected to possess highly specialized knowledge about such a daunting array of exceptionalities and developmental levels; even a bright, capable, and highly motivated special education teacher—like Judy—is unlikely to become a specialist in early childhood intervention, hearing impairments, communication disorders, orthopedic disabilities, health impairments, specific learning disabilities, ADHD, emotional and behavioral disorders, autism, intellectual impairments, and traumatic brain injury. And no teacher education program can adequately prepare an individual special education teacher to *specialize* in such a vast array of exceptionalities and developmental levels.

What we, as a distance-delivered teacher education program, can do, however, is prepare critically conscious, information literate special educators who recognize when they need highly specialized information about particular exceptionalities and developmental levels, and are able to locate, critically evaluate, and effectively use such information to develop culturally responsive instructional services that benefit their students.

Librarian and Faculty Collaboration

In the first year of their program, our candidates are immersed in the philosophical, historical, legal, theoretical, and pedagogical issues that form the foundations of special education practice; they read works by a variety of critical theorists and educators (Delpit, 1996; Gould, 1996; Kozol, 1991), disability rights activists (Brown, 2003; Grandin, 2006; Kunc, 1992), and Alaska Native writers (Hayes, 2006; Kawagley, 1995; Wallis, 2003); and they learn to develop and teach academic lessons based on the cultural traditions of Alaska's diverse Native peoples. Our students are also required to enroll in EDSE 694 (Special Education Practicum)—a clinical field experience—in the first year of their program. Jill (the practicum supervisor) flies to the villages where our candidates live and work; she visits our candidates in their school and classroom settings, observes them teaching students with exceptional learning needs, and offers them guidance and support. Many of our candidates are first year special education teachers, and they value their "face-to-face" visit with Jill, as this is often the only "face-to-face" contact that our teachers will have with UAS faculty.

In the second year of their program, our candidates are immersed in the development of information literacy skills and research strategies. Thomas (the coordinator) invited Jennifer (the librarian) to co-develop and co-teach the three research methods courses that comprise our candidates' second year of study; these three courses include: ED 626 (Classroom Research), EDSE 692 (Secondary Research Methods), and EDSE 698 (Master's Thesis Project). In ED 626, our teacher candidates conduct a phenomenological self-study in which they critically examine their work as special educators. In EDSE 692, our teachers learn to systematically collect and analyze secondary data sources related to the field of special education. In EDSE 698, our students conduct a metasynthesis of empirical and theoretical literature relevant to their current teaching assignments, and complete an action research project.

For the past several years, Thomas (the coordinator) and Jennifer (the librarian) have co-taught ED 626. As previously noted, all candidates in ED

626 are required to conduct phenomenological self-studies. In order to better teach our graduate students to conduct such studies, *we* conducted, and eventually published, a phenomenology on librarian and faculty collaborative instruction (Brown & Duke, 2005). Our interest in and commitment to information literacy, teacher education, and librarian and faculty collaboration led us to co-author additional publications (Duke & Brown, 2006; Duke & Ward, in press a; Ward & Duke, in press). As we prepared to teach EDSE 692 in the fall semester of 2008, we reviewed the literature on information literacy and teacher education (Duke & Ward, in press b), and used what we learned from conducting this review to help our candidates strengthen their information literacy and research skills. We offered our review of the literature to our candidates, along with our phenomenological self-study and other publications, so they could use them as templates as they conducted their own research projects in ED 626, EDSE 692, and EDSE 698.

Reducing Bias in Language

We (Jennifer, Thomas, and Jill) introduce our candidates to the American Psychological Association (2001) *Guidelines to Reduce Bias in Language*. These guidelines are meant to help authors "avoid perpetuating demeaning attitudes and biased assumptions about people … on the basis of gender, sexual orientation, racial or ethnic group, disability, or age" (p. 61). Because our candidates teach students with disabilities, we ask them to be especially mindful of "nonhandicapping" language. The APA manual explains: "The guiding principle for 'nonhandicapping' language is to maintain the integrity of individuals as human beings." We, therefore, urge our students to "avoid language that equates persons with their condition (e.g., *neurotics, the disabled*); that has superfluous, negative overtones (e.g., stroke *victim*); or that is regarded as a slur (e.g., *cripple*)" (p. 69).

Many of our teacher candidates live and work in predominately Alaska Native communities, so we devote a considerable amount of time to discussing respectful terms for Alaska Native individuals. The APA (2001) guidelines also state: "*American Indian* and *Native American* are both accepted terms for referring to indigenous peoples of North America, although *Native Americans* is a broader designation because the U.S. government includes Hawaiians and Samoans in this category" (p. 68). However, Thomas (the program coordinator) informed our students that Hawaiians and Samoans are "native" to Polynesia, and that Polynesia is separated from North America by thousands of miles of ocean; Hawai'i and Samoa were colonized by the U.S. government, but that does not in any way make Hawaiians or Samoans "native" to North America (Trask, 1999). Thomas and Jennifer (the librarian) both attended graduate school at the University of Hawai'i—Mānoa, and we assure our candidates that Native Hawaiians rarely (if ever) refer to themselves as *Native American,* preferring instead *Native Hawaiian* (or *kānaka maoli*) (Kame'eleihiwa, 1992). Likewise, Alaska Natives often prefer *Alaska Native* to *Native American;* some Alaska Native groups do refer to themselves as *American Indian* (e.g., Central Council of Tlingit and Haida Indian Tribes of Alaska), while others prefer *Eskimo* (e.g., Yup'ik Eskimo) or *Aleut* (e.g., *Unangax/Aleut*). Finally, the APA guidelines note: "There are close to 450 Native groups, and authors are encouraged to name ...specific groups" (p. 68). We, therefore, teach our candidates that it is respectful to use Athabascan, Yup'ik, Cupik, Inupiaq, St. Lawrence Island Yupik, Aleut, Alutiiq, Eyak, Tlingit, Haida, or Tsimshian when referring to particular individuals of Alaska Native ancestry.

Our Reflections

Jennifer: In his article *Critical Library Instruction: Implications for Instructional Practice,* the academic librarian and critical theorist James Elmborg (2006) noted:

> If literacy is the ability to read, interpret, and produce texts valued in a community, then academic information literacy is the ability to read, interpret, and produce information valued in academia—a skill that must be developed by all students during their college education. (p. 196)

Academic information literacy, as defined by Elmborg, is central to the three graduate-level research courses I co-teach with Thomas (the program coordinator). Students enrolled in these three courses learn to systematically collect and analyze a variety of primary and secondary data sources, conduct systematic and reproducible database searches, critically analyze and synthesize empirical and non-empirical literature, and write empirical reports that conform to APA publication guidelines.

We (Thomas, Jill, and I) share a common philosophy that guides and informs our work as teacher educators; we are preparing our graduate students to be *teacher researchers.* As part of our "teacher as researcher" approach to teacher education— which was inspired by the educator, researcher, and critical theorist Joe Kincheloe (2003)—I introduce our students to database research.

Database research.

Residents of the state of Alaska have access to a suite of databases known as the Statewide Library Education Doorway (SLED) Digital Pipeline Databases (http://sled.alaska.edu). This resource provides access to education and multidisciplinary databases—e.g., ERIC (EBSCOhost), the Professional Development Collection (EBSCOhost), and Academic Search Premier (EBSCOhost)—and databases related to Alaska Native issues (e.g., the Hubert Wenger Eskimo Database, Alaska Native Knowledge Network, Alaska's Digital Archives, Alaska and Polar Periodical Index), as well as business-oriented databases, databases related to health and medicine, reader's advisory resources, auto repair resources, and collections of interest to younger readers (e.g., Facts on File). While ED 626, EDSE 692, and EDSE 698 do not allow for an in-depth exploration of all these resources, I make sure that our teachers know they exist, and I encourage them to use the Digital Pipeline to develop resource-based learning experiences for their own K-12 students.

In ED 626, our graduate students are required to conduct a phenomenological self-study of their educational beliefs and practices. This phenomenological self-study—which includes a synthetic review of empirical and theoretical literature—is the pilot study for our candidates' Master's Thesis projects, so—in ED 626—Thomas and I teach our students the academic information literacy and research skills they will need to successfully complete their theses. Thomas and I co-teach every session of ED 626. There are days when I take the lead, and days when he takes the lead.

Students in ED 626 choose their research topics and—through in-depth class discussions (via audio-conference)—Thomas and I help them refine their purpose statements and develop research questions. During subsequent class sessions, we teach our students to use the ERIC Thesaurus to develop their search terms. We help them construct Boolean searches using ERIC subject descriptors, and they report back to us the following week on their search results and the challenges they encountered.

I emphasize the importance of taking detailed search notes throughout the semester; students must keep a log in which they document every database searched, and record every search term combination, any limiters used (e.g., peer-reviewed only, publication date ranges, grade levels), and the number of articles each search yielded. Our goal is to have our students construct strategic, systematic, and reproducible searches. Students are required to develop detailed selection criteria, and to include these selection criteria in their empirical reports—along with explicit search procedures—so that the general reader will be able to reproduce their search results; this is where our students' detailed note-taking really pays off.

We suggest that our students review 10-12 articles for their phenomenological self-studies. An important course objective in ED 626 is that students learn to *synthesize* the empirical and theoretical literature relevant to their research topics. We do not permit our teacher candidates to produce annotated bibliographies that summarize individual articles in isolation; instead, we teach our students to systematically analyze selected articles as a collective body of literature and identify emergent themes. For many students, this complex, strategic, and systematic approach to locating and synthesizing literature is new, and—at first—bewildering. I developed instructional handouts that begin to guide our candidates through this process (see Duke & Brown, 2006), and Thomas and I offer our candidates continuous guidance and instruction—throughout the entire semester—as they develop their synthetic reviews of the literature.

Most of our students select research topics that are frequently addressed in the critical theory literature on K-12 education. For example, one student developed the following purpose statement:

> The purpose of this phenomenological self-study is to describe the beliefs and practices of an early childhood educator who provides developmentally appropriate and culturally responsive educational services to young children and their families at a Tlingit and Haida Head Start Program in rural southeast Alaska.

We taught this student to conduct Boolean searches of ERIC using the following combination of subject descriptors:

1. ("Alaska Natives" OR "American Indians") AND ("developmentally appropriate practices");
2. ("Alaska Natives" OR "American Indians") AND ("culturally relevant education");
3. ("Alaska Natives" OR "American Indians") AND ("early childhood education");
4. ("developmentally appropriate practices") AND ("culturally relevant education"); and
5. ("early childhood education") AND ("culturally relevant education").

This particular teacher worked at an early childhood education program run by the Central Council of Tlingit and Haida Indian Tribes of Alaska, and the Tlingit and Haida peoples do refer to themselves as both Alaska Natives and American Indians.It should be noted, however, that we advise most of our teachers to use *both* subject descriptors (i.e., "Alaska Natives" OR "American Indians") when they are conducting their initial Boolean searches, even if they teach in Alaska Native communities where people do not typically describe themselves as American Indians (e.g., Yup'ik, Inupiaq, or Aleut communities). We explain to our students that there is a dearth of empirical and theoretical literature about the lives and experiences of Alaska Native individuals with disabilities; we also explain that while contemporary Alaska Native and American Indian peoples represent incredible cultural and linguistic diversity, they do share similar historical relationships with the U.S. government and its' public education systems, and these shared experiences can make the literature on American Indian individuals with disabilities relevant to the work of special educators who teach Alaska Native students. Pewewardy (2002) addressed the relevance of these similar historical contexts in his *Learning Styles of American Indian/Alaska Native Students*, and we encourage our teachers to read Pewewardy's excellent review of the literature to deepen their understandings of the historical contexts that influence their work with Alaska Native students and families.

Another one of our students developed the following purpose statement:

> The purpose of this phenomenological self-study is to describe the beliefs and practices of a special educator who provides instructional services to adolescents with emotional and behavioral disorders at a residential treatment facility for juvenile offenders in Anchorage.

We helped this student conduct a complex Boolean search of ERIC using the following combination of subject descriptors:

> ("adolescents") AND ("residential institutions" OR "psychiatric hospitals" OR "residential schools" OR "corrective institutions" OR "institutional schools" OR "delinquent rehabilitation") AND ("behavior disorders" OR "behavior problems" OR "emotional disturbances" OR "emotional problems" OR "antisocial behavior") AND ("special education").

Writing empirical reports. Our students submit multiple drafts of their self-studies to both Thomas and I for continual feedback—throughout the semester. We function as our students' co-editors, and we try to make their experience in ED 626 very similar to the process of submitting and revising an empirical article for publication in an academic journal. Our students learn that research is an exploratory, iterative process of revisiting and revising. Thomas and I strongly encourage our students to submit their studies for publication, and several have; recently, a study by one of our students was accepted for publication in the international, peer-reviewed journal *Review of Disability Studies* (Hauk, in press). We were *very* proud.

The most striking result of our collaborative approach to preparing "teachers as researchers" occurs at the end of each semester—when we ask our students to tell us what they learned from their research projects. Our students are able to discuss the empirical and theoretical literature with great confidence and authority. They have spent an entire semester gathering studies, synthesizing literature, reflecting on the research process in their journals, generating and analyzing knowledge forms related to their work as special educators, and connecting the findings of empirical and theoretical literature to their own instructional practice. In the beginning of the semester, many students are intimidated by the research process, and by the prospect of writing an empirical report; however, by the end of the semester, our students produce academically rigorous phenomenological research reports that reflect their voices and experiences.

Thomas: I earned two advanced degrees in special education—but never received any library instruction as part of my graduate education. Information literacy was not addressed in my Master's degree program (which prepared me to be a special education teacher), nor was it embedded in my doctoral program (which prepared me to be a teacher educator and educational researcher). I taught myself to use the ERIC database when I wrote the review of the literature for my doctoral dissertation, but I did not learn to efficiently and systematically search ERIC until I began co-teaching courses with Jennifer (the librarian).

In so many ways, I believe I received an excellent education in my doctoral program. I learned a great deal about the philosophical and theoretical foundations of social science research; I was introduced to critical theory; and I was taught to systematically gather and analyze primary data sources. However, one real area of weakness in my program of study was the total absence of information literacy instruction. I was never taught to systematically collect secondary data sources. The acquisition of information literacy skills just wasn't on the radar screen in either one of my graduate programs. I find that my lack of experience with information literacy instruction is typical of most other educators'—whether they be K-12 teachers or university-based teacher educators.

When I designed the M.Ed. in Special Education program, I wanted to make sure that our special education teacher candidates graduated with strong information literacy skills—that's why I embedded library instruction in ED 626, EDSE 692, and EDSE 698, and that's why I invited Jennifer to co-develop and co-teach these three research methods courses. As an academic librarian, Jennifer possesses a strong background in information literacy instruction, and our teachers benefit from her expertise with secondary research strategies. Together, Jennifer and I teach our candidates to locate, critically evaluate, synthesize, effectively use, and *conduct* educational research for the benefit of their K-12 students.

I also wanted to teach our candidates to critically evaluate information presented in textbooks and other curricular materials. So many of our candidates teach in Alaska Native communities; yet, the textbooks and curricular materials adopted by local school districts most often reflect the values and beliefs of the dominant European American culture. Our candidates teach students with disabilities, but many textbooks all but ignore disability culture and the contributions and experiences of people with disabilities. I want our candidates to have the information literacy skills necessary to locate and critically evaluate information resources that represent and affirm the life experiences and contributions of Alaska Natives, individuals with disabilities, and other historically oppressed peoples, and I want our candidates to effectively use these information resources as alternative curricular materials.

Jill: Early on in the process of designing the M.Ed. in Special Education program, I was assigned the task of developing and teaching ED 677 (Teaching Reading to Struggling Learners) and EDSE 610 (Assessment of Students with Disabilities). I began with the typical search for techniques and methods that would help special educators more effectively assess and instruct students who struggled with reading. The course structure consisted of texts, class discussions, a few research papers, and—fortunately for me— weekly reflective papers. The reflective papers were meant to be a means of determining if the teacher candidates engaged thoughtfully with the assigned readings and class discussions.

Many of the teachers enrolled in my courses live and work in remote Alaska Native villages. Most were inexperienced, and many were struggling with the demands of the now notorious No Child Left Behind (NCLB) Act—and the rather rigid implementation of this federal mandate by the state of Alaska and local school districts. Under NCLB, schools are evaluated for effectiveness based on the results of standardized tests in reading, writing, and math—and many of the schools represented by the teachers in my courses were designated "failing schools."

The anxiety and frustration expressed by the teachers in their reflective papers was unsettling. Many of the teachers were teaching predominantly Alaska Native children who were poor, and frequently subjected to abuse and neglect. In addition, many of the children were not receiving adequate nutrition and medical attention. The teachers were concerned that the rigid instructional methods adopted by many school districts were compounding the problems and creating an atmosphere of distrust in their villages. The teachers complained that they were forced to adopt instructional methods that were not culturally responsive and were required to teach content that was foreign to children growing up in rural Alaska.

Many of Alaska's 53 school districts have responded to NCLB mandates by adopting prepared (or "canned") reading programs that are highly "scripted" and "teacher proof." The topics and the methods of presentation are standardized, and are to be delivered by teachers but not enhanced or changed in any way. In essence, many of the teachers enrolled in our program had become robots; all too often, our teacher candidates were expected (or *required*) to be presenters of ready-made information (rather than facilitators of knowledge construction), and their students were passive consumers of other people's ideas (rather than active participants in the co-construction of knowledge). I was very troubled by the emphasis on compliance and conformity inherent in these "canned curricula." Teachers who dissented reported that they were promptly silenced. Teachers who did not comply were chastised. The parallels to Freire's (1970) descriptions of the "banking concept of education" in *Pedagogy of the Oppressed* were alarming.

As a result of the weekly reflective papers, I changed the format of my courses to one that maximized dialogue and critical thinking about educational policies. Jennifer (the librarian) taught our teachers to systematically search a variety of databases that index articles related to general and special education, indigenous education, and Alaska Native issues. The teachers collected and reviewed the literature on language and literacy in Alaska Native contexts. The teachers then interrogated the methodologies that were being used to teach reading from a variety of perspectives, and we discussed both diagnostic issues and issues related to the culture of power in schools. The courses shifted from "this is what the experts say about reading," and "this is what the experts say about assessment," to one of discussing the validity of various approaches to reading instruction, assessment, and the hidden agendas that frequently disadvantage children who come from historically oppressed groups. What began as rather traditional courses based on reading instruction and assessment techniques evolved into a rich dialogue about developing culturally responsive special education practices and empowering low-income, minority, and atypical learners.

Conclusion

Elmborg (2006) noted that "to be educators, librarians must focus less on information transfer and more on developing critical consciousness in students" (p. 192), while Kapitzke (2001) argued that "information literacy should not be in the domain of the teacher librarian alone," but "should be integrated across all subject areas" (p. 452). A primary goal of our M.Ed. in Special Education program is to prepare critically conscious, information literate special educators. Our special education teacher candidates receive critical library instruction throughout their program of study, and the academic librarian and special education faculty share responsibility for— and ownership of—our candidates' education. We believe that our program's emphasis on critical theory and information literacy—coupled with our student's exposure to librarian and faculty collaborative instruction throughout their program of study—makes the M.Ed. in Special Education program at UAS unique among special education teacher preparation programs in the U.S.

References

Ah Nee-Benham, M. K. P., and Heck, R. H. (1998). *Culture and educational policy in Hawai'i: The silencing of native voices.* Mahwah, NJ: Lawrence Erlbaum Associates.

Alaska Native Heritage Center. (n.d.). Cultures of Alaska. Retrieved January 6, 2009, from http://www.alaskanative.net/en/main_nav/education/culture_alaska//

American Psychological Association (2001). *Publication manual of the American Psychological Association* (5th ed.). Washington, D.C.: Author.

Assembly of Alaska Native Educators (1999). *Guidelines for preparing culturally responsive teachers for Alaska's schools.* Fairbanks, AK: Alaska Native Knowledge Network.

Brown, S. (2003). *Movie stars and sensuous scars: Essays on the journey from disability shame to disability pride.* Brookline, MA: iUniverse.

Brown, J. D., & Duke, T. S. (2005). Librarian and faculty collaborative instruction: A phenomenological self-study. *Research Strategies, 20*(3), 171-190.

Cannella, G. S. (1997). *Deconstructing early childhood education: Social justice and revolution.* New York, NY: Peter Lang.

Dauenhauer, R. (1997). *Conflicting visions in Alaskan education revisited.* Juneau, AK: Tlingit Readers.

Delpit, L. (2006). *Other people's children: Cultural conflict in the classroom.* 2nd ed. New York: New Press.

Doherty, J. J., & Ketcher, K. (2005). Empowering the intentional learner: A critical theory of information literacy instruction. *Library Philosophy & Practice, 8*(1), 1-10.

Duke, T. S., & Brown, J. D. (2006). Teacher as researcher: Librarian and faculty collaboration in teaching the literature review in a distance-delivered teacher education program. In D. Cook, & N. Cooper (Eds.), *Teaching information literacy skills to social sciences students and practitioners: A casebook of applications* (pp. 131-145). Chicago: Association of College and Research Libraries.

Duke, T. S., & Ward, J. D. (in press a). Haiku, self-reflection, and the research process. In D. Cook, & R. Sittler (Eds.), *The library instruction cookbook: 50+ active recipes for 1-shot sessions.* Chicago: Association of College and Research Libraries.

Duke, T. S., & Ward, J. D. (in press b). Preparing information literate teachers: A metasynthesis. *Library & Information Science Research.*

Elmborg, J. (2006). Critical information literacy: Implications for instructional practice. *Journal of Academic Librarianship, 32*(2), 192-199.

First Alaskans Institute Native Policy Center. (2006, October). *Alaska Native K-12 education indicators, 2005: Statewide summary report.* Retrieved January 6, 2009, from http://www.firstalaskans.org/documents_fai/05k12StatewideSummary.pdf

Freire, P. (1970). *Pedagogy of the oppressed.* Translated by M. B. Ramos. New York: Seabury Press.

Freire, P. (1974). *Education for critical consciousness.* Translated by M. B. Ramos. New York: Seabury Press.

Gould, S. J. (1996). *The mismeasure of man.* New York: W. W. Norton & Co.

Grandin, T. (2006). *Thinking in pictures, expanded edition: My observations on a life with autism.* New York: Vintage.

Hope, A., & Thornton, T. F. (2000). *Will the time ever come? A Tlingit source book.* Fairbanks, AK: Alaska Native Knowledge Network.

Hauk, A. (in press). Authentic inclusion: A celebration of exceptional teachers and student identity. A phenomenological self-study. *Review of Disability Studies: An International Journal.*

Hayes, E. (2006). *Blonde Indian: An Alaska Native memoir.* Phoenix, AZ: University of Arizona Press.

hooks, b. (2003). *Teaching community: A pedagogy of hope.* New York, NY: Routledge.

John, P. (1996). *The gospel according to Peter John.* Fairbanks, AK: Alaska Native Knowledge Network.

Kame'eleihiwa, L. K. (1992). *Native land and foreign desires. Ku Hawai'i ana a me na koi up'umake a ka po'e haole: A history of land tenure in Hawai'i from traditional times until the 1848 māhele, including an analysis of Hawaiian ali'i and American Calvinists.* Honolulu, HI: Bishop Museum Press.

Kapitzke, C. (2001). Information literacy: The changing library. *Journal of Adolescent & Adult Literacy, 44*(5), 450-456.

Kapitzke, C. (2003a). Information literacy: A positivist epistemology and a politics of (out)formation. *Educational Theory, 53,* 37-54.

Kapitzke, C. (2003b). Information literacy: A review and poststructural critique. *Australian Journal of Language & Literacy, 26,* 53-67.

Kawagley, A. O. (1995). *A Yupiaq worldview: A pathway to ecology and spirit.* Prospect Heights, IL: Waveland Press.

Kincheloe, J. (2003). *Teachers as researchers: Qualitative paths to empowerment* (2nd ed.). New York: Routledge.

Kozol, J. (1991). *Savage inequalities: Children in America's schools.* New York: Crown.

Kunc, N. (1992). The need to belong: Rediscovering Maslow's hierarchy of needs. In R.Villa, J Stainback, & S. Stainback (Eds.), *Restructuring for caring and effective education* (pp. 28-39). Baltimore: Brookes.

Lather, P. (1986). Research as praxis. *Harvard Educational Review, 56*(3), 257-277.

Napoleon, H. (1991). *Yuuyaraq: The way of the human being.* Fairbanks, AK: Alaska Native Knowledge Network.

Nieves, E. (2007, June 9). Indian reservation reeling in wave of youth suicides and attempts. *The New York Times.* Retrieved January 10, 2009, from http://www.nytimes.com/2007/06/09/us/09suicide.html?_r=1

Pewewardy, C. (2002). Learning styles of American Indian/Alaska Native students: A review of the literature and implications for practice. *Journal of American Indian Education, 41,* 22-56.

Skrtic, T. M. (1995). *Disability and democracy: Restructuring (special) education for postmodernity.* New York: Teacher's College Press.

Skrtic, T. M. (2005). A political economy of learning disabilities. *Learning Disability Quarterly, 28,* 149-155.

Trask, H. (1999). *From a native daughter: Colonialism and sovereignty in Hawai'i* (Revised ed.). Honolulu, HI: University of Hawai'i Press.

Wallis, V. (2003). *Raising ourselves: A Gwich'in coming of age story from the Yukon River.* Kenmore, WA: Epicenter Press.

Ward, J. D., & Duke, T. S. (in press). Interviewing: Getting past the surface. In D. Cook, & L. Farmer (Eds.), *Observe, reflect, act: A primer on applied qualitative research for libraries.* Chicago: Association of College and Research Libraries.

Information and Service Learning

John S. Riddle

Where's the Library in Service-Learning?

When I wrote "Where's the Library in Service Learning" in *Journal of Academic Librarianship* in 2003, I said there was a "research void" in the literature of both service learning and librarianship regarding the impact of service learning for library services. Since then a number of useful studies have appeared (e.g. Westney 2006, Herther 2008, Meyer and Miller 2008) and others have examined the use of service learning as a pedagogy for library students (e.g. Witbodi 2004, Burek Pierce 2006, Ball & Schilling 2006, Gerrish 2006, Yontz & McCook 2003). Still research needs to be guided by theoretical models and I would suggest that the literature is still here a bit thin. Though "Where's the Library in Service Learning?" did provide a nascent model, my goal here is to examine theoretical approaches that can guide both research and practice regarding the intersection of service learning and librarianship. These models are particularly valuable in that they bring a needed critical information literacy perspective to a service-learning pedagogy that is itself seeped in alternate and non-traditional modes of teaching.

A few initial questions present themselves. Can library services, such as the provision of information literacy instruction, benefit service-learning classes? Conversely, what might a pedagogy of learning through community service offer to the traditional mode of classroom teaching, particularly, for our purposes here, its affiliated library and research dimensions?

This becomes more than just a question of the degree of library interaction with service-learning classes, but of qualitative impact as well. Many service-learning scholars have argued that for service-learning to have a viable future in higher education it must continue to justify its value to academic teaching. It must show skeptical faculty and administrators a positive outcome on the subject learning taking place in classes; that students "learn" chemistry, composition, nursing, engineering, political science, etc. better by performing community service related to these subjects. Likewise, Edward Zlotkowski has long advocated a closer coherence of service-learning with subject-based instruction. His conviction that "there is probably no disciplinary area-from architecture to zoology-where service-learning cannot be fruitfully employed to strengthen students' abilities to become active learners" is the impetus behind the *Service-Learning in the Disciplines* series he has edited for AAHE (Zlotkowski, 1998, vi). In a more empirical vein, Abes, Jackson, and Jones (2002) have shown that the most significant factor motivating faculty to use service-learning is "increased student understanding of course material." Likewise, faculty who do not use service-learning cite "not relevant to subject matter" as a primary reason.

That service-learning contributes to students' moral and social development has been fairly well established, but, as Eyler and Giles (1999) ask, "where's the learning in service-learning?" In the final analysis, does service-learning have academic value? The answer depends largely on what is understood as the "academic value" service-learning can offer. Howard (1998) sees service-learning as effecting a fundamental transformation of the "information-dissemination" model of teaching (Pablo Freire's "banking model') when he writes that the "traditional classroom's orientation toward individual student learning is *replaced* by a commitment to the learning of the collectivity" (Howard, pp.23 and 27, emphasis added). Eyler and Giles, while acknowledging that "service-learning students may do as well academically as [students] in more traditional instructional settings," still suggest that service-learning offers a "value-added" dimension to traditional teaching. (Eyler & Giles, p. 63)

Both Howard's and Eyler and Giles' conceptions of service-learning's academic value, as distinct from traditional teaching, is limited by a surprising lack of a retained dynamism between the two teaching models. The case for the transformative nature of service-learning is well made by both, but it is less clear how the traditional mode of learning and its related research and library activities can be infused with the dynamism service-learning offers. Perhaps it is not a matter of "replacing" traditional teaching with service-learning or seeing service-learning as something "added" to traditional education, but is instead a question of retaining elements of both service-learning and traditional pedagogies in a sustained and dynamic ambiguity, neither privileged, each pushing its pedagogical envelope against the other. The central contention of this chapter is that what librarians call information literacy, especially in the variants of resource-based learning and critical information literacy, can help provide this important link between traditional teaching and service-learning.

A disclaimer: the nature of my argument is not strictly empirical, but hopefully a provocation, intending to foster dialogue, collaboration and research interests between librarians and service-learning faculty. As such, the conclusion will offer certain metaphors of service-learning that incorporate an information literacy and research focus. The use of metaphors reinforces the speculative nature employed here; eschewing definitive answers, a metaphorical conclusion intentionally leaves ground open for more study and reflection; it suggests rather than declaims.

Foundations of Information Literacy

The concept of information literacy emerged in the 1970's in response to a widely shared perception that the teaching of effective skills for the access and evaluation of information was declining in higher education. Information literacy posited that traditional literacy standards of reading, speaking, and mathematics are insufficient. Students must also become information literate as well to acquire the ability to effectively and efficiently locate, organize, evaluate, and communicate information. Since the 1970s libraries have been at the forefront of advocating information literacy as a standard for educational competence. An expansive attention to lifelong learning reinforced by a commitment that access to and critical evaluation of information is essential for an active citizenry lead two early champions to label information literacy "a revolution in the library" (Breivik & Gee, 1989).

In its initial concept information literacy was framed by certain models of learning theory and information seeking behavior, adapting much of its language and concepts from cognitive science, psychology, and communications theories. As such, information literacy tended to mirror certain paradigms of information processing in its epistemology while its teaching methodology benchmarked specific student competencies and empirically verified skills outcomes in the acquisition, use, and evaluation of information as its standards of success. Recently, however, librarians and library scholars have begun to challenge this information literacy model for its dependence on the restrictive languages of cognitive science and psychology. Two in particular will be discussed here, as their critiques are most pertinent for considerations of how information literacy can enhance the academic dimension of service-learning.

Resource-Based Learning and Critical Information Literacy

One of the first important advocates of information literacy, Patricia Breivik (1998) has refined her model to encompass new trends in higher education such as undergraduate research, inquiry learning, evidence-based learning, and service learning, all based on what she calls resource-based learning. Information literate students will need to access, organize, evaluate, and communicate information from a wide range of real-world resources including not only print, but also television, online databases, video and audio sources, internet and multimedia, community experts, government agencies, and others. At the same time students will need to recognize and critically assess the varied and generally conflicting economic, political, and social discourses which structure these information resources.

Critical use and evaluation of these resources are most effectively learned, argues Breivik, within the context of subject-based courses, mirroring the same call Zlotkowski has made for a greater linkage between service-learning and the disciplines. Essentially, Breivik and Zlotkowski, in their separate domains, argue that students will achieve more significant and relevant learning outcomes if they access and evaluate information resources or engage in service-learning activities within the contexts of specific disciplinary issues and problems. As such, a coherence exists between the pedagogies of service-learning and information literacy in terms of their common focus on disciplinary resources and experiences.

Whereas Breivik seeks to improve the information literacy model by making it more relevant to disciplinary teaching and resources, an Australian library scholar, Cushla Kapitzke (2003), seeks to bring the whole epistemology and practice of information literacy to a more sociocritical level. Challenging the older process based model of information literacy that was limited both by its orientation to a print culture and its language of cognitive science and psychology, Kapitzke (2003) has called for a transformative literacy practice. Traditional information literacy is driven by a linear "human capital" conception of competency or skills acquisition, which assumes that better training and education necessarily leads to greater productivity and growth. In this framework, traditional information literacy as a pedagogy is objective and externalized, its core values ("information," "facts," "knowledge") reified into book collections and databases, and its methodology instrumental. A transformative literacy practice, on the other hand, posits what we call knowledge and information as always culturally mediated, socially constructed, and especially now through digital technology, decidedly fragmented and non-linear. Molded from a Foucauldian critique, Kapitzke's transformative literacy practice renders knowledge as localized and discrete, embedded in particular sociohistorical contexts, ideologies, and practices, and structured by ties to power and capital.

For Kapitzke, a transformative practice effects an important shift in both the understanding and practice of information literacy. Foregoing its stance as a neutral instrumentality for transmitting what are deemed to be competency outcomes, this newer information literacy adopts a critical perspective not only to information resources but also to its own practice and methodology. "This approach," Kapitzke says, "requires a focus not on logic, but on ideology….information problem solving emphasizes processes in individual students' heads, whilst a critical information literacy would broaden analysis to socio-political ideologies embedded within economies of ideas and information." (p. 61). A critical information literacy will be conscious of how once neutral and universal concepts of "information," "fact," "knowledge," and even the role and function of the librarian, with his/her aura of authority and professionalism, have now become ideologically ambiguous through their intersection with structures of gender, class, ethnicity, power, and capital.

Likewise, a critical information literacy may transform the idea of the library itself, in both its physical and cyber manifestations. Kapitzke urges librarians to replace older notions of libraries as repositories of information, places where one goes to find information usually in a very private and even cloistered environment, with a new sense of libraries as socially active networked nodes "for communities of knowledge producers and distributors." (p. 53). Libraries become a central locus for the social construction of knowledge. In so many ways, Kapitzke's transformative literary practice destabilizes the very culture of libraries and the logic of information.[1]

---

[1] I should also note that Breivik and Kapitzke are not alone in attempting to reposition the idea of information literacy. Hubbard (1995) uses frameworks of textual criticism and sociology of knowledge to argue that libraries can be "laboratories" for studying information in the context of its position within academic discourses. Marcum (2002) argues that the very terms "information" and "literacy" are still ensnared in the information processing model, and he calls for a conceptual shift from information to learning and literacy for sociotechnical fluency. He calls upon librarians to refocus their practice to put greater emphasis on the visual, technological, and social components of learning. Using constructs from sociocultural theories, Simons, Young, and Gibson (2000) see learning as occurring in specific cultural environments. What they call the "learning library" becomes

Though neither Breivik or Kapitzke directly speak to service learning, I argue that they provide a framework for positioning service learning as a tool for engaging critical information literacy. It is in the sense of a transformative pedagogy that both critical information literacy and service learning come into play. I suggest that Kapitzke expands Breivik's model of resource based learning to include questions of ideology and transformative information literacy which speak directly to the service learning pedagogy. So, when joined, a framework emerges for seeing how service learning in a library context can work as a critical information practice within the structure of subject based learning, a call which, as noted above, people such as Eyler and Giles and Zlotkowski have made for the furtherance of the service learning agenda.

More broadly, there is the question of how service learning might inform our understanding of social justice, civic engagement, and citizenship. I would suggest that there are a number of variants to this argument. One, what we might call the conservative stance, situates service learning in an agenda of promoting volunteerism as a strategy of limiting government involvement in social problems. Service learning strengthens virtues of self-reliance and personal moral responsibility by inculcating at a young age the sense of duty and charity. Another more liberal model also links service learning to questions of individual character, but in the form of citizenship training and civic engagement. From working with community groups on pressing social issues, the student develops a broader perspective on possibilities of effective collective action as a force of amelioration. Yet what unites what I call the conservative and liberal variants of service learning are their conception of community service as applied problem solving, a focus on outcomes, and service learning as a venue of transformative social-consciousness.

Thirdly then, a more critical sense of service learning, though still necessarily focused on effective community based outcomes, is equally concerned with a repositioning of student self consciousness to include a sense of the Other. In one study, Ostrow (1995) analyzed over 790 journals kept by students who provided service at a homeless shelter. These face-to-

---

both locus and facilitator for programmatic partnerships between and among communities of learners. Westney (2006), pulling upon the work of a pioneer in public librarianship and service-learning, Kathleen de la Peña McCook, suggests that service-learning can play a vital role in forging community partnerships with the "engaged university," while Herther (2008) argues that service learning creates a new kind of "social contract" between libraries and users.

face encounters with people of starkly different experiences caused many students to become increasingly aware of how their own social and economic situations were a "distancing force" between themselves and their homeless clients, and so were compelled to revise previous opinions about what homeless people were "really like." This enabled transformations of students' own self-consciousness as they are "thrown back against themselves in their awareness" of what it means to be different (Ostrow, p. 374). In this, what I call a critical sense of service learning, social justice is achieved as much through a transformation of subjective consciousness as it is a resolution of local community problems.

It would seem there is a strong point of convergence between both Kapitzke's and Ostrow's sense of transformative pedagogy in service learning. Kapitzke brings to the service learning table a model of critical information literacy that, like Ostrow's understanding of how student social consciousness can be repositioned though community engagement, fosters a transformation of information-consciousness to include questions of ideology, power, authority, and even resistance. Likewise, though not writing directly about service learning, library scholars such as Elmborg (2006), Swanson (2004), and Jacobs (2008) have pulled upon concepts of critical theory to develop the "next evolutionary stage" for information literacy. In summarizing the values of critical literacy, Powell, Cantrell and Adams cite the same strengths service learning makes for its own contributions to questions of social justice and civic engagement:

> First, critical literacy assumes that the teaching of literacy is never neutral but always embraces a particular ideology or perspective. Second, critical literacy supports a strong democratic system grounded in equity and shared decision-making. Third, critical literacy assumes that the literacy instruction can empower and lead to transformative action. (as cited in Swanson, p. 264)

The Reciprocity of Information Literacy and Service Learning

A central question for this chapter is, how would a perspective of information literacy enhance service-learning pedagogy? That service learning can effect a change in the moral and social consciousness of students is fairly well acknowledged. But, as noted earlier, what is still a matter of debate is the contribution of service-learning to academic learning in the disciplines. (See, for instance, Kezar & Rhoads, 2001). Do service-learning students learn, for instance, chemistry, literature, or sociology better than students in traditional classes? Though the adoption of an information literacy perspective will not necessarily resolve this debate, it may bring a new and more rigorous focus to the learning perspective of service-learning.

Service-learning is advocated as an effective teaching tool for the immediacy of the community experience it affords. Placing students at the center of pressing social issues allows for experiences impossible to find in the more remote and cloistered classroom setting. At the same time, what sets service-learning apart from a broader conception of volunteerism is its engendering of vital learning opportunities. Students' community service is conducted within the structure of academic classes enabling them to reflect upon their experiences of local social problems within the context of broader disciplinary issues. It is here that a critical information literacy perspective can be particularly beneficial to service-learning students. Librarians can teach students to access and critically evaluate pertinent information resources relevant to their educational level. Critical information literacy will help provide the means for contextualizing the issues encountered in students' community experiences, map them into an ideological matrix, and more richly inform the reflective dimension of the service-learning course.

The conjunction of information literacy and service-learning also has important ramifications for perceptions of the library and its services. The library as an institution has traditionally been associated with particular cognitive activities, i.e. accessing, reading, and evaluating books, newspaper, articles, databases, websites, and other digital resources. Its service to the instructional dimension of the curriculum has been the prime motivation. However, a critical information literacy perspective, especially within a service-learning matrix that also stresses moral and social values of education, introduces questions of ideology and social position back into the library itself. If the library can help bring a strong traditional learning dimension into the pedagogy of service-learning, critical information literacy turns this process back on itself by leading the library to consider how the transformative nature of social engagement recasts traditionally abstract ideas of information, knowledge, and research into localized socio-cultural structures.

The introduction of information literacy, especially through Breivik's disciplinary resource-based model or Kapitzke's critical variant, to the service-learning paradigm can achieve a new and dynamic reciprocity between what are usually perceived as seemingly incommensurable modes of learning, community engagement, and information research, that is, the experiential and the rational, the doing and the thinking. Breivik's conception updates an older cognitive processing model of information literacy through the idea of context-sensitive resource-based learning in the disciplines. Highlighting even more the experiential nature of research, Kapitzke's critical information literacy sees the access, reading, and evaluation of information resources as localized, socially constructed, and ideologically infused forms of action. "Going to the library" and "doing research," instead of instrumental and relatively disengaged exercises, may become for service-learning students a significant kind of engagement infused with cultural and ideological meaning in some ways as socially informative as their community service. In adopting the approaches of Breivik or Kapitzke, three learning/experiential dimensions could be introduced to the service-learning class: community, classroom, and library, each with a unique physical locus (ontology) and epistemology. Metaphorically speaking, learning in the service-learning class becomes dynamically triangulated, with the challenge for the student to map the retained distinctness and reciprocity of each.

What Might An Information Literacy Perspective in the Service-Learning Class Look Like?: Examples and Suggestions

As noted earlier, there are few direct examples in the literature of how library services or information literacy in particular have been incorporated into service-learning in academic libraries. One is by Rhodes and Davis (2001), a librarian and English teacher respectively, at Hampton University of Virginia. In their service learning communications course, students developed and wrote online user guides for the library catalog and databases to help their own fellow students learn the new automated system recently installed by the library. Through instruction provided by librarians, the students had to become semi-expert information users themselves in order to effectively write the guides. An information skills component was integrated effectively into a service-learning context. In a similar mode, Meyer and Miller (2008) reported the partnership between a service-learning technical communication class and the campus library to instruct students on the use of RefWorks. They referred to their project as a "win-win collaboration" for both the library and the service-learning students and faculty.

However, since there are no reports in the literature of service-learning specifically using the disciplinary resource-based learning or critical information literacy perspectives outlined here, some suggestions of what these classes might look like will be offered. Breivik (1998) reports a number of subject courses that used a resource-based learning approach. It would not be difficult to imagine how a service-learning component could be added to these courses as well and so effectively integrate informational and experiential learning. For instance, librarians at Auburn University in Montgomery, Alabama developed a series of workshops for marketing courses to integrate research and information retrieval skills with the course instruction. A service-learning component of such courses, where for instance students develop marketing plans for local non-profit organizations, would benefit greatly from having an information literacy component to help students access and evaluate marketing-based resources in the library. Nursing students at Montana State University in Bozeman had classes in informatics, taught by librarians, in which they were shown how to access government health information resources. Again, a service-learning component in which students, for instance, create websites or print format resources of state and federal health information for clients of community health centers would find information literacy classes essential for mastering search and retrieval techniques.

More important, a critical information literacy could help students access and evaluate pertinent literature examining questions of the political and social context of information structures, such as information poverty, socioeconomic exclusion to information resources, and the information-seeking behaviors of particular social groups. Such questions would add an informational dynamic to students' community experience. They could explore the extent by which the ability to adequately address local community problems may be impacted through limitations for both the access and content of potentially transformative information. Furthermore, students may come to realize that what often appears to be a simple technological limitation may in fact be a manifestation of deeper social and political realities. In fact, drawing upon the complimentary arguments of Zlotkowski regarding service-learning and Breivik for resource-based learning in the disciplines, the learning dimension of almost any subject based class would benefit from linking an information literacy component with the experiential aspects of community service. Students would not only learn how to access, use, communicate, and evaluate valued information resources relating to the course subject matter, but then be given opportunities to experience their application in real-world situations.

Kapitzke (2003) has also imagined how a critical information literacy perspective could be incorporated into a service-learning type of class in which, for example, students rehabilitate an environmentally degraded playground:

Different attitudes and approaches to environmental degradation and regeneration could be explored by collaboration between teacher and teacher librarian to form working relationships with pro- and anti-conservation groups. These might include a local [development] group, indigenous communities, an environmental and/or civil engineer, a university ecologist, a town planner and a farmer. A critical information literacy would show students how each of these groups has different languages, values, interests, and agendas through which they view and work on the world....The work of the teacher, teacher librarian, and student is not to find the 'facts' about the environment, but to problematize and contextualize those differences through the study of discourse and text (Kapitzke, p. 61).

In an earlier paper, I have speculated on how a critical information literacy perspective could be incorporated into a number of actual service-learning courses as reported in the literature (Riddle, 2003). One such speculation was molded on an article by Rockquemore and Schaffer (2000) of Pepperdine University, who identified three distinct stages of learning development within a service-learning course (in their case, the service activities involved programs such as food delivery, residential geriatric care, youth mentoring or detention, and homeless shelters). The first is one of shock, emotional and social, in the initial rather disorientating stages of the community service experience. In the second, a normalization stage, shock is replaced by the development of certain relationships with their clients. Instead of generalizing about "those people," students found more personal descriptions of individuals with unique problems. With the final stage, engagement, causal explanations are sought to account for structural attributions of the clients' circumstances, which, Rockquemore and Schaffer note, are not too dissimilar from the students' own (e.g., political powerlessness, under-education, and low income).

An information literacy perspective could provide valuable assistance in each stage. Helping students find information about the agencies themselves (from local newspapers or magazines, web sites, program and service announcements, policy, staffing or budgetary descriptions collected by the library, etc.) would help ameliorate some of the shock on the initial encounter (though certainly not eliminate it, as this shock experience is a key goal for Rockquemore's and Schaffer's course objective). Likewise in the normalization and engagement stages a librarian could help students find contextual background on the particular social issues or benchmark how agencies elsewhere have addressed similar problems. The librarian would not only show students how to access and navigate information resources, print, digital, multimedia, etc., but to critically evaluate the information they found in terms of its relevancy to the pertinent social issues, and the ideological aspects of the resources themselves.

The idea here would not necessarily be that the students write a full blown traditional kind of research paper, which in some ways could be counter-intuitive to the service learning paradigm. But most service-learning courses contain a reflective assignment for students to consider the significance of their community experience. Research has suggested that this reflective aspect of the service-learning experience is most meaningful when integrated with subject matters of the particular course (Eyler & Giles, 1999). This integration can be effected by an information literacy component that would help transform apparently distinct kinds of experience, i.e. classroom, community, research, into interrelated modes of information for the student to reflect upon. Coming to an understanding of information research as a distinct kind of social/cultural experience points the way for the student to form a new conception of their own community engagement as in itself a certain mode of experiential information. Information research is recognized as itself a distinct mode of experience, and community experience as a mode of information. In this way critical information literacy can help service-learning students effectively link the disciplinary informational perspectives with the learning experiences from their community activities. In return, service-learning offers information literacy an arena to further develop an engaged and critical orientation.

Metaphors for the Integration of Service-Learning and Information Literacy

The approach of this chapter was to suggest possible lines of intersection between two modes of teaching, lines that I believe are more complementary and mutually reinforcing than might otherwise be suspected. Given the speculative nature I have adopted here, it is fitting to conclude with a metaphorical summary, one that intentionally and even obliquely points out connections between seemingly disparate elements. These metaphors can hopefully inspire collaboration and research between practitioners of service-learning and those who provide library services in general and information literacy in particular.

Joby Taylor (2002) has examined metaphors drawn from self-descriptions of community service programs to critique certain understandings of service-learning. Descriptive in nature, these are what Taylor calls "metaphors *of*" in that they tend to reify and normativize concepts of service-learning. For example, "national service is the moral equivalent of war" reductively imports connotations of destructiveness into an otherwise social building enterprise. Likewise, some who advocate a metaphor of "national service as citizenship development" also attempt to shift the metaphor from service to that of political reform, avoiding connotations of charitable benevolence historically associated with the word service. However, Taylor argues, this is more than a metaphor shift, but a conceptual repositioning, losing along the way the deep concern for social ills that foster nurturing relationships between people and communities. In response, Taylor urges new metaphors "*for* service" that are self-consciously chosen to frame the concept itself, rather than ascriptions from other kinds of practices. Two in particular spark reflections on the relationship of research and information literacy to service-learning pedagogy.

"Service is text" encourages a rethinking of the apparent dissonance between the concept of service as experience and traditional text-based classroom practices. That service can be "read" as part of the overall course content "highlights for faculty the need to integrate service with learning and offers metaphoric connections between [faculty's] traditional course construction activities and those of designing and implementing a service-learning course" (Taylor, p. 51).

Can we not also "read" the activity of research or the access and critical evaluation of information resources as part of the learning experience? Breivik's and Kapitzke's models of information literacy eschew an instrumentalist input-output definition of research for a more constructivist and sense-making approach that maps both the actions of the information-seeker and the structures of information resources themselves within broader socio-cultural matrices. "Reading" research as a distinct kind of learning experience becomes particularly resonant with service-learning as we can now see multiple learning experiences taking place: in the classroom, in the community, and in the library. The library itself, and its associated services including the provision of information literacy instruction, becomes a locus for unique learning experiences, with social, affective, and cognitive characteristics akin to, but not replicable through, the classroom or the community

This sense of the "place" of the library applies to another of Taylor's metaphors for service, that of "service as border crossing." Adopting Henry Giroux's idea of learning as taking place within social spaces whose borders shift with reconfigurations of culture, power, and knowledge, Taylor thinks service-learning's "situatedness within actual physical borderlands, in which diverse and unequal communities come together in collaborative action, particularly suits it as a context highlighting the links between education and progressive democracy" (Taylor, p. 52). He stretches this metaphor to include the crossings of social and epistemological borders, and re-conceptions of the idea of border itself.

For Taylor, this metaphor of learning experiences as social, physical, and conceptual border crossings is particularly appropriate for community service classes which challenge older notions of where on the campus learning actually takes place. By incorporating information literacy into its pedagogy, service-learning can create a new "research locus" within its scheme of border negotiations. An information literacy perspective is not just a matter of adding value to the academic learning of community service, though it certainly does this, nor can it fully replace the experiential characteristics of service-leaning. But just as with Taylor's notion that borders between communities become reconfigured through collaborative action, so the pedagogies of service-learning and traditional education can become dynamically integrated across the border provided by a critical information literacy.

References

Abes, E.. Jackson. G., & Jones, S. (2002). Factors that motivate and deter faculty use of service-learning. *Michigan Journal of Community Service-Learning*. *9*(1), 5-19.

Ball, M. & Schilling, K. (2006). Service learning, technology and LIS education. *Journal of Education for Library and Information Science*. *47*(4), 277-90.

Breivik, P. & Gee, G. (1989). *Information Literacy: A Revolution in the Library*. New York: American Council of Education.

Breivik, P. (1998). *Student Learning in the Information Age*. Phoenix, Arizona: Oryx Press.

Burek Pierce, J. (2006) Service learning sustains hope. *American Libraries*. *37*(10), 45.

Elmborg, J. Critical literacy: Implications for instructional practice. *The Journal of Academic Librarianship*, *32*(2), 192-199.

Eyler, J. & Giles, D. (1999). *Where's the Learning in Service-Learning?* San Francisco: Jossey-Bass.

Gerrish, B. (2006) Service-learning: a great experience for LIS students. *Colorado Libraries*. *32*(3), 32-5.

Herther, N. (2008). Service learning and engagement in the academic library: operating out of the box. *C&RL News* http://www.ala.org/ala/mgrps/divs/acrl/publications/crlnews/2008/jul/servicelearning.cfm. Accessed: 2/4/09

Howard, J. Academic service learning: A counternormative pedagogy. In R. Rhodes and J. Howard (eds.), *Academic Service Learning: A Pedagogy of Action and Reflection*. San Francisco: Jossey-Bass.

Hubbard, T. (1995). Bibliographic instruction and postmodern pedagogy. *Library Trends, 44*, 439-452.

Jacobs, H. (2008). Information literacy and reflective pedagogical praxis. *The Journal of Academic Librarianship, 34*(3), 256-262.

Kapitzke, C. (2003). Information literacy: A review and poststructural critique. *Australian Journal of Language and Literacy, 26*(1), 53-66.

Kezar, A. & Rhoads, R. (2001). The dynamic tensions of service-learning in higher education: A philosophical perspective. *The Journal of Higher Education*, 148-171.

Marcum, J. (2002). Rethinking information literacy. *The Library Quarterly. 72*(1), 1-26.

Meyer, N. & Miller, I. The library as service-learning partner: a "win-win" collaboration with students and faculty. *College and Undergraduate Libraries. 15*(4), 399-413.

Ostrow, J. (1995). Self-consciousness and social positioning: On college students changing their mind about the homeless. *Qualitative Sociology, 18*(3), 357-375.

Rhodes, N. & Davis, J. (2001). Using service learning to get positive reactions in the library. *Computers in Libraries, 21*(1), 32-35.

Riddle, J. (2003). Where's the library in service learning? Models of engaged library instruction. *Journal of Academic Librarianship, 29*(2), 71-81.

Simons, K., Young, J., & Gibson, C. (2000). The learning library in context: community, integration, and influence. *Research Strategies, 17*, 123-132.

Rockquemore, K. & Schaffer, R. (2000). Toward a theory of engagement: A cognitive mapping of service-learning experiences. *Michigan Journal of Community Service-Learning, 7*(Fall), 14-24.

Swanson, T. (2004). A radical step: Implementing a critical information literacy model. *Portal: Libraries and the Academy, 4*(2), 259-273.

Taylor, J. (2002). Metaphors we serve by: Integrating the conceptual metaphors framing national and community service and service-learning. *Michigan Journal of Community Service-Learning, 9*(1), 45-57.

Westney, L. (2006). Conspicuous by their absence: Academic librarians in the engaged university. *Reference and User Services Quarterly. 45*(3), 200-203.

Witbodi, S. (2004). Service learning in the library and information studies curriculum at the University of Western Cape: An exploratory study. *Mousaion. 22*(1), 89-102.

Yontz, E. & McCook, K. (2003). Service-learning and LIS education. *Journal of Education for Library and Information Science. 44*(1), 58-68.

Zlotkowski, E. (1998). About the series. In *With Service in Mind: Concepts and Models for Service-Learning in Psychology*, Washington D.C.: AAHE.

Critical Pedagogy and Information Literacy in Community Colleges

Gretchen Keer

Introduction

The community college information literacy instruction session is a unique environment for a number of reasons. Because the student body is drawn from the local community, it tends to reflect the community's diversity in terms of race, gender, class, and primary language. And because community colleges have open enrollment, the students' previous educational attainments vary. The students are, on average, older than the typical four-year college student and many are at a turning point in their lives. Some students are changing careers or in need of job training, some are trying to find focus after graduating high school, and some are interested in developing new hobbies and interests. Community colleges operate under the assumption that students want what they learn in their classes to be readily applicable to their lived experience. This is frequently read by educators and students alike as a desire for coursework to "be practical." This perceived desire sometimes creates a misperception that community college classes are not or should not be intellectually stimulating or too strongly emphasize theory. However, the need for practicality also creates an opportunity for the teacher/librarian to be very direct and honest in the classroom and to encourage her students to reciprocate.

There is also a philosophical dedication in community colleges to the development of "life-long learners." This dedication, which may be supported to varying degrees depending on the particular college environment, signals to the faculty that addressing the realities of our students' lives is at least part of the goal of the community college education process. It is, of course, up to the individual faculty member to take advantage of these attributes, but it is one of the things that make community colleges uniquely fertile ground for the introduction of critical pedagogy into the learning environment. Librarians in community colleges who are interested in incorporating critical pedagogy into their teaching practice have advantages that librarians in other higher education environments might not enjoy.

Critical Pedagogy, Information Literacy, and the Community College

Critical pedagogy is "a domain of education and research that studies the social, cultural, political, economic, and cognitive dynamics of teaching and learning." Specifically, it "emphasizes the impact of power relationships in the educational process" (Kincheloe & Steinberg, n.d.). This chapter will discuss the philosophical ties that relate critical pedagogy to the mission of the community college, and discuss ways in which community college librarians can apply critical pedagogy to their information literacy teaching, in order to develop what Kapitzke (2003a) calls a "critical information literacy" (pp. 48-50).

Like librarians in other institutions of higher education, community college librarians have assumed most of the responsibility for teaching information literacy. As a result, librarian educators have the opportunity to become more embedded than ever before in the classroom learning experience of their students. This also means that we must re-envision information literacy as more than just a handy set of skills for writing research papers. The ability to interact with, problematize, question, and evaluate information is also a necessary precursor to the development of a productive political consciousness. Critical thinking is one of the most valuable aspects of information literacy because it is the piece that students will most frequently need to apply to situations throughout their lives.

Community colleges, while historically associated with developing workers through vocational and technical curricula, tend to emphasize their ability to provide affordable education to life-long learners. This philosophy involves a dedication to meeting students where they are when they come to us and to encouraging them to be fully engaged as citizens. These stated goals are deeply rooted in the ethos of liberalism, but there is room for more radical educational interpretation and intervention. In community colleges, the concept of "student success" is ripe for expansion beyond its relevance to the business world or community life to the more amorphous but arguably more comprehensive goal of success through self-actualization. In order to fully participate in a democratic society, a person needs to be able to think critically about the information she encounters. For this reason, liberatory educational practices, such as critical pedagogy, are a good fit with information literacy.

Community college educators, in particular, try to look not only toward the student's subsequent educational goals, but also toward the student's future as a community member, family member, and independent thinker.

Students are also deeply concerned with how their education will impact their lives outside the classroom. Vanessa Sheared (1999) confirms that "because economic factors, family pressures and constraints, and environmental factors place significant pressures on potential learners, they need to know that what they are doing [in the classroom] will have a positive impact on these concerns" (p. 38). The more relevant the curriculum is to a student's real and pressing everyday concerns, the more fully the student will participate in the learning process.

Librarians propose to address a student's everyday concerns through information literacy instruction. The Association for College & Research Libraries (ACRL), in "Information Literacy Competency Standards for Higher Education" (2006), asserts that:

> by ensuring that individuals have the intellectual abilities of reasoning and critical thinking, and by helping them construct a framework for learning how to learn, colleges and universities provide the foundation for continued growth throughout their careers, as well as in their roles as informed citizens and members of communities. Information literacy is a key component of, and contributor to, lifelong learning. (p.4)

While the concept of critical thinking is mentioned here, the ACRL standards do not adequately address the fact that knowledge is socially constructed. The standards position the student as a person who doesn't know how to learn, and as a result assume that "improved education and training unproblematically translate into better productivity and economic growth" (Kapitzke, 2003b, p. 56). This could stem from the origin of the phrase "information literacy." Kapitzke (2003b) points out that, rather than reflecting carefully considered advances in library education pedagogy, the then-president of the American Information Industry Association, Paul Zurkowski, coined the term in reference to ways of addressing perceived "inadequate workforce skills" (p. 55). Inadequate workforce skills are undoubtedly a concern for community colleges, but two-year schools have for several decades now been experiencing philosophical tension between their traditional goal of building good workers and their current curricular emphasis on the concept of lifelong learning.

The information literacy standards also perpetuate a misconception that information literacy is a neutral force (Kapitzke, 2003a, p. 45). In addition, the official definition of information literacy is vague, and "despite its being the topic of numerous conferences and a considerable body of scholarly work, no consensus on its theoretical or practical dimensions has emerged" (Kapitzke, 2003a, p. 42). While the standards are limited and ill-defined, which are major failings in professional guidelines for best practices, the concept of information literacy lends itself easily to the development of alternate definitions and practical applications on the part of teaching librarians. In the classroom, we can develop what Kapitzke (2003a) calls "a critical information literacy" that would encourage students to "analyze the social and political ideologies embedded within the economies of ideas and information" (p. 49).

Education is, ultimately, the mechanism by which social order is reinforced. In order for the social contract to hold, a culture needs a way to encourage commonalities in its participants. Because the educational process is oriented around assimilation to, and the reproduction of, dominant cultural mores, becoming educated can be a double edged sword, especially for minority students who are often required to internalize not only the positive and liberating aspects of learning, but also the racist, classist, sexist, and heterosexist aspects of learning in order to succeed. However, as Guy (1999) observes, "because learning is essential to cultural reproduction, learning is also a central way of combating cultural domination and oppression" (p. 12). Encouraging students to recognize and question the ideologies that are all around us is a crucial part of helping them to combat domination and oppression. All educators should remain sensitive to these facts as they interact with students inside and outside the classroom.

Enacting Critical Pedagogy in the Community College Library

The students a community college librarian encounters tend to be those who inhabit an educational space outside the stereotypical "ivory tower" of the academy. They are often adults with jobs, children, aging parents, bills, and other concerns that often may not seem to directly mesh with the typical college curriculum. This collision of academia and community provides teaching librarians in these colleges with an opportunity to build an educational relationship that is based on real life shared experiences.

That relationship is initially difficult to build in the typical "one-shot" information literacy instruction session in a community college setting, which can easily devolve into a forty-five minute marathon during which the librarian desperately spews forth as many of the tenets of "How To Do Research" as is humanly possible while the class sits in anxious silence, hoping to figure out what possible relevance this litany could mean to their particular circumstances. When the librarian conceives of the information literacy session as a brief opportunity to frantically impart to students a veritable arsenal of techniques, shortcuts, and strategies, the students often feel that they have been plucked from the relative comfort of their regularly scheduled classes and deposited into a world of arcane codes and unfamiliar customs. What results resembles less a vigorous exploration of how to develop sound research skills and more a medieval ordeal that everyone is hoping desperately to survive.

What information literacy instruction is supposed to do, of course, is foster a student's capacity for and interest in seeking, finding, synthesizing, and evaluating information. These skills, which are closely related to those involved in critical thinking, are not only extremely valuable for the student who aims to be a good and productive collegian, but are also necessary traits of an informed, active, and engaged citizen as defined by Brookfield (2005), who insisted that:

> At the heart of a strong, participatory democracy is citizens' capacity to question the actions, justifications, and decisions of political leaders, and their capacity to imagine alternatives to current structures and moralities that are fairer and more compassionate. Such capacities are judged by some to develop as we learn to think critically. (p. 49)

The librarian can use information literacy instruction to provide students with the tools necessary to critically examine their environment. She can work to introduce students to their own powers of observation, questioning, interpretation, reasoning, and creative re-envisioning of the culture in which they are immersed. In a college classroom, these tools are important for succeeding at learning tasks. If the information literacy instruction is also culturally relevant, it can contribute to "helping learners from marginalized cultural backgrounds learn to take control of their lives and improve their social conditions (Hollings, King, and Hayman, 1994)" (qtd. in Guy, 1999. p. 5).

One of the challenges librarians face in providing culturally relevant information literacy instruction is that we have limited time in the classroom. Unlike classroom faculty, who typically have an entire semester to build relationships with their classes, librarians often address hundreds of students per semester and we address each class for only an hour or so, total. So how can we apply critical pedagogy concepts of community building within these strict time constraints? Teaching librarians must (1) address the emotional aspects of doing research, (2) be mindful of our language and word choice, and (3) encourage and facilitate conversations between students as an integral part of the classroom experience.

Emotion in the Library Classroom

Becoming educated is an intensely emotional process. Sometimes the emotional experience of education can be very negative. Students are often uncomfortable with the challenges the classroom offers to the complex histories and deeply held beliefs with which they arrive at college. The students tend to perceive this discomfort negatively, while educators generally take the view that ideas should be challenged and discomfort is sometimes necessary. However, a more insidious discomfort is that experienced by students who feel their complex personal histories are marginalized in the classroom. Students gain a sense of belonging within the classroom and within the college when the curriculum openly and positively addresses their cultural realities. Sheared writes that "students who found that their lived experiences were acknowledged by the program staff, teachers, and administrators not only participated, they persisted" (Sheared, p. 38). It stands to follow, then, that students who do not feel acknowledged may feel less inclined to participate and persist. The field of adult education has experienced some movement toward the realization that integrating students' social and cultural contexts into their educational experience does not merely provide the framework for effective learning, but is in fact the goal of non-oppressive education efforts.

Giving Voice in the Classroom

Education that appropriately recognizes and confirms a student's lived experiences allows the student to fully participate in her own education as a whole person. This means that the instructor does not deliberately or unintentionally silence the student and that the course material, teaching methods, and classroom atmosphere allow each student to retain her voice. In particular, minority students are well served by this effort. Vanessa Sheared (1999) calls this effort on the part of the educator, "giving voice:"

> Giving voice requires an acknowledgement that knowledge is inherently political and serves to socialize and condition behavior. Norms that often negate the voices of those who lack power and control over the discourse must therefore be reassessed and analyzed, by both teacher and students. (Sheared, 1999, p. 45)

Giving voice means not only giving the students the opportunity to speak, but also being aware, as an instructor, of one's own speech patterns, word choice, and attitude toward non-standard English in the classroom.

bell hooks (1993) asserts that "we must change conventional ways of thinking about language, creating spaces where diverse voices can speak in words other than English or in broken, vernacular speech" (p. 173-4). The librarian can be mindful of expressing concepts in ways that do not alienate students, and of offering practical definitions of library jargon when it must be used. For example, in my own teaching I describe how using the call number to locate a book works in much the same way as using a street address to find a friend's house. We should not cling too tightly to the professional terms we are comfortable with at the expense of the classroom community as a whole.

Classroom Interactions Between Students

Another important part of developing a non-oppressive classroom environment is for the librarian to be conscious of how students are able to communicate with each other as part of their learning experience. In order to make the information literacy session culturally relevant, the librarian must make a concerted effort to break the traditional classroom model and foster an environment in which all parties can participate in a dialog. Because the information literacy session often literally moves the student out of the classroom and into a new environment with a new teacher, the traditional interaction between teacher/librarian and student already has fault lines in it as soon as the students arrive in the library. Rather than looking at this as an obstacle, the librarian may, in her capacity a secondary authority figure to the professor, be able to encourage more flexibility in the ways her students interact with her and with the material being discussed.

To capitalize on this disruption of the traditional classroom power structure, the librarian could encourage the students to introduce her, as an outsider to their classroom dynamic, to their classmates. She might ask the students to introduce each other, as a way of getting them to acknowledge each other's presence in the classroom. She may be able to enter into a dialog with the students about what they are learning, and what they find most useful or problematic about the subject matter, or about the project at hand. The librarian can use her status as a classroom outsider to draw the students into interaction with each other, rather than relying so heavily on the authority figure at the front of the room. This kind of mutual participation in the information literacy curriculum can enrich the experience for all involved.

Teaching librarians who are interested in combating cultural domination in their classrooms must develop strategies to "minimize the potential for further exclusion and marginalization of learners" (Guy, 1999, p. 13). The first step in this endeavor is that "adult educators must formally acknowledge their inherent domination over the students and the knowledge that is introduced to the learner" (Sheared, 1999, p. 45). Teachers (including teaching librarians) are authority figures, and that is the first hurdle to be overcome in any effort toward building a liberatory experience in the classroom. Depending on the culture of the community college, the power-based relationship between librarian and students can be complicated to a lesser or greater degree. At the very least, the librarian can examine her own teaching philosophies and cultural background:

> Most adult educators have a philosophy that reflects their experience and knowledge but have not necessarily given much thought to how their philosophy affects their practice. Nor do educators necessarily give much thought to how their race, gender, class, or language influences their philosophy and what they do in the classroom (Sheared, 1999, p. 35).

Giving serious thought to one's own cultural, class, and gender background can make a great deal of difference to the tenor of the classroom.

Being willing to engage in spontaneous dialog with students whose backgrounds may not fit neatly into the traditional college script can also deeply enrich the classroom experience for all involved. For example, when the librarian asks the students what topics they are interested in researching, some students may make suggestions that sound sarcastic, or that are aimed at challenging the librarian's authority. If the librarian takes these comments in a spirit of fun, rather than reacting defensively, and acknowledges the student's contribution to the discussion by drawing him further into it, rather than shutting him out, these "throw-away" comments can enhance the feeling of community in the classroom. It might be pertinent to point out to the group that they can use their research skills to find information about absolutely anything they can think of, whether it's a "serious" course-related topic or something that might seem completely frivolous.

When my students suggest topics that could be considered inappropriate, such as celebrity sex scandals, or topics I'm not expert on, such as hip hop culture, I use the opportunity to acknowledge that I don't know a lot about those topics and to emphasize that research is for learning about things you don't understand or aren't familiar with yet. Following through on these topics for demonstration purposes also reinforces the idea that research skills can be used for things students care about on a personal level, as well as more task-oriented topics. These "inappropriate" topics can also hold hidden emotional significance for students because they are often related to the activities and interests that situate them in their personal cultures and subcultures.

As a result of the students' personal investment in the topics they suggest, these moments of challenge tend also to lend themselves to a discussion about the emotions that arise around research. When the conversation returns to assignment-related research topics, the librarian can ask how the students are feeling about researching unfamiliar topics. The students may express that the topics they are looking at are boring because they're not relevant, or that it makes them uncomfortable to be in a position of ignorance on a subject. If the librarian has been a good sport about researching topics that are outside her experience, she can then relate her own feelings of discomfort and hopefully normalize those feelings as just another part of the research process.

Conclusion

There are several reasons for teaching librarians in community colleges to embrace a philosophy of critical pedagogy. Liberatory education practices are closely related to and complementary with the goals of information literacy instruction. Community colleges are committed to fostering critical thinking skills in their students, and both critical pedagogy and information literacy provide methodologies for facilitating that goal. Also important is the fact that students who feel their education is relevant to their daily concerns are more likely to fully engage with their instructors, the material, and each other. Libraries are an important part of the student support network on community college campuses, and incorporating critical pedagogy into our information literacy instruction practice can only enhance our ability to encourage students to complete their educations. There is also a social justice component to integrating critical pedagogy into the information literacy classroom. It is vital, even essential, to make the classroom a place of dialog and mutual learning for learners of all backgrounds and cultural contexts. Critical pedagogy provides an opportunity for all students to fully interact with the curriculum, not only to obtain the maximum benefit from it but also to apply it constructively to enrich and change their own lives.

158

References

Association of College and Research Libraries. (2000). *Information Literacy Competency Standards for Higher Education.* Retrieved February 15, 2009, from American Library Association Web site: http://www.acrl.org/ala/mgrps/divs/acrl/standards/standards.pdf

Brookfield, S. (2005, Summer). Overcoming impostorship, cultural suicide, and lost innocence: Implications for teaching critical thinking in the community college. *New Directions for Community Colleges,* 2005(130), 49-57. Retrieved February 12, 2009, from Academic Search Premier database.

Freire, P. (1997). *Pedagogy of the heart.* New York: The Continuum Publishing Company.

Geismar, K., & Nicoleau, G. (Eds.). (1993). *Teaching for change: Addressing issues of difference in the college classroom.* Reprint series no. 25. Cambridge, MA: Harvard Educational Review.

Guy, T. C. (1999). Culture as context for adult education: The need for culturally relevant adult education. In *Providing culturally relevant adult education: A challenge for the twenty-first century:* Vol. 82. New directions for adult and continuing education (pp. 5-18). The Jossey-Bass higher and adult education series. San Francisco: Jossey-Bass.

hooks, b. (1994). *Teaching to transgress: Education as the practice of freedom.* New York: Routledge.

Kapitzke, C. (2003a). Information literacy: A positivist epistemology and a politics of outformation. *Educational theory, 53*(1), 37-53.

Kapitzke, C. (2003b). Information literacy: A review and poststructural critique. *Australian journal of language and literacy, 26*(1), 53-66.

Kinelchoe, J. L., & Steinberg, S. R. (n.d.). *The Freire international project for critical pedagogy.* Retrieved February 10, 2009, from McGill University Web site: http://freire.mcgill.ca/content/freire-international-project-critical-pedagogy

MCCC: About us. (2009). Retrieved April 15, 2009, from Montgomery County Community College Web site: http://www.mc3.edu/aboutus

Mercer County Community College - Educational philosophy (2009). Retrieved April 15, 2009, from Mercer County Community College Web site: http://www.mccc.edu/welcome_philosophy.shtml

Moeck, W. (2002, October 22). *R(e)Defining the Liberal Arts: Critical Thinking at the Community College Level.* (ERIC Document Reproduction Service No. ED471541) Retrieved February 14, 2009, from ERIC database.

Nettles, M., Millett, C., Association of Community Coll. Trustees, A., & American Association of Community Colleges, W. (2000, January 1). *Student access in community colleges. New expeditions: charting the second century of community colleges.* Issues Paper No. 1. (ERIC Document Reproduction Service No. ED438872) Retrieved February 12, 2009, from ERIC database.

Sheared, V. (1999). Giving voice: Inclusion of African American students' polyrhythmic realities in adult basic education. In T. C. Guy (Ed.), *Providing culturally relevant adult education: A challenge for the twenty-first century:* Vol. 82. New directions for adult and continuing education (pp. 33-48). The Jossey-Bass higher and adult education series. San Francisco: Jossey-Bass.

Shugart, S. (2008, January 1). Adult Students: A Priority Revisited. *Presidency*, 11(1), 18-22. (ERIC Document Reproduction Service No. EJ796092) Retrieved February 12, 2009, from ERIC database.

Swanson, T. A. (2004). Applying a critical pedagogical perspective to information literacy standards. *Community & Junior College Libraries*, *12*(4), 65-77.

Making a Home: Critical Pedagogy in a Library Internship Program for High School Students

Daren A. Graves, Mary McGowan and Doris Ann Sweet

Introduction

In 2001, following the lead of the U. S. Department of Health and Human Services, the Young Adult Library Services Association of the American Library Association promoted the issue of "positive youth development," encouraging libraries and young adult librarians to create library programs and services that fostered positive development (Family & Youth Services Bureau, 2001). There is very little in the way of empirical data about the rates of library use among youth, especially those of color in urban areas. If enrollment of students of color in library and information science programs is any indicator of youth of color's engagement with libraries, then the situation is bleak, as these numbers are very low, especially relative to the proportions of such populations in the greater U.S. population (Revels et al., 2003).

Revels et al. (2003) also argue that institutions that are serious about recruiting higher numbers of students of color into the library profession should develop initiatives that "would seek to recruit…minority high school students to receive training and experience working in the library" (p. 159). Verny (2002) reported that attempts to recruit youth through such programs "faced daunting challenges such as how to portray libraries as exciting places to work [and] how to persuade young adults to consider a career in library and information science." (p. 52) The U.S. and the world have been transitioning into an information economy, and libraries are increasingly becoming hubs for information access in low-income neighborhoods lacking easy access to computers and the Internet (The Boston Indicators Project). Given the difficulties described in getting youth of color engaged with libraries and librarianship, the following is a description of a program aimed at increasing high school students' of color engagement with libraries and librarians.

Relevant Literature

A pedagogical tool that has been shown to be useful in increasing the academic and civic engagement of youth of color and other marginalized communities is critical pedagogy. According to McLaren (1989),

> Critical pedagogy challenges the assumption that schools function as major sites of social and economic mobility. Proponents of this pedagogical theory suggest that schooling must be analyzed as a cultural and historical process, in which select groups are positioned within asymmetrical relations of power on the basis of specific race, class, and gender groupings. (p. 166)

In this vein, critical pedagogy is a teaching approach which attempts to help students question and challenge domination, and the beliefs and practices that dominate. Critical pedagogy poses a relationship between the teacher and the students where power and authority are relatively balanced. Unlike the "banking concept" in education (Freire, 1970) where teachers treat educational information similarly to economic capital by holding the information and depositing it into the heads of students who act as empty vessels waiting to be filled (i.e., like bankers depositing money into people's savings accounts), critical pedagogues recognize that students are experts on their own lives and conditions and have information. This expertise must be leveraged in order to help students analyze and deconstruct the conditions and hegemonic forces that serve to dehumanize and oppress marginalized and/or colonized peoples.

Research by Morrell (2004) has shown the effectiveness of employing critical pedagogy as a means to increase the academic engagement and displayed academic competencies of underserved high school students of color. The aim of Morrell's work with youth was for his students to move beyond achieving mastery in functional literacy to displaying "critical literacy." Morrell would define critical literacy as the act of decoding texts, analyzing the underlying power structures, and using the analysis to drive equitable change. As Morrell (2003) puts it, "There can be no liberation of self or other without tools or language to perform counter-readings of dominant texts that serve as the interests of power" (p. 5). In other words, for underserved students (especially those who are ascribed or ascribe for themselves cultural identities that are targeted and marginalized), it is not enough to be given the skills associated with functional literacy, because critical pedagogues argue that education is an inherently political act that those with hegemonic power use to reproduce the status quo. Carnoy and

Levin (1986) and Willis (1981) argue this point through the application of "cultural reproduction theory" to the analysis of the purpose of education in capitalist societies. As Willis (1981) posits in thinking about the roles that teachers have in schools reproducing a social, political, and economic status quo, where the hegemonic forces use schools as a means to continually oppress marginalized groups:

> Teachers should look at ways in which their own labour process and changes in it might be implicated in dominant or subordinate *Cultural Production* and *Reproduction*. Certainly the development of hierarchies and managerial systems turns subordinate *Cultural Production* into "social problems," "problems of control," and "pathology." (p. 66)

Educators who do not want their schooling practices to help reproduce hegemonic forces that oppress marginalized groups need to help their students develop critical literacy, which gives students literacy tools to help them decode and deconstruct such hegemonic forces. By helping students develop critical literacy Morrell (2004) and his students (many of whom were considered barely functionally literate) co-produced learning environments that ultimately led his students to present their work to graduate-level professors and researchers. These professors and researchers were so impressed by the work of Morrell's students, that many of them were inspired to re-visit and re-conceptualize their own theories around best practices in educational strategies geared towards underserved youth of color.

Drawing on the tenets of critical pedagogy and critical literacy, librarians who are interested in helping underserved youth to use libraries and information technology in ways that are truly useful to understanding their own worlds (and worlds they may not yet have access to) have been utilizing the concept of critical information literacy. Ward (2006) sees critical information literacy thus:

> [A] revisioning of information literacy would give birth to the future academic library—a place thoroughly integrated into the flow of campus learning where librarians, possessing diverse knowledge and expertise, would assist patrons in a multiplicity of information-related processes. These would include finding quality information, exploring the personal significance of a topic, framing an aesthetic experience of music, and facilitating personal awareness. (p. 402)

In this regard, Doherty (2007) argues that in a critical information literacy model, the traditional role of librarian as "gatekeeper" may have to change, as it perpetuates a "banking concept" of education. Rather than acting as "service providers" who limit access to information (e.g., a discriminatory form of information literacy where one has to be an expert in LOC call numbers) and determine for students and other library patrons what information is valid and how it should be organized, Doherty (2007) argues that librarians should act more as critical educators, drawing upon students' funds of knowledge and allowing students to bring their own expertise and literacies to the table, and "de-reifying certain forms of literacy" (p. 5) that leave underserved youth without access to key information and a sense of self-efficacy in the process of understanding the world(s) around them.

Some librarians have already begun to implement a critical information literacy model in their attempts to re-envision the roles of libraries in the 21st century. Swanson (2004) utilized a critical information literacy model with first-year college students in a composition course. Students were, as a result, able to sift through multiple sources and to more effectively evaluate their credibility and use them appropriately. While Swanson's example showed how critical information literacy models can impact college students' ability to effectively evaluate sources for college writing assignments, Giles (2002) showed that implementing a critical literacy model can impact the relationship between subordinated populations and the population that oppressed them. Using the example of the Australian Aborigines and the ANTaR reconciliation movement (where the Australian government resolved to bring to light and reconcile the systematic ways in which the aboriginal population was subordinated), Giles argues that if Australians were not to provide the aboriginal population with critical information literacy skills, the aboriginal population would not be truly empowered to obtain and utilize information about their systematic subordination. Furthermore, if the aboriginal population were dependent on their functionally literate White Australian counterparts, Giles wonders whether a truly equitable reconciliation would be possible. As Giles puts it, "Central to the movement supporting meaningful reconciliation in Australia will be the continued opening up of the story of Australia to non-dominant voices and to other viewpoints" (p. 210). Giles further asserts that both the Indigenous Australians and non-Indigenous Australians need to benefit from critical information literacy so that those on both sides of the equation can have access to counter-hegemonic portrayals of Australian history as well as those that have served as justification of the de-humanization of Indigenous Australians.

Overall, the research on critical pedagogy and critical information literacy sheds light on the importance of sharing power and authority and giving legitimacy to the lived experiences of traditionally marginalized communities. Critical pedagogy can serve as a means of deconstructing systems and institutions that have traditionally served as gatekeepers in ways that have denied access and promoted the oppression of those marginalized populations.

A New Paradigm

In the 2007-2008 academic year, Simmons College Library put the life experiences of eight Boston high school students at the heart of an already established library internship program funded by the Institute of Museum and Library Services and the H. W. Wilson Foundation. The program, called MassBLAST (Building Library Awareness and Staff for Tomorrow), was a program for high school students who are members of minority groups or are the first generation in their families to attend college (www.simmons.edu/massblast). The goal of the program was to create life-long library ambassadors, and possibly future librarians, by teaching the interns information literacy skills, introducing them to how a complex organization (the library) is organized and run, and imparting college and career skills. Two forty-hour internships were held each year, and four to six Boston public high school students participated in each session.

The first two years of the grant, library staff members made their own knowledge of the library and research the center of the program. Librarians determined the content to be imparted and how the interns should be taught. In traditional classroom settings, interns were taught how to use the online catalog and scholarly databases. Librarians showed interns how the library was organized and run by giving them short-term jobs in various departments.

In the summer of 2007, the MassBLAST staff met with Professor Daren Graves of Simmons College, who introduced them to the principles of critical pedagogy. Dr. Graves is an assistant professor in Urban Education at Simmons College and had been Assistant Director of the Simmons College Upward Bound program, where he helped coordinate the academic and college preparation components of this federally-funded after-school and summer program. The Simmons librarians, collaborating with Dr. Graves, worked to shift the learning paradigm and conceive of themselves as reciprocal learning and research partners, positioning the lived experiences and authentic interests of the interns as central to the internship. Interns would still learn about the library, but instead of having librarian knowledge dominate the process, the interns would create short research papers and media projects about their lives. Engaged with their stories, the interns would tell the librarians what they (the interns) needed to know.

Shedding the Gatekeeper Role

Staff had concerns as they embarked on this new program. How could they integrate the principles of critical pedagogy (i.e., reciprocal relationships, bringing in interns' lives-as-text) with the original goals of the program around learning and teaching library skills? What would be an active role for staff and how would they play it without becoming the authority? What structures could staff create to facilitate communication between librarians and interns?

The librarians first grappled with communication. In order to have the lived experiences and authentic interests of the interns drive the program, staff had to find ways of allowing the interns to tell them about their interests and lives. In a pre-internship meeting, librarians asked interns questions about their experiences in school and in their communities. These questions and their answers helped to create an environment in which the interns felt comfortable talking about their lives. For example, when asked about the first person to take them to a library, the interns responded with a discussion of their families and, for those interns who had immigrated to the U.S., about their countries of origin. The librarians then introduced themselves and talked about similar parts of their lives, keeping up this dialogue throughout the internship.

Librarians planned small group and one-on-one librarian/student "research partner" sessions to teach those research skills the interns actually needed to complete their projects. At this juncture, dilemmas arose around librarians assuming the gatekeeping role. One of the goals of the program was to impart library skills to the interns. Librarians served as experts and therefore as gatekeepers to this knowledge. Another goal was to endorse the interns' lived experiences as valid texts to be brought into the research and analytical processes. For this, interns, not librarians, were the experts. Therefore, librarians had to shed their traditional gatekeeper roles and become learners. In fact, interns became gatekeepers, choosing what information about their lives to share with librarians and putting librarians in a position of trying to connect what they were learning from their interns with the learning goals around libraries and research.

The Plan in Action

While it was important for librarians to shed the power and authority associated with their traditional gatekeeping role, the mere shedding of this would not mean that the interns would automatically assume authority and power. Librarians felt it would be important to structure the experience such that the youth would feel empowered to assume authority and feel comfortable bringing their own lives and issues into the library space. Both librarians and interns had to be able to reach a comfort point with letting the interns lead the way. To achieve this goal, librarians utilized three strategies: introducing the interns to youth-generated media, having librarians share their own life experiences, and helping interns with important issues that may not be library-related.

To help establish that the interns' lived experiences would be valid texts in the program, librarians introduced the interns to examples of youth-generated media. The web sites at *Stories for Change* and *Teaching to Change LA* are a rich source of digital stories made by filmmakers of similar ages and interests to the interns (Stories for Change, 2008; Teaching to Change LA, 2004-2005). Librarians chose videos to show and asked interns to consider the following questions:

- What are the filmmakers' concerns?
- What do the filmmakers want to tell us?
- How might libraries and librarians help them tell their stories?
- What resources do you think they need to tell their stories?

After that discussion the interns brainstormed answers to these questions:

- What interests you?
- What story would you like to tell about your life or your community?

Librarians recorded interns' answers. One of the librarians then showed a short digital story she had made about her father and talked about the process of making it. These exercises served the purpose of helping interns determine for themselves what they wanted to learn, while also validating that their lived experiences were central to the research process.

Over several days, interns developed their topics. One student was interested in teen pregnancy. Another wanted to persuade others that racism still exists and that affirmative action is a good way to combat it. Another intern wanted to research global warming since she had heard a lot about it in school. Another indicated that she wanted to explain the Muslim holiday Eid to Christians. Yet another said, after seeing the librarian's digital story about her father, that she wanted to tell a story about her mother in a similar way.

While the librarians established that interns' lived experiences were valid texts in the research process, they also felt a need to establish trust between themselves and the interns so the interns would feel comfortable sharing their lived experiences. Librarians did not want to ask interns to make themselves vulnerable to staff without doing the same in return. With this in mind, the librarians intentionally established relationships with interns where the librarians shared aspects of their own lived experiences. In structured times, such as weekly meetings, and in social times, such as snack break each day, librarians and interns had a chance to talk and listen. Tina later described her relationship with her partner librarian as, "Pretty good. Alyssa was telling me a couple things about her grandkids. And I was telling her about one of my friends that just recently passed." Lily described her relationship with her partner librarian by stating that she:

> was a good person. She helped me a lot. She's like my friend now. Because before I didn't know her. I was scared of her. She looked different. She looked serious. Then I found out she was really fun to work with...She told me about her family and I told her about mine. We shared things.

Clearly, Lily's perception of her partner librarian changed from a "different" and "scary" person to a "friend."

Librarians also became engaged with the needs of the interns, even if they were beyond the scope of the program. As Lucilia describes, "The day that Jean called me to come for the interview, I told her that I'm a senior and I haven't applied for college. And she told me if I want to come so she can help me to apply and look for colleges, and to see which colleges don't have a deadline." Lucilia went beyond calling her partner librarian a friend by expressing, "Our relationship is great I think. I always told her that she is one of my mothers. I always told her 'Oh, I got a lot of mothers and you are one of them.'" Librarians' engagement with the interns clearly fostered trust, as reflected in Lily's and Lucilia's use of the words "friend" and "mother."

This process of reciprocal sharing was an issue of sharing both power and authority. Librarians were used to a process whereby they set the agenda and executed requisite activities to help interns learn library skills. Leveraging interns' lived experiences as a way to teach library skills did not allow for the traditional process. Putting the student-driven process into an already existing library structure caused unease. For example, in reflecting on the process, Scott described the difficulty in helping interns both generate research topics that reflected their lived experiences and illuminate those experiences with traditional scholarly resources:

> And here I was trying to guide someone's thought process in developing a research topic. And I can't think of it in terms of, "You're in this college." I mean, sure they came here a few hours a week, but all the rest of the time that, if they're really gonna do a research project, all the rest of the time we should be doing work would be on these other scenarios [topics] which were not as conducive to the kind of research that I think of when I think of research.

Though a struggle, shedding the gatekeeper role and dealing with ambiguity yielded some amazing results.

Learning How the Library Works

According to their reflections, interns came to discover functions, processes, and purposes associated with the library of which they were not previously aware. In doing so, they made these new discoveries their own, gaining power with their new knowledge. Halimah and Nur's perceptions of librarians were influenced by the fact that they had no experience with libraries before emigrating from Bangladesh. Halimah describes this by reflecting,

> In this country I don't know how the library is going, because I have only been here two and a half years. So I don't know how, in this country's library, how they do the stuff. This country has lots of electronic stuff [in the library]. In Bangladesh, there is no computer. Maybe in the university library but not in school. We didn't have any library in our school. When I was there, there wasn't any library in two miles or three miles. So I never [went] there.

Nur echoed Halimah's assertion by saying of the program, "I learned how to find information in a book. How to order a book. If I had to request for a book that is not in the shelf." After completing the program, both Nur and Halimah were hired at a local public library branch to help students with their homework. Asked about how often they use the library now, Nur and Halimah responded,

> Nur: Every week, because I work [at the public library].
>
> Halimah: Me too.

Interviewer: How long have you been working at the library?

Halimah & Nur: Two and a half months.

Halimah: It's a program, like a help program. Homework assistance program. And every Saturday I go there to help the children from elementary school and middle school if they are having any problems with their homework, I help them.

Nur: And high school too...all grades.

Tina, who researched teen pregnancy, developed new strategies for conducting research as a result of the program, and put these strategies to work in the pursuit of academic excellence outside the program. Tina said:

I gained learning how to research better. Because I have a senior project due before I graduate so that would help me lot...Because mostly when I do research I go on the computer. But now that MassBLAST helped with going on the computer and looking in books, I'm just like, "Hmmm." Now when I do my senior project I can get more information by going in books and going on the Internet and just researching what I want. Choosing the right keyword for finding what I want to do.

Interns Challenging Domination

Interns had opportunities to put the library skills and knowledge to use by engaging in research projects of personal significance. At the end of the semester, interns presented their projects as short movies or slide shows to a university audience and described the processes involved in creating them. Interns stated that they learned more about themselves and the dominant forces that shape and impact their lives.

Tina approached this research opportunity to understand more about her own attitudes and behaviors, as well as those of her friend. Tina, who had already developed a specific plan to own and run her own business, actively pondered how her sexual behaviors might impact her professional goals. Her topic, teen pregnancy and sexuality, opened Tina's eyes as well as those of her (at the time) boyfriend. Tina describes this by saying,

I chose [my topic] because one of my friends at the time was having a kid. I was like hmmm....let me do this since I have a boyfriend and I'm sexually active so...let me just do this. It seems interesting, because not a lot of people talk about it ... Like, parents, they won't talk about it. They'll warn you about certain things but they won't really talk about it, you know. Unless it's an issue.

Interviewer: Do you ever talk about it with your friends?

Tina: Yeah, but then sometimes they're like, "You know, I wanna have a kid but not right now…but there were times where I had accidents." And I was just like, "Oh." Because I had an accident one time, but I didn't get pregnant or anything…This is something that could happen to me, so I wanted to get some more information about it.

Tina indicated that her research influenced her own sexual behaviors by stating,

It felt pretty good because I got to learn some information. And I actually took some responsibility on getting on some birth control, even though I'm still using condoms, which is good. So, in a way, it just brightened my eyes. And…my ex-boyfriend was actually there when I did my presentation and it opened his eyes. And he was just like, "…Wow."

From her words, it seems that Tina chose this topic both to better understand the issues that her friend faced with a teenage pregnancy, and to improve the chances that she did not face the same issues as her friend. Tina's research, as well as her own lived experiences, indicated that teenage pregnancy was an issue for many youth in her community and beyond. The phenomenon is exacerbated, from Tina's perspective, by her sense that "parents" or other adults may not talk about these issues with youth until pregnancy occurs, or as she put it when it is "already an issue." This opportunity allowed Tina to actively engage with adults, subverting the systemic lack of communication between youth and adults, to create a transformative space where she and librarians were both better educated about teen pregnancy. With interns' and librarians' raised consciousness around this issue, the library became a vehicle for more strategic youth agency with regard to how their behaviors impact their future. In Tina's case, this was exemplified by a young woman becoming more reflective about her sexual behaviors, which could ultimately empower her to fully realize her future personal and professional goals.

Lucilia's topic also had very personal significance. Lucilia, with her friend Lily helping her, described her research project by saying,

Lucilia: I was [researching] about global warming. If I do a project at school I always do global warming. I don't know…I'm interested in that… Because global warming is happening because of what we're doing like smoking, factories, and things like that.

Lily: She's worried about the world.

Lucilia: I was talking about my country and the United States. I was comparing which country would disappear first if global warming [continues to] occur. And I learned that my country would disappear first...It's a small country. It's not the same. This country is so big. And...people would come from my country to the United States.

In this case, Lucilia describes how her research on global warming led her to understand that if global warming continues, her native island nation of the Dominican Republic may no longer be suitable for human life, thus forcing a mass emigration of Dominicans to the U.S. Lucilia's research led her to understand the differential effects global warming could have on her country of origin and the country in which she currently resides. In listening to her talk about this topic, one could understand Lily's comment that Lucilia is "worried about the world," especially the Dominican Republic. Here, Lucilia describes how her research helped her to learn that unequal political-economic forces have unequal results on different populations. Lucilia clearly recognizes the United States as a political-economic power that is dominant in relation to her native Dominican Republic. And though Lucilia seems to indicate a global "we" (i.e., "global warming is happening because of what we're doing like smoking, factories, and things like that"), it became clear to her that the effects of global warming would have a more adverse impact on the less powerful Dominican population.

Librarians Challenging Domination

The librarians expressed that they too had learned a lot about life and gained respect for the interns throughout the process. Many of the librarians spoke of the enormous respect they had for the resilience interns displayed in spite of the challenges the interns faced in their lives. Scott expressed this by saying,

I guess I also, to some degree, learned [about]...this gap between where she is coming from and where I am coming from. I, of course, know...that anyone who has to rely on the public library in Boston, if it's not the BPL downtown, is gonna be in a tough position. And I, of course, know that there are people who don't have computers or Internet or whatever at home, and who go to high schools that are awful high schools. But, you know, I never actually had interacted with somebody who lived in that situation. And so I was able to put a little more specifics to something I read about in the newspaper. That was beneficial to me, just to know about.

Scott's experience humanized the disparities in access to quality education and libraries he previously had only read about. Meredith felt "incredibly angry" upon hearing about "some of the things that were going on in their schools and realized that they didn't have the support that they needed." In the cases of Scott and Meredith, they gained a deeper understanding of the social and economic forces that impeded access to information and information technology and led to a lack of overall resources and support in their interns' schools. Scott and Meredith's words indicate that in many ways these adults and youth, while living and working in the same city, existed in and navigated through different worlds. Jean appreciated the ways in which the program challenged the forces that create the perception that people from different communities reside in spaces (physical, psychological, or otherwise) that restrict access to outsiders.

> Everyone has a story to tell. But their stories...every one was different. And yet every one of their stories...makes the world a better place to be. When you talk with them and you hear these stories, it breaks down barriers... And I didn't just hear that from a novelist who's been working forever to try and say this. Or some news report. I heard it from, you know, a sixteen year-old who was talking about her own life... This...makes a connection for me with people that I haven't been connected to before.

Jean's words illustrate that librarians' attention to the interns' narratives simultaneously shed light on intern's lived experiences and the connections between the interns' and librarians' lives.

The act of librarians working with and learning from their interns created opportunities for the librarians to understand the hegemonic forces that had an impact on their own and the interns' lives. As noted above, Giles (2002) asserted that critical information literacy should result in the consciousness-raising of both the marginalized group and the group that traditionally served as gatekeepers. The process of empowering the marginalized groups is only facilitated when the gatekeepers have a heightened awareness of the marginalized group's narratives and understanding of the world. It is necessary for librarians to develop a more sophisticated understanding of these forces to better serve youth who do not traditionally engage with libraries.

Conclusion

The implementation of a pedagogy that put the life experiences of Boston high school students at the center of an educational endeavor yielded significant results for the librarians and interns alike. From the librarian perspective, the experience put a human face, voice, and spirit to issues of educational and digital disparities that were to some just something they read about. For the interns, the experience gave them valuable information about how libraries and librarians work, and how to leverage those resources toward the process of conducting academic research. Also, the process gave the interns chances to better understand themselves and their communities which, in turn, gave them opportunities to teach others about their communities, whether local or global.

Even more compelling, the elements of critical pedagogy embedded in the program gave interns the opportunity to investigate the local and global hegemonic forces that impact their lives as urban youth. A major component of investigating and challenging these forces was the agency the interns assumed in forging their own narratives. Ultimately, the intentional process of librarians ceding power and the interns assuming authority created spaces where the interns' lives, loved ones, customs, stories, and boundless spirits were welcomed, thus transforming the library. As Jean put it, in her reflections about what libraries can and should become for these interns and others like them, "[The library] is a place where these interns could find a home. But not just find a home. [It's a place] where they could make a home."

References

The Boston Indicators Project. (2006). Retrieved February 15, 2009 from http://www.tbf.org/IndicatorsProject/Technology/Indicator.aspx?id=3044.

Carnoy, M., Levin, H. M. (1986) Educational reform and class conflict. *Journal of Education, 168*(1), 35-46.

Doherty, J. J. (2007). No Shhing: Giving voice to the silenced: An essay in support of critical information literacy. *Library Philosophy and Practice, 9*(3), 1-8.

Family & Youth Services Bureau, Administration for Children and Families, Department of Health and Human Services. (2001). *Toward a blueprint for youth: Making positive youth development a national priority.*

Freire, P. (1970). *Pedagogy of the oppressed*, New York: Continuum.

Giles, G. (2002). 'Fair Go'? Equality? The people's movement for reconciliation (ANTaR) and critical information literacy. *The Australian Library Journal, 51*(3), 203-216.

MassBLAST. (2008). Retrieved February 15, 2009 from http://www.simmons.edu/MassBLAST/.

McLaren, P. (1989). *Life in schools: An introduction to critical pedagogy in the foundations of education.* New York: Longman.

Morrell, E. (2003). Writing the word and the world: Critical literacy as critical textual production. *Paper presented at Conference on College Composition and Communication*, 1-25.

Morrell, E. (2004). *Becoming critical researchers: Literacy and empowerment for urban youth.* New York: Peter Lang.

Revels, I., & LaFleur, L. J., & Martinez, I. T. (2003). Taking library recruitment a step closer: Recruiting the next generation of librarians. *The Reference Librarian, 39* (82), 157-69.

Stories for Change. (2008). Retrieved March 20, 2008 from http://storiesforchange.net/.

Swanson, T. A. (2004). A radical step: Implementing a critical literacy model. *portal: Libraries and the Academy, 4*(2), 259-273.

Teaching to Change LA. (2004-2005). Retrieved March 20, 2008 from http://tcla.gseis.ucla.edu/voices/1/features/student/videos.html.

Verny, C. (2002). Ohio goes recruiting for minority librarians. *American Libraries. 33*(7), 52-55.

Ward, D. (2006). Revisioning information literacy for lifelong meaning. *Journal of Academic Librarianship, 32*(4), 396-402.

Willis, P. (1981, January 1). Cultural Production Is Different from Cultural Reproduction Is Different from Social Reproduction Is Different from Reproduction. *Interchange on Educational Policy, 12*, 48-67.

Section Four

Unconventional Texts

Posing the Wikipedia "Problem": Information Literacy and the Praxis of Problem-Posing in Library Instruction

Heidi LM Jacobs

"So... is *Wikipedia* a good thing or not? I really need to know." An English Education Student (January 2009)

"The task of knowing is no longer to see the simple. It is to swim in the complex." David Weinberger, *Everything is Miscellaneous* (p. 198, 2007)

"If we remain too long recalcitrant Mr. Everyman will ignore us, shelving our recalcitrant works behind glass doors rarely opened." Carl Becker, "Everyman His Own Historian" (p. 235, 1932)

Introduction

In my job as an Information Literacy Librarian, I am struck by how often I hear "problem" and "*Wikipedia*" in the same sentence: "the problem with *Wikipedia* is..." or "what can we do about the *Wikipedia* problem?" The recurrence of these two words—*Wikipedia* and problem—has led me to consider the two main questions addressed in this article: one, how might *Wikipedia* be considered an information literacy "problem" and two, how might we think about this *Wikipedia* "problem" as an opportunity for developing a problem-posing information literacy praxis. As the *Oxford English Dictionary* reminds us, a problem can either be "a difficult or demanding question" or "a matter or situation regarded as unwelcome, harmful, or wrong and needing to be overcome" (Problem, 2009). This article contrasts what is at stake when we think about *Wikipedia* as an "unwelcome, harmful or wrong" problem to be "fixed" versus what is possible when we consider *Wikipedia* as a difficult or demanding question to be considered. Viewing *Wikipedia* as a difficult information literacy question allows us to consider how knowledge is created, produced, and disseminated, and to interrogate our current understanding of scholarship, scholarly authority, and the academy.

If we approach *Wikipedia* as something "unwelcome, harmful, or wrong and needing to be overcome," we run the risk of turning information literacy education into the kind of banking education that Paulo Freire (2000) cautions against in *Pedagogy of the Oppressed*:

> Education thus becomes an act of depositing, in which the students are the depositories and the teacher is the depositor. Instead of communicating, the teacher issues communiqués and makes deposits which the students patiently receive, memorize, and repeat. This is the 'banking' concept of education, in which the scope of action allowed to the students extends only as far as receiving, filing, and storing the deposits. (p. 72)

In talking with students about *Wikipedia*, it is clear to me that most of them have only been presented with rules about *Wikipedia* rather than open-ended questions. They have been told not to use it in their research and not to cite it in their papers: these are instructions they have patiently received, memorized, and repeated. By insisting that students "bank" a particular perspective on *Wikipedia*, we ask them to be passive consumers of knowledge rather than active participants. In my conversations with students about *Wikipedia*, I see that *Wikipedia* is a topic many of them are excited to talk about and eager to engage with on a range of levels. To forbid *Wikipedia* without discussing it critically and creatively is, I believe, a missed opportunity within our classrooms to foster precisely the kind of critical thinking we demand of our students and a missed opportunity to engage students' thinking about information literacy.

Approaching *Wikipedia* as a difficult or demanding question to be considered more closely aligns information literacy with the kind of problem-posing education Freire (2000) advocates:

> Banking education resists dialogue; problem-posing education regards dialogue as indispensable to the act of cognition which unveils reality. . . Problem-posing education bases itself on dialogue, creativity and stimulates true reflection and action upon reality, thereby responding to the vocation of persons as beings who are authentic only when engaged in inquiry and creative transformation. (p. 81)[1]

---

[1] When we read Freire, it is important to keep in mind what Kate Ronald and Hephzibah Roskelly (2001) observe in their article "Untested Feasibility: Imagining the Pragmatic Possibility of Paolo Freire": "As teachers struggle to connect world and word for ourselves, we need to remember and take heart from Freire's warning: 'To read is to rewrite, not memorize the content of what is being read' (*Critical Consciousness*, 100). Recognizing his popularity among educators in the United States, Freire cautioned: 'It is impossible to export pedagogical practices without reinventing them. Please, tell your fellow Americans not to import me. Ask them to

Freire's summoning of reflection and action reminds us of the importance of praxis—the interplay between theory and practice. As I (Jacobs, 2008) have argued elsewhere, reflective praxis is "vital to information literacy since it simultaneously strives to ground theoretical ideas into practicable activities and use experiential knowledge to rethink and re-envision theoretical concepts" (p. 260). Praxis is vital to the work we do since, as Antonia Darder, Marta Baltodano and Rudolfo D. Torres (2003) have described, "Cut off from practice, theory becomes abstraction or 'simple verbalism.' Separated from theory, practice becomes ungrounded activity or 'blind activism'" (p. 15). Further, as literacy scholar Rebecca Powell (1999) argues, "it is only through conscious reflection and critique, or what cultural theorists refer to as *praxis*, that genuine transformation is able to occur" (p. 4). Thinking about *Wikipedia* in terms of theories and practices allows us to see its potentials for developing a reflective information literacy praxis. This article argues that framing the "*Wikipedia* problem" as a difficult or demanding question is one way of working toward developing an iteration of such a praxis.

Wikipedia, the Miscellaneous and Information Literacy

For almost all of the twentieth century, university teachers could feel confident that students conducting research in their university's library would find information that had been, for the most part, vetted, evaluated, and approved. Before finding its way to library shelves, most resources in a college or university library had been evaluated by a series of trained experts such as peer reviewers, editors, editorial boards, book reviewers, and subject librarians. Since the rise of the Internet, university teachers can no longer assume that their students will be using materials that have already been extensively vetted. Instead, we have what David Weinberger (2007) calls "the miscellaneous." As Weinberger describes, "Authorities have long filtered and organized information for us, protecting us from what isn't worth our time and helping us find what we need to give our beliefs a sturdy foundation. But with the miscellaneous, it's all available to us, unfiltered" (p. 132). At the risk of over-simplifying matters, it seems to me that the unfiltered information universe can be approached in the university curriculum in one of two ways: either instructors and librarians can

---

recreate and rewrite my ideas' (*Politics of Education* xii-xix)" (p. 612). In LIS, it is important that we do not simply import his ideas but rewrite and recreate them.

continue to filter information for students by providing lists, rules, and guidelines related to information use, or they can learn about "the miscellaneous" alongside students and approach it through dialogue and problem-posing. As Freire reminds us, "Banking education treats students as objects of assistance; problem-posing education makes them critical thinkers" (p. 83). When seen through a lens of problem-posing, there are significant connections to be explored between *Wikipedia* and current discussions about critical thinking within information literacy.

Before proceeding, it is important to articulate some of the key concepts I see within current discussions of information literacy. Within the definitional writings on information literacy, I see two recurrent and mutually informing impulses. Both of these, I would argue, can be applied to using *Wikipedia* in the classroom. The first impulse is primarily centripetal and local: it generally focuses inquiries about information inward and is concerned with immediate tasks such as a particular assignment, information source, topic, or course. This first impulse is well-articulated in the Association of College and Research Libraries (ACRL) document from 2000, "Information Literacy Competency Standards for Higher Education." Here information literacy is described as: "a set of abilities requiring individuals to recognize when information is needed and have the ability to locate, evaluate, and use effectively the needed information" (p. 4). The ACRL document goes on to describe how an information literate individual is able to determine the extent of information needed; locate and access needed information; evaluate information and information sources critically; incorporate information into one's knowledge base; use information for a specific purpose; and use information ethically and legally (p. 4-5). In regard to *Wikipedia*, the most crucial outcomes and indicators are found in Standard Three: "The information literate student evaluates information and its sources critically and incorporates selected information into his or her knowledge base and value system" (p. 13). Of the performance indicators listed in this standard, I would argue that the second indicator is most crucial for thinking about *Wikipedia*: "The information literate student articulates and applies initial criteria for evaluating both the information and its sources" (p. 13).[2] In this context, thinking about *Wikipedia* is very much an information literacy concern.

The second impulse I see within information literacy is more centrifugal and global. Here, the focus is on information's outward movement and on how individuals can use information in their multiple locations in the world and, by extension, how information can have an impact on the world and its citizens. This impulse is best articulated in the United Nations Educational, Scientific and Cultural Organization [UNESCO] and International Federation of Library Association's [IFLA] document "The Alexandria Proclamation On Information Literacy And Lifelong Learning" (IFLA, 2005). The democratizing and social justice elements inherent in information literacy are foregrounded:

> Information Literacy lies at the core of lifelong learning. It empowers people in all walks of life to seek, evaluate, use and create information effectively to achieve their personal, social, occupational and educational goals. It is a basic human right in a digital world and promotes social inclusion of all nations. (para. 2)

Combined, the centripetal and centrifugal impulses within information literacy have the potential to help students think carefully, creatively, and critically about scholarly and historical information and how information is produced and reproduced.

Teaching "the *Wikipedia* Problem"

Students are extremely well-versed in the unofficial "rules" of using *Wikipedia* at university. Based on what students have told me, I expect many students follow this sort of usage guideline: use it as a starting place but never, ever cite it your papers.[3] When I ask them why they think their

---

[2] Outcomes of this indicator include: "Examines and compares information from various sources in order to evaluate reliability, validity, accuracy, authority, timeliness, and point of view or bias; analyzes the structure and logic of supporting arguments or methods; recognizes prejudice, deception, or manipulation; recognizes the cultural, physical, or other context within which the information was created and understands the impact of context on interpreting the information." (p. 13)

[3] My teaching in information literacy is primarily in the areas of History and English and thus the examples I provide in this article come from History and English. The arguments made in this article could be applied to other disciplines and modified to better connect with their discipline-specific ways of knowing.

professors do not want them to use *Wikipedia*, they are usually very quick to give these three reasons: *Wikipedia* can be full of errors, anyone can write, edit, or change entries at any time, and it is not a suitable scholarly resource. Students have learned—presumably from those of us who teach them—that *Wikipedia* is a resource that should not be trusted or used. Nevertheless, when I ask students how many of them have consulted *Wikipedia* in the past 24 hours, invariably 85-95% of them raise their hands. Almost always, my hand goes up too, as does that of their professor. When I ask why they use *Wikipedia*, they talk about the ease of access, the speed at which they can get information, the ability to get up-to-date information on just about any topic, and the ability of *Wikipedia* to give them the information they want as well as citations for where else to look. Occasionally a student will note that in contrast to our university's digital resources, which are guarded by password and available only to current faculty, students, and staff, *Wikipedia* is free to anyone with Internet access.

When we talk with students about *Wikipedia*'s place in universities, we are often unequivocal: we should not trust it; it is not scholarly. Indeed, *Wikipedia* has intrinsic limitations: it is an encyclopedia, it aims for a neutral point of view, it does not attempt to break new ground or convey new research, and its quality is uneven. Even *Wikipedia* (2009) says of itself, "We do not expect you to trust us" and admits "while some articles are of the highest quality of scholarship, others are admittedly complete rubbish. We are fully aware of this" (Ten Things).[4] However, as Margaret Conrad (2007) observes, "What is most remarkable about *Wikipedia* [is not] the number of errors in its entries, what is missing from the site, or even the vandalism that mars its reputation, but the sheer volume of reasonably good material that is available in multiple languages and how quickly errors and omissions get spotted" (p. 23). Clearly, within the academic setting *Wikipedia* is a resource that some love to hate and others hate to love.

The debates surrounding *Wikipedia* are both old and new. In many ways, the edicts against using *Wikipedia* in scholarly research are not unlike

---

[4] *Wikipedia* (2009) further notes, "We work hard to keep the ratio of the greatest to the worst as high as possible, of course, and to find helpful ways to tell you in what state an article currently is. Even at its best, *Wikipedia* is an encyclopedia, with all the limitations that entails. It is not a primary source. We ask you not to criticize *Wikipedia* indiscriminately for its content model but to use it with an informed understanding of what it is and what it isn't. Also, because some articles may contain errors, please do not use *Wikipedia* to make critical decisions." (Ten Things)

those that had long been made against reputable print encyclopedias like *Britannica* or *World Book*. The resistance against using these tools was not related to the authority or reputation of the publishers or authors, but instead emerged from the fact that general encyclopedias are general sources of knowledge.[5] More specific kinds of research require more in-depth sources of information with more specialized kinds of knowledge. In talking about the *Wikipedia* "problem," we need to articulate to ourselves and to our students precisely which elements we find problematic. As scholars and students have pointed out, one of the greatest limitations with *Wikipedia* is that it is—above all else—an encyclopedia. In this way it has as the same intrinsic limitations as other encyclopedias, esteemed, reputable, or otherwise. As Roy Rosenzweig (2006) reminds us, "should we blame *Wikipedia* for the appetite for predigested and prepared information or the tendency to believe that anything you read is true? That problem existed back in the days of the family encyclopedia" (p. 137). The most contentious issue (and from my perspective the most interesting) is not that our students are using an encyclopedia but that our students are using a resource that is written, rewritten, and overwritten by unknown writers with unknown credentials. It is only when we articulate what is problematic about *Wikipedia* that we can think critically and creatively about the questions and problems it raises.

When we talk about *Wikipedia* creatively and critically, the binaries begin to fall apart and we begin to see that, as Weinberger (2007) has argued, "The task of knowing is no longer to see the simple. It is to swim in the complex" (p. 198). The more we are able to move discussions of *Wikipedia* away from simplistic rules, the more we and our students will be able to swim in the complex issues *Wikipedia* raises. Thus, rather than having our conversations about *Wikipedia* be about rules or absolutes, I want to argue for our conversations to be question-based and centered around problem-posing. Through this approach, both teachers and students can collaboratively learn much about this "new old" resource and what it offers to our thinking about scholarship, teaching, and learning both today and in the future.

Wikipedia is a comparatively new resource that is continually evolving and one that both teachers and students can watch evolve. In this way,

---

[5] ODLIS (2007) defines an encyclopedia as "A book or numbered set of books containing authoritative summary information about a variety of topics in the form of short essays." (Encyclopedia)

Wikipedia can potentially help us resolve what Freire (2000) called the "teacher-student contradiction":

> Through dialogue, the teacher-of-the-students and the students-of-the-teacher cease to exist and a new term emerges: teacher-student with students-teachers. The teacher is no longer merely the-one-who-teaches, but one who is himself taught in dialogue with the students, who in turn while being taught also teach. They become jointly responsible for a process in which all grow. (pp. 79-80).

Further, as Freire notes, the teacher

> does not regard recognizable objects as his private property, but as the object of reflection by himself and the students. In this way, the problem-posing educator constantly re-forms his reflections in the reflection of the students. The students—no longer docile listeners—are now critical co-investigators in dialogue with the teacher. The teacher presents the material to the students for their consideration, and re-considers her earlier considerations as the students express their own. (pp. 80-81)

Because most of our students have a pre-existing relationship with *Wikipedia* before they enter the classroom, many of them feel more than willing and able to be "critical co-investigators" of the "*Wikipedia* problem." *Wikipedia* thus is a topic replete with opportunities to engage students as active participants within evolving discussions and debates related to information literacy and the production and dissemination of scholarly information and knowledge.

Teaching the Conflicts

When asked what we can do about the *Wikipedia* problem, I almost always summon Gerald Graff (1992) who, in writing about English literary studies, insists that educators need to teach the conflicts. More recently, Graff (2007) has argued that "controversial ideas are not tangential to academic knowledge, but part of that knowledge. That is, controversy is internal to the subjects or disciplines—it is the object of knowledge or is inseparable from it" (p. xv). Such an approach turns "problems" into sites of critical inquiry and reminds us of why thinking carefully and critically about *Wikipedia* is a rich locus for inquiry and engagement.

What intrigues me most about what students say about *Wikipedia* is that once we ask them to question *Wikipedia* as an information source, they are quick to ask these same salient questions of sources long thought reputable and "safe." Many of us have become complacent in our thinking about information sources we have grown accustomed to trust or see as authoritative. However, if we want students to engage in the critical thinking that information literacy demands, we cannot limit our parameters of critical inquiry to sources we distrust, like *Wikipedia*. As Weinberger (2007) daringly notes, "*Wikipedia* and *Britannica* derive their authority from different sources . . . the trust we place in the *Britannica* enables us to be passive knowers . . . *Wikipedia* expects the reader to be actively involved, alert to the signs" (p. 142). Being information literate requires that we be "actively involved, alert to the signs." In this way, teaching the "problems" of *Wikipedia* opens doors of active inquiry that are vital to the development of information literacy and critical thinking skills. *Wikipedia* also demands that we as librarians and professors model these processes when we approach information in our teaching and thinking. When we say "use this scholarly source over *Wikipedia*," have we ourselves undergone the critical analysis of both sources, or are we, too, relying on an inherited and passive trust of a long-respected tool or resource? Telling students not to use *Wikipedia* and to accept our judgments unquestioningly does not model or encourage the kinds of critical thinking we want our students to learn and practice. This is not to say that librarians and professors need to encourage or allow the use of *Wikipedia*. Rather, we need to allow room in our classes and curriculum for critical inquiry into our information sources be they subscription databases, university press monographs, librarian-selected websites or *Wikipedia*.

One way that this critical inquiry could be brought into classes is to have students compare a *Wikipedia* entry with an entry from a reputable scholarly reference work and discuss the differences between the two articles in terms of content, reliability, authority, and accuracy. When I teach a class on reference works for History courses, I bring in a topical *Wikipedia* entry and ask students to discuss and analyze it as a source of information. In the winter of 2008, for example, a first-year History class and I looked at the *Wikipedia* (2009) entry on Benazir Bhutto as a way of exploring *Wikipedia*. We compared the *Wikipedia* entry on Bhutto (who had been assassinated the previous month) with the entry found in the *Oxford Reference Online* (2009). [6] On that day, the information on *Wikipedia* was updated and edited

---

[6] Due to time constraints, I generally project the entries on a screen and we look at them as a class. One could also print off entries or have students find entries of their own to discuss. One could also use this exercise as a short class activity, an in-class group activity, or even develop it to be a larger out-of-class assignment.

numerous times within our class period while the *Oxford Reference Online* entries still listed Bhuttoas living. Students talked about why *Wikipedia* might not be the best source of information for them: contributors might not be experts, entries can be sabotaged, and sources for cited information are not provided. They also came up with instances when *Wikipedia* might actually be a very useful source: *Wikipedia* cannot be beat for its immediacy on current events, and on some topics, scholars may not be the most suitable experts to consult. Further, students noted that when we looked at the *Wikipedia* entry's history, we could see what changes were being made, undone, and redone. Often *Wikipedia* editors posted rationale as to why some changes were made and others overruled.

In class, we contrasted *Wikipedia*'s ability to be corrected, updated, and amended on an almost second-by-second basis with Oxford's (2009) policy: "If you notice an error in an entry, please contact us. We cannot usually correct errors in entries immediately. However, we will load the corrected text the next time we publish an update to the *Oxford Reference Online* website" (Oxford Digital Reference Shelf FAQs, para. 2). Significantly, after interrogating *Wikipedia*'s authority and accuracy so cogently, the students began to apply these same questions to more reputable publishers and resources, including those upon which many of us have grown to comfortably rely. After critiquing the relative anonymity of *Wikipedia*'s contributors and editors, several students noted that it is also not clear who actually wrote and approved the *Oxford Reference Online* entry on Bhutto. Another student pointed out that—no matter how carefully written and edited—there had to be errors in highly reputable reference works like the *Dictionary of National Biography*. How and when, one student asked, do these errors get caught and corrected? Asking critical information literacy questions of *Wikipedia*—a resource most students use and feel comfortable with—opens a door to asking other probing questions about other information sources, be it an Oxford University Press reference work or an open access digital archive. [7] These kinds of questions remind us not to be

---

[7] In 2008, *Encyclopaedia Britannica Online* (Academic Edition) launched a new format. It still has a number of features of the highly reputable print edition (attention drawn to its long-standing authority, a staff of respected and authoritative contributors and editors, and a clearly stated editorial ethos) yet some features of the 2008 edition are decidedly Wikipedian: users can easily link to sections where they may comment on entries, suggest revisions, and notify editors of corrections, typos, or factual errors. Unlike *Wikipedia*, where users may (with some exceptions) go in and directly edit the entries themselves, *Britannica*'s Editorial Mission states: "All

passive consumers of scholarly information and demand that we think critically about all kinds of information resources. Such a shift will help to illustrate to students that the production and dissemination of scholarly information is an active and evolving venture involving numerous decisions and choices, qualities that are often obscured by the fixed appearance of the printed page.

The Lessons of *Wikipedia*

The more we explore the idea of authorship in *Wikipedia*, the more questions we unearth about the production and dissemination of scholarly knowledge. In its inclusion of "history" and "talk" pages, *Wikipedia* shows students a rare "behind the scenes" look at the writing process.[8] Published scholars know first-hand that scholarly writing involves conversations, drafts, revisions, fact-checking, rewrites, editorial suggestions, agreements, and disagreements. When reading traditional print sources, students rarely get the opportunity to see the vital intellectual activities behind the fixed façade of a published piece. Good scholarly writers acknowledge or synthesize disagreements over interpretation or of the validity of source information, but they rarely devote valuable print space to alternative views they do not value. The seemingly limitless space of *Wikipedia* means that disagreements (both friendly and vituperative) over facts, sources, or interpretations can be made available and thus put into dialogue with the

---

comments are welcome; all suggestions will be read and taken seriously; all suggested text changes submitted through this system will be thoroughly evaluated and fact-checked; all approved changes will be published; and all readers using this system will receive a reply from our editorial department" (para. 2). It is not altogether surprising that *Britannica* now offers this interaction with its users since much was made of *Britannica*'s "static" qualities in Giles' article in *Nature* contrasting it and *Wikipedia* published in *Nature* (2005).

[8] Andrew Lih (2009) describes the *Wikipedia* talk pages as "a bulletin and discussion board for each individual page. . . . Talk pages are simply regular wiki pages that anyone can edit, but people quickly adapted them to act like 'threaded' discussion boards where comments and responses were posted to make up full-fledged conversation and debate" (pp. 75-76). The history pages are, as Lih describes, "the running log of all changes to a page. Every change is saved in *Wikipedia*— every addition, deletion or modification. For each page, there is a button that's labeled 'History' that reveals the complete lineage of an article" (p. 92-93).

entry itself. *Wikipedia* is, as Cass R. Sunstein (2006) writes, "in part a deliberative forum, with reason-giving by those who disagree and with deliberative 'places' to accompany disagreement" (p. 152). When looking at the talk pages of various entries, we see living examples of why writing, rewriting, editing, conversations, agreements, and disagreements are all a vital part of the processes whereby scholarly knowledge is created. For example, in the class where we looked at the *Wikipedia* entry on Benazir Bhutto, we scrolled back through the edit history to December 27, 2007, when news of her assassination first broke. Moments after the news was released, we could see the frenzied exchange between editors on whether there had been an assassination or an attempted assassination. Editors debated the merits of news sources and the accuracy of their information. Viewed as a whole, these editorial debates reveal these editors' deep commitment to accuracy and legitimacy of information, and underscores the importance of conversation within the production of scholarly knowledge.

As Weinberger (2007) asserts, "One of the lessons of *Wikipedia* is that conversation improves expertise by exposing weaknesses, introducing new viewpoints, and pushing ideas into accessible form" (p. 145). Nowhere is this lesson better illustrated than in the talk pages of many *Wikipedia* entries. Factual debates do not only happen about details concerning late-breaking news like the assassination of Bhutto, but also surrounding long-standing historical issues and topics. In the talk pages of the Sally Hemings entry[9], there is an energetic debate about the validity of cited sources. One Wikipedian called Moomot (2007) writes, "Has anyone bothered to read the article used for reference 2? This is not a legitimate source. The article is a diatribe that is not published anywhere except on some blog." There are also questions on the Hemings talk page about specific historical sources. Another Wikipedian, Welsh4ever76 (2006), writes, "I changed this entry to five children. Going by Thomas Jefferson's farm books there is not an entry

---

[9] Sally Hemings is an interesting and controversial historical figure. The Sally Hemings entry (2009) in *Wikipedia* offers this overview of her life: Sally Hemings "was an American slave owned by Thomas Jefferson. She is said to have been the half-sister of Jefferson's wife Martha Wayles Skelton Jefferson. Journalists and others alleged during the administration of President Jefferson that he had fathered several children with Hemings after his wife's death. Late 20th century DNA tests indicated that a male in Jefferson's line, likely Thomas Jefferson himself, was the father of at least one of Sally Hemings's children."

for a son born in 1789 or 1790. He only records five children ever being born to Sally Hemings." And elsewhere another Wikipedian, bww1, (nd) asks, "Do you ever wonder why Jeffersonian historians keep changing their minds, what is the real story? What are they dodging? And since they keep changing their story how do they retain any credibility?" These kinds of edits, readings, and comments are what Conrad (2007) calls "academic notions of team research and peer-review . . . carried to extreme levels" (p. 23). Being able to see the kinds of debates and discussions happening behind a *Wikipedia* entry and, indeed, behind pressing historical questions, allows students to see the vibrancy of historical and scholarly inquiry in ways that are often masked by the crisp, type-set pages of scholarly writing published in traditional print formats. *Wikipedia*'s talk pages make visible the often-invisible elements of scholarly debate, discussion, conversation, and exchange. The history and talk pages illustrate what we tell students about scholarly research: scholarly inquiry and the production of scholarly knowledge is iterative, collaborative, communal, and alive. As scholars, we get our bearings through others' cartographies, we chart new courses and others build on our explorations. The wiki model makes visible those long-standing ideals of scholarly communities.

Wikipedia has sparked a paradigm shift in the ways that we think about information resources. Furthermore, the presence of a resource like *Wikipedia* asks us to think critically about the parameters of scholarly knowledge and scholarly resources with an immediate and concrete example, the likes of which we have not quite seen. *Wikipedia* also demands that we consider difficult questions such as whether universities, scholars, and libraries are needed in the age of a resource like *Wikipedia*, when anyone with an internet connection can "be a historian" or access all the information one might need. Of course, librarians could easily enumerate the reasons why libraries are still urgently needed, and scholars could cogently articulate the limitations of *Wikipedia*, and historians could (and do) explain why writing *Wikipedia* entries on historical subjects and being a historian are hardly the same.[10] Although Rosenzweig (2006) notes that a "historical work without owners and with multiple, anonymous authors is. . . almost unimaginable in our professional [academic] culture" (p. 117), *Wikipedia* does ask us to consider what could happen if we apply 2.0 technologies to our own research and scholarly writings. For teaching

---

[10] Conrad (2007), for example, writes "The view that anyone can be a historian nevertheless sits awkwardly with those of us who have spent a decade or more mastering a discipline that has standards for practitioners" (p. 9).

faculty, what might the wiki model offer our scholarship and teaching?
Might a scholarly subject-based wiki be a more useful and flexible option
than a reference work or a textbook? For librarians, *Wikipedia* has shown us
that open access resources might be potentially viable options to the
incredibly expensive and highly restrictive scholarly resources we purchase,
renew, and support. *Wikipedia* also has a number of connections with some
of the core values of librarianship (ALA 2004) such as commitment to
education and life-long learning, the public good, social responsibility and,
most obvious, access to information. As Rosenzweig (2006) has noted,

> *American National Biography Online* may be a significantly better historical
> resource than *Wikipedia* but its impact is much smaller because it is
> available to so few people... The limited audience for subscription-based
> historical resources such as *American National Biography Online* becomes an
> even larger issue when we move outside the borders of the United States
> and especially into poorer parts of the world, where subscription fees pose
> major problems even for libraries. (p. 138)

In these ways, *Wikipedia* raises questions that have long simmered below the
surface for decades about academia, librarianship, the work we do, and the
ways in which we do that work.

Wikipedia's presence and ubiquity demands that we think critically and
creatively about the work we do, how we do it, and how we might do it in
the future. As Rosenzweig also notes,

> a much broader question about academic culture is whether the methods
> and approaches that have proven so successful in *Wikipedia* can also affect
> how scholarly work is produced, shared, and debated. *Wikipedia* embodies
> an optimistic view of community and collaboration that already informs
> the best of the academic enterprise. (p. 143)

"Could we," Rosenzweig goes on to muse, "write a collaborative U.S.
History textbook that would be free to all our students?" (p. 145). Or,

> Should those who write history for a living join such popular history
> makers in writing history in *Wikipedia*? My own tentative answer is yes. If
> *Wikipedia* is becoming the family encyclopedia for the twenty-first century,
> historians probably have a professional obligation to make it as good as
> possible. And if every member of the Organization of American Historians
> devoted just one day to improving entries in his or her areas of expertise, it
> would not only significantly raise the quality of *Wikipedia*, it would also
> enhance popular historical literacy. (p. 140)

In these ways, *Wikipedia* recasts problems that have long lingered in the
peripheries of our professional lives and repositions them in more urgent

and concrete ways. Further, asking our students and our selves to think about scholarly information in broader ways is a tremendous opportunity for critical thinking about our information literacy theories and practices. In short, *Wikipedia* demands that we think creatively, critically, and reflectively about praxis.

Conclusions

Whatever its limitations, it is imperative that we as educators pay attention to *Wikipedia* for a number of reasons. As Rosenzweig (2006) states: "One reason professional historians need to pay attention to *Wikipedia* is because our students do" (p. 136). Whether we like it or not, *Wikipedia* is here to stay. As the quotation from the English Education student at the beginning of this piece reveals, many of our students know they will need to negotiate questions related to *Wikipedia* and other similar resources in their lives outside of school. We are doing them a disservice if we ignore the complexities of *Wikipedia* and sidestep some of the vital objectives cited in the Alexandria Proclamation (IFLA, 2005) in our classrooms. Further, we need to think about the message we send to students when we banish, forbid, or ignore a resource in our classes that is firmly of their generation in favor of promoting resources of previous generations.

Asking specific questions about information sources, the structures behind them, and our assumptions about these information sources is a vital part of information literacy. As *Wikipedia* itself acknowledges, it does have limitations. However, unlike other more fixed resources, *Wikipedia* supplies us with the means to redress the limitations we see in it. Is there an absence of articles on a particular subject? We can write an entry. Is there a factual error? We can correct it. Limited or cursory information in an entry? We can rewrite the entry. Problematic resource for the academy? Invent a better model. Even if we don't use *Wikipedia* itself to redress the limitations of *Wikipedia*, we could, as *Britannica* appears to have done, use the *Wikipedia* model to recreate or revise an existing resource, or, perhaps, we could develop a new resource better suited to our purposes. As Conrad (2007) notes,

> It is our job to make sure that the Internet offers a little more comfort to historians. Ranting against Wikiality or even the likely eventual demise of *Wikipedia*, will not make the issues it raises about knowledge in the twenty-first century go away. (pp. 23-24)

Indeed, as Rosenzweig so cogently asserts, the "problems" associated with *Wikipedia* can be traced back to "the days of the family encyclopedia. And one key solution remains the same: spend more time teaching about the limitations of all information sources, including *Wikipedia*, and emphasizing the skills of critical analysis of primary and secondary sources" (p. 137). Whether or not we agree on *Wikipedia*'s various strengths and limitations is not the pressing issue. As Gerald Graff (2007) reminds us, "The real point we need to agree on is that good education is about helping students enter the culture of ideas and arguments" (p. xvii). In order for students to fully enter the culture of ideas and arguments related to information literacy, we need to provide means for them to become active participants in the debates and offer them opportunities for dialogues about the creation and dissemination of scholarly knowledge.

In thinking of *Wikipedia* (as well as other 2.0 technologies that encourage participation), I am often reminded of Walt Whitman's observation "That the powerful play goes on, and you may contribute a verse" (p. 410). *Wikipedia* is a resource that allows its readers an opportunity to "contribute a verse" to broader scholarly discussions and to participate in discussions that have been until fairly recently the sole purview of scholars and credentialed experts. What is most interesting and important to me about *Wikipedia* is that it foregrounds the importance of participation in relation to the creation of scholarly knowledge and information. Talking about *Wikipedia* in critical ways can help students to see that they can contribute a verse and be active participants rather than passive consumers within scholarly discussions and beyond.

As James Elmborg (2006) has noted, participation, action, and education should be vital parts of information literacy. In his article "The Other Dewey: John Dewey's *Democracy and Education* and Information Literacy," Elmborg notes that at the heart of Dewey's vision for public education is "the democratic citizen, educated for participation in a democratic society. Dewey envisioned these citizens as intellectually and physically engaged in creating a better world through intelligent action, and he imagined an education that could teach students to be such citizens" (p. 2). Could *Wikipedia* be part of that democratic participation? Could working with *Wikipedia* help students become intellectually "engaged in creating a better world through intelligent action"? Whether *Wikipedia* (or other wiki models) could actually achieve all of these things is certainly debatable. The possibilities, however, do exist and are thus worth considering. Talking creatively and critically about *Wikipedia* in our classrooms provides an excellent forum for students and teachers to actively work through a range of issues related to information literacy, education, and scholarly information.

Approaching the "problems" of *Wikipedia* as a series of difficult or demanding questions is an opportunity for us to develop a problem-posing information literacy praxis and for students to enter and participate in the larger culture of ideas and arguments related to information in the twenty first century. Just as bell hooks (1994) has noted, "Theory is not inherently healing, liberating or revolutionary. It fulfills this function only when we ask that it do so and direct our theorizing towards this end" (p. 61). *Wikipedia* is not healing, liberating or revolutionary unless we ask of it the questions that might make it so.

References

American Library Association (ALA). (2004) *Core Values of Librarianship*. Retrieved April 20, 2009 from ALA website http://www.ala.org/ala/aboutala/offices/oif/statementspols/coreva luesstatement/corevalues.cfm.

Association of College and Research Libraries. (2000). *Information literacy competency standards for higher education*. Retrieved February 10, 2009 from American Library Association Web site: http://www.ala.org/ala/mgrps/divs/acrl/standards/standards.pdf

Becker, C. (1932). Everyman his own historian. *American Historical Review*, 37(2), 221-236.

Benazir Bhutto. (2007, February 9). In *Wikipedia, the free encyclopedia*. Retrieved February 10, 2009, from http://en.wikipedia.org/wiki/ Benazir_Bhutto

bww1. (no date). Number of Children. Talk: Sally Hemings. In *Wikipedia, the free encyclopedia*. Retrieved February 10, 2008, from http://en.wikipedia.org/wiki/Talk:Sally_Hemings

Conrad, M. (2007). Public history and its discontents or history in the age of *Wikipedia*. *Journal of the Canadian Historical Association/ Revue de la Société historique du Canada*, 18(1), 1-26.

Darder, A., Baltodano, M., & Torres, R.D. (2003). Critical Pedagogy: An Introduction. In A. Darder, M. Baltodano, & R.D. Torres (Eds.) *The Critical Pedagogy Reader* (pp. 1-23) New York and London: Routledge.

Editorial Mission. (2009). *Encyclopaedia Britannica*. Retrieved February 12, 2009 from http://corporate.britannica.com/editorialmission.html

Elmborg. J. (2006). The other Dewey: John Dewey's *Democracy and Education* and information literacy. In C. Gibson (Ed.) *Student engagement and information literacy.* Chicago: Association of College and Research Libraries.

Encyclopedia. (2007, November 19). In Online Dictionary for Library and Information Science (ODLIS). Retrieved February 3, 2009, from http://lu.com/odlis/index.cfm

Freire, P. (2000) *Pedagogy of the oppressed* (D. Macedo, Trans.) New York: Continuum. (Original work published 1970).

Giles, J. (2005). Internet encyclopedias go head to head. *Nature, 438,* 900-901.

Graff, G. (1992). *Beyond the culture wars: How teaching the controversies can revitalize American education.* New York: W.W. Norton.

Graff, G. (2007). *Professing literature: An institutional history.* Chicago: Chicago University Press. (Original work published 1987)

hooks, b. (1994). *Teaching to transgress: education as the practice of freedom.* New York and London: Routledge.

International Federation of Library Associations (IFLA). (2005). *The Alexandria proclamation on information literacy and lifelong learning.* Retrieved February 10, 2009 from IFLA website http://www.ifla.org/III/wsis/BeaconInfSoc.html.

Jacobs, H. L. M. (2008). Information literacy and reflective pedagogical praxis. *Journal of Academic Librarianship, 34,* 256-262.

Lih, A. (2009). *Wikipedia Revolution: How a bunch of nobodies created the world's greatest encyclopedia.* New York: Hyperion.

Moomot. (2007, 3 January) Sources. Talk: Sally Hemings. In *Wikipedia, the free encyclopedia.* Retrieved February 10, 2009, from http://en.wikipedia.org/wiki/Talk:Sally_Hemings

Oxford Digital Reference Shelf FAQs. In *Oxford Reference Online.* Retrieved February 3, 2009 from http://www.oxfordreference.com./pages/ODRS_faq#c002

Powell, Rebecca (1999). *Literacy as a moral imperative: facing the challenges of a pluralistic society.* Lanham, MD: Rowman and Littlefield.

Problem. (2009). *Oxford English Dictionary.* Retrieved February 10, 2009 from http://dictionary.oed.com/cgi/entry/50189071

Ronald, K. & Roskelly, H. (2001). "Untested feasibility: imagining the pragmatic possibility of Paulo Freire." *College English.* 65, 612-632.

Rosenzweig, R. (2006). Can history be open source? Wikipedia and the future of the past. *Journal of American History, 93,* 117-146.

Sally Hemings. (2009, February 3). In *Wikipedia, the free encyclopedia*. Retrieved February 10, 2008, from http://en.wikipedia.org/wiki/Sally_Hemings

Stephen, L., & Lee, S. (Eds.) (1937-1939). *Dictionary of national biography*. London: Oxford University Press.

Sunstein, C. (2006). *Infotopia: How many minds produce knowledge*. New York: Oxford University Press.

Talk: Sally Hemings. (2009, February 3). In *Wikipedia, the free encyclopedia*. Retrieved February 10, 2009, from http://en.wikipedia.org/wiki/Sally_Hemings

Ten things you may not know about Wikipedia. (2001, February 1). In *Wikipedia, the free encyclopedia*. Retrieved February 3, 2009, from http://en.wikipedia.org/wiki/Wikipedia:Ten_things_you_may_not_know_about_Wikipedia#We_do_not_expect_you_to_trust_us

Weinberger, D. (2007). *Everything is miscellaneous: The power of the new digital disorder*. New York: Times Books.

Welsh4Ever76. (2006, 19 August). Number of Children. Talk: Sally Hemings. In *Wikipedia, the free encyclopedia*. Retrieved February 10, 2009, from http://en.wikipedia.org/wiki/Talk:Sally_Hemings

Whitman,W. (1982), "O Me! O Life!" In J. Kaplan (Ed.), *Walt Whitman: complete poetry and collected prose*. (p. 410). New York, NY: Library of America. (Original work published 1871)

Wikipedia. (2009). *Wikipedia main page*. Retrieved February 10, 2009 from http://en.wikipedia.org/wiki/Main_Page

Out of the margins...

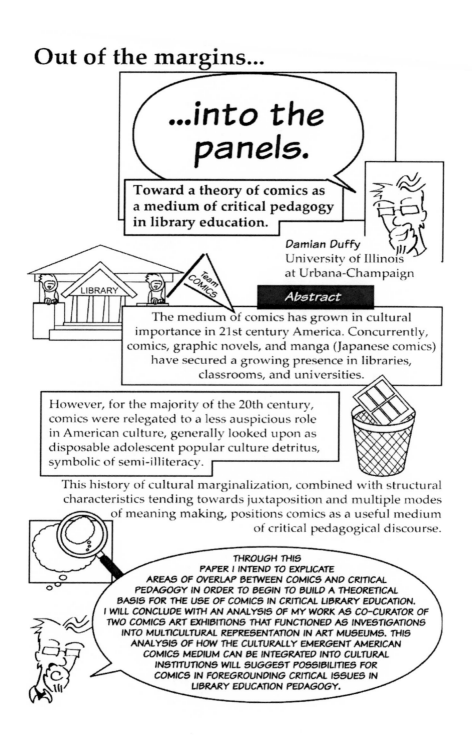

...into the panels.

Toward a theory of comics as a medium of critical pedagogy in library education.

Damian Duffy
University of Illinois at Urbana-Champaign

LIBRARY

Team COMICS

Abstract

The medium of comics has grown in cultural importance in 21st century America. Concurrently, comics, graphic novels, and manga (Japanese comics) have secured a growing presence in libraries, classrooms, and universities.

However, for the majority of the 20th century, comics were relegated to a less auspicious role in American culture, generally looked upon as disposable adolescent popular culture detritus, symbolic of semi-illiteracy.

This history of cultural marginalization, combined with structural characteristics tending towards juxtaposition and multiple modes of meaning making, positions comics as a useful medium of critical pedagogical discourse.

THROUGH THIS PAPER I INTEND TO EXPLICATE AREAS OF OVERLAP BETWEEN COMICS AND CRITICAL PEDAGOGY IN ORDER TO BEGIN TO BUILD A THEORETICAL BASIS FOR THE USE OF COMICS IN CRITICAL LIBRARY EDUCATION. I WILL CONCLUDE WITH AN ANALYSIS OF MY WORK AS CO-CURATOR OF TWO COMICS ART EXHIBITIONS THAT FUNCTIONED AS INVESTIGATIONS INTO MULTICULTURAL REPRESENTATION IN ART MUSEUMS. THIS ANALYSIS OF HOW THE CULTURALLY EMERGENT AMERICAN COMICS MEDIUM CAN BE INTEGRATED INTO CULTURAL INSTITUTIONS WILL SUGGEST POSSIBILITIES FOR COMICS IN FOREGROUNDING CRITICAL ISSUES IN LIBRARY EDUCATION PEDAGOGY.

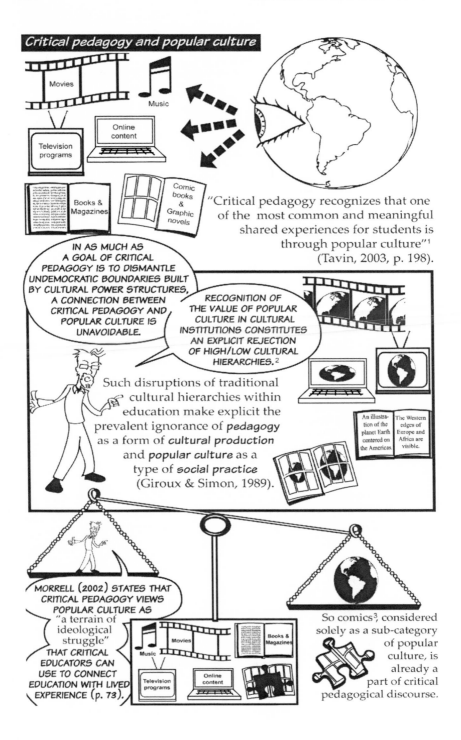

There are also *socio-political overlaps*. For example, a number of comics artists in the 1940s and 50s (e.g. Bernard Krigstein, Harvey Kurtzman, Will Elder, Gene Deitch) were politically affiliated with, and/or produced work which took part in, Leftist, often radical critique of American society (Buhle, 2007).

The functions of comics in contemporary socio-political critical discourse can be observed in multiple forms of comics, from editorial cartoons to comic books to graphic novels...

YOU'RE NOT FIGHTING A WOMAN NOW!

...e.g. early Superman[5] comic books embodied New Deal socially progressive views on issues like war profiteering and domestic violence (Daniels, 1995).

"The underground press comi[x]... of the 1960s and 1970s, which came into being partly to defy the restrictions of the Comics Code Authority...

IS NUCLEAR POWER THE ANSWER?

KID, I'D BET YOUR *LIFE* ON IT!

6

"...ironically failed to escape the basically political nature of American comic art"(Inge, 1990, p. xiv).

THE USE OF COMICS TO COMMUNICATE A SOCIO-POLITICAL PHILOSOPHY OF SOCIALLY TRANSFORMATIVE CRITIQUE ISN'T THE ONLY POINT OF SIMILARITY BETWEEN CRITICAL PEDAGOGY AND THE COMICS MEDIUM.

"In the dominant discourse, pedagogy is simply... methodology used to transmit course content... an afterthought reduced to the status of the technical and the instrumental. In a similar mode... popular culture is still largely defined in the dominant discourse as... the trivial and the insignificant of everyday life" (Giroux & Simon, 1989, p. 221).

PEDAGOGY AND POPULAR CULTURE ARE CONNECTED IN THAT BOTH ARE WIDELY VIEWED AS MARGINAL BY DOMINANT INTELLECTUAL CULTURES.

Comics as a marginalized medium

COMICS IN AMERICA WERE MARGINALIZED TO A UNIQUE EXTENT BY AN ANTI-COMIC BOOK MOVEMENT THAT ACHIEVED ITS PEAK IN THE EARLY 1950s WITH A PUBLIC OUTCRY OVER CRIME AND HORROR COMICS AS A CAUSE OF JUVENILE DELIQUENCY (see, e.g. NYBERG, 1998; HADJU, 2008).

The post-World War II American *anti-comic book movement* was popularized by child psychiatrist Dr. Frederic Wertham.

GENRE 10¢

DiversitySTUNTED

Jolting CENSORSHIP in the U.S. tradition!

Among other accusations, Wertham asserted that comic books constituted a public health problem akin to racial segregation (Beaty, 2005).

*There were public comic book burnings during this period (see, e.g. Zorbaugh, 1949; Haig. 1988).

Wertham published a number of articles and a best selling book, gave public speeches, and testified before both state and U.S. Senate hearings on comics, fanning the sometimes literal* flames of American anti-comics sentiment.

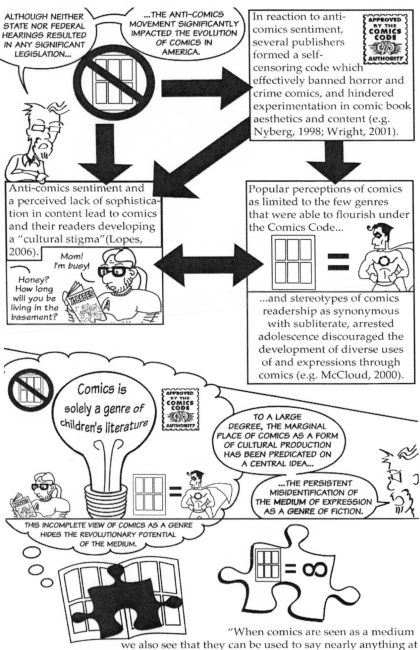

"When comics are seen as a medium we also see that they can be used to say nearly anything at all and that freedom can be disturbing or even threatening to those who are used to thinking of comics as essentially formulaic and juvenile" (Witek, 1992, p. 76).

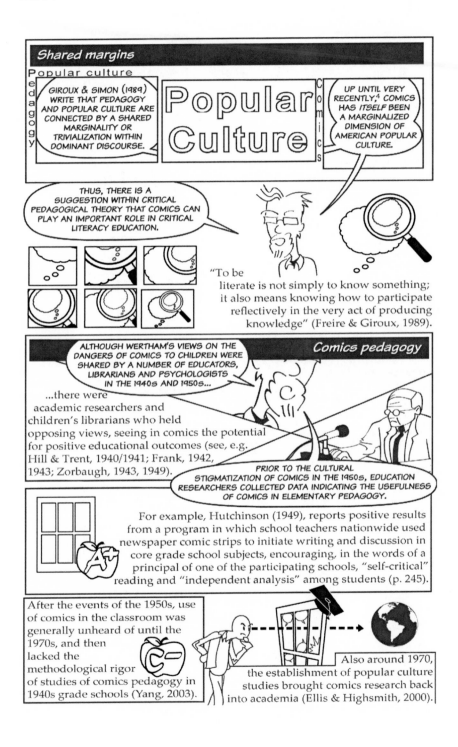

Shared margins

Popular culture

GIROUX & SIMON (1989) WRITE THAT PEDAGOGY AND POPULAR CULTURE ARE CONNECTED BY A SHARED MARGINALITY OR TRIVIALIZATION WITHIN DOMINANT DISCOURSE.

Popular Culture

UP UNTIL VERY RECENTLY,[4] COMICS HAS *ITSELF* BEEN A MARGINALIZED DIMENSION OF AMERICAN POPULAR CULTURE.

THUS, THERE IS A SUGGESTION WITHIN CRITICAL PEDAGOGICAL THEORY THAT COMICS CAN PLAY AN IMPORTANT ROLE IN CRITICAL LITERACY EDUCATION.

"To be literate is not simply to know something; it also means knowing how to participate reflectively in the very act of producing knowledge" (Freire & Giroux, 1989).

Comics pedagogy

ALTHOUGH WERTHAM'S VIEWS ON THE DANGERS OF COMICS TO CHILDREN WERE SHARED BY A NUMBER OF EDUCATORS, LIBRARIANS AND PSYCHOLOGISTS IN THE 1940s AND 1950s...

...there were academic researchers and children's librarians who held opposing views, seeing in comics the potential for positive educational outcomes (see, e.g. Hill & Trent, 1940/1941; Frank, 1942, 1943; Zorbaugh, 1943, 1949).

PRIOR TO THE CULTURAL STIGMATIZATION OF COMICS IN THE 1950s, EDUCATION RESEARCHERS COLLECTED DATA INDICATING THE USEFULNESS OF COMICS IN ELEMENTARY PEDAGOGY.

For example, Hutchinson (1949), reports positive results from a program in which school teachers nationwide used newspaper comic strips to initiate writing and discussion in core grade school subjects, encouraging, in the words of a principal of one of the participating schools, "self-critical" reading and "independent analysis" among students (p. 245).

After the events of the 1950s, use of comics in the classroom was generally unheard of until the 1970s, and then lacked the methodological rigor of studies of comics pedagogy in 1940s grade schools (Yang, 2003).

Also around 1970, the establishment of popular culture studies brought comics research back into academia (Ellis & Highsmith, 2000).

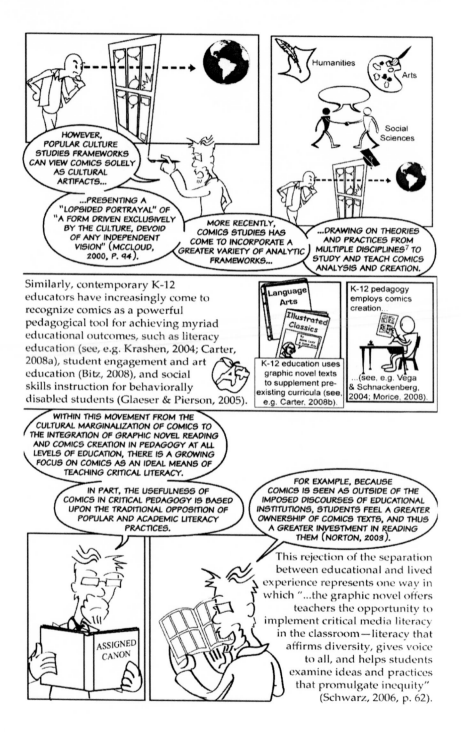

HOWEVER, POPULAR CULTURE STUDIES FRAMEWORKS CAN VIEW COMICS SOLELY AS CULTURAL ARTIFACTS...

...PRESENTING A "LOPSIDED PORTRAYAL" OF "A FORM DRIVEN EXCLUSIVELY BY THE CULTURE, DEVOID OF ANY INDEPENDENT VISION" (MCCLOUD, 2000, P. 94).

MORE RECENTLY, COMICS STUDIES HAS COME TO INCORPORATE A GREATER VARIETY OF ANALYTIC FRAMEWORKS...

...DRAWING ON THEORIES AND PRACTICES FROM MULTIPLE DISCIPLINES[7] TO STUDY AND TEACH COMICS ANALYSIS AND CREATION.

Humanities

Arts

Social Sciences

Similarly, contemporary K-12 educators have increasingly come to recognize comics as a powerful pedagogical tool for achieving myriad educational outcomes, such as literacy education (see, e.g. Krashen, 2004; Carter, 2008a), student engagement and art education (Bitz, 2008), and social skills instruction for behaviorally disabled students (Glaeser & Pierson, 2005).

Language Arts

Illustrated Classics

K-12 education uses graphic novel texts to supplement pre-existing curricula (see, e.g. Carter, 2008b).

K-12 pedagogy employs comics creation...

...(see, e.g. Vega & Schnackenberg, 2004; Morice, 2008).

WITHIN THIS MOVEMENT FROM THE CULTURAL MARGINALIZATION OF COMICS TO THE INTEGRATION OF GRAPHIC NOVEL READING AND COMICS CREATION IN PEDAGOGY AT ALL LEVELS OF EDUCATION, THERE IS A GROWING FOCUS ON COMICS AS AN IDEAL MEANS OF TEACHING CRITICAL LITERACY.

IN PART, THE USEFULNESS OF COMICS IN CRITICAL PEDAGOGY IS BASED UPON THE TRADITIONAL OPPOSITION OF POPULAR AND ACADEMIC LITERACY PRACTICES.

FOR EXAMPLE, BECAUSE COMICS IS SEEN AS OUTSIDE OF THE IMPOSED DISCOURSES OF EDUCATIONAL INSTITUTIONS, STUDENTS FEEL A GREATER OWNERSHIP OF COMICS TEXTS, AND THUS A GREATER INVESTMENT IN READING THEM (NORTON, 2003).

This rejection of the separation between educational and lived experience represents one way in which "...the graphic novel offers teachers the opportunity to implement critical media literacy in the classroom—literacy that affirms diversity, gives voice to all, and helps students examine ideas and practices that promulgate inequity" (Schwarz, 2006, p. 62).

ASSIGNED CANON

Of course, comics should not be taken into the classroom uncritically, but rather educators should "consider how comics can be incorporated into a curriculum that remains centrally concerned with learning, meaning making, and human possibility" (Norton, 2003, p. 146).

BERNSTEIN (2008) PROVIDES ONE EXAMPLE OF THE INCORPORATION OF COMICS INTO A CRITICAL CURRICULUM BY DESCRIBING HER USE OF THE GRAPHIC MEMOIR *PERSEPOLIS 2: THE STORY OF A RETURN* BY MARJANE SATRAPI IN A BASIC READING AND WRITING COURSE SHE TAUGHT AT THE UNIVERSITY OF CINCINNATI.

WITHIN THE CONTEXT OF A REMEDIAL WRITING COURSE IN WHICH THE INSTRUCTOR TREATED THE FIRST-YEAR STUDENTS AS SHE WOULD GRADUATE STUDENTS BY INVOLVING THEM AS PARTICIPANTS IN CURRICULUM DESIGN, BERNSTEIN FOUND THAT THE YOUNG WOMEN IN THE COURSE WERE ABLE TO RELATE MARJANE'S IDENTITY ISSUES AS AN IRANIAN WOMAN IN EUROPE WITH THEIR OWN PERSONAL EXPERIENCES IN LOW ECONOMIC MIDWESTERN URBAN SETTINGS.

Image based on the cover of *Persepolis 2*, with apologies to Marjane Satrapi.

IN PART, THE STUDENTS' RELATION OF PERSONAL LIFE EXPERIENCES WITH SATRAPI'S AUTOBIOGRAPHICAL TALE OF GROWING INTO ADULTHOOD IN EUROPE AND EVENTUALLY RETURNING TO IRAN CAN BE ATTRIBUTED TO THE *narrative content* OF THE GRAPHIC NOVEL.

FOR EXAMPLE, BERNSTEIN NOTES THAT, IN RESPONSE PAPERS, HER STUDENTS CONNECTED THEIR OWN FEELINGS OF ISOLATION IN THE NEW AND UNFAMILIAR COLLEGE SETTING WITH THE BOOK'S PORTRAYAL OF MARJANE'S DIFFICULT NEGOTIATIONS OF CULTURAL IDENTITY IN AN UNFAMILIAR COUNTRY AND CULTURE.

BERNSTEIN ALSO ASSERTS THAT THE *formal characteristics* OF COMICS—

—CONTRIBUTE TO STUDENTS' CRITICAL REFLECTIVE STANCE TO THE WORK.

BERNSTEIN WRITES OF READING COMICS AS AN "UNSTABLE PROCESS," OWING TO THE "CONTINUAL TRANSITIONS" OF MEANING CREATED BY THE MEDIUM'S VISUAL/TEXTUAL HYBRIDITY.

ONE EXAMPLE OF THIS UNSTABLE MEANING CAN BE FOUND IN THE PREVIOUS PANEL, IN WHICH I REAPPROPRIATE THE FRAMING DESIGN FROM THE COVER OF PERSEPOLIS 2 FOR USE AS A VISUAL SYMBOL OF THE FORMAL ASPECTS OF GRAPHIC NOVELS IN GENERAL.

formal characteristics

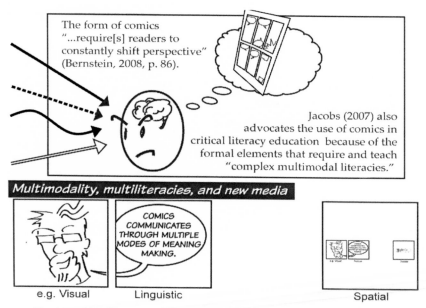

The form of comics "...require[s] readers to constantly shift perspective" (Bernstein, 2008, p. 86).

Jacobs (2007) also advocates the use of comics in critical literacy education because of the formal elements that require and teach "complex multimodal literacies."

Multimodality, multiliteracies, and new media

COMICS COMMUNICATES THROUGH MULTIPLE MODES OF MEANING MAKING.

e.g. Visual   Linguistic   Spatial

The New London Group (2000) describes a typology of five modes of meaning making that can be combined through multimodal design: *Linguistic design* (e.g. vocabulary, metaphor); *Audio design* (e.g. music, sound effects); *Spatial design* (e.g. elements creating geographic and architectonic meaning); *Gestural design* (e.g. bodily physicality, feelings and affect); and *Visual design* (e.g. color, background).

AND, IN FACT, COMICS CAN MAKE USE OF ALL FIVE OF THESE MODES OF MEANING.

Visual, Gestural[8]   Linguistic   Audio[8]   Spatial

Concepts of *multimodality*, and the ability to critically engage multimodal texts (*multiliteracies*) are often linked with *new media*, a term generally related to emergent information communication technologies (see, e.g. Kress, 2003; Selber, 2004).

"They [new media] make it easy to use a multiplicity of modes, and in particular the mode of image... as well as other modes, such as... sound effect ..." (Kress, 2003, p. 5).

SUCH SIMILARITIES PLACE COMICS AND NEW MEDIA IN DIALOGUE (*see, e.g.* GARDNER, 2006; DUFFY, 2009a).

New media hastens an increase in multimodal discourse that is by definition *socially transformative* because it causes "...deep changes in the forms and functions of writing" that can alter ways of thinking and structures of social power (Kress, 2003). Multimodal attributes of comics hold similar potentials.

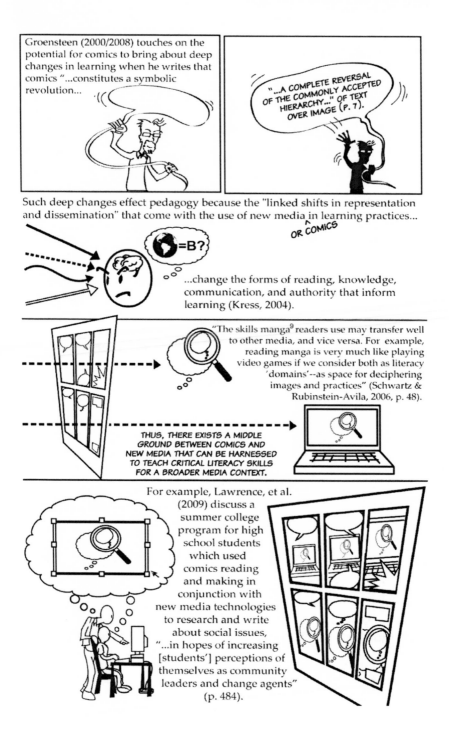

Groensteen (2000/2008) touches on the potential for comics to bring about deep changes in learning when he writes that comics "...constitutes a symbolic revolution...

"...A COMPLETE REVERSAL OF THE COMMONLY ACCEPTED HIERARCHY..." OF TEXT OVER IMAGE (P. 7).

Such deep changes effect pedagogy because the "linked shifts in representation and dissemination" that come with the use of new media in learning practices...
OR COMICS

=B?

...change the forms of reading, knowledge, communication, and authority that inform learning (Kress, 2004).

"The skills manga[9] readers use may transfer well to other media, and vice versa. For example, reading manga is very much like playing video games if we consider both as literacy 'domains'--as space for deciphering images and practices" (Schwartz & Rubinstein-Avila, 2006, p. 48).

THUS, THERE EXISTS A MIDDLE GROUND BETWEEN COMICS AND NEW MEDIA THAT CAN BE HARNESSED TO TEACH CRITICAL LITERACY SKILLS FOR A BROADER MEDIA CONTEXT.

For example, Lawrence, et al. (2009) discuss a summer college program for high school students which used comics reading and making in conjunction with new media technologies to research and write about social issues, "...in hopes of increasing [students'] perceptions of themselves as community leaders and change agents" (p. 484).

Lawrence, et al. (2009) had students read and respond to graphic novels, research social issues online, create projects in nontraditional formats, including poems written in Power Point slides, and comics made with a basic comics creation software program called Comic Life (http://plasq.com).

THE SUMMER PROGRAM TAUGHT BY LAWRENCE, ET AL. PROVIDES AN EXAMPLE OF WHAT RICE (2007) CALLS hip-hop pedagogy, A PEDAGOGY CENTERED AROUND WRITING THAT "PERFORMS" JUXTAPOSITIONS, RATHER THAN ENGAGING SOLELY IN ANALYSIS OF THE JUXTAPOSITIONS OF PREEXISTING TEXTS (p. 91).

By invoking hip-hop Rice seeks to shift the focus of critical composition and pedagogy into a philosophy of multimodal sampling and remixing found in popular culture in order to perform communicative acts created through juxtapositions.

I AM ARGUING FOR A SIMILAR USE OF COMICS IN CRITICAL PEDAGOGY; A CRITICAL PEDAGOGICAL PHILOSOPHY INFORMED BY THE SYSTEMS OF MULTI-MODAL JUXTAPOSITIONAL MEANING MAKING IN THE COMICS MEDIUM.

FOR MCCLOUD (1993) THE DEFINING CHARACTERISTIC OF COMICS IS THE juxtaposition OF IMAGES IN SEQUENCE.

THE HISTORY OF THE MARGINALIZATION OF COMICS IN THE U.S. MAKES THE MEDIUM ALSO CAPABLE OF PERFORMING CRITICAL CULTURAL JUXTAPOSITIONS THROUGH NEW FORMAL USES.

FOR INSTANCE, SMITH (2007) SUGGESTS THAT THE USE OF COMICS IN SCHOLARLY WRITING SUCH AS THE ONE YOU'RE READING CONFRONT READERS' PERCEPTIONS OF THE MEDIUM BY SUBVERTING EXPECTATIONS OF COMICS AS JUVENILIA OR POPULAR CULTURE.

THE INCLUSION OF COMICS IN CULTURAL INSTITUTIONS LIKE MUSEUMS AND LIBRARIES PROVOKE A SIMILAR INTERROGATION OF CULTURAL BOUNDARIES.

LIBRARY

MUSEUM OF THE ARTS

image adapted from p. 37, panel 3 of Smith (2007), another scholarly essay-in-comics-form.

However, Robins (2005) states that by recontextualizing museum art *into* communicative "stories of art," by focusing on how *curators' choices* and the *juxtapositions* created by display make *narrative meaning*, museums can elicit greater engagement from art and design students and teachers.

2 illustrations above and below based on photos of C. Hill's gallery comic *Blind Date* (2006).

C. Hill (2007) describes gallery comics as "…the intentional gathering of such a preponderance of comic art elements in 'made-for-the-wall' art so that audiences instantly sensed the kinship …to traditional comics" (p. 9).

In this approach, the walls of the gallery are considered "pages," while each individual art work is thought of as a single "panel" in the overall "comic" of the exhibition.[10]

The works are hung closer together than is traditional for museum installations so the pieces are displayed with the same spatial density as panels on a page.

THE RESULTING EXHIBITION DESIGN ENCOURAGES VIEWERS TO CONSIDER JUXTAPOSITIONS BETWEEN PIECES IN MUCH THE SAME WAY JUXTAPOSITIONS OF PANELS ARE READ WITHIN EACH INDIVIDUAL PIECE.

THUS, EACH PIECE IS CONSIDERED NOT JUST AS A SINGULAR ARTWORK, BUT ALSO AS AN ELEMENT CONTRIBUTING TO THE NARRATIVE MEANING OF THE EXHIBITION AS A WHOLE.

This narrative exhibition design was used not only because it *parallels* ways in which *comics* makes meaning...

...but also because it works well to *address* the critical pedagogical advocacy for *diversity* on which the exhibitions were based.

OUT =SEQ ≡NCE

The narrative of *Other Heroes* juxtaposes a *celebration* of the contributions of African-American comics creators with art that *interrogates* the concept of racial representation.

By integrating the juxtapositional nature of comics design into the unifying theme of the exhibition and presenting a *discourse on race,* as opposed to a collection of art circumscribed solely by demographic labels, we were able to avoid a curotorial philosophy wherein "... newly authorized voices are likely to continue to be marginalized, viewed as representative of particular identities rather than of the universal merit on which... canons are believed to be founded" (Detels, 1998, p. 44).

Other Heroes exhibition included, e.g. positive images of African-American heroes from small press comic books...

...juxtaposed with photographs interrogating similarities between comic book superhero masks and racial identity issues...

...juxtaposed with comic strips that explicity discuss racial politics.

(Th)ink

BEFORE SEPT. 11TH

TAXI!!

THIEF!! MURDERER!!

OFF DUTY!! OFF DUTY!!

AFTER SEPT. 11TH

TAXI

NEED A TAXI?! NEED A TAXI?!!

YIPE!! NO THANKS!!

TERRORIST!! MURDERER!!

WHAT A DIFFERENCE A DAY MAKES

Our comics narrative approach to curatorial design yielded an exhibition with a critical pedagogical foundation; we avoided marginalizing

Images[11] based on (clockwise) Jaycen Wise Cover by Mshindo Kuumba I, Daymask Revealed by LaTriece V. Branson, and (Th)ink: What a Difference a Day Makes by Keith Knight.

Original images (c) 2007 their respective creators. Jaycen Wise (c) 2009 Uraeus.

ALSO, ALTHOUGH HONORING AFRICAN-AMERICAN CONTRIBUTIONS WAS A PART OF THE EXHIBITION, SOME OF THE WORKS THAT CRITIQUED RACIAL INEQUALITIES WE INCLUDED WERE CREATED BY BY ARTISTS OF MULTIPLE ETHNIC BACKGROUNDS, PRESENTING A UNDERLYING NARRATIVE OF ACTUAL DIVERSITY.

artists by simultaneously asking how the margins are set in the first place.

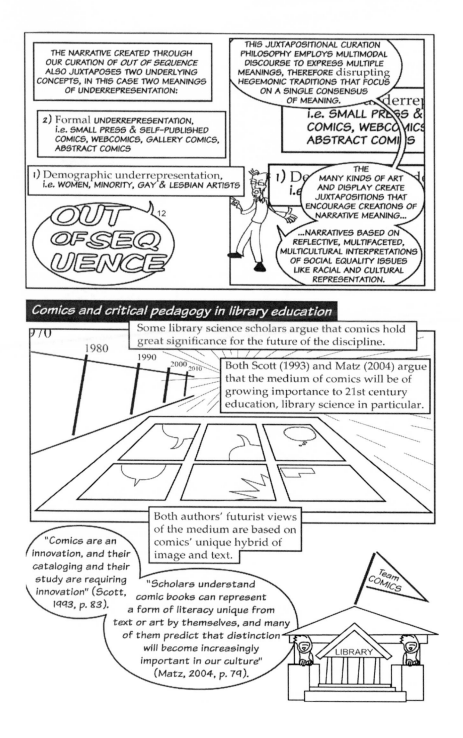

IN THE LAST DECADE, THE GRAPHIC NOVEL AND MANGA FORMATS OF COMICS HAVE BECOME A MAJOR AREA OF COLLECTION DEVELOPMENT IN PUBLIC AND ACADEMIC LIBRARIES, AND PARTICULARLY AS A COMPONENT OF YOUTH MEDIA SERVICES (see, e.g. GORMAN, 2003; GOLDSMITH, 2005).

BUT, DESPITE THIS INFLUX OF LIBRARY INTEREST IN GRAPHIC NOVELS AND MANGA, THERE ARE STILL LINGERING CULTURAL LIMITATIONS PLACED ON THE MEDIUM WITHIN BROADER LIBRARY CONTEXTS. FOR EXAMPLE, THE BENEFITS OF THE HYBRIDIZATION OF IMAGE AND TEXT IN TEACHING LITERACY TO RELUCTANT YOUNG READERS ARE SOMETIMES MISTAKENLY VIEWED BY LIBRARIANS AS THE ONLY USE OF COMICS (BRENNER, 2006).

IRIZARRY & ROBERTS (2007) TAKE ISSUE WITH A LIMITATION PLACED ON COMICS IN ACADEMIC LIBRARIES VIA THE CONCEPTION OF GRAPHIC NOVELS AS SOLELY LEISURE READING...

Image based on photo of display poster retrieved July 8, 2009 from http://www.flickr.com/photos/9037385@N05/706499401/in/photostream

...UNDERLINING THEIR POINT THROUGH A CRITIQUE OF A GRAPHIC NOVEL DISPLAY IN A STATE UNIVERSITY LIBRARY.

"It [the display] implies that comics are nothing more than disposable beach reads, to be savored in the summer and in between classes. It completely ignores the comic book's place as a scholarly resource" (Irizarry & Roberts, 2007).

THE APPLICATION OF A COMICS NARRATIVE DESIGN PHILOSOPHY TO LIBRARY DISPLAYS PRESENTS ONE AREA OF LIBRARY INSTRUCTION WHICH COULD USE THE MEDIUM TO FURTHER CRITICAL PEDAGOGICAL GOALS.

LIBRARIES GENERALLY SHELVE WORKS DONE IN COMICS FORM TOGETHER. LARGER COLLECTIONS WILL BE SEPARATED BASED ON THE AGE OF THE INTENDED AUDIENCE, BUT BEYOND AGE APPROPRIATENESS, DIFFERENCES IN SUBJECT AND GENRE ARE GENERALLY IGNORED (SEE, E.G. N.C.A.C ET AL., 2006; HOGAN, 2009). THIS IS LARGELY A PRAGMATIC MEANS OF ENSURING GREATER CIRCULATION FOR THE COLLECTION (E.G. IRIZARRY & ROBERTS, 2007).

However, library displays need not conform to such constraints. Displays concerning social issues, such as war, civil rights, gender, etc., should include comics among books, DVDs, and other relevant exhibited media. This would juxtapose a diversity of viewpoints through a diversity of media, composing a critical pedagogical multimodal narrative in an approach similar to the comics-based curatorial design framework of the exhibition comic.

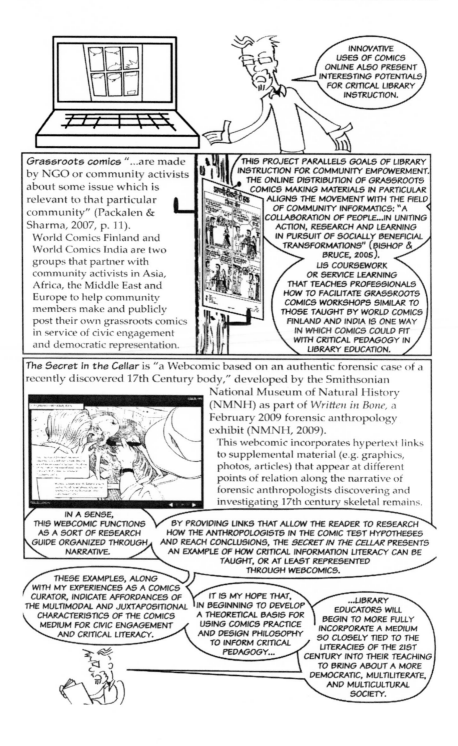

INNOVATIVE USES OF COMICS ONLINE ALSO PRESENT INTERESTING POTENTIALS FOR CRITICAL LIBRARY INSTRUCTION.

Grassroots comics "...are made by NGO or community activists about some issue which is relevant to that particular community" (Packalen & Sharma, 2007, p. 11).

World Comics Finland and World Comics India are two groups that partner with community activists in Asia, Africa, the Middle East and Europe to help community members make and publicly post their own grassroots comics in service of civic engagement and democratic representation.

THIS PROJECT PARALLELS GOALS OF LIBRARY INSTRUCTION FOR COMMUNITY EMPOWERMENT. THE ONLINE DISTRIBUTION OF GRASSROOTS COMICS MAKING MATERIALS IN PARTICULAR ALIGNS THE MOVEMENT WITH THE FIELD OF COMMUNITY INFORMATICS: "A COLLABORATION OF PEOPLE...IN UNITING ACTION, RESEARCH AND LEARNING IN PURSUIT OF SOCIALLY BENEFICIAL TRANSFORMATIONS" (BISHOP & BRUCE, 2005).

LIS COURSEWORK OR SERVICE LEARNING THAT TEACHES PROFESSIONALS HOW TO FACILITATE GRASSROOTS COMICS WORKSHOPS SIMILAR TO THOSE TAUGHT BY WORLD COMICS FINLAND AND INDIA IS ONE WAY IN WHICH COMICS COULD FIT WITH CRITICAL PEDAGOGY IN LIBRARY EDUCATION.

The Secret in the Cellar is "a Webcomic based on an authentic forensic case of a recently discovered 17th Century body," developed by the Smithsonian National Museum of Natural History (NMNH) as part of *Written in Bone*, a February 2009 forensic anthropology exhibit (NMNH, 2009).

This webcomic incorporates hypertext links to supplemental material (e.g. graphics, photos, articles) that appear at different points of relation along the narrative of forensic anthropologists discovering and investigating 17th century skeletal remains.

IN A SENSE, THIS WEBCOMIC FUNCTIONS AS A SORT OF RESEARCH GUIDE ORGANIZED THROUGH NARRATIVE.

BY PROVIDING LINKS THAT ALLOW THE READER TO RESEARCH HOW THE ANTHROPOLOGISTS IN THE COMIC TEST HYPOTHESES AND REACH CONCLUSIONS, THE *SECRET IN THE CELLAR* PRESENTS AN EXAMPLE OF HOW CRITICAL INFORMATION LITERACY CAN BE TAUGHT, OR AT LEAST REPRESENTED THROUGH WEBCOMICS.

THESE EXAMPLES, ALONG WITH MY EXPERIENCES AS A COMICS CURATOR, INDICATE AFFORDANCES OF THE MULTIMODAL AND JUXTAPOSITIONAL CHARACTERISTICS OF THE COMICS MEDIUM FOR CIVIC ENGAGEMENT AND CRITICAL LITERACY.

IT IS MY HOPE THAT, IN BEGINNING TO DEVELOP A THEORETICAL BASIS FOR USING COMICS PRACTICE AND DESIGN PHILOSOPHY TO INFORM CRITICAL PEDAGOGY...

...LIBRARY EDUCATORS WILL BEGIN TO MORE FULLY INCORPORATE A MEDIUM SO CLOSELY TIED TO THE LITERACIES OF THE 21ST CENTURY INTO THEIR TEACHING TO BRING ABOUT A MORE DEMOCRATIC, MULTILITERATE, AND MULTICULTURAL SOCIETY.

References

Beaty, B. (2005). *Fredric Wertham and the critique of mass culture.* Jackson, MS: University Press of Mississippi.

Bernstein, S. N. (2008). Material realities in the basic writing classroom: Intersections of discovery for young women reading *Persepolis 2*. *Journal of Basic Writing, 27*(1), 80-103.

Bigelow, W. (1992). Inside the classroom: social vision and critical pedagogy. In P. Shannon (ed.), *Becoming political: Readings and writings in the politics of literacy.* Portsmouth, NH: Heinemann.

Bishop, A. & Bruce, B. C. (2005). Community informatics: Integrating action, research and learning. *Bulletin of the American Society for Information Science and Technology, 31*(6).

Bitz, M. (2008). A rare bridge: The Comic Book Project connects learning with life. *Teachers & Writers, 39*(4), 3-10.

Brenner, R. (2006, March/April). Graphic novels 101: FAQ. *Horn Book Magazine.* Retrieved July 7, 2009 from http://www.hbook.com/magazine/articles/2006/mar06_brenner.asp

Buhle, P. (2007). Leftism in comics. *Science & Society, 71*(3), 348-356.

Carter, B. (2008a). Carving a niche: Graphic novels in the English language arts classroom. In B. Carter (ed.), *Building Literacy Connections with Graphic Novels: Page by page, panel by panel* (pp. 54-63). Urbana, IL: National Council of Teachers of English.

---. (2008b). Are there any Hester Prynnes in our world today? Pairing *The amazing "true" story of a teenage single mom* with *The scarlet letter.* In B. Carter (ed.) *Building literacy connections with graphic novels: Page by page, panel by panel* (pp. 1-25). Urbana, IL: National Council of Teachers of English.

Cassel, V. (2003). Between a bedrock and a nuclear power plant. In V. Cassel, (ed.), *Splat boom powl: The influence of cartoons in contemporary art* (pp. 17-29). Houston: Contemporary Arts Museum Houston.

Cherland, M. R. & Harper, H. (2007). *Advocacy research in literacy education.* Mahwah, NJ: Lawrence Erlbaum Associates.

Daniels, L. (1995). *DC Comics: Sixty years of the world's favorite comic book heroes.* New York: Bullfinch Press.

Detels, C. (1998). History, philosophy, and the canons of the arts. *Journal of Aesthetic Education, 32*(3), 33-51.

Duffy, D. (2009a). Remasters of American comics: Sequential art as new media in the transformative museum context. *SCAN Journal, 6*(1). Retrieved July 8, 2009 from http://scan.net.au/scan/journal/display.php?journal_id=130

---. (2009b). Learning from comics on the wall: Sequential art narrative design in museology and multimodal education. *Visual Arts Research, 35*(1), 1-11.

Ellis, A. and Highsmith, D. (2000). About face: comic books in library literature. *Serials review, 26*(2), 21-44.

Frank, J. (1942). Let's look at the comics. *Child Study, 19*(3), 76-77, 90-91.

---. (1943). The role of comic strips and comic books in child life. *Supplementary Educational Monographs, 57,* 158-162.

Freire, P. & Giroux, H. A. (1989). Pedagogy, popular culture, and public life: An introduction. In H.A. Giroux and R. I. Simon (eds.), *Popular culture: Schooling & everyday life* (pp. vii-xii). Granby, MA: Bergin & Garvey.

Gardner, J. (2006). Archives, collectors, and the new media work of comics. *MFS Modern Fiction studies, 52*(4), 787-806.

Giroux, H. and Simon, R. I. (1989). Schooling, popular culture, and a pedagogy of possibility. In H.A. Giroux and R. I. Simon (eds.), *Popular culture: Schooling & everyday life* (pp. 219-236). Granby, MA: Bergin & Garvey.

Glaeser, B. C. and Pierson, M. R. (2005). Extension of research on social skills training using comic strip conversations to students without autism. *Education and Training in Developmental Disabilities, 40*(3), 279-84.

Goldsmith, F. (2005). *Graphic novels now: Building, managing, and marketing a dynamic collection.* Chicago, IL: ALA Editions.

Gorman, M. (2003). *Getting graphic! Using graphic novels to promote literacy with preteens and teens.* Columbus, OH: Linworth.

Groensteen, T. (2006). *The system of comics.* (B. Beaty & N. Nguyen, Trans.) Jackson, MS: University Press of Mississippi. (Original work published 1999).

---. (2008). Why are comics still in search of cultural legitimization? In J. Heer and K. Worcester (eds.), *A comics studies reader* (pp. 3-12). Original work published 2000.

Hadju, D. (2008). *Ten cent plague*. New York: Farrar, Straus and Giroux.

Haig, D. (Producer), Harbury, M. (Producer), Lippincott, C. (Producer), & Mann, R. (Director). (1988). *Comic book confidential* [Motion picture]. United States: Cinecom.

Hill, C. (2007). Gallery comics: The beginnings. *International Journal of Comic Art*, 9(2), 6-12.

Hill, G. E. & Trent, M. E. (1940/1941). Children's interest in comic strips, *Journal of Educational Research*, 34, 30-36.

Hogan, J. (2009). Roundtable: Graphic novels in today's libraries. *Graphic Novel Reporter*. Retrieved July 7, 2009 from http://www.graphicnovelreporter.com/content/graphic-novels-todays-libraries-roundtable

Hutchinson, K. (1949). An experiment in the use of comics as instructional material. *Journal of Educational Sociology*, 23, 236-245.

Inge, M. T. (1990). *Comics as culture*. Jackson, MS: University Press of Mississippi.

Irizarry, P. & Roberts, J. (2007, October 19). Beyond leisure reading: Garnering support for comics scholarship from your academic library. Presented at the 2007 International Comic Arts Forum in Washington, D.C.

Jacobs, D. (2007). More than words: Comics as a means of teaching multiple literacies. *English Journal*, 96(3), 19-25.

Krashen, S. D. (2004). *The power of reading: Insights from the research*. Westport, CT: Libraries Unlimited.

Kress, G. (2003). *Literacy in the new media age*. London: Routledge.

---. (2004). Reading images: multimodality, representation and new media. *Information Design Journal*, 12(2), 110-119.

Lawrence, S. A., McNeal, K., and Yildiz, M. N. (2009). Summer program helps adolescents merge technology, popular culture, reading, and writing for academic purposes. *Journal of Adolescent & Adult Literacy* 52(6), 483-494.

Lopes, P. (2006). Culture and stigma: Popular culture and the case of comic books. *Sociological Forum*, 21(3), 387-414.

Matz, C. (2004). Are comic books a worthy consideration on scholarly grounds? *Against the Grain*, 16(1), 78-79.

McCloud, S. (1993). *Understanding comics*. Northampton, MA: Tundra.

---. (2000). *Reinventing comics*. New York: HarperCollins.

Morice, D. (2008). Three poetry comics exercises. *Teachers & Writers*, 39(4), 31-33.

Morrel, E. (2002). Toward a critical pedagogy of popular culture: Literacy development among urban youth. *Journal of Adolescent & Adult Literacy*, 46(1), 72-77.

National Coalition Against Censorship, The American Library Association, and The Comic Book Legal Defense Fund. (2006). *Graphic novels: Suggestions for librarians*. Retrieved July 6, 2009 from http://www.ala.org/ala/aboutala/offices/oif/ifissues/graphicnovels_l.pdf

National Museum of Natural History. (2009). *Written in bone – The secret in the cellar: A written in bone forensic mystery from colonial America*. Retrieved March 4, 2009 from Smithsonian National Museum of Natural History web site: http://writteninbone.si.edu/comic

New London Group (2000). A pedagogy of multiliteracies. In B. Cope and M. Kalantzis (eds.), *Multiliteracies: Literacy learning and the design of social futures* (pp. 9-38). London: Routledge.

Norton, B. (2003) The motivating power of comic books: Insights from Archie comic readers. *The Reading Teacher*, 57(2), 140-7.

Nyberg, A. K. (1998). *Seal of approval: The history of the Comics Code*. Jackson, MS: University of Mississippi Press.

Packalen, L. & Sharma, S. (2007). *Grassroots comics: A communication development tool*. Gummerus Kirjapaino Oy, Jyväskylä: Ministry for Foreign Affairs of Finland. Retrieved January 19, 2009 from http://formin.finland.fi/developmentpolicy/publications/grassroots_comics.pdf

Rice, J. (2007). *The rhetoric of cool: Composition studies and new media*. Carbondale, IL: Southern Illinois University Press.

Rifas, L. (2006, April). Cartooning and nuclear power: From industry advertising to activist uprising and beyond. *PS: Political Science and Politics*, 255-260.

Robins, C. (2005). Engaging with curating. *JADE*, 24(2), 149-158.

Scott, R. W. (1993). Comics and libraries and the scholarly world. *Popular Culture in Libraries*, 1(1), 81-84.

Selber, S. (2004). *Multiliteracies for a digital age.* Carbondale, IL: Southern Illinois University Press.

Schwartz, A. & Rubinstein-Avila, E. (2006). Understanding the manga hype: Uncovering the multimodality of comic-book literacies. *Journal of Adolescent & Adult Literacy, 50*(1), 40-9.

Schwarz, G. (2006). Expanding literacies through graphic novels. *English Journal, 95*(6), 58-64.

Smith, S. W. (2007). Academaesthetics: How the essay and comic can save each other. *TEXT, 11*(2). Retrieved January 12, 2008 from http://www.textjournal.com.au/oct07/smith.htm

Tavin, K. M. (2003). *Wrestling with angels, searching for ghosts: Toward a critical pedagogy of visual culture. Studies in Art Education, 44*(3), 197-213.

Thomspons, J. & Okura, A. (2007, October). How manga conquered the U.S., a graphic guide to Japan's coolest export. *Wired Magazine, 15*(11), 223-233.

Vega, E. S. & Schnackenberg, H. L. (2004). *Integrating technology, art, and writing: Creating comic books as an interdisciplinary learning experience.* Chicago, IL: Association for Educational Communications and Technology. (ERIC Document Reproduction Service No. ED485 026)

Witek, J. (1992). From genre to medium: Comics and contemporary American culture. In R. B. Browne and M. W. Fishwick (eds.), *Rejuvenating the humanities.* Bowling Green, OH: Bowling Green State University Popular Press.

Wright, B. (2001). *Comic book nation: The transformation of youth culture in America.* Baltimore, MD: Johns Hopkins University Press.

Yang, G. (2003). History of comics in education. *Comics in education.* Retrieved May 10, 2009 from http://www.humblecomics.com/comicsedu/history.html

Zorbaugh, H. (1944). Editorial. *Journal of Educational Sociology, 18*(4), 193-194.

---. (1949). Editorial. *Journal of Educational Sociology, 23*(4), 193-194.

Footnotes

1. The image in this panel is a visual rhetorical articulation of my definition of popular culture, although the list of forms of popular culture is not intended to be read as exhaustive.

2. By this I mean inclusion of creative work on its own merits, and not as a found object, as in, the use of comics panels or characters in Pop Art as symbolic of commerciality.

3. In this essay I will use the term "comics" as a singular to indicate the medium of expression found in the formats of comic strips, comic books, graphic novels, and manga (Japanese comics). This singular usage is suggested in key works of American comics scholarship, notably Witek (1992) and McCloud (1993).

4. With the growing cultural acceptance in America of graphic novels and Japanese comics, the stigma attached to comics as a harmful genre of children's literature appears to be largely a thing of the past (Lopes, 2006; Wolk, 2007). Comics in France went through a similar, albeit shorter period of marginalization as youth culture, ending in the 1960s (Groensteen, 2000/2008).

5. The illustration in this panel refers to a scene from Superman's first appearance in *Action Comics #1*, by Jerry Siegel and Joe Shuster.

6. The image is excerpted from the cover of *All Atomic Comics #1*, an educational comic critical of pro-nuclear propaganda in the classroom (see Rifas, 2006).

7. For example, contributors to *A Comics Studies Reader* (Heer & Worcester, eds., 2008) come out of such fields as sociology, media studies, art history, English and literature.

8. The face in the first panel incorporates gestural design elements listed by the New London Group (2000) through its representation of behavior, bodily physicality, feelings and affect. The audio of the word balloon is actually what the New London Group refer to as synaesthetic design, in this case visual standing in for audio.

9. Manga, or Japanese comics, are the most popular form of comics among American teens, particularly teenage girls. For more on the popularity of manga, see Thompson & Okura (2007).

10. These images have been significantly digitally altered to fit black and white printing constraints. The Other Heroes catalog is available online at http://tinyurl.com/otherheroescat

11. This is a digitally altered photograph of one of the walls in the Krannert Art Museum installation of *Out of Sequence*. The purpose of the image is solely to show the density of pieces on the wall. More detailed photos are available online at http://www.egamiphotos.net/gallery/6399703_RAZZz#404984486_tSszb.

12. For a more in-depth analysis of *Out of Sequence*, see Duffy (2009b).

Information Literacy Standards and the Politics of Knowledge Production: Using User-Generated Content to Incorporate Critical Pedagogy.

Maura Seale

> One of my colleagues is a quiet, diminutive lady, who might call up the notion of Marion the Librarian. When she meets people at parties and identifies herself, they sometimes say condescendingly, "A librarian, how nice. Tell me, what is it like to be a librarian?" She replies, "Essentially, it is all about money and power."

In his recent essay, "Google and the Future of Books," Robert Darnton relates the preceding anecdote. Although Darnton is primarily concerned with the politics surrounding access to information, the field of librarianship is, as his colleague notes, inescapably political. One of the most traditional roles of librarians—judging the value of information in order to create and maintain collections, helping users meet their information needs, and answering reference questions—is indeed highly politicized and powerful, even if it is not generally perceived as such. In 1989, the American Library Association (ALA) sought to shift some of this power to users by codifying the notion of "information literacy" and using it as the basis of instruction. The importance of information literacy and its centrality to the work of libraries and librarians were reaffirmed in a progress report created by the ALA in 1998. Following this, in 2000, the Association of College and Research Libraries (ACRL) developed the Information Literacy Competency Standards for Higher Education (hereafter ACRL Standards). This set of standards, indicators, and outcomes has become the most well-known and widely-used means of conceptualizing, teaching, and assessing information literacy within higher education, although individual libraries and librarians have developed other checklists and rubrics that seek to teach information literacy as well.

This increasing emphasis on instruction and information literacy within librarianship since the late 1980s, as exemplified by the actions of the ALA and ACRL, has led some librarians and library theorists to consider the relationship between information literacy and critical pedagogy. Cushla Kapitzke offers a nuanced and rich poststructuralist critique of information literacy, libraries, and librarianship (Kapitzke and Luke, 1999; 2001; 2003a; 2003b), and calls for "a critical information literacy" that "reframes conventional notions of text, knowledge, and authority" (2001, p. 453). Her work does not explicitly address the ACRL Standards but does critique other information literacy frameworks, such as the Big Six Skills, for emphasizing a hierarchical, generic, and positivist approach to information literacy, and for conceptualizing information as "unproblematic, atheoretical, and apolitical" (1999; 2003b; 2003a, p. 47). To Kapitzke (1999), the following are crucial to critical information literacy: "the social construction and cultural authority of knowledge; the political economies of knowledge ownership and control; [and] the development of local communities' and cultures' capacities to critique and construct knowledge" (p.483-484). In other words, critical information literacy must explicitly address the politics of knowledge production.

Other authors have considered the roles of knowledge production and the ACRL Standards within critical information literacy, but not in depth. Swanson's (2004b) description of an implementation of critical information literacy acknowledges issues around knowledge production (p. 267), but he also invokes the ACRL Standards unproblematically. Elsewhere (2004a), however, Swanson critiques standards such as those produced by the ACRL as overly simplistic and mechanistic, and emphasizes the need for students "to understand where information is created and how it arrives" in order to be truly information literate (p. 72). Simmons (2005) focuses on the role of genre theory in critical information literacy, but offers a similar critique of the ACRL Standards as positivist. These positivist standards erase aspects of information - specifically the politics surrounding its production - that are crucial to information literacy, such as ownership, access, and who can and cannot be published (Simmons, 2005, p. 300). Doherty and Ketchner (2005) and Ketchner (2007) contend that not only are the ACRL Standards decontextualized, they assume information is predominantly procedural and politically neutral and thereby act to reify traditional media. Moreover, the ACRL Standards highlight and legitimize the gatekeeping functions of librarians and their role as authority figures. Elmborg (2006) and Jacobs (2008) both critique the prominence of authority within library education, as well as the purported universality of various information literacy standards. Elmborg (2006) goes on to suggest that information literacy ideally "involves the comprehension of an entire system of thought and the ways that information flows in that system. Ultimately it also involves the capacity to critically evaluate the system itself," again placing a critical assessment of knowledge production at the center of the concept (p. 196). In contrast to these authors, Shanbhag (2006) does not address the ACRL Standards, or indeed any measures of information literacy explicitly, but instead focuses on the need to integrate discussions of knowledge production into information literacy: students "need to think beyond the singularity of the disciplinary model and understand multiple knowledge traditions and issues arising at the sites where they meet and create conflict" (p. 3).

While a majority of these authors discuss the ACRL Standards in some way and identify the need to critically engage with issues around knowledge production in an information literacy inflected by critical pedagogy, none articulates a substantial or substantive critique of the ACRL Standards themselves. This is necessary, because these are the guidelines by which many libraries and librarians, particularly within higher education, conceptualize, teach, and assess information literacy. It is unlikely that the ACRL Standards can or will be simply discarded, but careful analysis and critique can allow them to be more carefully deployed. Building on and extending the observations of these librarians and library theorists, this essay will carefully analyze and critique the ACRL Standards. Because politics and processes of knowledge production are central to a critical information literacy, and in order to incorporate the insights offered by antiracist, feminist, and queer theories, this essay will propose using user-generated content such as wikis, blogs, mash-ups, and message boards to highlight the inequities and power relations around knowledge production.

The ACRL Standards begin with a definition of information literacy:

Information literacy is a set of abilities requiring individuals to "recognize when information is needed and have the ability to locate, evaluate, and use effectively the needed information." Information literacy also is increasingly important in the contemporary environment of rapid technological change and proliferating information resources. Because of the escalating complexity of this environment, individuals are faced with diverse, abundant information choices—in their academic studies, in the workplace, and in their personal lives. Information is available through libraries, community resources, special interest organizations, media, and the Internet—and increasingly, information comes to individuals in unfiltered formats, raising questions about its authenticity, validity, and reliability. In addition, information is available through multiple media, including graphical, aural, and textual, and these pose new challenges for individuals in evaluating and understanding it. The uncertain quality and expanding quantity of information pose large challenges for society. The sheer abundance of information will not in itself create a more informed citizenry without a complementary cluster of abilities necessary to use information effectively.

> Information literacy forms the basis for lifelong learning. It is common to all disciplines, to all learning environments, and to all levels of education. It enables learners to master content and extend their investigations, become more self-directed, and assume greater control over their own learning. (Association of College and Research Libraries [ACRL], 2000, p. 2)

This definition is followed by a list of the standards themselves. As others have noted, this definition and the following standards conceive of information literacy as a "cluster of abilities" and mechanize and universalize a complex, recursive, and highly individual process. The definition also dichotomizes information—it is either authentic, valid, reliable, and of good quality, or not—and thus embraces a positivist notion of information as external and knowable and ready to be accessed, an approach that erases the ways in which the meaning and thus the qualities of information—including its authenticity, reliability, and validity—are socially and politically negotiated (Elmborg, 2006;Kapitzke, 2003a). This reification of information also acts to depoliticize it, as the social, political, and economic contexts in which it is produced and consumed are rendered invisible. These discursive moves, combined with the very act of definitively codifying information literacy, foreclose other possibilities, and ascribe authority and power to those that do the defining and make the distinctions between good and bad information. The emphasis on the dangers of "unfiltered information" likewise moves authority away from the individual and towards some external and objective arbiter (ACRL, 2000, p. 1). Information literacy, in this definition, is bound up with knowability, objectivity, truth, and authority.

The politics of information do come into play in this definition: "The sheer abundance of information will not in itself create a more informed citizenry without a complementary cluster of abilities necessary to use information effectively" (ACRL, 2000, p. 2) and indeed, because information literacy "enables learners to master content and extend their investigations, become more self-directed, and assume great control over their own learning" (ACRL, 2000, p. 2), it is seen as politically empowering. At the same time, however, the definition moves to depoliticize the notion of information literacy. In its evocation of "the contemporary environment of rapid technological change and proliferating information resources" (ACRL, 2000, p. 2), the definition uncritically repeats dominant discourse about the postindustrial and progressive "information society." However, May (2001) argues that this discourse is only made possible by a conflation of service work with information work and, more importantly, that long-standing relations of power between employers and employees have persisted in the so-called new economy; this new economy is characterized by the precarious nature of jobs and exacerbated by outsourcing and off-shoring, the replaceability of workers, and the increased surveillance and control of workers, made possible by better technology. The definition also emphasizes the "quantity," "abundance," and "diversity" of information resources that are available, thereby positing equal access to these resources for all. Both within the United States and globally, however, inequities in access to information persist, and this definition effectively writes out already-marginalized communities and peoples for whom the issue is not access to too much information, but access to any information at all. This reiterates Elmborg's (2006) argument that information literacy is always contextualized by the social, economic, and political. Similar inequities also exist within the realm of knowledge production and dissemination, and are completely ignored by this definition of information literacy. Despite the emergence and popularization of the content-creating technologies of Web 2.0—which have challenged dominant structures of knowledge production and dispersion—much of the means to create and distribute information continues to reside in the hands of the powerful and elite. MySpace may offer musicians a means of distributing their work outside of the mainstream record labels, but like the *Wall Street Journal*, HarperCollins, and Fox, it is owned by Rupert Murdoch's News Corporation ("News Corporation," 2009).

The standards themselves are briefly mentioned at the conclusion of this definition, and are then fleshed out with multiple performance indicators and potential outcomes in a different section. The standards are:

1. The information literate student determines the nature and extent of the information needed...

2. The information literate student accesses needed information effectively and efficiently...

3. The information literate student evaluates information and its sources critically and incorporates selected information into his or her knowledge base and value system...

4. The information literate student, individually or as a member of a group, uses information effectively to accomplish a specific purpose...

5. The information literate student understands many of the economic, legal, and social issues surrounding the use of information and accesses and uses information ethically and legally... (ACRL, 2000, p. 9-14)

What is most evident in the list of standards, performance indicators, and outcomes is how information literacy is constructed as a foregone conclusion; that is, the information literate student, the subject of these standards, is already information literate. The list of actions that constitute this document represent information literacy as a stable, closed, already-accomplished condition. This representation leaves no room for differences in ways of understanding or approaching it, instead universalizing through tautology. This document articulates what information literacy is, but erases the processes that create it. These processes are arguably the most central to the project of achieving a critical relationship with information. Instead, this definition moves immediately to standard, measurable end results, and consequently downplays variation and process. Moreover, as this critique will reveal, the standards are actively engaged in promoting an uncritical consumption of information. This list, as observed by other librarians and library theorists, also focuses almost exclusively on tasks and repeatedly uses words such as "defines," "constructs," "implements," and "participates" (ACRL, 2000). All of these tasks are performed in order to produce a product, as the performance indicators for Standard Four demonstrate (ACRL, 2000, p. 15). Kapitzke (1999) notes that this insistence on productivity embraces modernism and is thus outmoded, while Jacobs (2008) points out how this emphasis on compartmentalizing skills ignores the larger political and social goals of information literacy.

Despite the reference to "information choices" within "the workplace" and "personal lives" in the definition of information literacy that opens this document, the standards, indicators, and outcomes are consistently focused on libraries specifically—for example, by making reference to interlibrary loan and document delivery—and higher education more broadly (ACRL, 2000, p. 2). One outcome, for example, is "Differentiates between primary and secondary sources, recognizing how their use and importance will vary with each discipline;" several other outcomes also focus on disciplinary knowledge (ACRL, 2000, p. 8). This is not surprising given ACRL's orientation, but it does undercut the universality the Standards attempt to achieve by privileging academic literacy over other forms. Academic disciplines, as Doherty (2007) contends, are conservative and tend to resist change; by treating disciplines as authoritative, the Standards portray disciplinary discourse and knowledge as "static and monolithic" rather than highly political and contested, a move Simmons (2005, p. 300) perceives as anathema to critical information literacy. The erasure of diversity within disciplines and the privileging of already dominant processes, literacies, and epistemologies in the Standards can act, as Elmborg (2006) argues, to reproduce sociocultural, political, and economic hierarchies by creating good students with "standardized knowledge" and labeling "nonconforming students" as "rejects" (p. 194).

Knowledge production within the disciplines is thus ignored in the Standards, as is knowledge production more generally. The outcomes for Standard One, Performance Indicator Two gesture towards the issues of knowledge production but are uncritical: the information literate student "Knows how information is formally and informally produced, organized, and disseminated" and "Recognizes that knowledge can be organized into disciplines that influence the way information is accessed" (ACRL, 2000, p. 8) The student is not required to know or recognize how knowledge production and organization impacts content and is thus politically charged. This stress on information organization, access, format, and audience evokes traditional, print-based bibliographic instruction, which Kapitzke (2001) asserts may be obsolete. As with the definition of information literacy discussed previously, the standards understand information as being "out there," waiting to be accessed: "The information literate student extracts, records, and manages the information and its sources" (ACRL, 2000, p. 10).

In these instances, the Standards appeal to some sort of authority—the norms of the discipline or the systems that structure information. One of the outcomes for Standard Two explicitly refers to several types of authoritative entities, both academic and professional, including the library: "Uses specialized online or in person services available at the institution to retrieve information needed (e.g. interlibrary loan/document delivery, professional associations, institutional research offices, community resources, experts, and practitioners)" (ACRL, 2000, p. 10). Standard Three seems to be closely related to critical information literacy—"The information literate student evaluates information and its sources critically and incorporates selected information into his or her knowledge base and value system" (ACRL, 2000, p. 11)—but unquestioningly embraces the notion of authority. Indicator 2 and its outcomes deserve to be examined in depth:

Performance Indicator

2. The information literate student articulates and applies initial criteria for evaluating both the information and its sources.

Outcomes Include:

a. Examines and compares information from various sources in order to evaluate reliability, validity, accuracy, authority, timeliness, and point of view or bias

b. Analyzes the structure and logic of supporting arguments or methods

c. Recognizes prejudice, deception, or manipulation

d. Recognizes the cultural, physical, or other context within which the information was created and understands the impact of context on interpreting the information. (ACRL, 2000, p. 11)

Information is once again depicted as dualistic, as either reliable or not, valid or invalid, ignoring that all information is inherently limited and biased (Swanson 2004a). Outcome (a) specifically appeals to criteria of "reliability, validity, accuracy, authority, [and] timeliness," as though these characteristics are always transparent rather than situationally constructed. It also treats "point of view or bias" as though objectivity is possible, as though information can somehow be removed from the context in which is produced and consumed. Similarly, "prejudice, deception, or manipulation" in Outcome (c) are also understood to be transparent, objective, and obvious. It is not apparent whose criteria are being applied, but the language indicates some sort of authoritative entity—possibly, given the rest of the Standards, the library or university. By encouraging learners to approach information in this dualistic way and by invoking the existence of objective standards by which it should be assessed, the Standards inevitably lead to an uncritical consumption of information. Outcome (d) signals some form of cultural relativism or historical sensitivity, but explicitly ignores the political and economic context of knowledge production, which is central to critical information literacy. Indicator 4 continues in this vein, as does Indicator 6, in which "The information literate student validates understanding and interpretation of the information through discourse with other individuals, subject-area experts, and/or practitioners" after having "[determined] whether to incorporate or reject viewpoints encountered" (ACRL, 2000, p. 12). There is once again an appeal to some form of academic, professional, or disciplinary authority and the deployment of positivism. Truth and facts are perceived to be knowable and objective. They can be accessed and then simply accepted or rejected, rather than existing as the "raw material" learners can use to create their own views (Elmborg, 2006, p. 198). Throughout these standards, indicators, and outcomes, the student is constructed as the passive recipient of information in the form of truth or facts; the emphasis on authority, combined with the passivity of the learners, evoke Paulo Freire's notion of "banking education," with the library functioning as bank (Doherty and Ketchner, 2005; Elmborg, 2006; Jacobs, 2008).

In addition to focusing on traditional locations of authority, the ACRL Standards dwell on learning to use the systems that create and structure information—what Elmborg (2006, p. 197) refers to as the "grammar of information"—without any critical sense of those systems. One of the outcomes for Standard Two, for example, is "Constructs a search strategy using appropriate commands for the information retrieval system selection (e.g. Boolean operators, truncation, and proximity for search engines; internal organizers such as indexes for books)" (ACRL, 2000, p. 10). There is no sense here that teaching *about* information, including the ways in which these grammars of information deploy a particular worldview, is needed; being able to use the tools is sufficient (Swanson, 2004b; Elmborg, 2006). Standard Five is the potentially most significant in terms of critical information literacy. One of the indicators for this Standard demands that "The information literate student understands many of the ethical, legal, and socio-economic issues surrounding information and information technology" (ACRL, 2000, p. 14). However, the issues listed, while important, again emphasize the procedural rather than critical aspect of information literacy: privacy and security; censorship and freedom of speech; issues around intellectual property, copyright, and fair use; plagiarism and citation. One outcome gestures towards issues around knowledge production by referring to "free vs. fee-based access to information" (ACRL, 2000, p. 14), but there is no recognition that these topics are part of a system of information creation, production, distribution, and consumption, and no systemic critique, which Elmborg contends is key to a critical information literacy (2006, p. 196). The information literate student "follows laws, regulations, institutional policies, and etiquette related to the access and use of information resources," rules that are presented as natural and inevitable rather than socially produced and continually contested (ACRL, 2000, p. 14).

As this analysis demonstrates, traditional and institutionalized understandings of information literacy, as embodied in the ACRL Standards, do not adequately address the politics and processes of knowledge production. Instead, they emphasize a notion of information as dichotomous, objective, and apolitical, and appeal to traditional authorities such as libraries and academic disciplines. A critical approach to knowledge production is crucial to critical information literacy. As Kapitzke argues, "Considering the power of information networks to connect and disconnect, and to include and exclude, any pedagogy that ignores the political economy of information does a disservice to students" (2001, p. 453-454). In order to address this gap in the dominant conception of information literacy, and to incorporate critical pedagogy as well as antiracist, queer, and feminist perspectives, user-generated content such as wikis, blogs, mash-ups, and message boards, can be strategically employed in the library classroom to enable the discussion of inequities in knowledge production.

Swanson (2004b) observes that "Students enter our classrooms with their own experiences as users of information. This is a common ground from which we can enter a discussion about using and finding information" (2004b, p. 265). Similarly, Simmons (2005) advocates for using genre pedagogy to create a dialogue between the dominant discursive practices of higher education and those of students: "Teaching about genre fosters in students an awareness of the social construction of discourses so that the students can use but also challenge these genre distinctions [and] see that genres are social constructions that have developed in response to a social need" (p. 302). Doherty and Ketchner (2005) also emphasize the need for dialogue as opposed to "banking education" and suggest achieving it by relinquishing authority and building on the experiences of students. To each of these authors, critical information literacy necessitates some sort of dialogic process and creation of common ground between students and teacher; one way of creating this is through the discussion of user-generated content within the context of information literacy, as many students will have had some experience with this form of information.

The diffusion of knowledge production to locations outside of or marginal to traditional locations of power that has accompanied the increasing popularity of user-generated content has opened up space in which these types of inequities can be contested. Strategic use of user-generated content thus also offers the opportunity to incorporate antiracist, feminist, and queer perspectives into information literacy instruction, as well as prompting the questioning of inequities and hierarchies in knowledge production in two distinct, but related, ways. First, the content found in user-generated information itself can offer a challenge to dominant and mainstream discourse by introducing the words and perspectives of individuals who would otherwise not be heard. By listening to these voices, learners can begin to question the content of traditional and authoritative sources of information and move towards a critical understanding of information as always subjective, always political, and always inflected by social, political, and economic contexts. Second, the ways in which user-generated content is produced and disseminated can contrast and thus expose the otherwise invisible infrastructures of dominant forms of knowledge production, including whose voices and perspectives they validate, and whose they do not. The contrast between user-generated content and dominant systems of knowledge production open up a space in which learners can begin to grasp and assess the political, economic, and social inequities that inflect knowledge production, distribution, and consumption, and thus move towards a more critical view of information that challenges the emphasis within the Standards on information as objective and apolitical, as well as their embrace of authority.

Confessions of a College Call Girl is a blog written by an anonymous New York City sex worker between January 2007 and October 2008. (It is not currently being updated.) While many entries recount her experiences as a sex worker, College Call Girl also critically analyzes her childhood, her identity, her motivations for choosing sex work and the results of this choice, and the industry itself. In lighter moments, she comments on television shows and movies, and provides biographical sketches of "Hookers in History." The overall tone of the blog is ambiguous and conflicted; somewhat surprisingly, given the subject matter, the entries are open for comments. Many of those who comment self-identify as either current or former sex workers, while others seem to read the blog for narrative content. Here, College Call Girl responds to email from readers:

> I know I'm not the only reason you want to try sex work. But I know also that you're responding to something you've found in my writing–the vicarious thrill of someone who seems to have played with fire and barely singed her fingertips. That glamour exists–the empowerment of getting away with something, embracing your sexuality and behaving in a way society tells you you're not supposed to. It can be empowering to get something back on the body that has for so long been used and abused and objectified. And the money is good. But there's another side to this deal that I'm afraid I haven't shown you. (Confessions of a College Call Girl, 2007)

One of the final entries includes a letter to one of her customers, with whom she eventually became romantically involved:

> I liked it at first—it seemed easy and fun and I was a broke-ass arty chick in NYC driven to desperate measures. But I really started to hate myself, my body, sex, men, money...I've always been a huge sex-work advocate as a woman and a feminist but now I believe there really isn't a way to sell your body and be healthy. There isn't a way to keep from getting broken. ("Confessions of a College Call Girl," 2008)

These entries and the corresponding comments particularly, and the perspectives of sex workers themselves more broadly, can productively trouble second- and third-wave feminist analyses of sex work as either entirely oppressive or ultimately liberatory. Texts such *as* Confessions of a College Call Girl, when combined with others such as peer-reviewed women's studies journals, scholarly books on the subject of sex work, mainstream media coverage of the investigation and resignation of Eliot Spitzer, and films such as *Pretty Woman*, can help students ask questions about differences between the knowledge produced in each location, such as those Simmons (2005) poses: "Who owns and sells knowledge? Who has access to information? What counts as information or knowledge?...Whose voices get published?...Whose voices do not get published?" (p. 300). In this example, students could consider whether the perspective provided by College Call Girl could be heard through academic presses or mass media, if her blog could ever be a book in a university library, if her depressing narratives of repeated sexual assault would be depicted in a popular movie or television show. By articulating these issues, students can begin to engage with issues of knowledge production in a way that moves beyond the ACRL Standards; instead of searching for truth, facts, or authenticity, students encounter multivocality, the differential valuing of texts and voices, and the power disparities that characterize knowledge production. As Doherty (2007) suggests, "critical information literacy needs to de-reify traditional media and open up to all forms of knowledge" (p. 5). At the same time, however, the use of user-generated content within information literacy cannot be uncritical, nor can the use of more traditional academic or popular sources.

Other examples of user-generated content open up other realms of power and struggle. The blog Stuff White People Like explicitly satirizes whiteness and (less obviously) middle-class norms and markers (sea salt, National Public Radio, ironic tattoos), thereby challenging dominant discourses such as those found within mainstream media that render both as invisible, normal, and natural (Dyer, 1997; McIntosh, 2008). Racialicious critiques mass culture representations of race and gender—e.g. the ways in which drug use is tied to race in films such as *Dazed and Confused* and *Friday* and television shows such as *That 70s Show* and *The Wire*—and in doing so, opens up popular discourses around race and gender. A significant portion of the fan fiction at FanFiction.net and mash-ups such as "*Star Trek* + Nine Inch Nails = Closer" speak to the heteronormativity of mass culture, and make queerness the center of those narratives by reimagining the relationship between Harry and Snape in the *Harry Potter* series and that between Kirk and Spock in *Star Trek*. While these deconstructive analyses of mainstream and popular discursive practices and texts are not new to some academic fields, these texts present this information in ways that may be more accessible to students and allow them to critically engage with dominant and authoritative forms of knowledge. Comparisons between the types of entries found in Wikipedia (e.g. "diaper fetishism") that are localized to marginal social groups and those in a conventional, authoritative source such as the *Encyclopedia Britannica* can help students confront and assess the inequities and hierarchies intrinsic to contemporary knowledge production.

Produced in 2000, prior to the popularization and dispersal of Web 2.0 technologies that allow for wider participation in knowledge production, the ACRL Standards remain the prevailing means of understanding information literacy, particularly within higher education. There is undoubtedly value in a clearly articulated and institutionalized conceptualization of information literacy—in terms of defining professional identity, offering a clear, easy to explain and easy to promote instructional goal, and providing a way to think about library instruction in broader terms than just the ability to use the library catalog and databases. Still, the Standards are inadequate, incomplete, and inculcate complacency. The definition of information literacy that opens the document emphasizes the knowability and objectivity of information, the importance of traditional locations of authority, and the depoliticization of information and the systems in which it is produced and consumed. The standards, indicators, and outcomes are tautological, elide the politics around knowledge production, and ultimately promote an uncritical consumption of knowledge in lieu of any sort of systemic critique. The careful use of user-generated content in information literacy instruction offers a means of addressing these gaps, particularly those around knowledge production, as well as a way of incorporating some of the insights of antiracist, feminist, and queer theories and perspectives. User-generated content opens up a space in which to dialogue with students, in which hierarchies of race, class, gender, and sexuality inherent to knowledge production can be articulated and critically assessed, and in which multiple voices, including those of the margins, can be heard. The incorporation of user-generated content into information literacy instruction can assist librarians in moving beyond a notion of good, depoliticized information and into a more complicated and critical understanding of the politics and power of information.

References

Alexanderab. (2006). *YouTube - star trek + nine inch nails = closer*. [Video file]. Retrieved 2/11/2009, 2009, from http://www.youtube.com/watch?v=3uxTpyCdriY

Confessions of a college callgirl. (2009). Retrieved 2/11/2009, from http://collegecallgirl.blogspot.com.

Darnton, R. (2009). Google and the future of books. *The New York Review of Books, 56*(2).

"Diaper fetishism." (2009) *Wikipedia, the free encyclopedia.* Retrieved 2/11/2009, from http://en.wikipedia.org/wiki/Diaper_fetishism.

Doherty, J. J. (2007). No shhing: Giving voice to the silenced: An essay in support of critical information literacy. *Library Philosophy and Practice, 9*(2).

Doherty, J. J., & Ketchner, K. (2005). Empowering the intentional learner: A critical theory for information literacy instruction. *Library Philosophy and Practice, 8*(1).

Dyer, R. (1997). *White.* New York : Routledge.

Elmborg, J. (2006). Critical information literacy: Implications for instructional practice. *The Journal of Academic Librarianship, 32*(2), 192-199.

FanFiction.net: Unleash your imagination. (2009). Retrieved 2/11/2009, 2009, from http://www.fanfiction.net/.

Jacobs, H. L. M. (2008). Information literacy and reflective pedagogical praxis. *The Journal of Academic Librarianship, 34*(3), 256-262.

Kapitzke, C. (2001). Information literacy: The changing library. *Journal of Adolescent and Adult Literacy, 44*(5), 450-456.

Kapitzke, C. (2003a). Information literacy: A review and poststructural critique. *Australian Journal of Language and Literacy, 26*(1), 53-66.

Kapitzke, C. (2003b). Politics of outformation. *Educational Theory, 53*(1).

Luke, A., & Kapitzke, C. (1999). Literacies and libraries: Archives and cybraries. *Pedagogy, Culture and Society, 7*(3), 467-491.

May, C. (2002). *The information society : A sceptical view.* Malden, Mass.: Polity Press.

McIntosh, P. (2008). White privilege : Unpacking the invisible knapsack. In P. S. Rothenberg (Ed.), *White privilege : Essential readings on the other side of racism* (3rd ed, pp. 123). New York: Worth Publishers.

News corporation. (2009). Retrieved 4/6/2009, from http://www.newscorp.com/.

Racialicious - the intersection of race and pop culture. (2009). Retrieved 2/11/2009, from http://www.racialicious.com/.

Shanbhag, S. Alternative models of knowledge production: A step forward in information literacy as a liberal art. . *Library Philosophy and Practice, 8*(2).

Simmons, M. H. (2005). Librarians as disciplinary discourse mediators: Using genre theory to move toward critical information literacy. *Portal: Libraries and the Academy, 5*(3), 297-311.

Stuff white people like. Retrieved 2/11/2009, from http://stuffwhitepeoplelike.com/.

Swanson, T. A. (2004a). A radical step: Implementing a critical information literacy model. *Portal: Libraries and the Academy, 4*(2), 259-273.

Swanson, T. A. (2004b). Applying a critical pedagogical perspective to information literacy standards. *Community & Junior College Libraries, 12*(4), 65–78.

Critical Approach to Asia through Library Collections and Instruction in North America: Selection of Culture and Counter-hegemonic Library Practices

Hiromitsu Inokuchi and Yoshiko Nozaki

Introduction: Library as Selective Tradition, Library as Education

Contemporary cultural theories suggest that the selective representation of a culture, expressed in school textbooks, in history and literature instruction, and/or on film, reflects the power relations of a given society (e.g., Anyon, 1979; Apple, 1979; Fiske, 1987; Nozaki, 2001). Through the selective representation of culture, the dominant group(s) creates a certain tradition—what British cultural theorist Raymond Williams (1977) calls a "selective tradition" that serves to maintain the cultural hegemony of the dominant group(s).[1] As he puts it:

> Most versions of "tradition" can be quickly shown to be radically selective. From a whole possible area of past and present, in a particular culture, certain meanings and practices are selected for emphasis and certain other meanings and practices are neglected or excluded. Yet, within a particular hegemony, and as one of its decisive processes, this selection is presented and usually successfully passed off as "the tradition," "the significant past." (pp. 115-6)

A library is inherently selective, as it cannot house all of the documents (or books) available in the world. As such, librarians have to be discerning in their acquisition practices. Additionally, reference librarians have to select "appropriate" sources for their clients, recommending a few choice materials from the available books and articles. Through these processes, librarians tend to select and promote certain kinds of texts, cultural artifacts, and information. That is, a certain type of culture is promoted over others, and the selective traditions function as value systems, or sorting and organizing principles, for librarians in various cultures. Although most librarians in North America decry censorship, many of them are possibly

---

[1] This is also the case for school curricula. The concept of selective tradition is applicable to education in general (Apple, 1979).

unaware of the selective traditions in which they find themselves working, as they are perhaps deeply immersed in such traditions. In fact, librarians as a collective of professionals promote and maintain, almost instinctively, a certain type of culture in everyday life. For example, libraries as institutions usually promote a literate culture, thereby limiting illiterate people's access.[2] In this sense, librarians are the gatekeepers of culture, and inevitably, are involved in cultural politics. Hence, it would be best to proactively participate in such politics with a critical mindset (see Lewis, 2008).

A library is an educational, pedagogical space in which librarians—consciously or not—act to either maintain the selective tradition of the cultural hegemony by continuing business-as-usual, or enable social change by creating new selective traditions—alternative or oppositional (Williams, 1977)—that promote important values such as diversity, peace, and justice for the future. What Richard Shaull (1970) states about education generally applies to the idea of library as education:

> There is no such thing as a *neutral* educational process. Education either functions as an instrument which is used to facilitate the integration of the younger generation into the logic of the present system and bring about conformity to it, *or* it becomes "the practice of freedom," the means by which men and women deal critically and creatively with reality and discover how to participate in the transformation of their world. (p. 15)

In this chapter, we would like to discuss the issue of selective traditions of library collection development, because any instruction—including library instruction—involves two major elements: how to teach (i.e., instructional method or pedagogy) and what to teach (i.e., curriculum) (Bernstein, 1977; Whitty, 1992). The latter, what to teach in the library context, is largely determined by what libraries have in their collection. The issue of selective tradition in libraries as a vital concern for librarians interested in critical, counter-hegemonic instructional practices, since what is available—the kinds of cultures and knowledge represented—in a library often sets a practical limit upon what critical librarians can do. Simply put, it is not easy to foster critical approaches to dominant cultures if libraries do not have materials that exemplify these perspectives.

---

[2] We do not intend to criticize libraries' transformative efforts to promote literacy for the illiterate, but this kind of effort is still regarded as the promotion of a literate culture. Presently, aural-oral culture is not dominant in libraries while some libraries have developed good audio-visual collections or oral history collections.

Though one might examine the library collection development practice for any specific subject area, we would like to examine those of Asian Studies libraries in particular, and proceed to discuss some specific library collections that may counter the dominant, selective tradition. The notion of "Orientalism" (Said, 1978),[3] we would argue, is important when examining the value systems, or organizing principles, of such collections, because it explicates the hegemonic relations between the West and the Orient.[4] In the following section, we specifically focus on Japanese studies collections, though theoretically our arguments can also be applied to other Asian studies collections (e.g., Chinese studies collections) in the United States.

Orientalism and Study of East Asia

Orientalism is a well-known concept coined by literary theorist Edward Said. Said defines Orientalism as "a way of coming to terms with the Orient that is based on the Orient's special place in European Western experience" (1978, p. 1). One important aspect of Orientalism is that it comprises a mode of discourse, a body of knowledge, a political vision of reality—with supporting institutions, vocabulary, scholarship, imaginary, and doctrines— that expresses and represents the Orient. In other words, Orientalism is a style of thought, or a discourse, that serves to maintain "a Western style for domination, restructuring, and having authority over the Orient" (p. 2). In short, Orientalism is a type of Western discourse that constructs a cultural hegemony that justifies and maintains the political dominance of the West over the Orient. Libraries as institutions can play a powerful role in this discourse, supporting Orientalist scholarship and maintaining Orientalist languages and vocabularies. Indeed, libraries collect the texts of dominant cultures and scholarly publications that subscribe to the discourse of Orientalism. These texts are often referenced as part of the basic bibliography without serious criticism, or without simultaneously referencing materials that counteract Orientalism. Some prominent libraries may also present exotic pre-modern artifacts as if they are the essence of

---

[3] The relevance of the notion of Orientalism for critical educational studies has been recognized (McCarthy & Critchlow, 1993). However, only a few studies have used it extensively as a lens through which we may examine the issues of curriculum and teaching.

[4] Sociologist Stuart Hall (1992) also develops his notion of the West and the Rest discourse from Said's Orientalism. Hall's notion would be useful for the criticism of the cultural dominance of the West over the non-West.

Oriental (be it Japanese or Chinese) culture, thus taking part in the construction of the fixed image of the Orient.

While Said applies this concept to his analysis of the Middle East, a number of studies have also applied this concept to the analysis of East Asia (e.g., Lee, 1999). Richard Minear (1980) specifically examines this concept in the field of Japanese studies, as he discusses the writings of three influential scholars—Basil Hall Chamberlain, George B. Sansom, and Edwin O. Reischauer. These scholars' works are still considered "classics" by students learning about Japan. While noting "the striking differences in historical setting" (p. 514) between Said's Orientalism and the tradition of Japanese studies, Minear also demonstrates the resemblance between the two by analyzing Japanese studies discourse, or the way that the (Orientalist) binary opposition speaks through these scholars' works. Like Said's Orientalists, these scholars saw the world in a clear West ("us") and East ("them") binary, and essentialized Japanese culture, resulting in— unwittingly or not—the promotion of a view that assumes, or speaks of, the superiority of the West. These scholars also valued ancient or pre-modern Japan, but were critical of modern and contemporary periods. From their perspectives, Japan's "Westernization" or "democratization" would perhaps never be of the same quality as the West's.

The most significant difference between Said's Orientalism and the (selective) tradition of Japanese studies is that Japan has not been directly dominated by Western military power. However, Minear suggests that a resemblance exists, perhaps, because "the pursuit of knowledge involves the attempt to appropriate the reality of a subject, and is therefore aggressive; the subject is reduced, almost by necessity, to the status of object" (p. 516). Although Japan, unlike other "Oriental" countries, was never colonized, Orientalism as a cultural hegemony is applied to Japan as equally as if it were one of the "Oriental" countries. This is because Japan has never been associated with the West, and is therefore a cultural "other" of the West.[5]

The major feature of Orientalist discourse is the binary opposition between the West ("us") and the Orient ("them") (Inokuchi & Nozaki, 2005; Nozaki, 2009; Nozaki & Inokuchi, 1998). This discourse constructs the West and Orient as if they were mutually exclusive entities, where the culture of the Orient is essentialized and regarded as different from the West. It is

---

[5] Minear acknowledges that Japan succumbed to a Western use of force in the nineteenth century and, briefly, in the middle of the twentieth century. However, Japan is different from the region to which Said is referring, as Japan never became a colony.

perceived as something ancient or old (predating the influence of the West), and is objectified (as something to be examined) and looked at with curious eyes or exoticized:

> In a sense Orientalism was a library or archive of information commonly and, in some of its aspects, unanimously held. What bound the archive together was a family of ideas and a unifying set of values proven in various ways to be effective. These ideas explained the behavior of Orientals; they supplied Orientals with a mentality, a genealogy, an atmosphere; most important, they allowed Europeans to deal with and even to see Orientals as a phenomenon possessing regular characteristics. (Said 1978, pp. 41-2)

East Asian libraries are responsible for determining which aspects of East Asia will be represented. There is no neutral representation, but rather a common representation that tends to reflect the dominant values of society. Dominant U.S. views on other countries and cultures tend to be represented in a certain way, and U.S. views on East Asia are no exception (for example, Japanese people were represented as villains during the Pacific War, just as after 9/11, Middle Easterners were represented as villains). The representations of a particular cultural group depend upon social and historical contexts, but this particular representation of East Asia occurs because it is a cultural group that is not regarded as a part of "us," but as an "other" or "them"—those who are distinctively different from "us" (Inokuchi & Nozaki, 2005; Nozaki, 2009; Nozaki & Inokuchi, 1998). Though the recent economic advancement of East Asia can be attributed to a gradual change in power relations, historically, East Asian countries and people have been regarded as the "other," and the United States has maintained its cultural hegemony over the "other" part of the world for a long time. This cultural hegemony has shaped the study of Asia, and the forms in which the resulting knowledge is expressed.

In the case of Japan and the Japanese people, (western) cultural hegemony involves the production, circulation, and consumption of a particular kind of essentialized image. For example, the image of Japanese education as being a pressure cooker and culminating in "examination hell" has been prevalent in scholarly works, school textbooks, classroom discussions, and popular magazines (e.g., Nozaki, 2001; Tobin, 1986). The image of Japanese workers as robot-like, group-minded people has also repeatedly been portrayed in academia as well as popular media outlets (e.g., Kogure, 2008; Kogure & Nozaki, 2009). Movies and magazines alike have represented contemporary Japan as consisting of two opposites—the primordial, traditional culture and ultra-modern technology (e.g., *Lost in Translation*). These images are not completely false, but they are discourses that lead readers and viewers to a location where they can only see Japan in its essentialized and fixed forms (Fiske, 1987).

It is a challenge for Asian Studies libraries to value materials produced through oppositional and alternative cultures. For Asian libraries both support and are supported by the scholars and students of Japanese studies, who may not be able to completely shake themselves free from Orientalism.[6] Librarians select and acquire necessary books and documents for a scholarship that is still tainted by Orientalism, thus internalizing and reflecting its dispositions and preferences. By doing so, they participate in a selective tradition that maintains Western hegemony, or at least does not effectively counteract it.

Countering "Orientalism" in East Asian Libraries

How can East Asian libraries and librarians build library collections without falling into the trap of Orientalism? The major component of Orientalism seems to be the essentialist divide, the line drawn strictly between the West and the Orient that is one of the most fundamental operations of hegemonic power. The key problem here is that both essentialism and an essentialist view of culture regard a certain culture as monolithic, inherently and irreducibly different from other cultures. This view does not allow us to identify the diversity and conflicts within the culture. To counteract this essentialism, libraries need to focus on the variations, multiplicities, and contradictions within all Asian nations, peoples, and cultures. One useful approach here is to deconstruct a monolithic, fixed image of a given Asian nation by representing the multiplicity of cultures that exists within it.

Let us briefly introduce some of the innovative Japanese collections in North America. Hamilton Library at the University of Hawaii at Manoa retains the Sakamaki/Hawley Collection,[7] a compilation of more than 5,000 items of mostly Ryukyu source materials. Ryukyu (presently Okinawa

---

[6] Because the self is always constructed vis-à-vis the other(s), it would be difficult (and maybe unproductive) not to have the idea of Orient at all. The point should perhaps, be how to counter and deal with it. We discuss this point in detail elsewhere (Nozaki & Inokuchi, 1998).

[7] Frank Hawley was an English journalist and Shunzo Sakamaki was a professor at the University of Hawaii.

prefecture) has a distinct history and culture in Japan, and Hawley's Ryukyu Collection is considered very precious, since the majority of the Ryukyu/Okinawa materials were destroyed during World War II. In fact, a large percentage of Hawaii's Japanese Americans (the largest Asian ethnic group in Hawaii)[8] claim ancestral roots in Okinawa. Thus, when Professor Sakamaki attempted to purchase Hawley's collection, the United Okinawan Association of Hawaii helped by collecting donations. In this sense, this collection not only represents the multiplicity of Japanese culture, but also represents the multiplicity of Hawaiian culture. Other special collections include the Hokkaido Collection, Satsuma (presently Kagoshima prefecture) Collection, and Nan'yo (the Pacific Islands occupied by Japan during World War II) Collection. All represent the diverse historical and cultural experiences of Japan. Also, the Kajiyama Collection consists of the personal library of the late popular writer Toshiyuki Kajiyama, who was born in Seoul and educated through high school in Korea. Mr. Kajiyama was naturally attracted both to the culture and people of Korea and to issues on Japanese overseas migration. His collection, along with the others listed above, are very good resources for teaching about the different cultures (and subcultures) within Japan, and for challenging the dominant, essentialist view of Japanese culture. The Ryukyu/Okinawa collection, in particular, is an excellent resource for challenging the U.S. ("us") versus Japan ("them") binary, because many Hawaiian Japanese Americans have their roots in Okinawa. Although Japanese language materials are difficult to handle for non-Japanese speakers, critical librarians should make them accessible to students who are interested in Asia.

Another way to represent the multiplicity of a culture is to include material documenting subcultures. Though not housed within the East Asian Library, the Ohio State University library system includes the Cartoon Research Library, which has a substantial collection of Japanese Manga (comic books). Manga used to primarily target young people, but presently Manga are widely read by many adults, too, and incorporate a wide range of genres such as action-adventure, romance, sports, historical drama, science fiction, fantasy, mystery, horror, sexuality, food, and business. Japanese Manga are usually significantly longer than ordinary Western cartoons and a popular series of Manga can constitute several books. Popular Manga are often converted into animation movies. While

---

[8] According to the U.S. Census 2000, in the state of Hawaii, the population of Japanese Americans is 201,764. In comparison, the population of Whites is 294,102, and that of Filipinos is 170,635.

the origin of Manga dates back to as early as the 12th century, modern Manga appeared in the early 20th century (Aoki, 2009). However, the Manga genre experienced a revolution in the 1950s following the publication of Osamu Tezuka's *Tetsuwan Atomu* (Astro Boy) series, which was subsequently animated for television in the 1960s and became a tremendous hit. Today, Manga applies to both printed and animated forms, and is widely popular at both the national and global level. Although Manga is not seen as a part of high culture and contains some subversive material, for the most part, it reflects the dominant cultural and social values of contemporary Japanese society, making it a very valuable tool for the Japanese studies librarian who aims to introduce people to Japanese studies.[9] Following and documenting Manga's development is a very important task for the preservation of the cultural history of contemporary Japan, and not many libraries in Japan collect Manga. In the future, Manga—both printed and animated forms—should be collected more systematically, though it is not very easy to collect old Manga. For any teaching of contemporary Japan (including library instruction), Manga can be an excellent starting point, especially for those students who cannot read Japanese, as Manga is primarily a graphic form. Manga can be used as an introduction to contemporary Japanese literature or film, and can also be read as a form of social expression, and as such, a useful source for anthropological or sociological analysis. Hence, this kind of popular culture provides very good sources for critical analysis.

Some library collections focus on the contradictions or social conflicts within Japanese society. The East Asian Collection at Duke University's Perkins Library recently acquired an archival collection on Japanese student movements.[10] This collection consists of approximately 3,000 printed materials (books, periodicals, etc.) that span the severe confrontations that took place during the 1960s as a result of the Anpo treaty (The United States-Japan Security Treaty), through the protest movement's years of crisis and decay in the 1970s, and beyond. The protest movement against the Anpo treaty of 1960 was the largest political conflict in post-World War II Japan, and the subject is worth studying, as it is an important topic of history as well as social science. This kind of material will challenge the

---

[9] The OSU Libraries' Library Wiki page (http://library.osu.edu/wikis/library/index.php/Manga) on Manga provides excellent historical information, a bibliography and research examples on Manga.

[10] Detailed information about this collection can be found at http://library.duke.edu/digitalcollections/rbmscl/japanesepams/inv/.

common perception of Japan as a monolithic society that operates by the consensus. Political conflicts and social problems in Japan have been relatively neglected in the field of Japanese studies, but in many cases, related documents (such as court transcripts) are available (at least in Japan) and are relatively well organized. The collection development efforts of East Asian libraries in this area have not been strong, but recently some libraries have begun to acquire these kinds of documents; for example, the East Asian Library of UCLA acquired a multiple volume set of "Sengo Nihon kōgai Jiken Shiryō Shūsei [The Collection of Materials on Pollution Incidents in post-World War II Japan]." Even in Japan, very few university libraries systematically collect materials related to the political conflicts and social problems in Japan, though one exception is the Center for Education and Research in Cooperative Human Relations at the University of Saitama, which specializes in the collection of materials from a broad range of social movements in Japan.[11] It may be a good idea for a U.S. library to develop a special tie with the Center and make some duplicates from the collection.

Concluding Thoughts

In terms of the development of Japanese collections, the East Asian libraries of North American institutions have come to the point where they should begin—and some have already begun—focusing on the multiplicity of Japanese culture and on building more specialized collections that reflect the diversity of Japanese culture. In this way, they can counter the deep-rooted Orientalism in Western academia. It would also be a good idea for Japanese studies librarians to develop connections with special collection libraries in Japan that focus on heterogeneous aspects of Japanese culture and society in order to enhance their library's capability to be an active force in the critical transformation of the world. We would also suggest that librarians explore possibilities to develop counter-hegemonic collections in other fields, since the point about Japanese collection development also applies to other nationalities and ethnic groups in Asia (and, as a matter of fact, collection development in any part of the world).

Contemporary librarians of non-Western collections should be aware of a number of conceptual tools available for use as organizing principles for

---

11   The URL of the Center for Education and Research in Cooperative Human Relations is http://www.kyousei.iron.saitama-u.ac.jp/ (this site is in Japanese only).

their collection developments. Postcolonial studies provides a good set of conceptual tools. We have touched on the usefulness of Said's discussion on Orientalism and the importance of counteracting its essentialism, one tool available in postcolonial studies. Some critics and librarians may find other theoretical tools—such as the concept of hybridity or inauthenticity—useful in their respective contexts (e.g., Nozaki, 2009). Feminist and gender studies provide another set of useful tools, because looking at cultural practices from women's or from gay and lesbian perspectives inevitably challenges the construction of the Orient (and so the West) from the dominant (male) perspectives. It follows that a critical pedagogy of Asia in library instruction requires a multi-faceted, theoretical approach. These theories provide library educators with organizing principles of knowledge and a particular lens to examine library materials. These principles and lenses not only help us see clearly what is missing from already-existing collections and how materials circulating through dominant cultural institutions are part of Western selective traditions, but also enable us to use different search terms or develop a focus on different subject headings.

Regarding the training of librarians, while traditional professional training often emphasizes the importance of listening to the needs of the clients, the case of Orientalism shows that this approach is not enough. In order to critically examine current collection development policy and reference service practice—in addition to the major trends in, and the history of, a given subject area—expertise in critical sociology of knowledge—the area of study that examines knowledge and information circulating through the lenses of race, ethnicity, class, and gender—will be beneficial. Presently, work in critical sociology of knowledge is absent from library education, on the part of both teachers and learners. Libraries primarily deal with the circulation (and production to some extent) of knowledge, but the content and the process of circulation also have social consequences. Hence, librarians must develop the expertise to understand and proactively deal with such consequences from critical sociological perspectives.

References

Anyon, J. (1979). Ideology and United-States textbooks. *Harvard Educational Review*, 49(3), 361-386.
Aoki, D. (n.d.). History of Manga—Early origins of Japanese comics. Retrieved June 10, 2009, from http://manga.about.com/od/historyofmanga/a/mangahistory1.htm

Apple, W. M. (1979). *Ideology and curriculum*. London: Routledge & Kegan Paul.

Bernstein, B. (1977). *Class, class, codes and control vol. 3: Towards a theory of educational transmissions (2nd ed.)*. London and Boston: Routledge & Kegan Paul.

Fiske, J. (1987). *Television culture: Popular pleasures and politics*. London: Methuen.

Hall, S. (1992). The West and the Rest: Discourse and power. In S. Hall & B. Gieben (Eds.), *Formations of modernity*. (pp. 275-331). Cambridge: Polity Press.

Inokuchi, H. & Nozaki, Y. (2005). "Different than us": Othering, Orientalism, and US middle school students' discourses on Japan. *Asia Pacific Journal of Education*, 25(1), 61-74.

Kogure, S. (2008). *Othering in the technological environment: Techno-Orientalism, techno-nationalism, and identity formation of Japanese college students in the United States*. Tokyo: Tokyo-Kyogakusha Co.

Kogure, S. & Nozaki, Y. (2009). Techno-Orientalism and the images of Japan in National Geographic. *Comparative minds, critical visions: Center for Comparative and Global Studies in Education working paper Series 3* (2009):23-27.

Lee, R. (1999). *Orientals: Asian Americans in popular culture*. Philadelphia: Temple University Press.

Lewis, A. M. (2008). *Questioning library neutrality: Essays from Progressive librarian*. Duluth, Minn: Library Juice Press.

McCarthy C. & Crichlow, W. (Eds.), (1993). *Race, identity and representation in education*. New York: Routledge.

Minear, R. (1980). Orientalism and the study of Japan. *Journal of Asian Studies*, 39(3), 507-517.

Nozaki, Y. (2009). Critical teaching about Asia: Orientalism, the West and non-West binary, and postcolonial perspectives. *Journal of Intercultural Studies*, 30(2), 141-155.

Nozaki, Y. (2001). U.S. discourses on Japanese education: World geography textbooks and the representation of Japan as the "other" in the age of educational reform. In S. R. Steinberg (Ed.), *Multi/intercultural conversations: A reader* (pp. 136-165), New York: Peter Lang.

Nozaki, Y. & Inokuchi, H. (1998). What U.S. middle schoolers bring to the classroom: Students writing on the Pacific War. *Education about Asia*, 3(3), 30-34.

Said, E. W. (1978). *Orientalism*. New York: Vintage Books.

Shaull, R. (1970). Foreword. In P. Freire, *Pedagogy of the oppressed*. New York: Continuum.

Tobin, J. J. (1986). American images of Japanese secondary and higher education. In W. K. Cummings, E. R. Beauchamp, S. Ichikawa, V. N. Kobayashi, & M. Ushiogi (Eds.), *Educational policies in crisis: Japanese and American perspectives*. (pp. 262-274). New York, NY: Praeger.

Whitty, G. (1992). Education, economy, and national culture. In R. Bocock & K. Thompson (Eds.), *Social and cultural forms of modernity*. (pp. 267-309). Cambridge: Polity Press.

Williams, R. (1977). *Marxism and literature*. New York: Oxford University Press.

Section Five

Institutional Power

Teaching Against the Grain: Critical Assessment in the Library Classroom

Maria T. Accardi

Critical perspectives on assessment in higher education focus on its function as a regulator of the hierarchical structures that govern the university. Reynolds & Trehan (2000) observe that "[Assessment]'s function in providing the basis for granting or withholding qualifications makes it a primary location for power relations" (p. 268). And it is at the site of assessment that these power relations are validated and institutionalized, as Leathwood (2005) asserts: "Assessment has served, alongside a discourse of meritocracy, to legitimize and rationalize the unequal distribution of power and resources in society" (p. 310). In an institution of higher learning, assessment results serve to legitimize a course or an instruction program, provide evidence of student learning, substantiate effective instruction, and justify curricula. Not only do institutions require an ongoing process of programmatic and student learning outcome assessment for their own institutional purposes, institutions are also accountable to regional and disciplinary accrediting bodies, which places additional demands on an institution to demonstrate student learning.

This current dominant culture of higher education privileges a model of student learning that can be substantiated in standardized tests and other measures that similarly erase difference and reward conformity to immutable, uninterrogated standards. These measures serve to perpetuate the existence of the dominant culture. Understandably, many critical teachers chafe at such standards. Critical teachers seek to resist these political pressures that are concerned with churning out pasteurized processed student product and muting the flavors and colors of difference and diversity, but this resistance is often thwarted, rejected, or dismissed. As bell hooks (1994) observes, "[g]iven that our educational institutions are so deeply invested in a banking system, teachers are more rewarded when we do not teach against the grain" (p. 203). Teachers are indeed rewarded for supporting and perpetuating the banking model, so why does it matter to be critical? Why *should* critical teachers resist? Why should we seek alternative ways of teaching and assessing what we teach? Are there alternative rewards for these alternative approaches?

I believe we can begin answering these questions by examining the role of the library and the critical librarian who is embedded in this dominant culture of higher education. The library, while often regarded at least symbolically as the intellectual center of a campus, still has limited ability to resist. The library is charged with developing collections that support the curriculum and general education outcomes of the university, and with providing instructional services that help fulfill these general education outcomes. Libraries are rewarded for falling into lockstep behind chancellors, vice chancellors, trustees, and deans, the figures who control the budget that is the library's lifeblood. But despite the library's institutional demand to support the dominant culture of higher education, the *librarians* who work within that library may have some degree of freedom that teaching faculty outside the library do not. Librarians occupy a space that is separate but unequal, and quite different than that of teaching faculty. Even librarians with faculty status are not always accorded the same status as teaching faculty.[1] I contend that this marginal status can paradoxically allow for more opportunities for critical teaching and assessment. Because the primary educational outcome the library is usually expected to support—information literacy—is often overlooked, misunderstood, or minimally supported by the accrediting standards that legitimize the university, a librarian can leverage this marginal status and have the freedom to experiment with critical instructional methods and assessment strategies. Teaching against the grain, as hooks calls it, can have rewards for the critical teaching librarian.

The Pressures of Accreditation and the Place of the Library

When it comes to institutional accreditation, the academic library plays a role in providing evidence of teaching and learning, although this role varies by accrediting body. Laura Saunders's (2007) analysis of the ways in which regional accreditation organizations treat information literacy reveals

---

[1] Librarians in the Indiana University Libraries system have faculty status and are tenure track, but librarians are on 12-month contracts, while teaching faculty are on 10-month contracts. While many of their policies and procedures overlap, librarians and teaching faculty have separate faculty manuals and different requirements for the content of tenure dossiers. Teaching faculty dossiers include student evaluations of teaching in their dossiers, but librarians have no such official equivalent. And when faculty submit dossiers, teaching faculty dossiers travel a separate routing path than do librarian faculty tenure dossiers.

that all six major accrediting bodies in the United States address information literacy. However, not all of them use the term "information literacy," and instead refer to the importance of the library and its instructional role in the university (p. 321). And the degree to which each accreditation organization emphasizes the importance of information literacy varies as well. The Middle States Commission on Higher Education (MSCHE) "is the only accrediting organization to offer a comprehensive definition of information literacy," and "stresses the need for collaboration between faculty and librarians in the instruction and assessment of information literacy skills" (p. 321). Curiously, the accrediting organization that has the most regional oversight—the North Central Association of Colleges and Schools (NCACS)[2]—provides the least amount of emphasis on information literacy. Sanders observes that NCACS "uses the word library nine times throughout its standards, but only refers to the libraries' instructional role once, noting that institutions must employ sufficient library staff to maintain the resources and to 'train the students in their use'" (p. 323). The library's role is defined mainly in terms of its support of teaching and learning through "collecting and providing access to information resources" (p. 323). MSCHE and NCACS are at opposite ends of the spectrum, and these organizations, along with the other regional accrediting bodies in between[3], "place a high value on the skills associated with information literacy" (p. 323), according to Saunders. In addition, Saunders's analysis demonstrates that "all accrediting organizations devote large portions of text to expectations for outcomes assessment, in the library and beyond" (p. 325). Saunders notes that most organizations emphasize that "assessment should be institution-wide and include all programs, services, and offerings" (p. 325).

NCACS is the accrediting body that governs my current institution, Indiana University Southeast (IUS)[4], and, as discussed above, it provides the

---

[2] NCACS has regional authority over institutions of higher education in the following 19 states: Arizona, Arkansas, Colorado, Illinois, Indiana, Iowa, Kansas, Michigan, Minnesota, Missouri, Nebraska, New Mexico, North Dakota, Ohio, Oklahoma, South Dakota, West Virginia, Wisconsin, and Wyoming.

[3] New England Association of Schools and Colleges (NEASC), Southern Association of Colleges and Schools (SACS), North West Commission on Colleges and Universities (NWCCU), and Western Association of Schools and Colleges (WASC).

[4] IUS, located in New Albany, Indiana, is one of Indiana University's six regional campuses.

least amount of guidance when it comes to information literacy. However, as Saunders notes, NCACS "clearly states that the quality of the library is no longer measured by numbers of books, but by how well the library supports the teaching and learning of its parent institution" (p. 325). And while information literacy is marginalized by NCACS's standards—its use of the word "train" in reference to the library's instructional role is telling— I rely upon the NCACS's explication of Criterion Three for guidance on assessment. Criterion Three: Core Component 3a states, "The organization's goals for student learning outcomes are clearly stated for each educational program and make effective assessment possible" (3.2-9). Core Component 3a provides examples of evidence in this section as well, offering suggestions and best practices. These examples of evidence state and restate in several different ways the role of assessment: "Assessment of student learning provides evidence at multiple levels: course, program, and institutional," "Assessment of student learning includes multiple direct and indirect measures of student learning," and so on (3.2-10). The document does not, however, make provisions for methods of assessment, presumably leaving that to the discretion of the institution or program. This lack of specificity about assessment methods in particular and information literacy in general would seem to provide considerable freedom to library instructors at an NCACS institution, unless the institution itself provides more stringent guidelines and standards. And, indeed, the library instruction program at IUS has a very loosely defined General Education Student Learning Outcome, an extremely diluted distillation of the ACRL standards, to undergird its instructional practices and program assessment: "Information Literacy: Use appropriate tools and technologies to identify, access, and evaluate, and use information effectively. Use information responsibly, in accordance with legal and ethical principles" (IU Southeast General Education)[5].

Information literacy is one of the eight General Education Student Learning Outcomes approved by the Faculty Senate in 2004. General Education outcomes are reviewed on three-year cycles. The spring semester

---

[5] An interesting aside: For a time, the information literacy learning outcome mysteriously vanished from the IUS General Education website. It is believed that the site maintainers conflated it with "information technology fluency," a now defunct general education outcome, and thus deleted it from the site. No one knows how long "information literacy" was absent; I noticed it at some point last year. After bringing it to the attention of the Vice Chancellor of Academic Affairs, it was restored to the site months later.

in 2007 was the first time information literacy assessment was tapped for General Educational Committee review. As the coordinator of library instruction, I was charged with presenting an assessment report to the General Education Committee, but I had no example to follow. Given the perennial struggle faced by many library instruction programs to seek faculty buy-in and institutional recognition, I determined that a report containing numbers, charts, graphs, and quantitative data would be most appropriate and convincing, and I mined the assessment results of our pre- and post-test administered to First Year Seminar library session students to retrieve numbers to analyze. I submitted the report to the Committee, who apparently passed it onto the Faculty Senate, where it has apparently disappeared into oblivion. This is disheartening but not surprising. Despite its institutional validation by its inclusion in the General Education Learning Outcomes, and despite the positive relationships between the teaching faculty and the library and the resultant positive perceptions of our library's instructional services, information literacy continues to be dismissed as not equally important or as essential as other general education outcomes and learning goals.

Envisioning Critical Assessment

Keeping in mind that instruction program coordinators still must supply the evidence that institutions and accrediting organizations prefer—whether or not anyone will actually read it—the library instruction program's marginal position nonetheless provides it with a great opportunity to experiment with assessment practices and enact more critical methods that challenge the dominant modes of traditional assessment. Proponents of critical assessment methods contend that critical assessment flattens the hierarchy that is reinforced by traditional assessment methods. In conventional assessment models, the instructor deposits information in students and students retrieve that information in order to answer questions correctly and uncritically. Assessing in this way does not promote independent critical thinking (Reynolds & Trehan, 2000, p. 269). Critical assessment of student learning outcomes, on the other hand, disrupts that power relationship and challenges the way learning is defined, measured, and evaluated. Then, in turn, this approach provides an opportunity for critical programmatic assessment, where librarians can evaluate their instructional services in units other than numbers, percentages, and graphs.

One critical approach to assessment is participative assessment. As defined by Reynolds & Trehan (2000), participative assessment is "a process in which students and tutors share, to some degree, the responsibility for making evaluations and judgments about students' written work, gaining insight into how judgments are made and finding appropriate ways to communicate them" (p. 270). A participative assessment model, as explicated by Price, O'Donovan, and Rust (2007), employs a participative approach informed by social-constructivism, which posits that "knowledge is shaped and evolves through increasing participation within communities of practice, and that for students to truly understand the requirements of the assessment process, and the criteria and standards being applied, they need tacit as well as explicit knowledge" (p. 143). These student-centered approaches propose to encourage critical thinking and empower students to share responsibility for their learning. In addition, participating in the development of assessment criteria may provide students with the opportunity to influence the criteria (Reynolds & Trehan, 2000, p. 270). The model described by Reynolds & Trehan shows students in a management course collaborating in learning groups: "Peer assessment is intended to evaluate each student's understanding of their chosen topic and how it relates to the practice of management. They are expected to record the comments and grades that result from group discussions. In this sense, students' dialogue and social support is fundamental to the assessment process" (p. 270).

Critical assessment methods seem particularly designed for traditional courses in which classes meet more than once and students and instructor have ongoing relationships. But in library instruction, the librarian will teach a one-shot session for 50 minutes or slightly more, and then she may never see those students again. There isn't time for relationship-building, let alone collaboratively development of assessment criteria. How, then, might critical assessment methods work in a library instruction program? I envision using the focus group in conjunction with a portfolio assessment program as a critical assessment method. Below I will imagine such a model, using my current collaborative efforts in portfolio assessment as an example.

Focus groups assess the affective domain of learning. Understanding how students think and feel about their learning experiences is an important component of a critical pedagogical practice. As Kincheloe (2004) observes, "It is not an exaggeration to say that before critical pedagogy can work, teachers must understand what is happening in the minds of their students" (p. 20). Similarly, teaching librarians can employ focus groups in library instruction programs to illuminate student perceptions and experiences of library instruction services. Becher & Flug (2005) and Spackman (2007) describe using student focus groups for library assessment. Spackman discusses the evaluation of library instruction and library outreach through focus groups involving undergraduate students and graduate teaching assistants. Becher & Flug use focus groups in conjunction with a LIBQUAL analysis to evaluate student perceptions of library services. These examples, however, do not take into account student experiences of library instruction assessment.

Portfolio assessment in library instruction is a method of evaluating information literacy in the context of actual student work. This sort of direct, or authentic, assessment usually focuses on student research portfolios, where students submit a research paper together with a research log or an annotated bibliography, or some other sort of written work that documents and reflects upon the student's research process and the sources the student used. Librarian assessment of student research portfolios can be done in the context of a stand-alone credit-based library research course (Sonley, Turner, Myer, & Cotton, 2007), in collaboration with teaching faculty in a first year composition course (Scharf, Elliot, Huey, Briller, & Joshi, 2007; Sharma, 2007), or in other contexts, such as an undergraduate honors course (Snavely & Wright, 2003). Librarians can use a rubric to assess information literacy outcomes as evidenced in the student portfolio (Choinski, Mark, & Murphey, 2003; Knight, 2006; Diller & Phelps, 2008).

At my institution, I have been collaborating with the director of the honors program in assessing student e-portfolios submitted by students in the introductory honors seminars (Honors 103 and 104). In the first semester (Honors 103), I teach an instruction session focusing on the use of library research tools (the library catalog and article databases) and the evaluation of information sources. I also meet individually with students to talk about their research topics, helping them refine their topics and identify appropriate tools and resources for their research. Then, in the second semester (Honors 104), I conduct two additional library instruction sessions, which differ significantly from the more typical "here's the catalog, here's the database page" kind of sessions. The first session consists of an activity inspired by Troy Swanson's (2004) example of a critical information literacy model. In this activity, students are presented with six information sources all on the same topic (in this case, the local food movement), and they are asked to describe what type of sources they are—scholarly, popular, site on the open web, and so on. Then, the students are presented with information need scenarios and are asked to decide which of the sources reviewed earlier best meets the information need in the described scenario. In the second session, I use an activity inspired by the example described by Reeves,

McMillan, and Gibson (2008), where students are responsible for learning how to use a research tool and teaching the class how to use it.

After these two sessions, students in Honors 104 continue working on the same topics they developed in the Honors 103 sessions and the research consultations I held with them. Then, when students actually conduct their research and submit research papers as a part of a comprehensive research e-portfolio, I review the papers, looking at the types of sources used and their use and integration into the paper. I conduct this evaluation using a rubric I developed that is mapped to the ACRL information literacy standards.[6]

What would happen, though, if I invited students to contribute to and shape the way I assess their information literacy skills? And what would happen if students were given the opportunity to self-assess their information literacy skills? By the second semester in Honors 104, I have developed a relationship with students. I have gotten to know them, I know their research topics, and they see me as a resource for their projects. They stop me when they see me in the library and say, "Ms. Accardi, I got those books you helped me find," or they friend me on Facebook and send me messages asking how to do interlibrary loan. So, by this time, after all of the work we have done together, when it comes time to assess their work, there is an opportunity to build upon the collaborative, participative, student-centered model we've been developing. Radcliff et al. (2007) notes that "it is important that students understand how their work will be assessed," (p. 139), and it is here that I can take the opportunity to not just inform students about how their work will be evaluated, but invite them to participate in the development of assessment criteria. Here I return to the focus group and imagine it as a participative tool that gives students a voice in influencing the way they are assessed.

A plan for such a strategy might look like this: In the spring semester, I will invite students in Honors 104 to participate in an information literacy assessment focus group. In this focus group, the facilitator—who may or may not be me—will define information literacy and briefly summarize the ways in which information literacy is assessed. I will have developed a list of questions that invite students to 1) comment on the concept of information literacy and its relevance to their research and writing projects, 2) imagine ways in which information literacy might be evaluated in the context of

---

[6] Critical teaching librarians must take care to critique the standards that we use to conduct our own critical assessment practices, as I briefly discuss later, and as other authors in this collection discuss more thoroughly (TK pp. #).

their work, 3) evaluate the information literacy rubric I've previously developed, and 4) make suggestions for revisions to assessment methods and instruments (including the aforementioned rubric). The overarching goal governing these discussions will be to help students understand learning outcomes I wish for them to achieve and to provide them with an opportunity to play a role in critiquing these learning outcomes and defining how they will be assessed. But I also want them to learn that the ways in which they are assessed, measured, and determined to be successful (or not) are created by the people who create and perpetuate the dominant culture of higher education. This is an opportunity for students to experience and learn from a teacher who, in the words of hooks (1994), "[has] the courage to transgress those boundaries that would confine each pupil to a rote, assembly-line approach to learning" (p. 13).

Teachers who empower students at the assessment level do more than just expose students to alternative models of thinking and learning in the dominant culture of higher education. They also teach students that their voices matter, that they are more than just numbers or units or statistics. They are people, not products, with valid thoughts and important ideas. The promise of hooks's (1994) model of engaged pedagogy seems particularly relevant here: "To teach in a manner that respects and cares for the souls of students is essential if we are to provide the necessary conditions where learning can most deeply and intimately begin" (p. 13). Put differently, empowering students at the assessment level honors the individual and unique voices of each student in a way that the dominant culture of higher education does not.

I had the opportunity to pilot the information literacy assessment focus group described above and I was able to witness how student involvement in assessment has an empowering impact on those students. In the focus group, I distributed to the students the rubric I have used previously to assess information literacy skills as exemplified in portfolios and asked them to evaluate and comment on it. It was pleasing and exciting to see students make very astute observations about the rubric. One row of the rubric, based on ACRL Standard 1, concerns the variety of sources used in a research paper. The ratings for this characteristic is as follows: "1—Uses sources from only one source type, 2—uses mix of two source types, and 3—Uses mix of more than two source types." This rating clearly privileges using multiple source types. The students quite rightly pointed out that the number of source types used in a research paper depends on context. For example, one student was researching the history of a particular animal breed. Most of the valid, credible sources available on her topic were websites. She should not be penalized for using the best sources possible for this topic just because she didn't use more than one type of source. When I conceded this point to the students, acknowledged its importance, and informed them that I was going to remove or edit how source type variety was evaluated in the rubric, it was clear that students were pleased that they were consulted and that their opinions made a difference in how they were going to be assessed. This affective impact is difficult to quantify, but this respect and care for the souls of students, to use hooks's words, contributes to a positive, successful, and empowered learning environment.

Now that I've concluded the focus groups, my subsequent evaluation of these students' portfolios will occur in conjunction with the students' self-assessment of their portfolios using our collaboratively-designed criteria. Students are already expected to provide meta-cognitive letters reflecting upon all submitted work in the portfolio, which includes a video of a speech they delivered in class and their favorite piece of written work for the course, as well as their research paper. An additional meta-cognitive letter will prompt them to reflect on their research process and information literacy skills.

After students have submitted the e-portfolios, complete with their self-assessment, and I have completed my evaluations, I will follow up with an electronic survey asking students to reflect on my evaluations and how they felt about participating in developing the assessment criteria. Given that this will take place after the semester is over, it will be difficult to get student participation, but I think it is important to make the effort to get feedback after the completion of the initial assessment. This feedback can be used to inform future assessment methods and practices.

Critiquing the Critique

And it must be noted, too, that critical methods of assessment are not immune to their own critique. Self-assessment, for example, is typically regarded as "empowering." Tan (2004) notes, "The student's lack of power is framed as an impediment to their learning and student self-assessment is commonly advocated as an opportunity for students to gain a measure of power or control in the assessment process. The assumption is that student participation in the assessment process enhances student empowerment" (p. 651). However, Tan's examination of differing notions of power—sovereign, epistemological, and disciplinary power—indicates that student empowerment is dependent on the type of power exercised. Tan notes, "Power should be appreciated for its productive pedagogical potential. It is not simply an evil to be shunted away in order for students to learn freely" (p. 660). Rather, the emphasis should be on how power can be best used for the benefit of students (p. 660). That is, it is not sufficient to merely empower students; instead, the issue is whether self-assessment has provided any benefit to students. The emphasis should be on learning: "Focusing on learning allows all parties to consider the various impediments to students benefiting from their self-assessment in terms of learning and not in terms of autonomy" (p. 660). For all of our desire to trouble the power relations we see in the hierarchy of assessment, student learning must be at the forefront of any of our efforts.

While I concede this point, I would argue here that student learning in a critical assessment context involves more than just learning the curricular content of the classroom. It includes learning about the inevitability of power structures that govern the university, and how teachers and students alike might find room in this power structure to resist the status quo. This awakening to the dominant culture of power—an awakening not unlike Freire's concept of conscientiziation—is an opportunity for students to learn that universities are concerned with producing graduates so that they can meet their institutionally-driven retention targets, which, in turn, result in more or less state funding. Students might arrive at the cynical realization that for all of its posturing about a caring, nurturing environment, many universities mostly care about numbers, not about the self-actualization of students.

The primary shortcoming of this focus group + portfolio assessment model is the impossibility of conducting it on a scale much larger than one class. The demands of limited time and resources hamper the librarian's ability to thoughtfully experiment with formative assessment models such as the one imagined above. What, then, can we do with the results of the assessment, and how generalizable are the assessment findings to the larger pedagogical strategies of an instruction program? How meaningful is a sample of one? Moreover, this sort of model is dependent on a good working relationship with a member of teaching faculty; my project is impossible without a relationship that encourages and fosters collaboration and innovation. And while the institutional and accrediting requirements that govern my institution create space for enriching assessment methods in a critical way, other libraries may not have that freedom. Laboring under the demands of accrediting and institutional requirements, libraries may have little choice but to input information into students' heads and then request that the students regurgitate it. Even so, as I've discussed throughout this chapter, libraries might have more freedom to do critical assessment work than they think.

At the heart of the pre- and post-test measure, portfolio assessment, focus group discussion, and rubric development is an investigation of what standards or criteria we use to evaluate information literacy. Reliance on using the ACRL information literacy standards—and reliance on the very concept and definition of information literacy—is not without its problems, as Maura Seale and Benjamin Harris discuss elsewhere in this volume. Critical assessment methods demand interrogation of the assumptions that shape the standards employed to organize, validate, and measure student learning. Again, here we have a site where the the marginal status of the library instruction coordinator has some freedom to both challenge institutional requirements while still conforming to the required framework. Standards are developed in the context of dominant cultures and discourses that privilege certain kinds of knowledge and learning while marginalizing others. Cushla Kapitzke's (2003) critique of the concept of information literacy helpfully identifies the problems inherent in this approach. Kapitzke argues, "Information literacy, as a method of approaching textual work, is not autonomous and neutral; it intersects with variables of gender, age, socioeconomic status, ethnicity, religion, and geographic location to generate different learning outcomes in different classrooms and education and educational contexts." (p. 49). I see my critical model described above as a place where the focus group has particular value. Conducting honors student focus groups as a way of collaborating and shaping assessment criteria is one way in which I might trouble the monolith that is the concept of information literacy and the student as conceived within the ACRL standards.

Embracing the Margins

At our place in the margins, where we contribute to general education but are not of general education, where we are forgotten or misunderstood, where we are subject to uninterrogated standards, there can be, paradoxically, great freedom. We cannot dismantle the repressive strictures of accreditation, or secede from the institution and refuse to comply with the legitimizing practices to which we are subject. We can, however, in our own ways, however small, clear out space for creative disruption, for thoughtful experimentation, and for subtle but satisfying interruptions of the structures that govern us, and, ultimately, contribute to student learning in a positive and long-lasting way.

References

Becher, M. L. & Flug, J. L. (2005). Using student focus groups to inform library planning and marketing. *College & Undergraduate Libraries, 12*(1/2), 1-18

Choinski, E., Mark, A. E., & Murphey, M. (2003). Assessment with rubrics: An efficient and objective means of assessing student outcomes in an information resources class. *portal: Libraries and the Academy, 3*(4), 563-575.

Diller, K. R. & Phelps, S. F. (2008). Learning outcomes, portfolios, and rubrics, oh my! Authentic assessment of an information literacy program. *portal: Libraries and the Academy, 8*(1), 75-89.

Indiana University Southeast. General Education. http://www.ius.edu/generaleducation/outcomes.cfm. Accessed 14 February 2009.

hooks, bell. (1994). Teaching to transgress. New York: Routledge.

Kapitzke, C. (2003). *I*nformation literacy: A positivist epistemology and a politics of *out*formation. *Educational Theory, 53*(1), 37-53.

Kincheloe, J. L. (2004). *Critical pedagogy primer.* New York: Peter Lang.

Knight, L. A. (2006). Using rubrics to assess information literacy. *Reference Services Review, 34*(1), 43-55.

Leathwood, C. (2005). Assessment policy and practice in higher education: Purpose, standards, and equity. *Assessment & Evaluation in Higher Education, 30*(3), 307-324.

North Central Association Higher Learning Commission. Exploring the criteria and the core components. *The Handbook of Accreditation*, 3.2-1-3.2-20. http://www.ncahigherlearningcommission.org.

Price, M., O'Donovan, B., & Rust, C. (2007). Putting a social-constructivist assessment process model into practice: Building the feedback loop into the assessment process through peer review. *Innovations in Education and Teaching International, 44*(2), 143-152.

Radcliff, C. J., Jensen, M. L., Salem Jr., J. A., Burhanna, K. J., Gedeon, K. J. (Eds.). (2007*) A practical guide to information literacy assessment for academic librarians.* Westport, CT: Libraries Unlimited.

Reeves, L., McMillan, J., & Gibson, R. (2008). Keep them engaged: Cooperative learning with the Jigsaw Method. In D. Cook & R. Sittler (Eds.), *Practical pedagogy for library instructors: 17 innovative strategies to improve student learning* (77-86). Chicago: Association of College and Research Libraries.

Reynolds, M., & Trehan, K. (2000). Assessment: A critical perspective. *Studies in Higher Education, 25*(3), 267-278.

Saunders, L. (2007). Regional accreditation organizations' treatment of information literacy: Definitions, collaboration, and assessment. *The Journal of Academic Librarianship, 33*(3), 317-326.

Scharf, D., Elliot, N., Huey, H. A., Briller, V., & Joshi, K. (2007). Direct assessment of information literacy using writing portfolios. *Journal of Academic Librarianship, 33*(4), 462-477.

Sharma, S. (2007). From chaos to clarity: Using the research portfolio to teach and assess information literacy skills. *Journal of Academic Librarianship, 33*(1), 127-135.

Snavely, L. L. & Wright, C. A. (2003). Research portfolio use in undergraduate honors education: Assessment tool and model for future work. *Journal of Academic Librarianship, 29*(5), 298-303.

Sonley, V., Turner, D., Myer, S., & Cotton, Y. (2007). Information literacy assessment by portfolio: A case study. *Reference Services Review, 35*(1), 41-70.

Spackman, E. (2007). Utilizing focus groups to evaluate an information literacy program in a general biology course. *Science & Technology Libraries, 27*(3), 3-28.

Swanson, T. (2004). A radical step: Implementing a critical information literacy model. *portal: Libraries and the Academy, 4*(2), 259-273.

Tan, K. H. K. (2004). Does student self-assessment empower or discipline students? *Assessment & Evaluation in Higher Education, 29*(6), 651-662.

Information Is Personal: Critical Information Literacy and Personal Epistemology

Troy A. Swanson

Paulo Freire (1970) challenged educators to move beyond the banking concept of education. The banking concept views students as a sort of knowledge repository where instructors deposit facts, figures, definitions, and thoughts for later use. Not only does this view remove the autonomy of the individual over her or his own education, but it takes away any notion of active learning and personal creativity. The instructor is the actor and the student is the receiver. The banking concept refuses to explore the role of culture, socio-economic status, and systemic power that underlie all concepts of knowledge and information.

In terms of information literacy, the banking concept would situate understanding, finding, and using information as rote skills that are to be performed with machine-like precision by students churning out research papers. Several writers, including myself, have suggested *critical information literacy* approaches that reframe knowledge and information in terms of societal power structures, economic factors, and political systems (Luke and Kapitzke, 1999; Kapitzke, 2001; Swanson, 2004; Elmborg, 2006). These approaches see information systems—including libraries and educational systems—as structures that tend to reinforce the societal status quo by supporting the values behind it and limiting access to media outlets and mass distribution of information. The statements' various stances toward critical information literacy recast information literacy skills as a means to individual empowerment by challenging and rethinking the status quo and the ways of knowing that they represent. These writers view the librarian-to-student interaction as a problem-posing journey that allows librarians to act as partners in the meaning-making process along with students.

The various critical information literacy approaches present arguments aimed at librarians and the education community. They assume that a fully-realized critical information literacy model presents an opportunity to make information literacy more vital to higher education, and they assume that this means more vital to students. I suggest that this assumption may not be well-founded. The significant challenge to a fully realized critical information literacy perspective does not lie in convincing librarians, faculty members, administrators, or professional organizations about the benefits of a critical approach, although this is important. It lies with convincing our students by shifting the focus of critical pedagogy toward student belief about knowledge and worldview.

Paulo Freire Doesn't Live in the Suburbs

Several scholars have noted that many students enter higher education with a systemic view of education where their college environment is a system to be navigated. Many students hold anti-intellectual and anti-learning attitudes. Some students go so far as to express attitudes of practically open defiance (Kohl, 1994; Leo, 1996; Arvidson, 2008; Elias, 2008). This matches some of the experience I have had in the classroom and in the attitudes demonstrated by students in focus groups I've conducted. "Is this going to be on the test," is not an uncommon feeling. Luckily, open hostility is not common, but polite perseverance and kind-hearted humoring of the instructor or librarian is more common. Many students who are engaged in their education do so because they see education as a large job-training program that teaches work skills (Shapiro, 2005; McNay, 2006). Higher education is not about improving society or the self, but it is about jumping through hoops with the hopes that a larger paycheck lies ahead.

This is hardly an environment where discussions of "oppression" and political-power structures carry much weight with students. It is not a stretch to say that many students prefer the banking model of education. The "is-this-on-the-test" attitude pervades. Students may view education as a way to change their economic conditions but they have no desire to examine what values and assumptions dominate our political or economic systems. They are not interested in using education to challenge these systems. In fact, I would argue that many students see education as a way to access and become a part of these systems.

So, what do we do when students prefer the banking model? If we see critical pedagogy as an avenue to a more meaningful approach to information literacy, how do we engage students in the larger discussion about the nature of information and the ways that information is created? I do believe that the problem-posing approach that has been proposed by many critical pedagogy practitioners (Luke and Kapitzke, 1999; Kapitzke, 2001; Swanson, 2004; Elmborg, 2006) can provide an avenue for this engagement. I believe that the starting problem is to ask the question "how do you know what you know?" From a critical pedagogical standpoint, this question encourages us to consider the nature of information sources and the societal influences on these sources, but this question encourages us to do more than that. This question also encourages us to be introspective and to consider how our beliefs interact with information sources. I have asked myself this question in my own research, and I have considered how my beliefs dictate my own research.

A Personal Story

I am currently in the midst of my doctoral research in community college leadership, and for this research, I have selected a model that frames community colleges as loosely coupled systems as defined by organizational psychologist Karl Weick (1976). When I initiated the dissertation process, I imagined myself reviewing the literature on organizational theory and determining how that literature may be applied to community colleges. I envisioned a process that weighs the benefits of one model against the benefits of another model. The picture in my mind was of a checklist that included models and attributes. I would carefully consider these models and discuss them with my committee chair.

As a librarian, I should have known better. This is not at all what happened. The reality is that I reviewed a few articles that described organization models on higher education, and I stumbled upon the model that I would use for my own research. In one of those "ah ha" moments, I immediately knew that this was the model I needed and this would be the model I would use. After that, I performed a cursory review of the remaining major organization models of higher education partly to satisfy myself and mostly to satisfy my committee, and I started to gather as many sources as possible on loosely coupled systems. The decision that I made was practically instantaneous. My imagined checklist never existed. There was no cost/benefit analysis between models. Something in my mind clicked and that was that.

Looking back, I asked myself: why did this one model standout from all of the others? Why did I immediately recognize that this was the model that I needed? As information literacy practitioners, we may explain this in terms of the characteristics of the information source matching my information need. Information scientists may explain this through human computer interaction models, information processing behaviors, information exchange theory, recognition of cognitive authority, and any number of other models and frameworks that are applicable and offer way to view this decision (Spink, 2000; Wilson, 1983).

There is value in all of these explanations, but as someone who greatly values critical theory and critical pedagogy, I also have to step back and think about how the ideas in these sources have made their way to me. The higher education literature is not exempt from the systemic pressures that impact how we view this industry. Too often the views of minority groups, support staff, students, and part-time faculty are absent from the conversation. The impact of campus, local, and national politics are not acknowledged, and the dominance of formal methodologies based on scientifically sound assumptions is assumed. Our role in addressing injustice in our society too often takes a backseat to the needs of industry. To some degree, the higher education model I chose does address some of these criticisms that I hold of higher education and the higher education literature. It does look at individual actors and their motivations for carrying out their responsibilities, and in my own research, it would provide me with an opportunity to seek out some of the unheard voices within the higher education literature. But, this is only part of the reason that I find this model attractive, and it is not really the cause of that "ah ha" moment.

Perhaps the most important reason that I selected this source is that I recognize how this framework matched my understanding of how community colleges operate. It offers explanations for how individuals perform their own responsibilities, how they work together in organizational units and groups, how values and beliefs are communicated within the organization, how interests of individuals and groups are negotiated, and how decisions are made at the grassroots and the topmost levels of the organizational chart. The bottom line is that this framework closely matched my *experiences and understandings* of how community colleges actually operated. It matched the reality that I perceived. It had little to do with costs and benefits, little to do with unheard voices in higher education, and everything to do with my own beliefs and perceptions.

Most of us who have conducted research, especially extensive research, are quite familiar with this "ah ha" moment when lightning strikes. This is not a moment when logic and analysis align with outside sources, but belief and worldview do so. As we filter the multitude of information sources that come our way, there are external factors that we must consider about how information is made, but we also must recognize the ways that our own personal values help us filter the cacophony of information that comes at us. This is something that we must consider with our students.

Information is Personal

When librarians teach students to think about and evaluate information sources, we tend to teach characteristics about those sources including author credentials, publication, date, peer reviewed or "popular," and a number of other criteria. We tend to challenge students to review source characteristics and then make some sort of judgment as to the usefulness of the source in the light of their information need (Rieh and Belkin, 1998; Ensor, 1997; Metzger, 2007; Olaisen, 1990; Rieh, 2002; Swanson, 2004 & 2005).

Critical pedagogy would rightly view this exercise as reproducing or reinforcing the dominant social order. These criteria give away authority to traditional academic and media forms and ignore the voices that are left out of the conversation. Kellner (2005) calls for the implementation of "multiple forms of computer, information, and communication literacies that will empower students to develop their potentials, create communities of learning, and work toward democratizing society" (p. 64). Elmborg (2006) does just that by challenging librarians to not view the library as part of the educational assembly line that casts the learner as a passive observer in a standardized, generic, and meaningless information literacy process. He challenges librarians to apply information literacy in a way that "can generate important critical questions about its own conclusions, assumptions, or methods" (p. 194).

Critical pedagogy in general and critical information literacy in particular may challenge us to apply feminist, class, postcolonial, postmodern, poststructural, or emancipatory approaches to education (Apple, 2005; Kellner, 2005; McLaren, 2005) and the library community may apply these to information and research, but we must be prepared for the realities we will face in the classroom.

For example, will our students be accepting of discussions of class domination and oppression? The answer to this question will largely depend on the beliefs that students hold about the nature of social class. When students examine sources about social class, their beliefs about social class will impact the sources they select, their understandings of how these sources were created, and the participation (or lack of participation) of individuals in debates surrounding these issues.

As I described above, it was my own beliefs about the nature of community colleges that led me to my "ah-ha" moment in my dissertation research. When I chose Weick's model of loosely coupled systems to frame my research, I did so because it aligned with my experiences. Since that first "ah-ha" moment, I have read many criticisms of Weick's model. I have been in the position of weighing Weick's model against his critics, but I have not found any of them to be strong enough to dissuade me from using it. In my manuscript, I have taken pains to counter the critics in order to build an argument for my reader about why I think that this model is pertinent to my research. But what is the driving force behind my well-crafted argument? The driving force stems from my beliefs about community colleges that are drawn from my experiences. Unlike most undergraduate researchers, I recognize the role of belief in this process, and I sought out opposing viewpoints. I recognize the influences of the political and economic environments through which this model was created. Even though I didn't find the critics to be convincing, this is not to say that my beliefs have not changed. If anything, they have grown richer and more focused thanks to my research. This is an example from my own educational experience of beliefs guiding learning.

We cannot escape the fact that critical pedagogy, information, and learning are entangled with belief. Interactions with information are highly personal and highly value-laden. Beliefs tend to reinforce existing knowledge by acting as a filter that catches sources that agree with these pre-existing beliefs. Contradictory evidence is easily passed over or ignored. Beliefs form early in life and, as they self-perpetuate, they become increasingly difficult to change in adulthood (Pajares, 1992). Changes in core beliefs about the nature of the world only happen with deep-learning experiences that are time consuming and difficult to enact in the classroom (Dole and Sinatra, 1994).

Students, especially traditionally-aged college students, tend to enter college with an absolutist or dualistic approach to knowledge. They think that one "truth" must exist for all questions so they are trying to ferret out fact and fiction. They apply this belief about knowledge, or this *personal epistemology*, to the information sources they encounter. Over time, this view about knowledge grows more complex. Initially, students tend to move to a more relativistic view where they refuse to make judgments about the merits or deficiencies of information sources. They eventually reach a more reflective standpoint where they make judgments about information that allow them to take stands on issues (Brabeck and Wood, 1990; King and Kitchener, 2004; Perry, 1970; Schommer-Aikins, 2004).

Educational psychologist Baxter Magolda (1992; 2004), who studies personal epistemology, identifies three factors in this area of social psychology that very much help us as we consider the impact of belief on knowledge and learning. First, knowledge is socially constructed, complex and deeply intertwined with the individual's views of the world. It follows, then, that the conceptualization of the self is necessarily involved with how knowledge is viewed, accepted, challenged, and ultimately created. Finally, authority and expertise are concepts that form within community and larger peer groups.

These personal epistemological explorations provide a needed level of explanation for our understanding of critical information literacy. Elmborg (2006) and Luke & Kapitzke (1999) both advocate for a critical information literacy approach and both state that knowledge is not an external entity to the learner. They do not delve into how that impacts learning and how this impacts our conceptualization of a critical information literacy approach. If information is tied to belief and those beliefs are tied to community and society, librarians and instructors who are developing a critical approach to information literacy skills with students need to form avenues of instruction that get students to recognize the beliefs they hold and how those beliefs impact their view of information sources. The question we face is the *how* question. How do we engage student beliefs in the classroom?

Problem Posing, Ill-Structured Problems, and Critical Questions

Elmborg (2006) notes that "ultimately, critical information literacy involves developing a critical consciousness about information" (p. 198). He notes that librarians must "problematize" the library by recognizing how the library plays a role in the many discourses and knowledge-construction processes that occur on college campuses. He suggests that librarians should follow Freire's problem-posing approach that moves students away from a "single-knowable reality." I would suggest that librarians must actively view this consciousness as pointing inward for students toward the single-knowable reality that they hold in their own worldviews.

Hofer (2004) emphasizes the need for instructors to set up instances of knowledge conflict during the learning process. When external information conflicts with the understandings that students hold, they begin a process of internal monitoring when they reconsider what they believe and the nature of the information sources before them. They engage in a complex construction process where they discard some beliefs, combine new sources with existing knowledge, ignore aspects of external sources, and recast their views on the topics they are exploring.

Researchers note that this conflict happens when students are presented with *ill-structured* problems which they set in contrast to *well-structured* problems. Well-structured problems tend to be solved by skills that emphasize logic and formal argument. Ill-structured problems do not have single answers and, therefore, require students to make judgments about the validity of information sources. The answers that students present to these ill-structured problems will depend on the ways that information sources appeal to the beliefs that students hold (Brabeck and Wood, 1990; King and Kitchener, 2004).

The problem-posing approach suggested by critical information literacy practitioners is enhanced when it is paired with ill-structured problems. I would suggest exercises that seek to expose students' beliefs about knowledge. On any given subject, the following critical questions should be applied.

- How do you know what you know?
- What information do you trust?
- What causes you to disagree with a piece of information?
- What counts as expertise?
- Who can publish on a specific issue?
- Who cannot and why?
- Whose voice is included/excluded?
- What information is trusted by society?[1]

These questions could be considered in research proposals, annotated bibliographies, or perhaps writing journals, but they may be even more powerful when they are at the heart of class discussions. They have the potential to become the core of a learning community that shares and constructs knowledge around ill-structured problems.

---

[1] I want to acknowledge and thank the Critical Information Literacy Work Group sponsored by the Illinois Center for Information Literacy for their work in creating these questions. I want to especially thank my two primary co-collaborators in their formulation, Adam Burke of Waubonsee Community College and Rob Morrison of National-Louis University.

An Example: the Rwandan Genocide and the Media

In the Spring 2009 semester, I collaborated with a history faculty member on a project that focused on the 1994 Rwandan genocide as part of a 20th century history course that aimed to move students toward a more critical consciousness. For this project, students started by watching the PBS Frontline documentary, *Ghosts of Rwanda*. While this documentary was fairly well-done, we felt that its main point, that the genocide could have easily been avoided if the rest of the world had the political will to act, is somewhat simplistic. One thing that the documentary does well is to bring to life the horrors of the genocide and instill the feeling that someone should have done something.

After watching the documentary, students worked together in groups to review media coverage from 1994 as the genocide unfolded. The students searched a number of research tools including library subscription databases and Google News to locate articles from the time period. They were asked to identify which voices were most prominent within each article. These articles were contrasted with primary documents from the National Security Archives that revealed some of the behind the scenes communications about Rwanda that was occurring during the genocide. Each student group created a short, written group report and they gave a presentation to their classmates. Then, each student was asked to write a larger reflection that included the perspectives from *Ghosts of Rwanda*, their findings on their media reviews, the primary documents from the National Security Archives, and their own reflections about the interrelationships between government, media, and the public.

The goals of this project were to situate the Rwandan genocide in post-colonial Africa and to challenge students to examine the choices that media make about what and how to report. The student groups found a range of different voices reflected in the media reports, but all groups found that Western government leaders were given more prominence than victims. The students were very critical of the choices made by journalists about which voices to include and which voices to exclude. Students also indicated that they previously held simpler views of the role of the media in that they had thought that the media "just told us what happened."

The popular histories of the Rwandan genocide tend to place blame on the UN, on President Bill Clinton, or on other outside groups for not acting. The accounts that students wrote were impressively more complex not only implicating political leaders, but also implicating the power structures in which they operate. They considered the responsibilities of voters, media outlets, and leaders. Students clearly examined their beliefs about how information is created, how it is transmitted, and how it is utilized by citizens. Several students reflected on media reports about the wars in Iraq and Afghanistan. These are outcomes that could not be achieved through the banking approach.[2]

The Critical Consciousness and the Reasoning Apparatus

We have to be realistic in what we can expect in one class or one semester. The creation of a critical consciousness is an ongoing process that develops and deepens over years, but we should work to move students toward that goal. The example given above is one example that attempted to move students in this direction. It was more than a one-shot library session. The librarian was deeply involved in the creation of the project and co-taught three different sessions. The time commitments of this project definitely posed challenges. But, these are challenges that must be overcome if we are to see the growth in our students that we desire.

Instructors and librarians should pose questions and create assignments that make implicit beliefs more explicit. Then students should be challenged to examine the origins and implications of these beliefs. How do these beliefs align with other beliefs? What outcomes and worldview arise from these beliefs? How should they be altered in the light of new information sources?

Students may enter our classrooms preferring the banking approach to learning and after one or two semesters (or even one or two years) this preference may not undergo extreme shifts. However, our goal and our hope should be that by examining and addressing personal belief we can make learning more meaningful. This must be part of a critical information literacy approach, and it must be central to convincing students to abandon the banking concept of learning. This can enable us to fully engage learners as active partners in the learning process and truly engage the learner as equal partners in learning. It will not be an easy task, but I believe it is necessary.

The end goal is Freire's *praxis* that merges theory and premeditated action. This broadens *the Pedagogy of the Oppressed* to move beyond economic oppression and to address the "oppression" of social and historical context. Peters (2005) warns us to not shift critical pedagogy too far away from its

---

[2] I would like to thank Merri Fefles, Professor of History at Moraine Valley Community College, for her partnership and inspiration on the Rwanda Project.

origins and his warning may be a worthy critique of the approach I am proposing. However, he also warns us that at the heart of critical theory must be reason and reason's "capacity to examine its own reasoning apparatus, be it the method of science, critical thinking, or the social mind" (p. 47). Engaging personal belief is the first step to examining the reasoning apparatus as it lies at the core of the reasoning apparatus.

References

Apple, M. (2005). Making Critical Pedagogy Strategic. In I. Gur-Ze'ev, Ed. *Critical theory and critical pedagogy today: Toward a new critical language in education.* Haifa, Israel: University of Haifa, p. 95-113.

Arvidson, P. (2008, October 3). Students 101. *Chronicle of Higher Education,* 55(6), A20-A20.

Baxter Magolda, M. (1992). Students' epistemologies and academic experiences: implications for pedagogy. *The Review of Higher Education.* 15(3), 265-287.

Baxter Magolda, M. (2004). Evolution of a constructivist conceptualization of epistemological   reflection. *Educational Psychologist.* 39(1), 31-42.

Brabeck, M. and Wood, P. (1990). Cross-sectional and longitudinal evidence for differences between well-structured and ill-structured problem solving abilities. In M.L. Commons, C Armon, L. Kohlberg, F.A. Richards, R. A. Grotzer, and J. D. Sinnott (Eds.) *Adult development 2: Models and methods in the study of adolescent and adult thought.* (133- 146.).

Dole, J. and Sinatra, G. (1994). Social psychology research on beliefs and attitudes: implications for research on learning from text. *Beliefs about text and instruction with text.* R. Garner and P. Alexander (eds). Hillsdale, NJ: Lawrence Erlbaum Associates.

Elias, R. (2008). Anti-intellectual attitudes and academic self-efficacy among business students. *Journal of Education for Business,* 84(2), 110-117

Elmborg, J. (2006). Critical Information Literacy: Implications for Instructional Practice. *Journal of Academic Librarianship.* 32 (2), 192-199.

Ensor, P. (1997). Database commentary: Credibility and accuracy on the Web: The librarian's role. *Technicalities.* 17 (4), 6.

Freire, P. (1970). *Pedagogy of the oppressed.* New York: Herder and Herder.

Hofer, B. (2004). Epistemological understanding as a metacognitive process: thinking aloud during online searching. *Educational Psychologist.* 39(1), 43-55.

Kapitzke, C. (2001). Information literacy: The changing library, *Journal of Adolescent & Adult Literacy* 44(4), 452.

Kellner, D. (2005). Critical theory and education: historical and metatheoretical perspectives. In I. Gur-Ze'ev, Ed. *Critical theory and critical pedagogy today: Toward a new critical language in education.* Haifa, Israel: University of Haifa, p. 49-69.

King, P. and Kitchener, K. (2004). Reflective judgment: theory and research on the development of epistemic assumptions through adulthood. *Educational Psychologist.* 39(1), 5-18.

Kohl, H. R. (1994). *I won't learn from you: And other thoughts on creative maladjustment.* New York, NY: New Press.

Leo, J. (1996). No books, please; we're students. *U.S. News & World Report.* 121,11, p. 24.

Luke, A., & Kapitzke, C. (1999). Literacies and libraries: Archives and cybraries. *Pedagogy, Culture and Society.* 7, 467-492.

McLaren, P. (2005). Critical pedagogy in the age of terror. In I. Gur-Ze'ev, Ed. *Critical theory and critical pedagogy today: Toward a new critical language in education.* Haifa, Israel: University of Haifa, p. 70-94.

McNay, I. (2006). We sacrifice our souls on the altar of employability. *Times Higher Education Supplement,* 1766, pp. 12,12.

Metzger, M. J. (2007). Making sense of credibility on the Web: Models for evaluating online information and recommendations for future research. *American Society for Information Science and Technology.* 58 (13), 2078-2091.

Olaisen, J. L. (1990). *Information quality factors and the cognitive authority of electronic Information.* Oslo: Bedriftsøkonomisk institutt.

Pajares, M. (1992). Teachers' beliefs and educational research: Cleaning up a messy construct. *Review of Educational Research.* 62(3), 307-332.

Perry, W. (1970). *Forms of intellectual and ethical development in the college years: A scheme.* New York: Holt, Rinehart, and Winston, Inc.

Peters, M. (2005). Critical pedagogy and the futures of critical theory. In I. Gur-Ze'ev, Ed. *Critical theory and critical pedagogy today: Toward a new critical language in education.* Haifa, Israel: University of Haifa, p. 35-48.

Rieh, S. Y. (2002). Judgment of information quality and cognitive authority in the Web. *American Society for Information Science and Technology.* 53, 145-161.

Rieh, S. Y., & Belkin, N. J. (1998). Understanding judgment of information quality and cognitive authority in the WWW. *Proceedings of the ASIS Annual Meeting.* 35, 279-89.

Schommer-Aikins, M. (2004). Explaining the epistemological belief system: Introducing the embedded systemic model and coordinated research approach. *Educational Psychologist.* 39(1), 19-29.

Shapiro, H. T. (2005*). A larger sense of purpose: Higher education and society.* Princeton, N.J.: Princeton University Press.

Spink, A. (2000). Toward a theoretical framework for information science. *Informing Science.* 3, 73-76.

Swanson, T. A. (2004). A radical step: Implementing a critical information literacy model. *portal: Libraries and the Academy.* 4 (2), 259-273.

Swanson, T. (2005). Teaching students about information: Information literacy and cognitive authority. *Research Strategies.* 20 (4), 322-333.

Weick, K. (1976). Educational systems as loosely coupled systems. *Administrative Science Quarterly.* 21 (1), 1-19.

Wilson, P. (1983). *Second-hand knowledge: An inquiry into cognitive authority.* Contributions in librarianship and information science, no. 44. Westport, Conn: Greenwood Press

Encountering Values: The Place of Critical Consciousness in the Competency Standards

Benjamin Harris

Introduction

The *Information Literacy Competency Standards for Higher Education* (2000) published by the Association of College and Research Libraries (ACRL) has been a valuable tool for information literacy instructors in the planning and assessment of local instruction programs. More than the theoretical, anecdotal, and empirical literatures in library and information studies, these standards have been the primary means for information literacy advocates to develop teaching and learning goals related to the location, selection, evaluation, and use of information. In some ways, the standards have taken the place of pedagogy in library instruction, resulting in a profession-wide dependence on lists of educational outcomes to define both the theory and practice of information literacy instruction.

In an effort to extend beyond assessment-focused teaching and learning, and with the hope of developing teaching and learning strategies that contextualize information literacy in the continuing lives of people beyond the environment of formal education, librarians and others have directed their attention toward "critical information literacy." Critical information literacy moves beyond assessable objectives to question the social, political, and economic forces involved in the creation, transmission, reception, and use of information. Ultimately, this deployment of critical pedagogy should result in information literate activity that recognizes the complicity of the individual—and the individual as a community member—in information-based power structures and struggles.

In an effort to create a dialogue between critical pedagogy and the ACRL's *Competency Standards*, I contend that Standard 3 allows us to explore how critical information literacy instruction might work in practice. Standard 3 states that the "information literate student evaluates information and its sources critically and incorporates selected information into his or her knowledge base or value system" (ACRL, 2000, p. 11). Of the outcomes and indicators associated with this objective, Performance

Indicator 5 deals with the learner's awareness that new information can have an impact on one's beliefs and values. While many teachers have focused on training students to evaluate sources, the process of integrating the information from these sources into one's "value system" is rarely addressed. Here, at the "dead center" of the standards, lies an opportunity to revise the way we view information literacy development objectives.

While practical strategies for the application of a critical pedagogy will differ based on context and environment, I suggest an approach that bridges the gap between theory and the classroom. To achieve this end, it is useful to draw upon Paulo Freire's concept of "critical consciousness." International information literacy standards such as the *Information Literacy Framework* from Australia and New Zealand and the "Seven Headline Skills" from Great Britain (rubrics for teaching and assessment that were drafted after the publication of the ACRL's *Competency Standards*) also inform this chapter. While these documents have received little attention outside of specific geographical locations, international standards represent innovation and varying perspectives on information literacy development. This extension of our perspectives on teaching and learning standards facilitates the development of a critical information literacy pedagogy, and allows us to consider alternative pedagogical strategies, such as reflective practice and dialogic interaction, as key activities in the development of critical consciousness.

Critical Pedagogy and Consciousness

Critical pedagogy has received widespread attention in the education literature for a number of decades. Brazilian educator Paulo Freire continues to be one of the key figures associated with critical theory and teaching, and his work has been adapted by educators worldwide since the 1970s. In influential publications such as *Pedagogy of the Oppressed* (1970), *Education for Critical Consciousness* (1973), and *The Politics of Education: Culture, Power, and Liberation* (1985), Freire outlined an educational agenda that sought to offer learners political, social, and cultural enfranchisement via educational opportunities.

For Freire, one of the few predetermined "outcomes" of critical pedagogy is the learner's development of a critical consciousness. Unlike other forms of consciousness described in Freire's research, a being of critical consciousness is able to set aside fictive or naïve thinking in favor of a critical reality. He contends that some individuals and communities view reality as a context "out there" in the world, separate from the human being. Conversely, the development of critical consciousness allows one to "enter into" reality and "look at" it from within (Freire, 1973, p. 103).

While some will be satisfied with the recognition that social and political inequality exists between peoples, the being of critical consciousness will also act in response to these findings. "Critical understanding leads to critical action," Freire explained, suggesting that critical action would not be forced but would be a natural result of a critical literacy (1973, p. 44). With this approach in mind, the main objective in critical information literacy development would not be the achievement of learning or the performance of tasks related to a prefabricated outcome. Rather, the process of development, and a conscious awareness of that development in the learner—even if the experience and outcome of that development are highly individualized for learners and learning communities—would be of greater interest.

The shift to a pedagogy that facilitates the development of critical consciousness in learners may seem challenging given the dominance of assessment-based pedagogies in information literacy instruction. However, as assessment strategies have improved and adapted during the last 20 years, information literacy advocates have proven themselves to be open to explorations of new and innovative teaching strategies. In considering critical pedagogy and information literacy instruction, we need an avenue to guide our connection between the teaching and learning standards that define our practice and unexplored realms of information literacy development. As one path toward this discussion, the ACRL competency standard related to values (specifically, how learners evaluate and integrate information, and how this information shapes their value systems in turn) may allow us to correlate these seemingly disparate pedagogical approaches.

Values in the ACRL Standards

The *Competency Standards* serve as a profession-wide standards and outcomes tool, created to help librarians, instruction coordinators, and others efficiently assess information literacy development in learners and also gauge the impact of their instructional programs. Of course, there have been numerous critiques of the *Standards* and their uses in information literacy instruction. The limitations of assessment-based pedagogies seem to be clear. As Tara Brabazon contends, "Teachers cannot assume that there is a single method to construct curriculum, assemble a reading list, or express an ideology. Generic competencies undervalue and unravel the social diversity and plural complexity of our classrooms and libraries" (2005,

p. 16). Gorman and Dorner (2006) continue this line of critique and extend it to include any standards-based educational philosophy drawn from Bloom's *Taxonomy*. A number of authors have focused on the "Western-centric" character of the *Standards* (Luke and Kapitzke, 1999; Mokhtar and Majid, 2008; Virkus, 2003), contending that an application of these standards outside of a genericized white academic situation is tantamount to "a kind of educational imperialism" (Gorman and Dorner, 2006).

Any set of standards designed for assessment purposes are necessarily specific in character. Those who might critique educational standards for being restrictive, prescriptive, or limited are more than likely correct. However, educational standards have specific goals, and are not meant to be a comprehensive or holistic representation of a particular literacy, subject, or skills set. For this reason, standards designed for assessment purposes are not intended to extend beyond assessable measures. It is not reasonable to expect an educational taxonomy to measure the immeasurable or to quantify experiences that cannot be reduced to numerical or similar data.

While the majority of performance indicators and learning outcomes included in the *Standards* are drawn toward a focus on assessment, an opportunity exists to expand and reinterpret what we assess and how we might choose to assess it. Often thought of specifically as the standard related to the evaluation of sources, Standard 3 in the ACRL's *Competency Standards* states that the information literate student "determines whether the new knowledge has an impact on the individual's value system and takes steps to reconcile the difference" (2000, p. 12). With the inclusion of this performance indicator, the values standard offers something of a "loophole" through which instructors can expand the types of data that are normally collected, and the types of objectives around which information literacy programs are often organized. For the most part, instructors have failed to exploit this opportunity. The relationship between knowledge, the learner's values, or the values of the information's creator is rarely discussed in theoretical or practical literature on information literacy instruction.

Also, the indicators and outcomes related to the values standard are inconsistent with the assessment-based approach of the *Competency Standards*. Performance Indicator 5 states that "the information literate student determines whether the new knowledge has an impact on the individual's value system and takes steps to reconcile differences" (ACRL, 2008, p. 12). The outcomes provided with this performance indicator, outcomes designed to help librarians and others assess the performance of a particular task or process, state that the information literate individual will "investigate differing points in the literature" and then "determine whether to incorporate or reject viewpoints encountered" (ACRL, 2008, p. 12). There is no real provision for assessing whether or not the learner has actually defined a personal value related to new information and then participated in some process of reconciliation.

To be true to the spirit of the ACRL *Competency Standards*, we must consider the route through which values and value systems came to be included as a point of assessment in information literacy development. Bloom's *Taxonomy of Education Objectives*, a highly influential text in the development of assessable curricular structures, was a guiding influence in the development of the ACRL standards (ACRL, 2000, p. 6). In the *Taxonomy*, values are ideas or beliefs that hold a specific position in the individual's system of motivation. At the basic level, an individual can "accept" a value, whereby the individual's motivation and action based on the value itself will be tentative (Krathwohl, Bloom, and Masia, 1964, p. 141). Following acceptance of a value, an individual may develop a "preference" for a value. At this stage of valuing, an "individual is sufficiently committed to the value to pursue it, to seek it out, to want it" (Krathwohl, Bloom, and Masia, 1964, p. 145). Finally, when an individual accepts a belief at a high degree of certainty, they have reached what Bloom refers to as "commitment" to the value (Krathwohl, Bloom, and Masia, 1964, p. 149).

After specific values develop, systems of values that correlate into an individual's "philosophy of life" are then constructed (Krathwohl, Bloom, and Masia, 1964, p. 159). The development of a philosophy of life, whereby cognitive and affective education objectives are internalized and achieved, allows the individual to act as a global citizen based on this "mode of conduct" (Krathwohl, Bloom, and Masia, 1964, p. 165). Bloom's *Taxonomy* provides a number of example assessment strategies to determine the level of "valuing" given to a particular belief.

Values-based teaching and learning has a place in information literacy theory and practice, but there has been little in the literature to suggest that librarians and teachers in the U.S. have recognized this opportunity. There is evidence, however, that educational standards adopted by other international organizations have considered the issue of values in relation to information literacy development. In fact, the consideration or removal of learning outcomes related to values may be seen as a response to the current manner of addressing these issues in the ACRL *Competency Standards*.

Values in the Australia and New Zealand *Framework* and SCONUL

Information literacy advocates both in the United States and abroad have been remarkably loyal to the ACRL *Competency Standards*—at times, without critical analysis. As organizations have adopted and revised the *Competency Standards*, it is clear that not all have agreed that the relationship between information literacy and values development is a necessary or even desirable inclusion. For example, the information literacy assessment standards created by the ALA's Anthropology and Sociology section (2008) and its Science and Engineering section (2006) remove the consideration completely, and instead, use the word "value" in relation only to whether an item possesses "value" for the researcher. With this change in usage and the definition of the word, the implications of information beyond its immediate application are set aside.

SCONUL, the Society of College, National and University Libraries in Great Britain, published their "seven pillars" or "seven headline skills" in 1999 to help librarians and others understand information literacy development in higher education environments (Webber, 2008). SCONUL's seven pillars are meant to be more of a "model" of the information literate individual's abilities, and the drafters attempted to refrain from claiming that these were "standards" in any common sense of the word. Still, the relationship between this model and the ACRL *Competency Standards* is clear. The seven pillars, or seven tasks that act as support for information literate activity, do not extend beyond the skills-based model of information literacy development and do not suggest a relationship between information and the values of either the information provider or the information literate person.

While the ACRL *Competency Standards* offer limited consideration for the integration of values development and the relationship between information literacy and values systems, and while other standards neglect this consideration entirely, the Australian and New Zealand *Framework* takes a very different approach. The original version, published in 2001, mirrored the current ACRL standards in structure as well as content. However, a revision published only 3 years later in 2004 exhibits a dramatic shift in the purpose, organization, and content of information literacy development standards. No longer focused on skill-based or assessment-oriented indicators and outcomes, the 2004 *Framework* offers instructors a higher benchmark for the instruction and assessment of students in higher education. The revised *Framework* should be of great interest to teachers interested in critical pedagogy.

Closely related to Standards 3 and 5 in the ACRL guidelines, Standard Six in the Australian and New Zealand *Framework* states that "the information literate person uses information with understanding and acknowledges cultural, ethical, economic, legal, and social issues surrounding the use of information" (Bundy et al., 2004, p. 22). However, the performance indicators and outcomes of Standard Six in the *Framework* go well beyond the task-focused or classroom-based character of the ACRL guidelines. The second performance indicator for Standard Six states that the information literate individual "recognizes that information is underpinned by values and beliefs" (Bundy et al., 2004, p. 23). If *all* information is underpinned by the values of its creator or transmitter, then *all* information is likely to be biased in some manner. The information literate individual must recognize that the values associated with the information are not always presented in an obvious way.

The *Framework* then goes on to offer outcomes that depict a process of valuing in the information literate individual that is more closely aligned with the process described in Bloom's *Taxonomy*. First, the information literate individual "identifies whether there are different values that underpin new information or whether information has implications for personal values and beliefs" (Bundy et al., 2004, p. 23). Then, one "applies reasoning to determine whether to incorporate or reject the viewpoints encountered" (Bundy et al., 2004, p. 23). The final outcome states that the information literate individual "maintains an internally coherent set of values informed by knowledge and experience" (Bundy et al., 2004, p. 23).

Clearly, the outcomes for each of the standards are progressively more sophisticated and they are sequenced so that the higher order activity appears as a final "step." This process-oriented approach is not promulgated by the ACRL Standards.

The inclusion of an outcome related entirely to maintenance of a "coherent set of values" also suggests that information literate activity requires learners to consistently recognize and consider how the receipt, selection, evaluation, and use of information is a process that is shaped by—and shapes—their own personal set of values. Values are not static, obviously, and will change based on time, experience, and the new knowledge gained by the learner. The individual must be cognizant of their personal values, how these values work with one another, and how information literacy involves a constant and continuing process of values assessment and reconciliation. To be information literate, one must participate in a constant dialogue between the values that underpin information and the values one presently holds.

Toward Critical Information Literacy

As librarians and others continue the discussion connecting critical pedagogy and the current state of information literacy theory and practice, there are a number of practical strategies that can assist learners in the development of a critical consciousness about information and information sources. Specifically, Freire presents two strategies to help foster critical consciousness: reflection and dialogue. These critical activities may be thought of as the "praxis" of critical consciousness, and offer an ideal starting point as we move toward a critical information literacy pedagogy.

Reflective practice describes the inward activity that is performed in an outward fashion during dialogue. One questions oneself, and through the process of understanding one's actions, one is able to develop a "theory of actions" (1973, p. 112). "We must have a clear and lucid grasp of our action...whether we wish to or not," wrote Freire on the topic of reflective practice (p. 112). In this process, one can become more sensitive to one's own reasons for action, while developing the ability to understand the actions of others. Critical reflective practice allows us to consider our own beliefs and the beliefs of the other with a certain amount of equality. Here, the outcome is less important than the process of reflection on engagement with information and the relationship between the information and one's value system.

For many learners, guided reflection will be the most effective way to introduce reflective practice during early instructional experiences. Teachers may ask learners to use specific questions to reflect on their information-related activities. As students look back at their experience, they might consider the following questions: How does this information reflect, contradict, or change my beliefs about this issue or topic? What can I learn about the author's values based on the information provided? How do the author's values reflect, contradict, or change my beliefs about this issue or topic? Does this information relate to the value systems of any communities in which I participate or maintain membership?

While asking these questions in a direct way may seem challenging, these are the kinds of queries that people who practice critical information literacy would ask upon receiving any type of information. Learners are often more sensitive to locating information that either contradicts or reinforces their current value system. For example, a politically conservative reader may immediately locate the differences in values in a resource created by a more liberal author. Another reader who is committed to beliefs that are more liberal may find immediate connections. Ideally, a source that aligns with one's personal values should receive the same critical attention directed toward those sources with which one immediately disagrees.

Teachers must also engage in similar critical reflective practice about information literacy instruction. One strategy for doing this is to consider the multiple audiences for information literacy instruction. For example, numerous authors have discussed the "West-centric" character of the information literacy standards in their current form. The information literacy instructor may, in this case, choose to reflect on the ways that their own instruction favors a Western perspective on information literacy. One may ask questions about teaching and professional activities as a part of reflections on teaching and pedagogy: How does my teaching (approach, style, curriculum, etc.) speak to some but not all of the students in a class? How can I be more aware of the range of cultural, social, and political differences between students? How will I model critical practices that include and invite these diverse communities of learners? Teachers that experiment with critical reflective practice for their own development are better able to encourage and inspire learners to follow suit.

Along with reflective practice, dialogue is the second primary method Freire advocated as a means toward critical consciousness. Dialogue, in Freire's terms, requires a horizontal communicative relationship between interlocutors. In this relationship, communication and intercommunication are connected by an openness and empathy for the other position. In a loving, humble, hopeful, trusting, and critical environment, these interlocutors will struggle to come to a shared understanding of reality (1973, p. 45). By entering into an intimate communication with another, with a focus on questioning the positions of all participants, one can enter into a critical exchange of ideas. This type of dialogue may happen with two people, five people, or a student and their sources. Dialogue, thought of in terms of the human being/text relationship, requires that one question the source and then question their own reactions and responses to the source. The goal is not to argue a position, but rather, to be open with ideas and to be equally open to the ideas of others.

Freire's work makes clear that dialogue should not have a specific outcome. In fact, outcomes—in and of themselves—are a challenging component of Freire's pedagogy, since the liberated learner should "find themselves" at an outcome during the process of dialogic inquiry. As a practice of critical consciousness, dialogue with another person, within a community, or even with information sources requires that the critical subject ask questions of others. As a resolution to this process, those in the dialogue should come to a point of shared reality. While two people will be of two minds, may hold different positions, or are subject to different social conditions, change happens when people see the same situation in a shared way from their varying subject positions.

As a practice of critical information literacy, dialogue between two interlocutors might begin with a discussion of a particular issue and an exploration of the values each person holds in relation to that topic. A speaker may not even realize that their position is associated with a personal value, and this discussion can be an enlightening experience before the interlocutors even consider additional information. Then, the instructor can add a new source of information related to that topic that both speakers can discuss. To facilitate the dialogue, the instructor can encourage speakers to consider the ways that the information reflects or contradicts their position and the personal values that underpin that position.

In the abstract, this activity may sound rather involved. As an example of how this might work in practice, one can consider the border wall between Mexico and the United States as a topic. An instruction librarian might pose the following questions to foster reflection and dialogue: What are your positions on the construction of the border wall? How do these positions reflect a value to which you are committed, a commitment that transcends the discussion of the wall? Maybe an opponent of the wall values the protection of the environment, and believes that the wall is detrimental to the continued existence of certain animals whose habitat exists on both sides of the border. Maybe a proponent of the wall holds the value that the economic stability of citizens of the United States is of greater importance. The proponent may still agree with the opponent of the wall, and may agree in some part with the values of that opponent, but their level of commitment in relation to specific values is different.

After establishing a position, locating the personal values that relate the position, and discussing these in an open and accepting forum, the instructor may introduce new information related to the construction of the border wall. The instructor can then encourage both speakers to consider this information in light of their position as well as the values that determine this position. In many ways, this activity can be conducted like any issue-specific discussion; however, on reflection, participants will be able to locate how information has an impact on the way we view the world as well as the values that dictate our worldview.

There are two primary challenges involved in using dialogue to explore how critical consciousness, personal values, and information literacy work together. Without question, there is a time commitment involved in such activities. An open dialogue and the creation of this situation can take time. In addition, the discussion of controversial topics—especially as they relate to one's personal values—can be difficult for learners. In some cases, an instructor may also find it difficult to delve into the personal, and often emotionally-based, values that define one's position on a topic. While Freire does not directly describe this as an alternative or an option to replace dialogue, a more manageable strategy may be found in modeling this kind of situation for learners, either through the presentation of examples or personal narratives. Whether one adopts a praxis of critical consciousness in the personal or professional spheres of life, it is not expected that the deployment of these strategies will be identical to the use of the same strategies by another person. Critical consciousness is a way of thinking and being and is highly subjective. The exploration of these strategies in information literacy will have numerous benefits, even without a rigid process model as a guide. As Troy Swanson has written, "information literacy does not need to be truly Freirean, nor does it need to fully embrace a critical pedagogy" but there is "much to gain by drawing from the critical pedagogical school of thought" (2004, p. 75). The infusion of multiple perspectives into our teaching and reflective practice allows us to work toward greater diversity and intellectual heft in pedagogies of information literacy instruction.

Conclusion

In a 2002 editor's column for *Research Strategies*, Lisa Hinchliffe advocated that librarians should not only "teach" information literacy but should live and model information literate habits of mind for other learners (p. 96). Heidi Jacobs has written that "one of the ways we can do this in our daily teaching lives is to work toward creating habits of mind that prioritize reflective discussions about what it is that we are doing when we 'do' information literacy" (2008, p. 258). Concerned that teachers and learners refrain from becoming "boxed in and compartmentalized" by standards and assessments, information literacy advocates should be "thinking about pedagogy and talking about how we might work toward making the global local, the visionary concrete, the theoretical practicable, and perhaps, the ideal possible" (Jacobs, 2008, p. 258). The recognition of information literacy learners as beings of potential critical consciousness facilitates a correlation between assessable objectives and "habits of mind" practices. Through habitual experience, dialogue and reflection become a way of living, a way of participating in the world—a constant stream of communication that challenges and revises one's values systems, while also inspiring critically conscious action.

References

Anthropology and Sociology Section, Association of College and Research Libraries (2008). *Information literacy standards for anthropology and sociology students.*Retrieved   from   http://www.ala.org/ala/acrl/ acrlstandards/anthro_soc_standards.cfm

Association of College and Research Libraries. (2000). *Information literacy competency standards for higher education.* Chicago: American Library Association.

Bahruth, R.E., & Steiner, S.F. (2000). Upstream in the mainstream: Pedagogy against the current. In S.F. Stainer, H.M. Krant, P. McLaren, & R.E. Bahruth (Eds.), *Freirean pedagogy, praxis, and possibilities* (pp. 119-146). New York: Falmer Press.

Brabazon, T. (2005). Burning towers and ashen learning: September 11 and the changes to critical literacy. *Australian Library Journal 54*(1), 6-22.

Bundy, A. (Ed.). (2004). *Australian and New Zealand information literacy framework: Principles, standards, and practice.* Adelaide: Australian and New Zealand Institute   for   Information   Literacy.   Available   from http://www.caul.edu.au/info-literacy/publications.html

Council of Australian University Librarians. (2001). *Information literacy standards.* Canberra: Council of Australian University Librarians. Available from http://www.caul.edu.au/info-literacy/publications.html

Doherty, J.J., & Ketchner, K. (2005). Empowering the intentional learner: A critical theory for information literacy instruction. *Library Philosophy and Practice 8*(1), 1-10.

Freire, P. (1973). *Education for critical consciousness.* New York: Seabury Press.

Freire, P. (1970). *Pedagogy of the oppressed.* (M.B. Ramos, Trans.). New York: Herder and Herder.

Freire P. (1985). *Politics of education: Culture, power, and liberation.* (D. Macedo, Trans.). South Hadley: Bergin and Garvey.

Gorman, G.E., & Dorner, D.G. (2006). Information literacy education in Asian developing countries: Cultural factors affecting curriculum development and programme delivery. *IFLA Journal 42*(4), 281-293.

Hinchliffe, L.J. (2001). Information literacy as a way of life. *Research Strategies 18*, 95-96.

Jacobs, H.L.M. (2008). Information literacy and reflective pedagogical praxis. *The Journal of Academic Librarianship 34*(3), 256-262.

Krathwohl, D.R., Bloom, B.S., and Masia, B.B. (1964). *Taxonomy of educational objectives: The classification of educational goals, handbook II: Affective Domain.* New York: David McKay.

Luke, A., & Kapitzke, C. (1999). Literacies and libraries—archives and cybraries. *Pedagogy, Culture & Society 7*(2), 467-491.

Mokhtar, I.A., & Majid, S. (2008). Information literacy standards, guidelines and their implementation: An analysis. *DESIDOC Journal of Library and Information Technology 28*(2), 5-12.

Science and Technology Section, Association of College and Research Libraries. (2006). *Information literacy standards for science and engineering/technology.* Retrieved from http://www.ala.org/ala/acrl/acrlstandards/infolitscitech.cfm

Swanson, T.A. (2004). Applying a critical pedagogical perspective to information literacy standards. *College and Undergraduate Libraries 12*(4), 65-77.

Virkus, S. (2003). Information literacy in Europe: A literature review. *Information Research 8*(4). Retrieved from http://informationr.net/ir/8-4/paper159.html

Webber, S. (2008). *The seven headline skills expanded.* Retrieved from http://www.sconul.ac.uk/groups/information_literacy/headline_skills.html

Disintermediation and Resistance: Giroux and Radical Praxis in the Library

Ruth Mirtz

One of the current challenges to libraries in the United States is finding ways to make the library more central to the lives of students, faculty, staff, and administration, while managing a reduced budget for ever more-expensive resources. Librarians have realized that hiding their light behind the stacks and authority control only makes their mission to provide knowledge more difficult. Part of this new realization comes from seeing the internet do an "end-run" around the library and librarians: users think everything is on the 'net, so all they need is computer instruction and an internet connection from the library.

This self-service movement has led to efficiencies such as self-checkout and automated ILL. But it may also be encouraging students and patrons to stumble through databases and to assume information is NOT available because they can't find it. These situations lead people such as William Miller (2007) to decry the state of information literacy, to point out the ignorance and brazen over-confidence of non-librarians to find and use information, and to then rally the cry of "we must teach them our way of doing things." Librarians who see their role as more corrective than educative might see disintermediation as a threat to their source of income, their status as knowledge workers, and their mission in the world at large. Under those terms, disintermediation must be either stopped at once or grudgingly recognized, so that it then may be ignored.

Given this prevailing wind gusting through libraries, the issue of disintermediation becomes quite problematic, even paradoxical. Libraries need to reduce costs and increase usage; librarians want to pursue their calling, which is as expensive and time-consuming as any other highly-skilled individualized instruction. Most librarians recognize, however, that disintermediation is not going to be stopped by wishing it away; some librarians have embraced it as a greater good for both libraries and users, because it frees time for librarians to do other important work; some librarians have already begun looking at the possibilities of studying disintermediation in order to re-imagine the library's mission. Because disintermediation and critical pedagogy both place a claim on human agency, rather than simply a choice of "roles" in the library, they offer a place to tease out the educative mission of reference service and library instruction, as well as other "hidden" curricula in collection development and knowledge management practices.

A Brief History of Disintermediation

Disintermediation began as a concept in banking, as people began to invest directly in financial products without going through the bank, according to Gellman (1996). In the early and mid 90s, many librarians were taking a hard look at disintermediation, mainly because of the changes wrought by technology, including how to define the phenomenon and identify its effects. Gellman (1996) defines disintermediation as "the diversion of information users from centralized physical repositories to alternate sources available directly through computers and computer networks" (p. 2). Disintermediation was painted as a fearful and damaging event in library science, described as the end of the profession and a kind of technological outsourcing. If students can search databases from anywhere, at any time, and with any level of understanding of their topic, of what use is a librarian? Among librarians, the term originates with those who see it as a bad thing; users more likely call it "eliminating the middle man" and quite favorable to them, just as in warehouse stores which claim to have lower prices because they deal directly with the manufacturer of the products.

While some (such as Kieft, 1995) see disintermediation as the "death" of libraries, most others (such as Gellman, 1996; Fourie, 1999) point out that disintermediation brings with it opportunities for libraries to expand their services in new directions, and that it also brings profound and permanent changes to what librarians do. When librarians spend less time on the questions users can answer independently, they can concentrate on training users, evaluating new resources, and making disintermediated practices more successful. The librarian's role changes from answering all users' questions to helping users answer their questions. The new role does not necessarily mean less "face time" between users and librarians, though. Sturges (2001) points out that most information seekers prefer human contact and realize they need human interpretation and intervention: "When the information they require is crucially important to their lives and their work, people deliberately seek out intermediaries in whom they place particular trust" (p. 64). Thus, there are natural limits to disintermediation, and eventually thoughtful users will recognize when they need human interpretation and evaluations. He also suggests that "reintermediation" is the goal and that librarians can become managers and leaders in this new future with improved value-added service. He reassures us that intermediaries and similar roles such as gatekeepers will always be needed because they are a natural and required part of information processes (p. 65). Unfortunately, a more frequent justification of reintermediation is to secure library jobs which will otherwise disappear (see, for example, Veldof, 2008).

Sturges' (2001) prediction may be reassuring, but if librarians are to become merely a different kind of gatekeeper, they may also lose the power of disintermediation to change the way librarians think about information-seeking. Because disintermediation disrupts traditional power structures among librarians and users and information, it also exposes us to new ways of thinking about those relationships. This essay argues that only some kinds of reintermediation are appropriate and that our mission as librarians requires that we support disintermediation, as we support our users through disintermediating experiences.

Approaching Disintermediation through Critical Pedagogy

Most of those writing about disintermediation in library services are stressing the change that comes with disintermediation and librarian's reactions to the changes—that is, how to cope. These thinkers are basing their strategies on a rather traditional view of information, however, a view that is widely viewed as too narrow to support a technologically-driven library. The narrower view of information as commodity or product (as opposed to a generative, interpretive view of information or knowledge) speaks to many librarians' view of themselves as brokers or trainers, with information being a neutral, abstract object. In contrast, much of what critical pedagogy offers is a critique of learning as a static object capable of being placed into "learning modules" and worksheets. Paulo Freire described this version of impoverished education as the "banking concept" of learning, where one can collect ideas into bags and carry them around as one might a bag of coins. This kind of education assumes the teacher is the absolute authority, with or without the knowledge that would give him or her the authority, while the goal for students is to become "manageable beings" (Freire, 1986, p. 60). Students learn to accept reality, not to ask questions, and to remain objects in the world, not agents with the power to influence reality (p. 61-62).

Critical pedagogy, however, as an approach to educative mission of the library, moves information, knowledge, and learning out of this narrower, positivist view of how the world works. As one of the spokespeople for critical pedagogy, Henry A. Giroux has analyzed, interrogated, and theorized about the nature of education, particularly the institutionalized and politicized version of education present in much of higher education in the United States. In recent years, Giroux has turned his attention to a critique of the consumerist, anti-youth, neoliberal politics of recent administrations and the influence of the media on the commodification of life, yet his call for profound and radical transformation of democracy and culture remains strong. He has been influenced by theorists in a variety of disciplines such as Antonio Gramsci, Edward Said, and Paulo Freire. Although I may do grave injustice to Giroux's thinking, I will summarize a few of the tenets of Giroux's critical pedagogy:

Institutional power, such as that wielded by universities, libraries, and faculty, creates the "possibility of struggle, resistance, and transformation." Institutions, however, are not just monolithically benign or totalitarian evil. The power wielded by institutions can both conceal and reveal the workings behind that power (Giroux, 1983, p. 137). We, along with students, must work between the lines of oppressive power and creative power and develop continual self-examination practices that question our social relations, including our personal histories, our habits of mind, and our experiences (Giroux, 1983, pp. 149-150). These acts of self-examination should not lead to cynical, destructive analyses, though. The ultimate purpose of dismantling dehumanizing and un-reflective structures and artifacts is to reassemble them as radically new ways of acting and thinking (Giroux, 1983, p. 160). Along with self-examination, "transmission modes" of education have to be replaced with "classroom social relationships" which allow students to critique information, examine their own histories and "frames of reference" for the sources of their beliefs, and challenge the dominant culture (Giroux, 1983, pp. 202-203).

Transmission modes of learning and unexamined relationships maintain the status quo, not allowing for greater participation from those who have been historically left out of higher education (Giroux, 1983, p. 9). Critical thinking plays out in material constraints and opportunities, such as computer access and hiring practices. Questions of material wealth, support networks such as welfare and health insurance, and the outsourcing of education services are other examples of these material conditions. Many of these critical pedagogical practices happen when faculty members, including librarians, see themselves as public intellectuals with the responsibility to speak out against forces that work against empowering students. (Giroux, 2006, pp. 94-95).

Disintermediation, by reducing the authoritarian role of the librarian, is theoretically a positive change from the standpoint of critical pedagogy. This reduction of outside authority allows students to ask critical questions about their knowledge and empowers them to question, for example, the corporatized nature of knowledge on some academic databases or the difficulty of making connections across databases based on disciplinary boundaries. There is no intervening authority to constrain or restrict their search or their questions, no tutorial that shows them a "recommended" search process. Students don't have to wait for instruction or an assignment to pursue questions of importance to them. They don't have to pass a basic skills test before they are allowed to launch a complex search. They are free to gain searching skills from trusted friends in a highly contextual environment, the same way most of them learned to use Facebook. For instance, when my students use Google Scholar, they are sometimes led to sites that offer full-text articles, but for a price. They quite rightly balk at paying $12. 95 for an article they haven't read. They immediately question the marketing of access. Students create their own intermediation needed at that point of challenge, and not just the economic one, although the economic story is an important one. Librarians know students ask these questions because the questions come to the reference desk. I have often explained why they don't need to pay for the article (because our library has free access), but I have rarely taken the time to explain the connection between Google Scholar, pay-for-access sites, and "free" access (which students have actually paid for already through taxes and tuition). In this same situation, students will often choose research materials based on what's free, rather than what they need to know, but again that moment of decision-making is one full of challenge to the institution's idea of appropriate research. In what ways do students "buy" their education at the university, and especially at the library? Asking that question when making decisions about licensing, accessibility, balancing the collection, and database training means seeing the library through the lens of critical pedagogy. Our answers depend on whether we primarily see the library as a service to students (to get them through the next paper deadline) or as an approach to lifelong learning (to guide students to action through the freedom and responsibility that comes with knowledge).

In other words, disintermediation provides one of many locations for "radical praxis" (Giroux, 1983, p. 155) in library instruction where students can "critically interrogate their inner histories and experiences" (p. 150). Critical pedagogy is based in a utopian vision of democracy as an extension of justice and freedom, rather than based on a capitalist, consumerist society which desires workers rather than thinkers (Giroux, 2006, p. 250). Students' previous experiences of libraries may well have been as subjects rather than agents. Their understanding of the library as institutional power is being reproduced and challenged simultaneously when they experience the empowerment and disillusionment of "doing it themselves" in a database search engine. The process shapes the thinking; databases don't ask questions. The point at which most librarians become intermediaries is a point of resistance: students' struggle to find resources at the library is part of their struggle to find a voice within the discourse of their discipline, to control their position in the classroom, and to accommodate or subvert their teachers' desires for them. Students (and many librarians) prefer to work with a positivist, commodifying theory of knowledge; if they can get a "thing" from their research, then they can place/paste it in their papers and get a result/grade. Questioning the authority of traditional library research leads us to such questions as how database search engines determine inquiry processes and why students and teachers use Google and Wikipedia even when they know how to use academic databases and evaluate websites.

Giroux's theory of critical pedagogy includes more than a dismantling of the structures and thought processes behind disintermediation issues. For Giroux, critical pedagogy should reconstruct "transformative activities" and new categories (p. 161) for thinking about libraries, research, and the nature of academic study. Critical pedagogy needs "to link the language of critique to the language of possibility" (Giroux, 2006, p. 5). This language of possibility and hope is what sets critical pedagogy apart from post-structuralism and other critiques of institutionalized education: a utopian vision for education in a democracy is not an impossibility. Of course, even though humans have the capacity to turn critique into action, we also have the capacity to turn every learning opportunity into a hoop to be jumped. Our students are often encouraged by standardized tests and rigid policies to see their education as a series of meaningless gestures. The language of possibility may appear as very small steps in the face of such resistance. As a librarian, simply showing genuine interest in a student paper topic, while helping navigate a database, can make a difference, because the student then sees an authentically possible audience outside of the classroom for what he or she is learning. Freire (1998) reminds us that without hope, we are left with fatalism, determinism, and nothing to learn from history. "Joy does not come to us only at the moment of finding what we sought. It comes also in the search itself. And teaching and learning are not possible without the search . . ." (p. 125). Librarians don't have to accept distintermediation as an inevitability, nor assume they can't learn from its processes.

Transforming the workings of disintermediation, rather than praising its inevitability or despairing in its newness, means analyzing its history, its context, how it works, how users perceive it, and so on. In practical terms, this means the work of revealing the inner motivations and structures of the institution, demystifying intermediating practices, and the creation of materials by those who use them (librarians should be writing their own stuff); provide ways to critically examine common practices such as using Google. Changing the question from the rhetorical "why can't students do this?" (which is another form of the question "why can't students be more like me?") to "what is keeping students from understanding this?" How can we break down the structures that create distance and de-motivate students? How are gender and class and cultural differences creating stronger intermediation than librarians?

How Librarians Can Empower Students

Librarians have to rethink their "deficit" model of students, where students are seen as empty vessels to be filled at the library. They need to go beyond imagining new roles for themselves as gatekeepers or coaches or trusted colleague (all roles suggested as adaptations to disintermediation). Librarians can help students develop the critical self-awareness needed in order to create "radical needs" and new "social relations to sustain them" (Giroux, 1983, p. 149). Some one-shot bibliographic instruction tries to do this with a quick discussion of the myths and misperceptions students hold about libraries, but a discussion of Google's marketing strategies and their relation to students' purposes might be equally helpful in developing such social relations with fellow students and librarians. For librarians, this kind of critical self-awareness may require teaching faculty that students don't stop using Google when instructed in a more complex, lengthy research process; the fact that we (students, librarians, faculty) all use Google creates a shared ground for starting social relationships and a much more engaged instructional session.

Users need to engage with the library as text, not conduit to the text. Library space planners have created socialized physical spaces for learning, and today most new libraries have information commons where students can work together. However, research processes are rarely seen as socialized spaces where gender and class can intrude, react, and transform. Here's a typical scenario: A student comes to the reference desk because she can't find any scholarly journal articles on a topic. After looking online, neither can the librarian. The student becomes even more frustrated with the lack of success. What does the librarian say in response, in order to continue the social relationship initiated by the student?

> 1) Ask the students to leave an email address and see if she can find something when she has a break.

> 2) Explain what the problem is so that the student understands the nature of the scholarly conversation she's entering and why her school has not paid for access to the database that would allow her to more quickly find articles on her topic.

> 3) Apologize for the inadequacy of the library's holdings.

> 4) Sympathize with the student and explain that she needed to start this search two weeks ago.

Some of us might try to do all four! In fact, any of the four responses might start an excellent conversation challenging the student's conceptions about libraries, librarians, research, or academic deadlines. The disintermediation of academic research hasn't failed, but rather presented the first challenge to this student. Each of the four responses to the student is also a response to the disintermediation issue. The first response might show the student how a librarian is a collaborator in research processes and how librarians are also interested parties in undergraduate knowledge-building. The second response might show a student how the nature of her own construction of the topic is different from how scholars have approached the topic, making it possible for her to see new connections between her life and scholarly research. The third response, if extended, might show students that they have original and unusual ideas of their own that may not have been taken up by scholars, and that they may need to use primary sources for their research because of the individualized spin they are interested in. The fourth response, particularly if paired with the first response, helps expose the inner workings of academic research. For first-generation college students and non-traditional students, learning the tacit knowledge of academic work and study skills, which better-prepared students were told in high school, is invaluable. Many students need what librarians received or seek out: repeated, intensive, low-stakes, successful encounters with databases.

Here's another typical scenario: The librarian is facing the usual first-year college English class of 25 students who are working on their first research paper, for a one-shot library instruction session. She knows she can't cover everything, so how does she choose? How does a librarian best prepare students for the disintermediated environment of academic online research? She could 1) give a demonstration on how to use the library webpage as a portal and how to navigate two general academic databases or 2) give a lecture on the basic research process of moving from abstract to specific information sources and how print and online materials are related, or 3) describe how an experienced researcher would handle the paper as opposed to a less-experienced researcher (comparing a Lexis-Nexis search to a Google search, for instance) or 4) give students the first third of the class period to try their own searching strategies, followed by a discussion of which strategies worked better, and then followed by some specific suggestions for library research based on what the students found challenging. The librarian's choice will depend on how she sees the issue of disintermediation. None of the options are wrong, if they are the result of a librarian asking how disintermediation has already created myths and misconceptions in students' minds, how it will create barriers and exclude some students while reinforcing other students' sense of entitlement, and how it could reinforce a static, linear, unreflective research process for students. The option that gives the librarian a chance to collaborate with students in their research and demonstrate common learning goals in a social environment will support the goals of critical pedagogy as well.

All of the options for the scenario described above take up valuable time, however, and a librarian often can't reduce the amount of material to cover. When there is no time in a one-shot bibliographic session for straying away from the faculty member's agenda or the curricular requirements for the session, establishing a critically thoughtful and socializing environment for thinking about information will have to happen outside the session in one-on-one conferences, or in a 3-minute exercise to fill out a card with questions for the librarian about what was covered, or perhaps a micro-theme where students describe, and thus reflect on, the most important thing they learned during the session. One of the most powerful lessons from librarians, which takes up very little classroom time, comes from asking students how long they should work in a database without getting anywhere and discussing why a certain frustration level is counterproductive. In other words, when does the self-service impulse from users hit a disintermediated emotional flashpoint?

One final example examines the problem of class differences between librarians and students. Most libraries provide research guides or fliers on every discipline and academic major, to guide students in the absence of a human intermediary. But few or none of the fliers are on topics of interest to students, such as hunting, extreme sports, or the latest celebrity scandal. These are not scholarly topics but they give librarians the opportunity, in the disintermediated environment that the flier operates in, to model effective and efficient research processes, including evaluating sources and asking critical questions about issues. Librarians may feel these topics are not academic or life-altering or too "everyday," but the library's ignoring of such topics may be a class difference as well and why some students do academic research at their local public library. By limiting research models not only to academic or "serious" topics, but to topics that have been the subject of serious research and thinking, we model a non-problematic research process that then frustrates students when they try the topics that are important to them. In other words, librarians too often model successful searches, not failed ones. Whenever students have to eliminate topics of primary interest to them or adapt topics to fit what they can find literature on (such as switching from the topic of deer baiting to bovine tuberculosis) instead of pointing students to other professional sources of information (such as Department of Natural Resources reports on stakeholders' meetings about deer hunting regulation changes), the library has missed the chance to intermediate with users in a critically supportive way. The search process then fails to engage a citizen in a collective process or in ethical questions that could alter the status quo. The library hasn't encouraged or provided a challenge to disintermediation, but encouraged failure. The library hasn't, in Giroux's terms, "offer[ed] a discourse of possibility, a way of providing students with the opportunity to link meaning to commitment and understanding to social transformation—and to do so in the interest of the greatest possible justice" (Giroux, 2004, p. 73). The library has thus, in this situation, failed to help students negotiate the movement between scholarly, individual, and public spheres, nor to create a conversation among the data created by researchers, the values a student brings from home, and the potential to enact change in the world.

Beyond Critical Library Instruction

Disintermediation needs the lens of critical pedagogy. More than a decade ago, John Buschman (1994) used Giroux's vision of education in a democracy and called for librarians to "critically analyze our library technologies in order to capture their democratic potentials" and "make our institutions and our profession active participants in an energetic public democracy" (p. 18). In addition, librarians need to historicize accurately their own understanding of disintermediation, which was powerfully present in the imposing wooden card catalog, physically standing between the student and the books. After analysis, however, as Giroux (1983) reminds us, we have the task of reconstructing the useful actions and ideas into new knowledge and new constructions of experience (p. 160).

So how can librarians construct a new experience? Not by embracing disintermediation mindlessly nor to rejecting it out of hand, but by studying it carefully and thoroughly and making a conscious, critical choice about each connection between users and information. Disintermediation does empower students, especially in the hands of a persistent student with flexible goals who sees value in the process as well as the product. We can assist students working in a disintermediated environment by teaching the habits of mind, such as asking "why?" and "why not?" and "whose agenda is being served here?" and "am I ready for help?". We can assist faculty by encouraging assignments that allow time and varied approaches to information, in order to encourage a fuller, not a more superficial, answer to questions. For the foreseeable future, librarians will remain the intermediaries, with the most power to elaborate or dissolve that role from one that preserves the status quo to one that actively questions whether disintermediation is creating an exclusionary or inclusionary library, as well as what can be done about it. This means continually re-asking and re-solving similar problems, continually pounding against the wall of positivist and debasing influences of institutionalized education. Librarians need to plan and manage for information equity as much as information access. Librarians have to ask if their fears of disintermediation are about their feelings of professional isolation, or insulation from other disciplines on campus or their marginality in faculty governance, or economic exploitation by the university, or their fears of being pushed out of their socioeconomic and intellectual status in the community.

None of these questions is easy. They are, in Paulo Freire's words, "unquiet" questions: "a pedagogy will be that much more critical and radical the more investigative and less certain of 'certainties' it is. The more unquiet a pedagogy, the more critical it will become" (Kutz and Roskelly, 1991, p. x). Disintermediation is already an unquiet, disquieting phenomenon in libraries, deeply embedded in the reification of education as a consumable commodity, something that can be bought and sold. Thus, according to critical pedagogy, disintermediation gives us the seeds of challenge and resistance, at the same moment that it contains the power to rule us.

References

Buschman, J. (1994). Taking a hard look at technology and librarianship: Compliance, complicity, and intellectual independence of the profession. *Argus, 23*(2), 13-18.

Fourie, I. (1999). Should we take disintermediation seriously? *The Electronic Library, 17*(1), 9-16.

Freire, P. (1986). *Pedagogy of the oppressed*. New York: Continuum.

Freire, P. (1998). *Pedagogy of freedom: Ethics, democracy, and civic courage.* Lanham, MD: Rowman & Littlefield.

Gellman, R. (1996). Disintermediation and the internet. *Government Information Quarterly, 13*(1), 1-8.

Giroux, H. A. (1983). *Theory and resistance in education: A pedagogy for the opposition.* South Hadley, MA: Bergin and Harvey.

Giroux, H. A. (2004). Cultural studies, public pedagogy, and the responsibility of intellectuals. *Communication and critical/cultural studies, 1*(1), 59-79.

Giroux, H. A. (2006). *America on the edge: Henry Giroux on politics, culture, and education.* Gordonsville, VA: Palgrave Macmillan.

Kieft, R. K. (1995). The death of the librarian in the (post)modern electronic information age. In *Information for a new age: Redefining the librarian* (pp. 15-22). Englewood, CO: Libraries Unlimited.

Kutz, E., & Roskelly, H. (1991). *An unquiet pedagogy*. Portsmouth, NH: Boynton/Cook.

Miller, W. (2007). Reference services over the past century: Moving from the center to the fringes. *The Reference Librarian, 48*(2), 3-7.

Sturges, P. (2001). Gatekeepers and other intermediaries. *Aslib Proceedings, 53*(2), 62-67.

Veldof, J. R. (2008). From desk to web: Creating safety nets in the online library. In S. K. Steiner and M. L. Madden (Eds.), *The desk and beyond: Next generation reference services* (pp. 120-134). Chicago: ACRL.

The Library as "Stuck Place": Critical Pedagogy in the Corporate University

Cathy Eisenhower and Dolsy Smith

Working closely with faculty in a first-year undergraduate writing program, some of whom teach courses expressly construed in terms of critical pedagogy and social justice, we use the word *pedagogy*, and to a lesser extent, *critical pedagogy*, to rally ourselves and our library colleagues around approaches to teaching research that go beyond the bounds of typical library instruction. We use *pedagogy*, moreover, as a wedge to open space—in a discursive field dominated by the rubrics of "information literacy"—for a more intellectually sustaining and reflective way of thinking about what we do, a more fruitful praxis. "Praxis," as described by Lather (1998), is "about philosophy viewing itself in the mirror of practice" (p. 497). To claim critical pedagogy as a practice and a theoretical position, and to undertake this mirror test, we must first consider what we mean by the phrase and how we engage with it specifically as librarians.

Historically, critical pedagogy and its attendant literature rose up as a critique from the

> "radical" educator who recognizes and helps students to recognize and name injustice, who empowers students to act against their own and others' oppressions (including oppressive school structures), who criticizes and transforms her or his own understanding in response to the understandings of students. (Ellsworth, 1989, p. 300)

According to this model, such a pedagogy works to create a democratic public sphere in which citizens debate critical issues and transform civil society into a more socially just network. Ellsworth's feminist critique of critical pedagogy literature, including the work of Henry Giroux and Peter McLaren, takes issue with the lack of context for these abstract goals, with the absence of serious reflection on how teachers are necessarily implicated in the oppressive formations to which they draw attention, and with the heavy dependence on rationalism as the means for students to arrive at critiques that lead to social action.[1]

In the course of trying to write an essay about the links between critical pedagogical theory and our own teaching practices, we came to realize that we do not exactly teach what we preach, and that the very possibility of a critical pedagogy of library instruction would seem to hinge on a prior critique of the aims and conditions of library instruction, a critique that we have not made explicit to ourselves. This essay, then, is our gesture toward such a critique, putting the work we do—as instruction librarians, and as critical pedagogues engaged in library instruction—in the context of contemporary labor, capital, and the corporatizing university.

We take as our starting point a claim Lather (1998) makes, quoting Ellsworth (1997): not only is "critical pedagogy in the field of schooling…impossible," but teaching itself is also impossible. According to these writers, the entire educational project is paternalistic, and as teachers we must "[come] up against 'stuck place after stuck place' as a way to keep moving within 'the impossibility of teaching' in order to produce and learn from raptures [sic], failures, breaks, and refusals" (p. 495). If this seems true, and to us it does, then the librarian as critical pedagogue must ask herself these questions: how are librarians to work toward social justice in the library classroom, if when we hold our educational philosophies—and our very selves—up to meet our practices in the mirror, those practices are very often not our own but those of the faculty with whom we collaborate? Is such social justice work even a reasonable desire given the particular ways librarians are suspended in the bureaucratic structures of a corporate university?

The Classroom as Technology: The Reproduction of the Corporate Subject

Working in the classrooms at our large urban university, many of which sit in the basement of office buildings—classrooms without windows, awkward polygons full of motley furniture, with dry-erase boards now

---

[1] For Ellsworth, the critical pedagogy discourse that posits student "empowerment" as the central purpose of this teaching practice has succumbed to a model in which the teacher has the "consciousness-raising power" and must enlighten the student, while outside real classrooms, far from teachers' hopeful eyes, students participate in discourses and take action based on their own desires for social justice not granted legitimacy by the authority of the critical pedagogue.

useless after years of neglect—one gets a distinct impression of the relation between a university education and the corporate structure it supports. No longer is the former intended to be a sphere apart, a world of intellectual pursuits from which students descend to the more mundane concerns of bourgeois livelihood, having been formed as self-reliant citizens in a crucible of liberal subjectivity. Even as we acknowledge the many limitations of that model, and the exclusions and inequities that it has tended to reproduce, we should note that it serves rhetoric and marketing far more than it describes practice. These classrooms suggest, on the contrary, that higher education makes up the bottom rung of the corporate ladder.

Education today does not "form" students into something (responsible workers or citizens). It informs them. Beyond communicating disciplinary content, education imparts "skills" necessary to stay afloat in a fluid and contingent workforce. And this is a workforce tasked, above all, with the arts of communication, with handling information. ACRL's Information Literacy Standards, much like the model of standardized testing universalized by No Child Left Behind, make this link between school and work abundantly clear: the reflective self-reliance of the sometime bourgeois subject becomes the potential for "life-long learning" and its corollary, continuous "self-assessment." To what else does "life-long learning" refer, but the need for workers to stay productive by re-tooling in response to the demands of capital and changes in the modes of production? And what does "self-assessment" mean, other than that the worker must absorb the burdens of management, learning to measure her own performance by abstract rubrics, learning even to quantify it—instead of following the intrinsic and elusive voice of what was once called "responsibility," and before that, "craft"? In these examples of the fate of labor after Ford and Taylor, discussed widely in the critical literature (see, for example, Dyer-Witheford, 1999, pp. 78-82), one thing stands out in particular. As the finessing of information occupies more and more of the labor in virtually every field, labor itself is turned into an informational potential. It is not only counted and broken apart into discrete quanta—that, of course, has been true since at least the Industrial Revolution—but also abstracted into "skills," "knowledge," "abilities," "networks," "connections," etc. Marx talked about labor-power in terms of time, but capital seeks subtler mechanisms to measure and absorb that power, sending its tendrils deep into the reservoirs of intelligence and personality.

As an agent of communication/information, the worker is no longer a cog in an industrial-style machine—or as a cog, she puts different parts of herself into play. Lazzarato (1996) offers the following assessment:

> In today's large restructured economy, a worker's work increasingly involves, at various levels, an ability to choose among different alternatives, and thus a degree of responsibility regarding decision making. The concept of 'interface' used by communication sociologists provides a fair definition of the activities of this kind of worker—as an interface between different functions, between different work teams, between different levels of the hierarchy, and so on. What modern management techniques are looking for is for "the worker's soul to become part of the factory." ... workers are expected to become "active subjects" in the coordination of various functions of production, instead of being subjected to it as simple command. We arrive at a point where a collective learning process becomes the heart of productivity…" (p. 134)

Workers, not only white-collar professionals but also workers in the service and manufacturing sectors, are expected to collaborate, to manage themselves, to contribute to teams and working groups convened for specific tasks. They are part of an increasingly contingent and amorphous collective medium, in which the work demands greater performance of the "whole" self. Virno (1996) calls this performance "sentiments put to work" (p. 14): whether for the fast-food cashier expected to offer her customers a "real" smile, or the hedge-fund manager whose bonus depends on "thinking outside of the box," or the librarian charged not just with helping patrons track down sources and facts, but with empowering students to "think critically."

The discourse of information literacy links the selective consumption of information to the production, pedagogically speaking, of autonomous subjects. But information is a commodity—and not only *a* commodity, but the preeminent commodity-form of contemporary capitalism, insofar as the production and exchange of all commodities increasingly depends on sophisticated techniques of information-gathering, from the surveys and focus groups that precede product design to the sales data that are used to create increasingly complex (and personal) profiles of consumers. We argue that the *a priori* commodification of information—and the technology that it depends on—raise questions about the form of subjectivity that information literacy can produce. As Virno (1996) writes, the material conditions of an "informed," endlessly mediated mass culture render a certain ideal of self-awareness, of intellectual autonomy, less and less viable:

> The superabundance of miniscule perceptions becomes systematic in an
> environment of artificial actions. In a workplace dominated by
> information technologies, thousands of signals are received without ever
> being distinctly and consciously perceived. In a completely analogous way,
> our reception of the media does not induce concentration, but dispersion.
> We are crowded with impressions and images that never give rise to an
> "I." (pp. 28-29)

We may take issue with the scope of Virno's rhetoric, but all the same we
can acknowledge the ubiquity of superfluous experience in our daily lives.
Shopping malls, supermarkets, animated billboards, video games,
television's thousand channels, the vast thirsty sea opened up by Google, the
satellites that make it possible, in theory, to triangulate anything on the
planet—what do all these signals communicate? Even before they can be
parsed as messages, they are measured as facts of production. In other
words, they are the voices in which capital speaks to itself. And how much of
what we feel and take to be fact comes from the media, from Hollywood,
from commodities that live and die according to market trends? And when
we consider that by "market trends" we mean only a rule of information,
information that we ourselves supply by consuming—hence by desiring and
communicating—we can begin to see how the totality of social life is
involved in what Lazzarato (1996) calls "immaterial labor". If culture was
once opposed to the material stuff of life, to the forks and spoons and beans
and roofs and automobiles, the concept of information dissolves this
distinction (Schiller, 1997). Information technology establishes feedback
loops that convey nuances of need and desire on the part of consumers,
nuances which can then be analyzed and used to make new products, the
ideal being a product that responds to a need consumers did not yet know
they had. Through these mechanisms, both consumers and producers take
part in the process of production with an intimacy that belies the
importance accorded the factory by classical economic and organizational
theory. Likewise, the close suture between work and leisure calls into
question the role of the school. As Lazzarato (1996) cannily observes,

> If production today is directly the production of a social relation, then the
> "raw material" of immaterial labor is subjectivity and the "ideological"
> environment in which this subjectivity lives and reproduces. The
> production of subjectivity ceases to be only an instrument of social control
> (for the reproduction of mercantile relationships) and becomes directly
> productive, because the goal of postindustrial society is to construct the
> consumer/communicator—and to construct it as "active." (p. 143)

On the laptops that we supply them with, our students update their Facebook status ("Bored in the library!"), check the stats on ESPN, search for the best value on holiday flights, etc.—all behaviors that replicate, on the explicitly "personal," "subjective," or social level, the components of "information literacy." A *critical pedagogy* of information literacy might help our students explore what it *means* and what it *does* to consume particular information, which is at the same time to produce it—Facebook being a golden example of a product woven almost entirely out of the humble straw of its own consumers, out of their very desires, moreover, and their strange self-fashioning. The consumers of Facebook supply the labor whose product they consume, in a circle much crazier, though of course much less oppressive, than that between factory and factory-store.

Here labor is, in a funny way, immediately social; it manages to exist without needing to be disciplined. In fact, it flourishes by virtue of being a non-discipline: as a student (or a librarian) you go to Facebook when you want a diversion from your "work." (That is not to say that using Facebook involves no discipline; rather, the discipline involved is social and ideological.) If above we said that a critical pedagogy *might* take this labor for its object, we said so because by and large in *our* classroom, the demands of a rigorous supplementarity still hold sway. Our students come there to learn the discipline of constructing a scholarly, "literate," academic, critical self, a subject of discourses far removed, ostensibly, from the anecdotage on Facebook and the twitter on Twitter. With some exceptions, they come to retrieve books from the shelves and articles from scholarly journals, to practice formulating academic arguments, to apprentice themselves to the pleasures of bibliography. This is true even though many of the courses we work with take some form of popular culture as their critical object: horror films, conspiracy theories, comic books, video games. All of which evokes a set of further question: What labor does or can the "critical" perform, in the discursive forms in which it is currently given? How might we give it new forms to work with?

The Biopolitics of the Classroom: Critical and Affective Labor

On the one hand, the classroom is a space full of discrete subjects: a space for different bodies, voices, names, ID numbers, genders, races, nationalities, etc.; and, of course, a space for the differentiation that it is the business of schools to accomplish through the various mechanisms of assessment and discipline. On the other hand, we have the "class" that comprises these subjects, considered as a part of social life. It is a network woven of various discourses, some of them explicit (the disciplinary/curricular discourse), and many more that go unarticulated (discourses of fear and desire). The network exists long before the students enter the room. But once the class period begins, one is aware—one's body is aware—of certain resonances that travel from person to person, and which lend the space itself a "character" (like the "scene" at a party or in a bar) touched by the immanence of discipline, torqued in the direction of those particular passions of the school: boredom, anxiety, ennui. A joke or a topic of idle chat rumbles from one table to another, or else a complaint about the assignments. A tacit mood of irritable distraction or, more rarely, of genuine enthusiasm, communicates itself from those already there to those now walking in, or vice-versa. Naturally, these phenomena are impossible to pin down, being highly fluid, subject to sudden shifts and accumulations that dissipate just as quickly. Mechanisms of anxiety—and here we are speaking as instructors, whose anxieties occupy a privileged place in the classroom—may very well magnify this data emanating from the others (Are they laughing at me? Do I look bad today? Do I sound like I don't know what I'm talking about?), but each magnification or projection only adds in turn to the store of resonance, affecting the others, too, in ways they cannot not perceive.

As Lazzarato (1996) observes, "immaterial labor constitutes itself in forms *that are immediately* collective, and we might say that it exists only in the form of networks and flows" (p. 137). As political phenomena, these flows both serve and pose challenges to the forms of power that circulate through society in the age of neoliberal government. This government and its apparatuses of security, as Foucault (2008) calls them, aim to control society at the level of the population, by adjusting and intervening in social life through the analysis of norms and trends, of desires, interests, and behaviors. These analyses divide the social mass into units that are not subjects per se, but rather strata or bands of subjectivity: number of people who eat oatmeal for breakfast, who suffer from eczema, who have been convicted of shoplifting, who watch *Desperate Housewives*. These bands of experience, derived from "statistically significant" samples, not only yield new products and services, but also inform policy, programs, and infrastructure aimed at optimizing life: at extending the number of lives that fall within a certain range of longevity, health, mobility, fertility, etc., and that conform to certain patterns of behavior and belief—lives that, above all, are conducive to the overarching goal of unchecked social and economic growth. For at stake in these rational analyses is the reproduction of the structures of rationality from which they derive—accomplished through the ceaseless flow of information, multiplying and refining itself.

The collaboration, the active learning, the critical discussion that prospective donors glimpse through the windows of our classrooms would thus be in tune with the informational milieu of global capitalism. Or to imagine it another way, pedagogy adjusts the index of refraction in its subjects, making them more (or less?) efficient media for the flow of information. The horizon of this adjustment can be found in the contemporary workplace, where, as Lazzarato (1996) puts it, "The subject becomes a simple relayer of codification and decodification, whose transmitted messages must be 'clear and free of ambiguity,' within a communications context that has been completely normalized by management" (p. 135). The discourse of "information literacy," of course, stakes its whole appeal on the pertinence of this process. But even the "critical"—in "critical thinking," and perhaps, its radical claims notwithstanding, in "critical pedagogy,"—can be seen to serve the reproduction of a society managed and governed according to neoliberal models. Again following Foucault (2008), we can think of (neo)liberalism as "a tool for the criticism of reality":

> criticism of a previous governmentality from which one is trying to get free; of a present governmentality that one is to reform and rationalize by scaling it down; or of a governmentality to which one is opposed and whose abuses one wants to limit. (p. 320)

The critical is the preeminent mode of neoliberal rationality because the latter tends toward a perpetual anxiety of regulation, of adjustment, of optimization—and toward reason's perpetual self-improvement. But how does this critical engine handle—except by excluding it from its analysis—what falls outside of the realm and the scope of reason, what refuses to be reasonably governed: i.e., emotion, feeling, affect? Feminists have long recognized the ways rationalism excludes women, people of color, and so on, and teachers, even critical pedagogues, have unquestioningly valorized rational discourses in their classrooms as the logical path to the teacher's own conception of social justice and how to act toward and on it. Perhaps many of the "raptures [sic], failures, breaks, and refusals" in our classrooms, and between our ideas about teaching and what happens in our classrooms, happen where reason fails and reveals feeling—not illegible or incomprehensible, but frustrating "stuck places" rooted in intuition and experience. For Ellsworth (1997), the term "critical" itself masks the particular work scholars and teachers are doing by coding anti-racist, anti-sexist, anti-capitalist, etc., with the ambiguous word that surely represents critique, but of what sort?

The Classroom as Workplace: Pedagogy and the Post-Fordist Organization

In our particular library's case, we are caught in a learning organization—a post-bureaucratic organizational governance model that links power, within an ostensibly flexible institutional structure, to demonstrable learning: self-development embodied by discursive prowess, innovation, and self-management, among other attributes. The learning organization bases its work on shared vision with leaders that, rather than heroically driving the institution into the future, function as teachers, stewards, designers, "*managers of the creative tension* between what is and what might be" (Coopey, 1995, p. 195). Coopey outlines the "learning culture" based on his survey of learning organization literature:

> A 'learning culture' encourages the development of individuals and the transformation of the organization by nurturing a questioning spirit, experimentation, differences, openness and a tolerance of disequilibrium. Shared mental models of how the organization might best function within its environment inform the processes and structures. (p. 195)

But the minimally structured, flexible learning organization cannot fulfill its promise, as Coopey discovers, and as we have found here. A lack of usefully articulated performance appraisal standards exacerbated by leaders whose relish of the exercise of power is camouflaged by a rhetoric of shared vision, democratic collaboration and policy-making, and non-hierarchical operations, results in conformity to managers' tacit expectations and an informal social jockeying for political power. To rank-and-file eyes, management appears to wield its power arbitrarily: not based on the knowledge that individual learners glean from external networks, but responsive primarily to those learners' discursive facility for rationalizing their function and value within the organization.

A rhetoric of critical pedagogy put into play in the context of this particular learning organization, in meetings and informal interactions between instruction librarians inside a corporate university, positions us as educators in opposition to organizational goals linked to external professional measures and neoliberal values—assessable outcomes, metrics, efficiency, economy. But this rhetoric also provides an occasion to demonstrate our discursive facility/power before our colleagues. Part of our counterhegemonic work, or at least our talk about such work, is possible because of our library's structure of ostensible self-governance and our labor contracts, which make firing librarians difficult. Speaking out, or up, in the learning organization, we "critical pedagogues" vocally resist institutional mandates for programmatic assessments that quantify student learning in ways passionately ignorant of knowledge as a "structural dynamic ... not a substance" (Ellsworth, 1997, p. 68) and heavily invested in the consumerist model of student as customer. Maybe the question is, What kind of work does our "defiant speech" do? Is it defiant *enough*? Is it defiant at all, or simply the expected "questioning spirit" that is finally disciplined by power arbitrarily executed, or by the disciplinary conventions and ideologies and identities of those of our faculty colleagues who resist considerations of "pedagogy" at all?

Librarians entwined in social and labor relations with faculty grounded in shared critiques of such institutional power, commitments to social justice broadly conceived, and social constructivist approaches to knowledge produce a kind of value for the library as an organization, despite our attempts at defying it. The library as an enterprise and librarians as professionals, both individually and collectively, must constantly justify their worth to university administrations, municipalities, and corporate trustees to ensure continued funding and self-preservation. Much of library literature takes up this task of how librarians can convince the powers that be of their value and, even more important, how they can revise their identities to serve the needs of a constituency formed by cultural trends, social policies, and economic shifts. As we enter discursive communities on campus (largely humanities-related because of their often leftist social theoretical approaches) as allies in the struggle against "oppressive formations" (Ellsworth, 1997), we become more in demand as intra-institutional collaborators, which administrations generally deem "innovative," and as co-teachers of research. The bottom line is that our counterhegemonic work results in our insinuating ourselves more into committee work, classroom teaching, and, ironically, the bureaucratic structures of the university. What we mean to the library, then, are increases in teaching, in numbers of students taught, in departmental collaborations, in university-wide committee work, and thus quantifiable efforts that demonstrate the library's support of the work of the university. Our discursive resistance to the corporatization of higher education and its implicit distortions of learning and knowledge—its obsession with quantitative assessment, student satisfaction, outcomes, and consumerist attitudes toward learning—is subsumed in its Foucauldian way into numbers that scaffold the very discourse we critique.

The numbers (metrics), though, also disguise the intimate publics we have built:

> One of the striking things about academic life is the way its institutional spaces and relations of professional labor support the production of intimate publics. That is, they become public contexts of collective life on which people come to rely for sustaining their identities, their opinions, and their relations to power, as well as their fantasies, rages, and desires. Usually without realizing it, workers invest in these scenes anxieties and needs for mirroring one normally associates with the institution of privacy and domestic intimacy (Negt and Kluge, 32-38). But because most intimate publics are generated in institutions that seem merely instrumental to people's survival, they tend not to experience their own institution-based intensity as something emanating from *themselves*, their needs and desires. (Berlant, 1997, p. 150)

The formations of our own subjectivities, according to Berlant, rely heavily on these intimate publics and our conceiving of our "work" as counterhegemonic. We call attention to this word because of the particular labor that teaching librarians do and do not do in the classroom and in the educational institution itself. In many ways, our subjectivities and their formations are so closely tied to those of faculty that the relationship feels parasitic at best, in conflict with our own praxis at worst. We feel supplemental, marginalized, undisciplined, and though we may have capacities for playing out critical pedagogy in the classroom, our ability to do so is almost completely determined by the desires, fantasies, identities, opinions, and relations to power of our faculty counterparts. If I teach library instruction with a faculty member in the business school who, if he ever encountered critical pedagogy, would regard as counter to his job the "politicization of the classroom," do I engage him about it? The clear answer is no. Instead, I resist voicing my opinions, desires, my need for mirroring, and enact his banking pedagogical fantasy in a room full of students while he looks on and perhaps corrects my performance, if necessary. My authority to teach comes out of his silent observation and controlling presence, and my ventriloquism and silencing of critical teaching practice result from assessing my own relationship to his power within the institution: he is faculty, a masculine profession, and I am a librarian, a feminine profession, perceived to be servile and self-effacing. Whereas he develops bodies of abstract knowledge, I "[serve] others through applying and communicating [that] knowledge" (Holbrook, 1991, p. 203). Moreover, he controls my access to classroom teaching, as all faculty ultimately do. Even faculty engaged in the feminized work of composition and the impossibility of teaching often regard library instruction in instrumentalist terms because they have not considered how discourses of "information" and the critique of such discourses can open alternative spaces in the classroom for thinking about the labor of scholarship and our relation to the infrastructures and systems that discipline it.

As librarians, our affective investments, and hence the forms of subjectivity we employ in the classroom (or during office hours or on the reference desk), are by and large a sort of supplement to the flows of pedagogical power and authority: our virtues are chiefly those of patience, active listening, understanding, the willingness to help; our discourse is one of encouragement and suggestion, not prescription, inspiration, and charismatic authority. Publicly interrogating our own positions in classroom power relations—based on what the institution grants us along with our gender, race, class, etc.—as one piece of a critical pedagogy would likewise reveal that as our authority is vicarious; in the intimate public of the classroom, because of our limited time there, librarian-workers look to faculty to interpret students' mirroring of our needs and anxieties because faculty have built the intimate public, we have not. On the other hand, our work is perhaps less visible than that of our faculty colleagues to the disciplining forces of efficiency: it is difficult to make more efficient the work of someone whose job it is (at the reference desk, for instance) to stand and wait. As parts of the pedagogical apparatus, our labor is, in the sense defined above, immaterial, but because our impact on the production of subjects (corporate or critical) is, by and large, rather small, our labor can seem immaterial in another way: i.e., does it really matter?

In the end, our position remains profoundly ambivalent. As librarians, our engagement (with pedagogy) is not given but must be wrested from situations that would reduce such engagement to the motives of efficiency, even if the place of that efficiency, in the overall "business" of teaching at the university, seems at times to verge on the negligible. Or if not negligible, then a smooth surface to which nothing sticks. Thus, the perennial complaint by librarians about how little students learn from them becomes, when considered in the inverted mirror of praxis, the ideal role of information literacy in the corporate-educational imaginary: a point that reduces friction in the flow of potential labor and (future) capital, a Teflon funnel through which the noise of thinking and wondering and not-knowing and resistance gives way to the signal of productive work. So to return to the metaphor from which we began, perhaps the most that we can hope for is to hit those "stuck places" where thinking occurs. For praxis is only ever the messiness of philosophy and practice as they confront forces (capital, gender, bodies, etc.) in dissonance, and the value of praxis comes from seeing what can happen when we defer, a little while, the recuperation of force into value.

References

Berlant, L. (1997). Feminism and the institutions of intimacy. In E. A. Kaplan & G. Levine (Eds.), *The Politics of Research*. New Brunswick, NJ: Rutgers University Press.

Coopey, J. (1995). The learning organization: Power, politics, and ideology introduction. *Management Learning, 26*(2), 193-213.

Dyer-Witheford, N. (1999). *Cyber-Marx: Cycles and circuits of struggle in high-technology capitalism*. Urbana: University of Illinois Press

Ellsworth, E. (1989). Why doesn't this feel empowering? Working through the repressive myths of critical pedagogy. *Harvard Educational Review, 59*(3) 297-324.

Ellsworth, E. (1997). *Teaching methods: difference, pedagogy, and the power of address*. New York: Teacher's College Press.

Foucault, M. (2008). *The birth of biopolitics: lectures at the Collège De France, 1978-79* (G. Burchell, Trans.). New York: Palgrave Macmillan.

Holbrook, S. E.(1991). Women's work: The feminizing of composition. *Rhetoric Review, 9(*2), 201-229.

Lather, Patti. (1998). Critical pedagogy and its complicities: A praxis of stuck places. *Educational Theory, 48*(4): 487-497.

Lazzarato, M. (1996). Immaterial labor. In P. Virno & M. Hardt (Eds.), *Radical thought in Italy: A potential politics*. Minneapolis, MN: University of Minnesota Press.

Schiller, D. (1997). The information commodity: A preliminary view. In J. Davis, T. A. Hirschl, & M. Stack (Eds.), *Cutting edge: Technology, information capitalism and social revolution*. London: Verso.

Virno, P. (1996). The ambivalence of disenchantment. In P. Virno & M. Hardt (Eds.), *Radical thought in Italy: A potential politics*. Minneapolis, MN: University of Minnesota Press.

About the Contributors

Maria T. Accardi is Assistant Librarian and Coordinator of Instruction at Indiana University Southeast in New Albany, IN. She holds an MLIS from the University of Pittsburgh and an MA in English from the University of Louisville. She may be contacted at maccardi@gmail.com.

Jill Burkert is an Assistant Professor of Education at the University of Alaska Southeast, where she teaches graduate courses in special education and provides onsite classroom support for teachers in Alaska's remote, rural, and Native communities.

Jason Coleman is Service Coordinator at Kansas State University Libraries. He earned his MLS from Emporia State University in 2007. His research interests include reference interviewing in virtual settings, staff training through social software, motivation in information literacy instruction, and knowledge-management for reference.

Jonathan Cope is a reference/instruction librarian at the College of Staten Island, CUNY. He can be contacted at jonathan.cope@csi.cuny.edu

Emily Drabinski is Electronic Resources and Instruction Librarian at Long Island University, Brooklyn. She sits on the board of *Radical Teacher*, a socialist, feminist, anti-racist journal of teaching theory and practice.

Damian Duffy is a PhD candidate in the University of Illinois at Urbana-Champaign Graduate School of Library and Information Science and a founder of the Eye Trauma Comics collective (http://eyetrauma.net). He is also a comics creator and comics art curator. He can be reached at duff@eyetrauma.net.

Thomas Scott Duke is an Associate Professor of Education at the University of Alaska Southeast, where he coordinates graduate programs in special education and teaches courses in special education, multicultural education, and qualitative research methods.

Cathy Eisenhower is author of the poetry collections *clearing without reversal* (Edge 2008) and *would with and* (Roof 2009), and co-translates the works of Argentine poet Diana Bellessi. She has published articles on gaming and research pedagogy, and, along with Dolsy Smith, started open-access scholarly publishing at GWU's Gelman Library.

Sara Franks received two Master's degrees, in Library Science and English, from Indiana University- Bloomington in 2007. She is currently the Instruction and Outreach Librarian at Saint Joseph's University in

Philadelphia, where she develops the information literacy program, acts as liaison to the English and Sociology departments, and teaches composition.

Dr. Daren Graves is the Director of the Urban Master's Program at Simmons College. As a teacher educator, he is committed to preparing teachers who see urban youth as assets in the teaching and learning process. His research interest involves the interplay of school culture and racial identity on the academic performance of students of color.

Benjamin R. Harris is an Assistant Professor and Instruction/Liaison Librarian at Trinity University's Coates Library in San Antonio, Texas. Aside from research on the relationship between values and information literacy development, he has published and taught courses on visual information literacy.

Lisa Hooper graduated from Indiana University with a master degree in library science emphasizing in music librarianship. She also holds an MM (University of Illinois at Urbana-Champaign). Her research in music and archival ethics has been presented at various conferences. Lisa is head music and media librarian at Tulane University.

Hiromitsu Inokuchi (Ph.D. University of Wisconsin-Madison) has recently earned his MLS at the State University of New York at Buffalo. Currently, he is a visiting professor of Asian Studies at the SUNY-Buffalo and a volunteer cataloger at the Far Eastern Library at the Royal Ontario Museum (Toronto).

Heidi LM Jacobs is an Information Literacy Librarian and the English subject librarian at the University of Windsor's Leddy Library. Her current research involves information literacy, literary history, and digitization.

Gretchen Keer is Instruction Services Librarian at Humboldt State University in Arcata, CA. She also has five years experience teaching and planning information literacy curricula in a community college setting, and a deep investment in progressive education. She can be contacted at Gretchen.Keer@humboldt.edu.

Bryan M. Kopp, Ph.D., is Assistant Professor of Rhetoric and Writing, Coordinator of University Writing Programs, and former Associate Director of the College Lesson Study Project at the University of Wisconsin-La Crosse. His current research focuses on the rhetoric of teaching and learning across the disciplines.

Alana Kumbier is a Research and Instruction Librarian at Wellesley College. She holds a Ph.D. in Comparative Studies from The Ohio State University, where she worked in the areas of critical archival studies, science studies, disability studies, and visual cultural studies. Alana earned her M.L.I.S. from Kent State University.

Sharon Ladenson is the Gender Studies and Communications Librarian at Michigan State University. She has researched and presented on the history of Michigan women library leaders, and gender and library management. She contributes regularly to the American Library Association's *Library Instruction Round Table News*, and writes reviews for *Feminist Collections*.

Mary McGowan was the Coordinator of the MassBLAST program at Simmons College. She has a Master of Science in Library and Information Science from Simmons College and a Master of Science in Film from Boston University.

Ruth Mirtz is Education Librarian and Assistant Professor at J. D. Williams Library at the University of Mississippi. Her most recent work in library science include the presentation "College students encounter databases: Major and minor obstacles in academic searches" at the Michigan Academy in 2009 and a chapter forthcoming entitled "The changing scholarly article and the Googlization of student search skills."

Yoshiko Nozaki is Associate Professor of comparative and international education at the State University of New York at Buffalo. Her recent book, *War, Memory, Nationalism, and Education in Postwar Japan, 1945-2007* won the AERA Division B Curriculum Studies Outstanding Book Award.

Kim Olson-Kopp, M.L.S., M.F.A., is the Outreach and Technology Librarian at Viterbo University in La Crosse, Wisconsin.

Mary Caton Lingold is a Master's candidate in English at the University of Colorado at Boulder. She has worked as an instructor for the University Libraries' information literacy program for two years.

Elisabeth Pankl is a Humanities Librarian at Kansas State University Libraries. She received her MLS from the University of North Texas in 2005. Ms. Pankl's research interests include rhetorical literacy, spatiality, and literary geography.

Elizabeth Peterson is a Humanities Librarian at the University of Oregon. She is the Subject Specialist for Literatures in English, Comparative Literature, Cinema Studies, Creative Writing, and Folklore.

John Riddle is the Head Librarian of the Penn State University Fayette campus. He received a B.A. from Drew University and an M.L.S. from Rutgers University. He also has Master's Degrees in Political Science and Film Studies.

Maura Seale is currently Research and Instruction Librarian/Bibliographer for American History, American Studies, and African American Studies at Georgetown University. She received an

M.S.I. from the University of Michigan in 2007 and an M.A. in American Studies from the University of Minnesota in 2005.

Caroline Sinkinson is Assistant Professor at the University of Colorado at Boulder University Libraries. She is the Instruction Coordinator/Research and Instruction Librarian at Norlin Library. Her main responsibility is coordinating the Information Literacy component of the first year writing class offered by the University Program for Writing and Rhetoric.

Dolsy Smith is a reference and instruction librarian at The George Washington University.

Troy A. Swanson is Teaching & Learning Librarian at Moraine Valley Community College, where he teaches information literacy and coordinates the library's online presence. Among his other publications, his article "A Radical Step: Implementing A Critical Information Literacy Model" published in portal: Libraries and the Academy was selected for the Library Instruction Round Table's list of top instruction articles for 2004.

Doris Ann Sweet is Associate Director for Research Services at the Simmons College Library. From 2005-2009, she was also the Director of the IMLS-funded MassBLAST project, promoting library internships for high school students, based at Simmons College and carried out with nine partner libraries in Massachusetts, www.simmons.edu/massblast.

Margaret Rose Torrell is Coordinator of Writing Programs and an Assistant Professor of English at the State University of New York: College at Old Westbury, where she teaches courses in composition, disability studies, and multicultural literature. She has forthcoming book chapters on the intersection of disability studies and masculinity studies.

Jennifer Diane Ward is an Associate Professor of Library Science at the University of Alaska Southeast, where her main responsibility is to support distance-delivered education. She believes that librarians need teachers and teachers need librarians to achieve critical consciousness in our future generations.

Author Index

Subject Index

DATE DUE

DEMCO, INC. 38-2931

CPSIA information can be obtained at www.ICGtesting.com
Printed in the USA
BVOW071115170212

283167BV00002B/60/P

9 781936 117017